New Labour

in power

MANCHESTER
UNIVERSITY PRESS

New Labour in power

edited by

David Coates
and
Peter Lawler

Manchester University Press

Manchester and New York

distributed exclusively in the USA by St. Martin's Press

Published by Manchester University Press
Oxford Road, Manchester M13 9NR, UK
and Room 400, 175 Fifth Avenue, New York, NY 10010, USA
http://www.man.ac.uk/mup

Distributed exclusively in the USA by
St. Martin's Press, Inc., 175 Fifth Avenue, New York,
NY 10010, USA

Distributed exclusively in Canada by
UBC Press, University of British Columbia, 2029 West Mall,
Vancouver, BC, Canada V6T 1Z2

British Library Cataloguing-in-Publication Data
A catalogue record for this book is available from the British Library

Library of Congress Cataloging-in-Publication Data
New Labour in power / edited by David Coates and Peter Lawler.
     p.   cm.
   Includes bibliographical references and index.
   ISBN 0-7190-5461-3 – ISBN 0-7190-5462-1 (pbk.)
   1. Labour Party (Great Britain)   2. Great Britain – Politics and government – 1997
   I. Coates, David.   II. Lawler, Peter James
   JN 1129.L32 N49   2000
   324.24107–dc21   00-022268

ISBN 0 7190 5461 3 *hardback*
     0 7190 5462 1 *paperback*

First published 2000

07 06 05 04 03 02 01 00   10 9 8 7 6 5 4 3 2 1

Typeset by Servis Filmsetting Ltd, Manchester, England
Printed in Great Britain by Biddles Ltd, Guildford and King's Lynn

Contents

Contents

Figures and tables

Figures

Tables

Preface

The election and subsequent performance of the Blair Labour Government demands commentary. Prior to the election, the Labour Party underwent a process of reform which just a few years earlier would have seemed improbable. Then, having promised a great deal – no less than 'New Labour, New Britain' – Tony Blair's government was given one of the clearest electoral mandates this century. As with his predecessor, Blair's impact on the British political scene has already been sufficient to generate a new adjective that has, in accordance with his own vision, also rapidly acquired international currency. The British political lexicon has had to expand considerably to account for the changes in the style and language as well as the substance of British politics today.

The New Labour Government presented the electorate with a reform programme that stretched across all of the key policy domains. It is appropriate, then, that one of the largest and most diverse political science departments in the UK should attempt to come to some judgement of the promise and performance of the Blair Government at the mid-point of its first term in office. To this end, it was agreed that individual members of staff would examine the policy areas of most interest to them guided by two simple questions: what did New Labour promise, and what have they delivered so far? The project was conceived in an egalitarian and collective spirit (the contributors range from a doctoral student through to a pro-vice chancellor) and was intended to produce an assessment that would have value beyond the narrow confines of the academic community. Consequently, contributors were asked to err on the side of clarity and brevity and, furthermore, to bear strongly in mind the needs of both students and the ubiquitous 'informed reader'. First drafts were presented at a series of seminars during 1998 with final versions delivered in mid-1999. The editing process allowed some further updating and, by and large, the various chapters cover events up until September 1999. The completion of the book also coincided with the fiftieth anniversary of the founding of the Department of Government at the University of Manchester.

What follows, then, makes no claims to be the most comprehensive account of New Labour into power. The range of policy domains covered in this collection imposes limits upon the depth of analysis possible in a single volume. Equally, we did not set out to come to a singular, collective judgement of the Blair Government's performance, although at a later date we might contemplate such a task. The editors left the individual contributors to draw their own conclusions and, not surprisingly, they are mixed. It is hoped, however, that this collection of essays will help the reader form her or his own assessment of New Labour in power.

The production of a volume such as this incurs the usual debts. First of all, the editors wish to thank the contributors for making their job so much easier than it might have been. The contributors, bar one, come from the same department but, of course, were rarely in the same place at the same time. Nonetheless, the project was conceived in a co-operative spirit and this was maintained throughout its execution in spite of the fact that the two editors were both overseas during the final stages of the project. Thanks are due also to the various members of the administrative staff in the Department of Government for ably assisting both the editors and the contributors. Nicola Viinikka, commissioning editor at Manchester University Press, enthusiastically supported the project from the outset and Pippa Kenyon, assistant editor at MUP, was an invaluable and patient link between editors and publishers. The final edit was carried out in Stockholm and the editors would like to thank Björn Bergman, General Secretary of the trade union Ledarna, for graciously providing essential office facilities there. Finally, thanks to Gillian Andrews for her efficient handling of the copy-editing process and to Stephen Young for suggesting the project in the first place.

This project was largely conceived and produced in a university department situated in the heart of a British city with long and deep associations with the British labour movement and Labour Party. It is a city that is unequivocally part of the Labour Party's traditional heartland, one in which the New Labour vision of a 'New Britain' will be received with considerable interest and probably considerable circumspection. It is also a city that is going through its own process of comprehensive rejuvenation. It seems fitting, therefore, to dedicate this volume to the city and people of Manchester.

David Coates and Peter Lawler

1

The character of New Labour

David Coates

The return of the Labour Party to power on 1 May 1997 will undoubtedly prove to be one of those watershed events regularly cited by subsequent political historians. It is destined to be treated as a defining moment in the life of late twentieth-century Britain, a moment when one important chapter of recent British political history decisively closed and another equally decisively opened. Certainly the result drew a sharp (and at the time, unexpectedly deep) line in the electoral sand. It sent into opposition a Conservative Party that had hitherto enjoyed almost two decades of unbroken political power, and one which in its Thatcherite heyday only two elections before had seemed to many to be electorally invincible. It brought into power a Labour Party that had hitherto failed to win a general election for over twenty years, and gave that party a parliamentary majority of unprecedented scale. New Labour entered office with a parliamentary majority of 179, and faced a Conservative opposition with fewer seats than that party had known since the 1830s. In terms of seats won (if not in terms of votes captured), landslide elections don't come much bigger than this; and governments rarely enter office with their electoral mandate so clearly endorsed. The purpose of this text is to monitor how true to that endorsement New Labour in office is proving to be.

The arrival of New Labour

Among its supporters, desperate for a release from the seemingly endless years of Conservative political ascendancy, New Labour's electoral victory was widely hailed at the time as being of epochal importance. It was presented both as a clear statement of a nation's preference for a new direction in politics and as 'an immense opportunity' for the incoming Labour Cabinet 'to redefine the terms of political debate and recapture the language of political exchange' (Rawnsley, 1997). It was 'the people's victory', Hugo Young euphorically announced in the immediate wake of the election: one in which the UK electorate, in 'bringing in the centre-left, despatched the right into outer darkness with a conclusiveness that has never been done to it in time of prosperity and peace' (Young, 1997:10). 'Dilute the excitement with whatever doses of scepticism you feel appropriate,' Andrew Rawnsley wrote, 'and there is still no question that on Friday morning Britain woke up a different country. It may be a trick of the light but it feels like a younger country' (Rawnsley, 1997:2).

Rawnsley's reference to the UK as a 'younger country' was a deliberate invocation of what had become by then a distinctive theme of the Labour Party leadership, one heralded explicitly in the title of Tony Blair's collection of pre-election speeches: *New Britain: My Vision of a Young Country*. New Labour coming into power promised to modernise Britain, and to re-energise it (to make the country 'young' again). As Harold Wilson had done a generation before, Tony Blair understood his task as party leader as one primarily focused on what George Bush once famously called 'the vision thing': on the clarification, that is, of a distinct and alternative vision of Britain's future to that canvassed by Labour's political opponents. Harold Wilson had toured the UK in 1964 laying out the various dimensions of Labour's modernising project (what he termed then its 'economic purpose, social purpose, world purpose'), promising if elected to:

> mobilise the entire nation in the nation's business . . . to create a government of the whole people . . . to replace the closed, exclusive society by an open society in which all have an opportunity to work and serve, in which brains will take precedence over blue-blood, and craftsmanship will be more important than caste. Labour wants to streamline our institutions, modernise methods of government, bring the entire nation into a working partnership with the state. (Wilson, 1964:9–10)

A generation later and in a different idiom, Tony Blair did the same thing; and in pulling together those speeches as part of the pre-election build up, described New Labour's ambitions for 'my kind of country' as resting on:

> four cornerstones . . . four building blocks of a more secure and successful Britain. First, we want to improve the standards of living of all Britain's families through an economic strategy based on investment in people, infrastructure and industrial research and development. . . . Second, we want to build a new social order in Britain, a genuine modern civic society for our own time, based on merit, commitment and inclusion . . . Third, we seek to decentralise and make accountable the institutions of political power in Britain . . . Finally, the condition of Britain at home is intimately connected to our influence abroad . . . We should say loud and clear that Britain has a lot to offer, especially in partnership with other countries. . . . These are the building blocks of the young country I want to lead – confident in itself, and confident in its future. (Blair, 1996:xii–xiii)

These four cornerstones constituted a coherent 'New Labour' policy package: the first signalling new economic policies, the second a new social agenda, the third a programme of political and constitutional reform, and the fourth a new foreign policy. Both individually and collectively they were presented to the UK electorate in 1997 as qualitatively different from the policies on offer from the then Conservative government, and from policies offered to previous UK electorates by earlier Labour Party leaderships. New Labour presented itself in 1997 as a new 'third way' in British politics that was neither Thatcherite nor old Labour; and in doing so transformed the electoral fortunes of both. It sent the Conservative Party into the political wilderness for at least one election, and maybe more: leaving it with a share of the popular vote (30.7 per cent) lower than that party had ever fallen to since the modern party system began in 1832. And it pulled Labour back from the electoral depths into which it had slipped by 1983: giving it a share of the popular vote (43.2 per cent) that no Labour Party had obtained since Harold Wilson's landslide victory of 1966.

The creation of New Labour

The arrival of New Labour in power was itself the culmination of a long (and at times confrontational and traumatic) process of internal party reform, a process triggered by the scale and character of the 1983 election result. That process of reform went through a number of stages, initiated first by Neil Kinnock and then by John Smith. In particular it involved:

- *A strengthening of the position of the party leader* (initially against a National Executive Committee (NEC) dominated in the early 1980s by left-wing forces within the party). This was achieved by the creation in 1983 of a Campaign Strategy Committee answerable to the leader, the post-1985 re-organisation of party headquarters and expansion in the size and resources of the Leader's Office, the re-structuring of NEC policy-making (after 1987, policy emerged from a full Policy Review organised through just 7 NEC committees, each jointly chaired by a shadow cabinet member and a senior NEC figure) and by the establishment after 1988 of a shadow cabinet economic secretariat (from which, by the early 1990s, party economic policy largely derived).
- *Incremental moves away from forms of party government based on affiliated organisations towards direct individual membership participation* (around the notion of OMOV – one member one vote). In 1987, candidate selection was re-organised on an electoral college model, with individual members contributing 60 per cent of the votes cast, and affiliated unions controlling the rest. In 1993, this residual trade union vote was removed from candidate selection, union block votes at conference were reduced from 90 per cent to 70 per cent and the rules for leadership selection were amended (to give union members, voting as individuals, one-third of the vote, with MPs, Euro-MPs and constituency party members contributing the rest).
- *A steady shift of policy commitments away from the 1983 programme*: to leave the party, by 1992, no longer opposed to EC membership or to the UK's retention of nuclear weapons and no longer committed to the revocation of Conservative policies on industrial ownership and industrial relations reform.

> ## Box 1.1 *The revision of Clause 4*
>
> ### The original Clause 4 (1918)
>
> To secure for the workers by hand or by brain the full fruits of their industry and the most equitable distribution thereof that may be possible, upon the basis of the common ownership of the means of production, distribution, and exchange, and the best obtainable system of popular administration and control of each industry and service.
>
> ### The new Clause 4 (1995)
>
> 1 The Labour Party is a democratic socialist party. It believes that by the strength of our common endeavour, we achieve more than we achieve alone so as to create for each of us the means to realise our full potential and for all of us a community in which power, wealth and opportunity are in the hands of the many not the few, where the rights we enjoy reflect the duties we owe, and where we live together, freely, in a spirit of solidarity, tolerance and respect.
> 2 To these ends we work for:
>
> - a dynamic economy, serving the public interest, in which the enterprise of the market and the rigour of competition are joined with the forces of partnership and co-operation to produce the wealth the nation needs and the opportunity for all to work and prosper, with a

With Tony Blair as party leader, the pace of internal party reform then intensified. The leadership group around Tony Blair were convinced that the full transformation of the party's constitution and programme was a vital prerequisite to the transformation of the party's electoral performance. Modernisation, in Blairite terms, had to start at home. Party modernisation in the Blair era has so far included the following changes:

- *the replacement of the old Clause 4* by a new statement of party values and aims (see Box 1.1);
- *the creation of a new mass membership base for the party*, with a target of half a million party members by 2001;
- *the resetting of decision-making processes within the party*. This has involved a reduced reliance on trade unions as sources of party funds (for the first time in 1997, they became responsible for less than 50 per cent of party funding), the ending of trade union sponsorship of MPs, direct appeals by the party leadership to the membership for policy ratification (on the pre-election *Road to the Manifesto* document in 1996), the redesign of NEC membership to include a wide range of party 'stakeholders' and the resetting of the role of the annual

thriving private sector and high quality public services, where those undertakings essential to the common good are either owned by the public or accountable to them;
- a just society, which judges its strength by the condition of the weak as much as the strong, provides security against fear, and justice at work; which nurtures families, promotes equality of opportunity and delivers people from the tyranny of poverty, prejudice and the abuse of power;
- an open democracy, in which government is held to account by the people; decisions are taken as far as is practicable by the communities they affect; and where fundamental human rights are guaranteed;
- a healthy environment, which we protect, enhance, and hold in trust for future generations.

3 Labour is committed to the defence and security of the British people, and to co-operating in European institutions, the United Nations, the Commonwealth and other international bodies to secure peace, freedom, democracy, economic security and environmental protection for all.
4 Labour will work in pursuit of these aims with trade unions, co-operative societies and other affiliated organisations and also with voluntary organisations, consumer groups and other representative bodies.
5 On the basis of these principles, Labour seeks the trust of the people to govern.

conference. Under proposals placed before the party in 1997 (in the documents *Labour into Power* and *Partnership in Power*), future policy will emerge from a two-year rolling programme of policy review organised through committees reporting to a new broadly-based (and regularly re-elected) National Policy Forum of 175 party members, with the annual conference restricted to a bi-annual discussion of the resulting policy outcomes and otherwise encouraged to play a 'showpiece role' free of 'gladiatorial . . . and deeply divisive conflicts'.
- *more generally, the establishment of 'a huge distance in reality and in public perception'* (Kinnock: 1997) *between itself and 'Old Labour'* in both its 1983 Bennite and its 1974–79 Wilson/Callaghan manifestations.

Central to the establishment of this 'huge distance in reality and in public perception' has been the adoption by the Labour Party under Tony Blair's leadership of the term *New Labour* and the associated rhetoric of modernisation and change. The term 'new' appeared no less than 107 times in the *Road to the Manifesto* document; and was equally present in major Blair speeches throughout the pre-election period. It was used, for example, 37 times in the Blair address to the 1995 party conference (Harrison, 1996:2). Such usage was not accidental. The New Labour leadership were very conscious, as Tony Wright MP later put it, that 'a lot of people [had] simply walked away from the Labour Party' in the 1980s, 'walked away emotionally from it, and something had to be done about that' (Wright, 1997b). New Labour became convinced that the electorate was sending it a strong set of messages to which the party *had* to respond if it was ever to regain office:

> There was an assortment of messages . . . That a party agenda that seemed to revolve only around more state control and higher taxes was out of tune with the times. That it was not enough to be a caring party if the caring could not be paid for or priorities clearly established. That a party that seemed to be the prisoner of outside interests could not pursue the public interest. That a party that represented producer interests could not properly represent consumer interests, not least in the public sector. That a party that seemed more interested in defending yesterday's economy than in creating the conditions for tomorrow's was on the wrong track. That a party whose instincts on so many fronts appeared defensive and conservative was unlikely to be a source of radical ideas. That a party that seemed to be on an ideological trip from somewhere in the past . . . was increasingly irrelevant to a changed world. (Wright, 1997a: 23–4)

In relation to the economy, New Labour has positioned the party well to the right of its policy stance in 1983. The 1983 Labour Party presented itself to the UK electorate as a party of state ownership and control. It was committed to the creation of a five-year national plan to be negotiated primarily with the trade unions, to the re-nationalisation of all firms and industries privatised by the Conservatives and to the withdrawal of the UK economy from the EC. It was also committed to exchange controls and to the use of selective import quotas. New Labour, of course, is not. Far from seeking to control private industry and regulate market forces, New Labour is committed to the creation of 'a new partnership between government and industry, workers and managers – not to abolish the market but to make it dynamic and work in the public interest, so that it provides opportunities for all' (Blair, 1996:32). And far from actively seeking what the 1983 manifesto called 'a partnership with the trade unions', New Labour has actively distanced itself from any special relationship with them. New Labour is not anti-union in a Thatcherite sense. Tony Blair certainly made clear to the 1997 TUC that his government wants to work with trade unions in the pursuit of industrial competitiveness. But New Labour will not reverse the Conservative industrial relations legislation, or abandon its pursuit of labour market flexibility. There is to be no going back 'to the days of industrial warfare, strikes without ballots, mass and flying pickets, secondary action and the rest'. New Labour, the Prime Minister told his union audience, 'will keep the flexibility of the present labour market. It may make some shiver, but I tell you in the end it's warmer in the real world' (Blair, 1997a: 8) – a message far removed from Labour's 1983 endorsement of trade unions as standing 'at the heart of our programme'.

The 1983 Party was also heavily committed to the redistribution of wealth and power, and to the provision of an extensive and largely unreformed set of welfare services. New Labour is committed to neither of these things (except in so far as its 'welfare-to-work' proposals were seen as inherently redistributive). In 1983 the party proposed to increase public spending (and to borrow extensively to finance this spending), to tax the rich, to raise child benefit, to tie pensions to inflation/average earnings (whichever was rising faster), to phase out health charges and to extend the range of disability benefits. New Labour, on the other hand, has sought to 'put the final nail in the coffin of the old tax and spend agenda' (Tony Blair, quoted in the *Guardian*, 4 April 1997, p. 13). It has adopted the spending ceilings of its Conservative predecessor. It has refused to increase income tax for the duration of its first parliament; and it has set about a major review/reform of the entire welfare and benefit system. New Labour has its own ambitious welfare programme; but it is also of the view that 'we have reached the limits of the public's willingness simply to fund an unreformed welfare system through ever higher taxes and spending' (Tony Blair, quoted in the *Guardian*, 14 May 1997). New Labour in power is committed to a new deal for the unemployed that will move them from welfare to work, and to a major overhaul of the modes of provision of health care and high educational standards.

The 1983 Party had been opposed both to membership of what was then the EEC and to the UK's retention of nuclear weapons. Its election manifesto had committed the next Labour Government to the full repeal of the 1972 European Communities Act and to the establishment of a non-nuclear defence policy for the UK. No such commitments informed the election manifesto of 1997. On the contrary, New Labour went to the country promising constructive leadership *within* the European Union and a strong defence stance within NATO. Against the Conservative Party's increasingly strident opposition to greater European integration, New Labour made clear in 1997 its commitment to the rapid completion of the single market and to acceptance of the Social Chapter, while indicating its continued opposition to the idea of a European federal super-state and its caution in relation to immediate European monetary union. And while the 1997 manifesto was as keen as the 1983 manifesto had been on international negotiations to reduce nuclear stockpiles, it simply declined to follow the 1983 initiative of unilaterally cancelling the Trident programme. Instead, it offered a strategic defence and security review (which would allow British nuclear weapons to be included in any multilateral arms reduction talks), the banning of production and trade in anti-personnel mines, and a foreign policy in which human rights, environmental concerns and the combating of global poverty, would all move up the policy agenda.

In breaking so distinctly with the left face of old Labour, New Labour has not chosen, however, to realign its policies with old Labour's more moderate faces either. On the contrary, New Labour has been keen to put a distance between its policy stance and the main economic policies of previous Labour governments. Those governments, and particularly the 1974–79 governments, were ultimately corporatist in thought and intention. New Labour is not. The Wilson and Callaghan governments were committed to the building of a strong national manufacturing base via extensive state involvement in industry. New Labour is not. There is to be 'no going back to nationalisation or to corporatist management of the economy in which the state created industrial strategies designed to "pick winners"', and no return to 'tripartite institutions or beer and sandwiches at No.10' (Tony Blair, quoted in the *Guardian*, 8 April 1997, p. 1). For New Labour is a keen exponent of the thesis of globalisation, and of the need for investment in human capital as the key to economic competitiveness. In economic terms, it sees itself as pursuing a middle way between the statism of old Labour and the unbridled individualism of its Thatcherite alternative – a 'third way' as Tony Blair likes to describe it. The intellectual gurus of New Labour are prone, moreover, to present this 'third way' as new and uncharted territory. Tony Wright again:

> In the past the Left believed that its job was broadly to embrace the state and to attack markets, and the Right on the whole believed it was its job to embrace markets and attack the state. I think we've reached a politics which understands the limitations of both those analyses, that it's possible to see what the state might do and possible to see what the market might do. That's where politics is at now, trying to find a way in which states and markets can be constructed for the public good. But that's very different from the old way we used to talk about the mixed economy . . . which simply said there shall be a market economy and there shall be a state sector, and there shall be co-habitation between the two. (Wright, 1997b)

In its economic and social policies, as well as in its European and international ones, New Labour sees itself as a major reforming force on the UK Centre-Left. One that is still firmly rooted in the values of the Labour tradition, but one whose re-renewed radicalism comes from its willingness to forge new modes of delivering those values, modes appropriate to the realities of the modern age. 'I challenge anyone to deny that this is a radical programme', Tony Blair announced when launching the Party's 1997 election manifesto, but 'it is a radicalism of the centre – one entirely in tune with the needs and aspirations of the British people'. The emphasis placed by the leadership of New Labour on the underlying continuities of its policy proposals is a strong one. As Tony Blair (1996:18) put it, when steering the reform of Clause 4 through an initially sceptical party conference: 'our values do not change. Our commitment to a different society stands intact. But the ways of achieving that vision must change. The programme we are in the process of constructing entirely reflects our values. Its objectives would be instantly recognisable to our founders.' But the claim for radicalism and novelty is equally strong. New Labour sees itself as possessing an unprecedented sensitivity to the need to prioritise the building of strong communities, conventional families and a widespread respect for law and order. It talks a language of stakeholding, duty and responsibility in ways that previous Labour governments did not. Consequently, it is drawn towards active policies on youth crime, school truancy, even inadequate parenting, which were missing from the policy portfolios of earlier Labour administrations. It also possesses an unprecedented scale of commitment to a major package of constitutional reforms. This includes not just the reform of the House of Lords and Scottish and Welsh devolution (as with the Labour Party in the 1970s), but also a Freedom of Information Act, the incorporation into UK law of the European Convention on Human Rights, and the possibility of major changes to the rules governing the electoral system.

It is not that New Labour created these commitments afresh in the three years of Blair leadership, but rather that New Labour inherited a momentum in policy formation under all these headings. Furthermore, it was prepared both to accelerate that momentum and to consolidate its outcomes into what it now sees as a great reform package. The incremental movement of party position over time is clear. In the key area of industrial policy, for example, the 1983 position (of re-nationalising all firms privatised by the Conservatives) stealthily gave way to merely the social ownership of stakes in privatised companies (1987), to the stronger regulation of privatised utilities (1992) and to the advocacy of joint public-private partnerships (1997). Similar patterns of change are discernible across the whole sweep of party policy as is shown in Appendix 1.

The promise of New Labour

So against what set of general commitments and specific promises did New Labour by 1997 ask that its performance be judged?

The general commitments against which its performance in government can legitimately be set emerged steadily from New Labour figures in the run up to the 1997 election. Indeed some of New Labour's more general ambitions were foreshadowed earlier still. For example, long before there was any question of him leading the Labour Party and in the context of a wide-ranging interview with *Marxism Today*, Tony Blair had already 'sketched out the headings of a new policy agenda . . . fundamentally different from the issues that dominated debate in the past' (Blair, 1991:33). That interview would, of course, now constitute only a forgotten moment in the history of Labour Party modernisation but for Blair's later elevation to party leadership. In the light of that subsequent history, however, it does offer an intriguing insight into the continuities of thought (and policy concerns) of what we now treat as the New Labour project. Asked for his new agenda, Blair in 1991 foreshadowed his later 'four cornerstones' in the following manner.

• A modern society requires a modern constitution . . . There is a clear case for a written constitution, including the guarantee of certain inalienable civil liberties. Decision-making should be devolved as far as is practical from the centre and as close to the impact of the decision as is sensible . . . Constitutional reform can no longer be treated as peripheral. If it is right that we need a modern view of society and its relationship with the individual, then the constitutional question becomes central.

- In economic policy . . . we need to develop a new economics of the public interest, which recognises that a thriving competitive market is essential for individual choice . . . but without seeing it as an ideology in itself which we must obey even if it conflicts with the objectives we as a community have identified as part of the public interest. . . . The government should play a full and active part assisting industry to grow and modernise . . . [in] a partnership between the public and private sector . . . There is a real case for investment in training, not just for economic success, but to allow each individual the opportunity to develop his or her talents to the full and thus have much greater power over their own future.
- The crusade against poverty is not simply one of compassion for the poor . . . or even of some loose notion of a safety net for the most disadvantaged . . . The existence of an underclass of deprived and poor, with vast disparities of wealth existing between rich and poor, is seen not just as morally wrong but as an obstacle to the creation of the social cohesion necessary for society to function effectively.
- A new settlement between individual and society must recognise, more than ever before, that it is a settlement not just within our own nation but with Europe and the wider world . . . If Britain was confident in itself, in its modern identity as a European nation, it would be supporting the movement towards a single currency and closer European integration, but focusing the debate where it should be – on the measures that must accompany monetary union to make it work, and up-dating radically the institutions of the European Community to insist that, as its power increases, so must its democratic accountability. (Blair, 1991: 33–4)

These characteristically Blairite concerns and formulations then resurfaced in the Labour Party leadership election campaign in 1994, where they were presented in Tony Blair's personal manifesto, *Change and National Renewal*, as giving 'modern voice to Labour's values' (*Guardian*, 24 June 1994). In that campaign, Tony Blair linked arguments about economic policy to arguments about community, and linked arguments on rights with arguments about duties and responsibilities, in a way that would later becoming defining of the core of New Labour's project. 'Over the last few years' he announced in the first speech of his leadership campaign,

> there has developed a keen belief that we have lost our sense of purpose and direction as a country. One reason surely is that we have lost our identity as a country. The growth of social division, inequality and the disintegration of the family and the community have torn us apart. The task of the Left is not to replace the Tories' crude individualism with old notions of an overbearing paternalistic state. The task is rather one of national renewal, rebuilding a strong civic society and basing it on a modern notion of citizenship, where rights and duties go hand in hand, where the purpose of social action is to develop individual potential, not subjugate it. We have to counter the belief that action by society to improve social conditions and notions of personal responsibility are incompatible. (*Guardian*, 25 May 1994)

By the time of the 1997 election campaign, there is a discernible coherence to much of what New Labour was by then promising, a coherence rooted in a distinctive understanding of how modern nations work. They work – or rather they work well – according to New Labour if they are based on a dynamic economy and a developed civic society. They work badly if economic dynamism is blocked and social cohesion is undermined. A dynamic economy requires the encouragement of enterprise, the development of skills, and an active partnership between business, workers and government. A strong civic society requires stable families, strong communities, and well-resourced public services. It also requires a widespread respect for law and order. In a New Labour understanding of the world, economic dynamism is a casualty of over-regulated product and labour markets, and inadequate systems of education and training; and social cohesion is a casualty of persistent poverty, social exclusion and widespread criminality. For New Labour, economic dynamism and social cohesion go together. Each is enhanced by policies which recognise that 'the role of government has changed: today it is to give people the education, skills, technical know-how to let their own enterprise and talent flourish in the new market place' (Blair, 1997b). As Gordon Brown told Roy Hattersley, 'today, in an economy where skills are the essential means of production, the denial of opportunity has become an unacceptable inefficiency, a barrier to prosperity' and 'the long-term root cause of poverty' (Brown, 1997:9). In such a world, equality of outcome is less important than equality of opportunity, and New Labour can best help the poor by combining a commitment to strong public services with one to maximise opportunity by tackling 'at source the denial of work to millions of people'.

> That is why by far the biggest new expenditure commitment by the Government is our welfare-to-work programme – the largest employment programme for decades. At the heart of the programme is a commitment to equality of opportunity – helping those out of work to realise their potential through fulfilling employment. . . . We will not succeed by repeating old solutions that fail to address the problems of the 1990s and simply try and compensate people for poverty. Roy Hattersley says Britain needs a party which speaks up for the poor and for greater equality. Britain has such a party. It is in government, and it has begun systematically to meet the challenge of reuniting a divided society. (Brown, 1997:9)

Of course, by the time that Tony Blair and Gordon Brown were delivering these statements of New Labour's underlying analysis of modern capitalism, the General Election had already been won: on a manifesto which had begun life (in 1996) with a statement of five early pledges made in the policy statement *New Labour, New Life for Britain*. These are listed in Box 1.2. Those five were then expanded, in the full manifesto, into Labour's ten-point 'contract with the people'. The ten pledges are shown in Box 1.3. Each of the ten was then accompanied, in the full manifesto, with a linked series of more detailed policy commitments, as shown in Box 1.4.

Box 1.2   *The five early pledges*

1 Cut class sizes to 30 or under for 5, 6 and 7-year-olds, by using money from the assisted places scheme
2 Fast-track punishment for persistent young offenders, by halving the time from arrest to sentencing
3 Cut NHS waiting lists by treating an extra 100,000 patients as a first step by releasing £100 million saved from NHS red tape
4 Get 250,000 under-25s off benefit and into work by using money from a windfall levy on the privatised utilities
5 Set tough rules for government spending and borrowing; ensure low inflation; strengthen the economy so that interest rates are as low as possible

---

Box 1.3   *New Labour's 'Contract with the People'*

1 Education will be our number one priority, and we will increase the share of national income spent on education as we decrease it on the bills of economic and social failure.
2 There will no increase in the basic or top rates of income tax.
3 We will provide stable economic growth with low inflation, and promote dynamic and competitive business and industry at home and abroad.
4 We will get 250,000 young unemployed off benefit and into work.
5 We will rebuild the NHS, reducing spending on administration and increasing spending on patient care.
6 We will be tough on crime and tough on the causes of crime, and halve the time it takes persistent juvenile offenders to come to court.
7 We will build strong families and strong communities, and lay the foundations of a modern welfare state in pensions and community care.
8 We will safeguard our environment, and develop an integrated transport policy to fight congestion and pollution.
9 We will clean up politics, decentralise political power throughout the United Kingdom and put the funding of political parties on a proper and accountable basis.
10 We will give Britain the leadership in Europe which Britain and Europe need.

Box 1.4 *New Labour's manifesto – key policy commitments*

Education	• Cut class sizes to 30 or under for 5, 6 and 7-year-olds
	• Nursery places for all four year olds
	• Attack low standards in schools
	• Access to computer technology
	• Lifelong learning through a new University for Industry
	• More spending on education as the cost of unemployment falls
Personal Prosperity	• Economic stability to promote investment
	• Tough inflation target, mortgage rates as low as possible
	• Stick for two years within existing spending limits
	• Five-year pledge: no increase in income tax rates
	• Long-term objective of ten pence starting rate of income tax
	• Early budget to get people off welfare and into work
Business	• Backing business: skills, infrastructure, new markets
	• Gains for consumers with tough competition laws
	• New measures to help small business
	• National minimum wage to tackle low pay
	• Boost local economic growth with Regional Development Agencies
	• A strong and effective voice in Europe
Welfare-to-work	• Stop the growth of an 'underclass' in Britain
	• 250,000 young unemployed off benefit and into work
	• Tax cuts for employers who create new jobs for the long-term unemployed
	• Effective help for lone parents
Health	• 100,000 people off waiting lists
	• End the Tory internal market
	• End waiting for cancer surgery
	• Tough quality targets for hospitals
	• Independent food standards agency
	• New public health drive
	• Raise spending in real terms each year – and spend the money on patients not bureaucracy
Crime	• Fast track punishment for persistent young offenders
	• Reform Crown Prosecution Service to convict more criminals

	• Police on the beat not pushing paper
	• Crackdown on petty crimes and neighbourhood disorder
	• Fresh parliamentary vote to ban all handguns
Family Life	• Help parents balance work and family
	• Security in housing and help for homeowners
	• Tackle homelessness using receipts from council house sales
	• Dignity and security in retirement
	• Protect the basic state pension and support secure second pensions
Quality of life	• Every government department to be a 'green' department
	• Efficient and clean transport for all
	• New arts and science talent fund for young people
	• Reform the lottery
	• Improve life in rural areas
	• Back the World Cup bid
Politics and the Constitution	• End the hereditary principle in the House of Lords
	• Reform of party funding to end sleaze
	• Devolved power in Scotland and Wales
	• Elected mayors for London and other cities
	• More independent and accountable local government
	• Freedom of information and guaranteed human rights
Foreign policy	• Referendum on a single currency
	• Lead reform of the EU
	• Retain Trident: strong defence through NATO
	• A reformed United Nations
	• Helping to tackle global poverty

Labour went to the country in 1997 claiming that in government it would tell the truth, make tough choices, insist that the public sector live within its means, take on vested interests, resist unreasonable demands, and give a moral lead in those areas where government had responsibilities it should not avoid (Labour Party, 1997). It went to the country too asking to be judged against what Tony Blair called the 'traditional aims of the Labour Party – namely extending opportunity, social justice, progress, a sense of community rebuilt' (Blair, 1997c). The task of the chapters that follow is to assist you to decide if – when set against its election manifesto commitments and its own declared criteria of performance – New Labour in power is actually delivering on its central promises. It is also to enable you to judge the degree to which – in responding to issues which the manifesto did not/could not anticipate – the policy trajectory of New Labour remains consistent with the values and policy-lines on which the Party fought and won its 1997 landslide.

References

Blair, T. (1991), 'Forging a New Agenda', *Marxism Today*, September, pp. 33–4.
Blair, T. (1996), *New Britain: My Vision of a Young Country*, London, Fourth Estate.
Blair, T. (1997a), *Speech to the TUC*, Brighton, 9 September.
Blair, T. (1997b), *Speech to the European Socialists Congress*, Malmö, Sweden, 6 June.
Blair, T. (1997c), 'Not a Promised Land', *Guardian* (1 May), p. 26
Brown, G. (1997), 'Why Labour is Still Loyal to the Poor', *Guardian* (2 August), p. 9.
Harrison, R. (1996), *New Labour as Past History*, Nottingham, European Labour Forum Pamphlet No. 8.
Kinnock, N. (1997), *The 1997 Election: Tradition, Failures and Futures*, BBC/OU television interview, Brussels, 23 October.
Labour Party (1997), *New Labour: Because Britain Deserves Better*, London, Labour Party.
Rawnsley, A. (1997), 'We Are a Nation Reborn', *Observer* (4 May), p. 2.
Wilson, H. (1964), *The New Britain: Labour's Plan Outlined*, Harmondsworth, Penguin.
Wright, T. (1997a), *Why Vote Labour?*, Harmondsworth, Penguin.
Wright, T. (1997b), *The 1997 Election: Tradition, Failures and Futures*, BBC/OU television interview, London, 20 October.
Young, H. (1997), 'The People's Victory', *Guardian* (2 May), p.10.

2

New Labour and the electorate

Andrew Russell

The general election of 1 May 1997 saw Labour return to power after a period of opposition spanning eighteen years and four previous elections. Moreover, the New Labour Government was elected on a seemingly massive mandate, with a majority in the House of Commons of 179 which apparently put them in the driving seat for electoral contests into the next century. The scope of the Labour victory was so immense in parliamentary terms that the immediate reaction to the result was characterised by talk of Labour's landslide and the triumph of the New Labour agenda driven by Tony Blair. However, more detailed scrutiny of the dynamics of Labour – and critically Conservative – support reveals that the landslide majority may have been delivered by public disenchantment with the Conservatives as much as via popular synchronicity with the New Labour project.

Deconstructing Labour's victory

On 2 May 1997, Tony Blair became Prime Minister after a remarkable turn-around in British electoral politics. After a fourth successive defeat in the 1992 general election, and the prospect of the redistricting of parliamentary constit-uencies to Conservative advantage before the next election, Labour seemed doomed to perpetual opposition. Even the extensive programmatic renewal and image revamps since 1983 had not delivered electability. Any resurgence in Labour's fortunes needed to be centred around areas of electoral weakness (for instance from voters in the South of England), and the in-built Conservative advantage in policy areas such as economic management and in the service sector economy would need to be diluted. Between the 1992 and 1997 elec-tions both conditions were fulfilled to produce a set of favourable conditions for New Labour that previous leaders could only have dreamt of.

New Labour secured a majority of 179 in the Commons. The epitome of this remarkable victory was in the Enfield Southgate constituency where former student activist and 'Blairite' candidate Stephen Twigg defeated Conservative

Table 2.1 *The 1997 general election*

	Votes (%)	Seats
Conservative	30.7	165
Labour	43.2	419
Liberal Democrat	16.8	46
Others	9.3	29

Secretary of State for Defence, Michael Portillo – a man widely tipped to be the next Conservative leader. The imagery derived from Enfield was just as potent as that from the 1992 Conservative success in Basildon which became the *leit-motif* for John Major's unlikely victory then.

Nevertheless, New Labour received less votes nation-wide than John Major's Conservatives had gained in 1992. Labour's share of the vote (43 per cent) was their best electoral performance since the re-election of Harold Wilson's Government in 1966 but still fell some way short of their typical pre-election poll standing. Of the 73 opinion polls conducted by the five major polling organisations throughout 1997, including 44 during the election campaign itself and 2 exit polls, only one (ICM's poll 2 days before the election) forecast Labour's share of the vote to be as low as the final result (see Figure 2.1). The vast majority of pre-election polls predicted that Labour's support would be significantly higher than the actual result. Although Britain may have ceased to be 'the nation of liars' that Crewe talked of after the 1992 election (Crewe, 1992) and despite a general decline in Labour support during the campaign, a classic 'spiral of silence' still existed around the public's reported vote intention to pollsters and their actual behaviour in the polling booth. The fact that, unlike in 1992, the British public were not markedly inclined to conceal their support for the Conservatives when talking to pollsters, prevented the kind of inquest that followed the 1992 general election.

Turnout at the general election was low. In fact the official turnout of 71.4 per cent was the lowest of any post-war general election. Debate is currently raging over whether the decline in turnout is linear or trendless but a complex picture of electoral turnout emerged from the 1997 election. A common perception might be that the low turnout was due to large-scale abstention from Conservative voters, and some individual constituency returns seem to back this up. For instance, nine of the ten British constituencies with the largest turnout were Conservative losses while high profile Conservative Alan Clark returned to the Commons in Kensington & Chelsea from a turnout of only 50 per cent. On the other hand, the Conservatives held on to Stone, Surrey South-West, and Wantage where turnouts of 78 per cent were significantly higher than the national average, and as a rule of thumb middle class constituencies generally saw a higher turnout rate than seats characterised by working class occupants (Denver and Hands, 1997a). Some inner-city safe Labour seats suffered from low turnout but this did not set a trend that could be applied

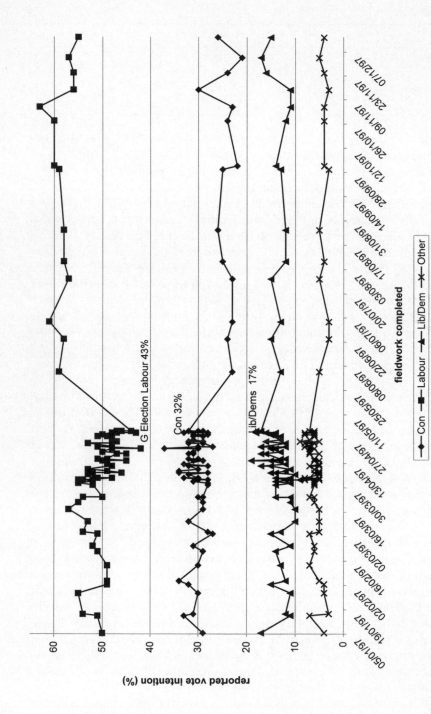

Figure 2.1 *Public opinion polls 1997*

Source: Denver et al., *British Elections & Parties Review*, Volume 8, pp. 264–7

Box 2.1   *Labour's campaign successes*

- *The professional campaign.* A surge in campaign spending was accompanied by an increasingly effective electoral strategy as the effects of political marketing techniques contributed to an efficient and well-targeted campaign.
- *The economy.* Conservative economic failures were highlighted and traditional barricades to Labour's ability to mobilise the economic vote were overturned.
- *Europe.* The issue of European integration and the social and political development of the EU were turned against the Conservative government as Labour made much of Conservative division on the question of Europe.
- *Sleaze.* The outgoing government were almost exclusively held responsible for sleaze, being associated with financial and sexual scandals and misdemeanours. The Labour opposition was not tarnished with the same brush.
- *The social agenda.* Traditional Labour strongholds such as education, health and welfare services continued to be profitable campaign issues for New Labour in 1997.
- *Leadership.* New Labour and its leader, Tony Blair, became synonymous in the public's perceptions. Blair's leadership of Labour was a key electoral asset and contrasted sharply with John Major's apparent inability to force the Conservative Party into line.

---

throughout the country. Denver and Hands (1997b), following the work of Denver and Halfacree (1992), suggest that the variance in turnout in inner-city areas was likely to be the result of 'floating populations' and the age of the electoral register rather than political factors. Despite some clear-cut exceptions, the most obvious influence on rates of turnout appears to be the marginality of any particular seat (Denver and Hands, 1997b). This would imply that voters were using logical judgements in determining whether to vote or not (asking the classic rational choice question 'what difference is my vote likely to make?') rather than implying that the low turnout in 1997 was solely the result of apathy.

The campaign

The professional campaign
Much has been made of the 'professionalisation' of the 1997 Labour campaign. The central control exerted by Millbank Tower – and particularly from the offices of Philip Gould and Peter Mandelson – seems to have been a central

plank of Labour's electoral strategy in 1997. The strategy of 'rapid rebuttal' – which sought to counter all Conservative election stories as quickly as possible – acquired almost mythical status in post-election analysis (even the computer software system that enabled rapid rebuttal was given a legendary title – *Excalibur*). Furthermore the party's determination to mount a 'modern' campaign translated as an expensive, televisual campaign. Labour's campaign spending (£7.4m) betrays two crucial aspects of Millbank Tower's attitude to the election. Firstly, Labour had significant resources and were prepared to spend almost two-thirds as much as the Conservatives. Secondly, the party was not prepared to appear complacent about the likelihood of victory. Spending money on an elaborate campaign was a vital aspect of being 'seen' to be fighting a serious modern campaign. As such the 'marketisation' of the 1997 campaign became shorthand for the changes in – and therefore the newly found electability of – Labour under Blair.

The effect of the media on the 1997 campaign is hard to measure. What is clear, however, is that the traditional hostility of the national press to Labour had been diluted. The approval for Blair (interestingly they focused on the leader rather than the party) granted by the *Sun* sparked some interest in the role played by the tabloids in the 1997 election. It is probable that the thawing attitude to New Labour of the tabloids reflected a change among the papers' readerships rather than among their editorial boards, but Labour, to be sure, would rather have the support of the *Sun* and the *Daily Star* than their hostility as in 1992.

The economy

As the explanatory power of social class seems to have diminished, and as debate has raged on the extent to which newer cleavages such as geography can explain variance in British voting, one particular theory – economic voting – has recently gained favour in psephological circles. Most of the focus for these studies has concentrated upon personal economic expectations, but the basis for economic voting lies in the economic credibility of the political parties.

In 1992, Labour had a clear lead on most of the issues that dominated the election, having in-built advantages on the social agenda of education policy, the NHS and unemployment. The Conservatives only led on economic issues such as income tax policy. Despite this apparent imbalance, the Conservatives were able to cash in on their one policy advantage in 1992 and designed their main campaign strategy around the issue of taxation. Despite apparently unfavourable economic conditions in 1992, the heartland of Conservative support – the service sector based electorate in the south of England – failed to turn against the Conservatives. Choosing to absolve the Major Government from blame for the new recession, the electorate (particularly in the south) was likely to rate the Conservatives as the best party to deal with the economy. This economic competence question was a key feature of most explanations of the 1992 election.

Britain's expulsion from the European Union's Exchange Rate Mechanism (ERM) in September 1992 dealt a fatal blow to the Conservatives ability to mobilise voters around economic issues. Previous post-war financial and economic disasters (the sterling crises of 1947 and 1967–68, and the IMF loan of 1976–78) had been associated with Labour in office. The ERM crisis not only made a mockery of Conservative pledges to cut tax 'year on year', it was the most serious economic disaster presided over by a Conservative government since the war. Since 1952, GALLUP has asked the public which party was best equipped to handle Britain's economy. Until September 1992 (with one single exception – during the poll tax protests of 1990) the Conservatives were comfortably ahead of Labour on this question. This decisive lead was wiped out immediately after the ERM crisis. In an instant, the basis of successive Conservative electoral victories had been undermined. The Conservative failure to redress the question of economic competence robbed them of the potential advantage from other economic indicators that would normally have been considered good news for an incumbent government. Hence, falling unemployment, manageable inflation, a more favourable balance of payments and an upturn in the housing market could not save the Conservatives in 1997. The 'feelgood factor' gave way to a determination to punish the government. If the issue of economic management was the key reason why the Conservatives were victorious in 1992, it was crucial to their defeat when the election was replayed five years later. The fact that the economic crisis had a European issue at its core served only to heighten the disquiet in the Conservative Party and exacerbate its image as unmanageable. In short, the Conservatives were stymied by the ERM crisis and the collapse of the Conservative vote in 1997 had the loss of control over the public perception of economic competence as its root cause.

For their part, Labour was anxious to present itself as the party of economic responsibility. Incredibly the Labour opposition promised to stick to the spending plans of the Conservative government, at a stroke reducing their scope for spending plans. Gordon Brown's pledge to leave unaltered the top and basic rates of income tax for the duration of the next parliament was widely praised even from traditionally hostile sources. The *Daily Mail* hailed the Shadow Chancellor's tax pledge as a watershed. It was 'as significant an act of exorcism as we have witnessed in the post-war history of British politics'. The newspaper's leader comment declared that the Conservatives had 'destroyed their own credibility as tax-cutters' and had rendered themselves 'most ill-qualified to mock New Labour's new-found fiscal restraint' (Jones, 1997:96). Clearly Labour had moved significantly to defuse the 'tax bombshell' that cost them so dearly in the 1992 campaign.

Europe

New Labour's main European strategy was to point to the disunity among the Conservatives and stress their own unity. In reality this was not an onerous task since the Conservative campaign appeared on the point of self-destruction over

Europe on several occasions. Seldom can a government have been so ill served by its own elite as the Conservatives were in the 1997 campaign. Forced into an official 'negotiate and decide' policy on future European integration (renamed 'wait and see' by almost everyone but the Prime Minister), John Major suffered the indignity of having two cabinet ministers stray from the adopted line on the single currency. The dissension of John Horam and James Paice would normally have resulted in their expulsion from the cabinet, but coming in the middle of the election campaign, the Conservatives could not risk even more internal dispute. Consequently – and under pressure from the Referendum Party at the constituency level – over 100 Conservative election candidates used their election addresses to reject in principle a single European currency. Conservative unity had been sacrificed for political expediency but the electoral costs of appearing so divided were immeasurable. In contrast, Labour presented a relatively united front; a remarkable turnaround from their 1983 stance saw New Labour promise closer relations with the EU, and the delivery through the Community of greater worker's rights and the minimum wage.

Education

Tony Blair's mantra that the election would be about 'education, education, education' hit the headlines in 1997, and Labour's well-publicised pledge to reduce class sizes played well with the British electorate. In fact, although education might have been seen to have been a profitable area for the party to campaign on, they were in danger of being outflanked by the Liberal Democrats whose promise to raise income tax by one penny in the pound to finance an improvement in education allowed the third party to pose as the most radical of all alternatives. Nevertheless, Labour ran a sure-footed campaign on education issues and their traditional lead on educational matters was not seriously threatened.

Sleaze

The issue of political 'sleaze' swamped the 1997 campaign. Furthermore, sleaze was an issue that almost exclusively hit the incumbent Conservatives rather than the Labour opposition. Dunleavy and Weir (1995:55) divided sleaze into eight categories:

1 Alleged financial wrongdoing by ministers and MPs, shady deals and the misleading of others
2 The perception of a dramatic surge in lobbying and the intermediary role of certain MPs
3 The alleged 'packing' of 'quangos'
4 'Jobs for the faithful', and tactical use of the honours list
5 Company directorships for retired ministers and senior civil servants
6 The murky world of party fund-raising
7 Unconventional sexual behaviour
8 Salary increases for 'fat cats' in the privatised public utilities

Using only three points in this list – those relating to money (points one and two) and sex (point seven), Farrell *et al.* were able to identify no less than 24 Conservative MPs whose re-election was threatened by sleaze in the 1997 election, a figure that does not include those who opted not to stand for re-election. (Farrell *et al.*, 1998:80) Although they conclude that these 24 were almost as damaged by their association with Conservatism as with sleaze, the connection between sleaze and Conservatism was clearly a major disadvantage to the government in 1997. Labour were quick to capitalise, even standing down their candidate in the Tatton constituency (as did the Liberal Democrats) so that Neil Hamilton could be opposed by an 'independent' anti-sleaze campaigner, Martin Bell. Bell's remarkable victory illustrated the degree of public disenchantment with the level of sleaze with which the incumbent government had become entwined.

Health and welfare

A curious feature of the 1997 campaign was that Labour's victory was secured without reliance on the social features of Labour's traditional electoral strength. In particular, health and welfare issues – where Labour had grown used to outperforming the Conservatives in election campaigns – were relegated behind issues such as Europe and sleaze. That is not to say that this particularly disadvantaged Labour since many of the headlines about Europe and sleaze contained anti-Conservative subtexts. Even when the Conservatives appeared to be making some headway with an anti-federalist stance on European integration, it served to simultaneously highlight Conservative divisions on the issue of Britain's EU partnership. Moreover, where welfare issues did connect with the electorate, they continued to be advantageous for Labour, as the party retained their traditional 'ownership' of the social agenda whilst making inroads into the economic domain of the Conservatives (see Russell, 1995; 1997 for a fuller discussion of these domains).

Leadership

An inescapable truth from the electoral contest of 1997 was that it was a contest as much between the party leaders as the parties themselves. Clarke *et al.* (1998:30–1) report that despite sophisticated attempts to analyse the impact of economic perceptions on electoral choice in 1997, economic effects were outweighed by 'a powerful combination of anti-Conservative and pro-Labour political factors' and that Labour's chief asset was its popular leader. Nevertheless, the increasing presidentialisation of elections in Britain should not mask the conclusion that a popular leader of an unpopular party is not a recipe for electoral success. Naturally, New Labour's success at the polls in 1997 was Tony Blair's triumph but only because New Labour had been built in his own image. John Major – while lagging behind Blair in public affection – continued to be significantly more popular than the party he led to defeat. Crucially, Major lacked credibility because of the antics of his party since the 1992 election.

Table 2.2 *Evaluations of the 'Best person for Prime Minister' during 1997 (%)*

	Major/Hague	Blair	Ashdown	Don't know
Jan.	28	39	14	19
Feb.	28	39	13	20
Mar.	25	41	12	22
Apr.				
May.*	10	62	13	14
Jun.				
Jul.	11	61	15	14
Aug.	11	59	15	15
Sep.	12	63	13	11
Oct.	8	67	11	14
Nov.	8	60	15	16
Dec.	8	59	16	17

* Question relates to William Hague after his succession.
Source: GALLUP 9000

When asked which of the three party leaders would make the best prime minister, the response of the public was a definite and resounding endorsement of Tony Blair, his approval rating being more than three times the magnitude of either John Major or Liberal Democrat leader Paddy Ashdown (Table 2.2). Blair's performance since the election – and against the new Conservative leader William Hague – has been even more impressive.

During the campaign, Labour was naturally keen to exploit Tony Blair's popularity. Aspects of the party's publicity drew on Blair as much as the party's name – the posters advertising Labour's pledge not to raise income tax even contained his picture and signature. In his exhaustive account of the campaign, Jones reports that Labour became obsessed with the question of leadership – using it as a symbol of Blair's hold on the party and the apparent inability of John Major to impose firm leadership on the Conservatives. The epitome of this obsession was the press conference where Gordon Brown's use of the phrase 'leadership' reached epidemic proportions. One answer began,

> It is a question of leadership and John Major has to explain if he makes an issue of leadership, how he has failed to show leadership in Europe. Tony Blair has shown he can lead, and has shown by his magnificent reform of the Labour Party that he can lead and get results, if the issue is one of leadership.

By the end of the news conference, Brown had made 24 separate references to leadership (Jones, 1997:228). Labour was comfortable with the electoral image of their leader and played the issue to maximum effect.

All in all, the campaign went extremely well for New Labour. Traditional strengths, including the social agenda of health, welfare and education, were maintained, while traditional weaknesses – on the economic and international

---

Box 2.2   *The demographic nature of Labour's vote*

- *Social class.* By 1997 Labour had become the 'superclass' party that the reforms since 1983 had been striving for. New Labour made significant inroads into the Conservative stronghold of the middle class electorate.
- *Age effects.* Labour's attempts to woo young voters bore fruit. Only the eldest sections of society resisted the forward march of New Labour.
- *The gender gap.* The much heralded propensity of women voters to favour the Conservatives over Labour was significantly diluted in 1997 as Labour benefited from its new 'catch-all' appeal.
- *Geography.* Traditional Labour heartlands in Scotland, Wales and northern England held firm, while Labour had some remarkable successes in the south of England, overturning many aspects of the 1980s' electoral geography of Britain.

---

agenda – were obliterated. Control of the campaign from the centre was unquestioned and their opponents seemed determined to take every opportunity to shoot themselves in the foot. The tables had been reversed so completely from 1983 that it was the Conservatives who emerged from the election with little chance of an immediate return to power, while Labour assumed the mantle of the natural party of government.

The basis of Labour support

Clearly, an important task to perform is to unearth the nature of support for Labour in 1997, to attempt to ascertain the source of New Labour's electoral mandate. This section will attempt to deconstruct the profile of the New Labour vote in 1997, and assess the extent of its electoral success across different social classes, regions, age groups and genders.

Social class

Whatever the outcome of the class dealignment debate in the 1980s, Labour under Neil Kinnock clearly adopted a 'superclass' electoral strategy, attempting to widen their appeal from the narrow confines of the 1983 debacle. The extended search for votes continued under the brief leadership of John Smith but gathered pace dramatically after Tony Blair's ascent to the leadership of the party in 1994. Evidence taken from the NOP exit poll, presented in Table 2.3, shows that while the British electorate can continue to be characterised by social class, Labour does appear to have made significant inroads into the voting profile of those from the top of the class scale. Over one-quarter of managers and administrators were prepared to vote Labour according to the exit poll, while Labour enjoyed a significant lead over the Conservatives in all other class

Table 2.3 *Reported vote by social class in the 1997 general election*

	Conservative (%)	Labour (%)	N
Managers/administrators	40	29	555
Office workers	25	44	308
Skilled manual	24	50	379
Semi-unskilled manual workers	20	57	250
N	618	874	1492

Source: NOP exit poll

Table 2.4 *Reported vote by age group in the 1997 general election*

Age group	Conservative (%)	Labour (%)	N
18–29	21	53	273
30–44	25	46	474
45–65	31	40	526
65+	41	31	343
N	668	948	1616

Source: NOP exit poll

categories. Critically, Labour found it easier to recruit from the managerial classes in 1997 than in previous elections.

Age

Table 2.4, which shows Conservative and Labour support according to age, reveals that the standard age group cleavage with the youngest sections of the electorate being more likely than their older cohorts to support Labour held fast in 1997. Russell *et al.* (1992) suggested that those elements of the electorate socialised under Thatcherism were more likely to develop pro-market, anti-collectivist attitudes than the standard pattern would suggest. Hence Labour's success in attracting the youngest sections of the electorate would have been welcomed by the party, although the rightward shift in economic thinking within the party may not have hindered this. Only the eldest section of the electorate was more likely to favour the Conservatives under Major than Labour under Blair in 1997. Nevertheless, and as Table 2.5 shows, the hostility of the over-65s to New Labour was diluted when some control for relative deprivation was introduced, so that the voting patterns of those reliant on state pensions differed little in the choice between Conservative and Labour.

Gender

A common explanation for Conservative success in 1992 was the gender gap. Major and the Conservatives were more popular with women voters than with

Table 2.5 *Reported vote of those reliant on state pensions in the 1997 general election*

	Conservative (%)	Labour (%)	N
Retired on state pension	38	35	413
Non-OAPS	27	44	1264
N	691	986	1677

Source: NOP exit poll

Table 2.6 *Reported vote by gender in the 1997 general election*

	Conservative (%)	Labour (%)	N
Male	29	42	710
Female	30	42	899
N	667	942	1609

Source: NOP exit poll

men. Much of the evidence for this relationship was debatable and counter-claims were posted that the so-called gender gap could be explained largely with reference to other social cleavages such as trade union membership and age structure. Table 2.6 shows that no such controls are necessary for the 1997 election, male and female voters being almost equally likely to favour Labour over the Conservatives. Labour's efforts to increase female representation in parliament may have aided their electoral chances here. It is certainly worth noting that, before being declared illegal in the High Court, Labour's all women short-lists contributed to a much higher proportion of female candidates in winnable seats in 1997 than had previously been the case. Of the 120 Women MPs in the Commons after 1 May 1997, 101 represented the Labour Party.

Geography

Perhaps the most striking feature of the changing electoral dynamics of the 1980s was the geographic gulf in voting behaviour, as the Labour vote retreated to the industrial heartland of the north and Celtic nations, while the Conservative vote was consolidated in the service sector-dominated south of England. Labour failed to make significant in-roads into the Conservative vote in the south in 1992 despite the new recession of the 1990s which dispropor-tionately hit the service sector. Thus, one of the biggest challenges facing New Labour was to make headway in the very areas that had resisted Labour voting since 1979. Table 2.7 shows that New Labour can be very pleased with its geo-graphic outreach in 1997 – the south of England became as fertile ground for Labour voting as Conservative voting – especially as Labour had come from third place in many of these seats. Indeed, after supposedly controlling for social

Table 2.7 *Reported vote by geographic region in the 1997 general election*

Region	Conservative (%)	Labour (%)	N
South	35	34	661
Midlands & Wales	21	56	458
North	31	46	438
Scotland	26	28	120
N	691	986	1677

Source: NOP exit poll

structure, McAllister claims that the southeast and southwest of England now constitute Labour territory (McAllister, 1997:137). At the same time, the drive for target seats in southern England did not adversely affect Labour's hold on their traditional heartlands. Conservative representation in Scotland and Wales was eliminated altogether in 1997 and while the national swing to Labour was 9.9 per cent, and 11.8 per cent in Labour's 91 target seats, the swing to Labour in the 54 non-target seats won by Labour was typically 14.3 per cent (Whiteley and Seyd, 1998:191).

Since the 1997 general election, the Scottish electorate has overwhelmingly endorsed Labour's recommendation for a devolved parliament in Edinburgh, while the Welsh assembly was also backed (albeit by a much narrower margin) in the referendums in Scotland and Wales. These heartlands of support – especially the Scottish Labour vote – could pose a serious threat to the party in the near future. Poll evidence since the election has shown that Labour support in Scotland is waning faster than anywhere else in the country. Moreover, with the inaugural Scottish parliament, the Scottish National Party has been given a focal point around which to mobilise anti-Labour sentiment. If the solid Labour vote in Scotland, founded in opposition, begins to erode in government, the search for new voters in England will become even more critical.

The geographic cleavages of the 1980s were clearly redrawn by the 1997 election result, but the story is as much one of Conservative disaster as Labour success. McAllister has noted that 'the Conservatives performed proportionately worse in the regions where they had secured most of their gains during the 1980s' (McAllister, 1997:136). Meanwhile Labour closed the north–south divide sufficiently to suggest the success of their targeting campaign had finally overcome the polarisation of the electorate evident in 1987. In 1997 Labour were victorious in many seats which seemed unwinnable in the 1980s the party taking St Albans, Warwick and Leamington and even Margaret Thatcher's old seat Finchley and Golders Green.

Ownership of shares and houses

In other areas of the profile of the vote, New Labour took the battle directly to the Conservatives. Owning shares was a surprisingly poor predictor of propensity to vote Conservative rather than Labour in 1997 (Table 2.8). Strikingly, while the

Table 2.8 *Reported vote of share owners in the 1997 general election*

	Conservative (%)	Labour (%)	N
Share owners	39	34	235
Non-share owners	27	44	1342
N	691	986	1677

Source: NOP exit poll

Table 2.9 *Reported vote by housing tenure in the 1997 general election*

Tenure status	Conservative (%)	Labour (%)	N
Home owner with mortgage	30	41	703
Own outright	39	33	457
Rent – council	12	61	186
Rent – housing assoc'n	28	47	54
Rent – private sector	22	49	116
Rent – other	26	43	102
N	668	950	1618

Source: NOP exit poll

Thatcher governments had cashed in electorally on the home owning boom, Labour enjoyed a majority of votes from mortgage holders in 1997 (Table 2.9).

After Labour's victory

The enigma of Blair and New Labour's popularity is reflected in events after the election. All governments and new Prime Ministers are likely to enjoy a brief honeymoon period. On succession from the Thatcher governments, John Major's honeymoon period lasted about four months. The Blair honeymoon period has endured to an unprecedented length. Throughout 1997, Blair enjoyed a massive approval rating advantage over the Conservatives that showed little or no sign of decay – not even the change in Conservative leadership could dent Blair's advantage. Figure 2.2 derived from the Gallup Political and Economic Index shows that Blair's personal lead over the Conservative leader was unassailable throughout 1997. The net scores are based on responses to the questions: 'Are you satisfied or dissatisfied with Mr. Major (Mr. Blair) as Prime Minister?'; 'Do you think that Mr. Blair (Mr. Hague) is or is not proving (will or will not prove) a good leader of the Labour (Conservative) Party?'; and 'Do you think that Mr. Ashdown is or is not proving a good leader of the Liberal Democrat Party?'.

Approval of the Government's record also endured throughout 1997. Indeed, winning the election in May was a platform for an enduring honeymoon period between the electorate and the Government (see Figure 2.3). Indeed, it was only on 9 September 1998 that the *Guardian* was finally able to claim that 'Blair

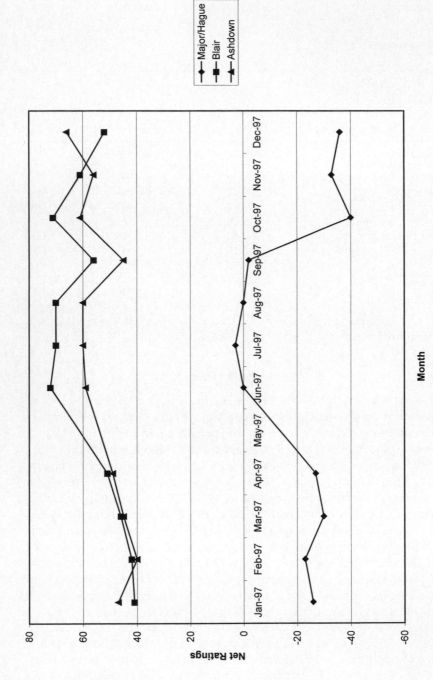

Figure 2.2 *Ratings of party leaders 1997*
Source: Gallup Political and Economic Index

Month

Net Ratings

Major/Hague
Blair
Ashdown

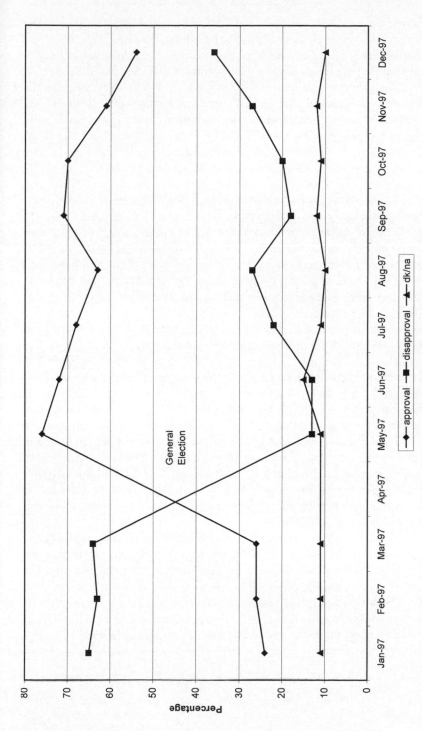

Figure 2.3 *Assessment of Government's record*
Source: Gallup Political and Economic Index

approval ── disapproval ── dk/na

Bubble Bursts – State of Nation Poll Shows PM as "Just Another Politician"'. The basis for this front-page story was that '[t]he poll shows that his personal ratings, particularly those for honesty and empathy with the voters, have plummeted to levels more in keeping with ratings for past prime ministers'.

In fact Blair's ratings remained good. Comparing the ICM/*Guardian* poll to its predecessors reveals that Blair's ratings on questions asked of the British public under Major, outperformed the Conservative prime minister by between 5 and 15 per cent. The honeymoon period with the British electorate may finally be over officially, but its duration and degree of intensity will have made Labour very confident of repeating the 1997 victory at the next election.

The next election and beyond: implications for the future

If the basis for Labour's remarkable return to power in 1997 was to be found in the haemorrhage of Conservative support rather than in Labour's own electoral strategy, it might be thought that Labour's electoral hegemony could be threatened by a reversal in Conservative fortunes. However, the enduring honeymoon period, the continued popularity of the Prime Minister, and, above all, the task facing the Conservatives in opposition, suggest that Labour should hold onto power at the next election.

Since his accession to the Conservative leadership in June 1997, and a good reputation as performer in the Commons notwithstanding, William Hague has failed to deliver a significant upturn in Conservative approval ratings or in reported vote intention in opinion polls. At the campaign level he seems to have eschewed public popularity in favour of a policy review and programmatic renewal straight from the Labour tactics employed by Kinnock, Smith and Blair. The Conservatives seem to consider 1997 the same way that Labour looked at 1983: a critical election from which the road back to power would be long and hard. In fact, the similarities between Hague and Kinnock are striking, both decided early on that the party image and personnel needed attention at a fundamental level before short-term electoral advantage could be pursued. It remains to be seen whether the Conservatives will contest Labour at the next election in a meaningful sense.

As far as Labour are concerned, the electoral work has been done and borne fruit. The hardest task was to persuade those sections of the electorate resistant to Labour to allow them the chance to govern. Once in office, Labour ought to find it easier to keep their support. After so much effort to secure approval for Labour's economic management skills – and with such a soft electoral mandate – it is perhaps not surprising that a safety first policy of economic management has been employed in order to secure a second term for New Labour.

References

Clarke, H., M. Stewart and P. Whiteley (1998), 'Political Change and Party Choice: Voting in the 1997 General Election' in D. Denver, J. Fisher, P. Cowley and C. Pattie (eds), *British Elections & Parties Review, Volume 8: The 1997 General Election*, London, Frank Cass.

Crewe, I. (1992), 'A Nation of Liars? Opinion Polls and the 1992 Election', *Parliamentary Affairs*, 45:475–95.

Curtice, J. (1995), 'What Future for the Opinion Polls? The Lessons of the MRS Inquiry' in C. Rallings, D. Farrell, D. Denver and D. Broughton (eds), *British Elections & Parties Yearbook, 1995*, pp. 139–56.

Denver, D. and G. Hands (1997a), *Modern Constituency Electioneering*, London, Frank Cass.

Denver, D. and G. Hands (1997b), 'Turnout' in P. Norris and N. Gavin (eds), *Britain Votes 1997*, Oxford, Oxford University Press.

Denver, D. and K. Halfacree (1992), 'Inter-Constituency Migration and Turnout at the British General Election of 1983', *British Journal of Political Science*, 22:248–54.

Denver, D., J. Fisher, P. Cowley and C. Pattie (eds) (1998), *British Elections & Parties Review, Volume 8: The 1997 General Election*, London, Frank Cass.

Dunleavy, P. and S. Weir (1995), 'Media, Opinion and the Constitution' in F. Ridley and A. Doig (eds) *Sleaze: Politicians, Private Interests and Public Reaction*, Oxford, Oxford University Press.

Farrell, D., I. McAllister and D. Studlar (1998), 'Sex, Money and Politics: Sleaze and the Conservative Party in the 1997 Election' in D. Denver, J. Fisher, P. Cowley and C. Pattie (eds) *British Elections & Parties Review, Volume 8: The 1997 General Election*, London, Frank Cass, pp. 80–94.

Jones, N. (1997), *Campaign 1997: How the General Election was Won and Lost*, London, Indigo.

McAllister, I. (1997), 'Regional Voting' in P. Norris and N. Gavin (eds), *Britain Votes 1997*, Oxford, Oxford University Press, pp. 133–49.

Russell, A. (1995), 'Spatial Variation in Economic Attitudes and Voting Behaviour in Britain', 1983–92, PhD, University of Sheffield.

Russell, A. (1997), 'A Question of Interaction: Using Logistic Regression to Examine Geographic Effects on British Voting Behaviour' in C. Pattie, D. Denver, J. Fisher and S. Ludlam (eds), *British Elections & Parties Review, Volume 7*, London, Frank Cass, pp. 91–109.

Russell, A., C. Pattie and R. Johnston (1992), 'Thatcher's Children: Exploring the Links between Age and Political Attitudes', *Political Studies*, 40:742–56.

Whiteley, P. and P. Seyd (1998), 'Labour's Grassroots Campaign in 1997' in D. Denver, J. Fisher, P. Cowley and C. Pattie (eds), *British Elections & Parties Review, Volume 8: The 1997 General Election*, London, Frank Cass, pp. 191–207.

Acknowledgements

The assistance of the polling organisations in providing data is gratefully acknowledged.

3

New Labour and the Clinton Presidency

Douglas Jaenicke

Robert Reich, Clinton's first Secretary of Labor (1993–96), contends that Clinton in the US, New Labour in the UK, and left-of-centre governments in continental Europe all represent a distinctive third way of governing (Reich, 1999:46). This chapter examines the Clinton Presidency in that light, less to establish a causal influence between it and New Labour, than to provide comparative benchmarks for understanding and evaluating New Labour in government.

There are obvious connections between Bill Clinton and Tony Blair, and between American New Democrats and British New Labour. In 1997, New Labour received campaign advice from Clinton's campaign advisers and adopted many of Clinton's campaign techniques. In 1998, the New Labour Government worked with the Clinton White House to organise the third way conference at New York University, in which both leaders participated. Furthermore, the two leaders have established a good personal relationship, and, more importantly, both apparently occupy similar locations in political time and are pursuing similar political strategies (despite the obvious differences between the US and UK political systems). According to Skowronek (1993), two dimensions define a president's location in political time: first, whether the existing political regime (or order) is vulnerable or resilient, and second, whether a president is affiliated with or opposed to the existing political order. Both President Clinton and Prime Minister Blair came to power opposed to the raw economic neo-liberalism of their predecessors, at a time when that neo-liberalism was vulnerable but continued to effectively constrain policy choices. Furthermore, both leaders apparently subscribe to the view that their parties had to adopt new policies in order to fashion new winning coalitions in the 1990s and beyond, and also that their countries now need new economic policies in order to prosper in a more globalised economy. Since the New Deal of the 1930s, the Democratic Party has sought to unite the working class and middle class around the issue of economic security while simultaneously attracting substantial capitalist financial backing for the party and its candidates. Clinton's health security bill sought to resurrect that successful cross-class political strategy in the new context of global capitalism and fiscal austerity imposed by large budget deficits and public opposition to tax increases. With its courting of middle England voters and its overt appeal to some capitalists in order to diversify the economic investors in New Labour and its agenda, New Labour appears to be pursuing a similar cross-class coalition strategy.

A third way? Neo-liberalism plus active government

According to Reich (1999:46–8), 'third way' governments in both Western Europe and the US have accepted five tenets of economic neo-liberalism:

1 A reduction of budget deficits
2 A preference for less government regulation in the US and a rejection of state ownership in European countries
3 An acceptance of expanded global trade and capital mobility
4 An acceptance of flexible labour markets and, finally,
5 A reduction of the welfare safety net.

Confirming Reich's judgement that the Anglo-American version of the third way is more conservative than its continental counterpart, Clinton and New Labour have both added to that list the eschewing of enforceable obligations upon the winners of economic globalisation and the acceptance of growing inequality.

Despite embracing much of the neo-liberal agenda, the third way is not simply economic neo-liberalism. Rather, if its advocates are to be believed, third way policies seek to combine market-driven economic change with a new form of government activism that addresses the economic anxiety and costs of neo-liberal policies. Although accepting market-driven economic change and therefore rejecting the old left's hostility to the market, advocates of the third way also insist that government has a positive role to play in helping individuals cope with economic change. This is to be achieved primarily by ensuring that individuals have the opportunity to obtain the necessary skills and education to adjust successfully to new economic conditions. This new form of government activism is supposedly different from the so-called tax and spend policies traditionally associated with the Democratic Party in the US and old Labour in the UK precisely because it relies more upon the private sector and individual responsibility.

Clinton's version of active government has sought to recreate the successful New Deal Democratic coalition, which used government-provided economic security to forge a cross-class alliance between the middle class, working class and the poor. In his 1996 State of the Union address, Clinton (1996a:5,10) declared that although 'the era of big government is over . . . we can't go back to the era of fending for yourself', insisting instead that 'people who work hard still need support to get ahead in the new economy. They need education and training for a lifetime. They need more support for families raising children.

They need retirement security. They need access to health care. More and more Americans are finding that the education of their childhood simply doesn't last a lifetime.' Two years later Clinton further declared: 'we have moved past the sterile debate between those who say government is the enemy and those who say government is the answer. My fellow Americans, we have found a third way. We have the smallest government in 35 years, but a more progressive one' (Clinton, 1998a:2). Clinton's version of positive government has thus far demonstrated three central policy concerns: enabling Americans to exploit the economic opportunities created by neo-liberal policies, providing economic security in the new context of economic globalisation, and finally ensuring that 'work pays' for the poor (Table 3.1).

Education and economic opportunity

Reich (1997) has argued that in the new context of intensified globalised economic competition, economic growth and falling unemployment are insufficient to address the problem of increasing economic inequality; and that government needs instead to prioritise policies which enhance investment in human capital. Echoing Reich, President Clinton has regularly emphasised increased education as essential for economic success in the contemporary globalised economy. In his very first presidential address to Congress, Clinton (1993a:400–1) stressed the need for more post-secondary education in order for the US to be competitive in the global economy. According to him, government should be responsible for making available the education and training which are necessary for both economic opportunity and security. Instead of curbing the economic changes wrought by global capitalist competition, government should help prepare Americans for employment in a changing economy by ensuring good quality state schools and an opportunity to secure post-secondary education.

Improving state schools

Like New Labour in the UK, Clinton has therefore proposed a number of policies intended to improve the quality of the state schools and to increase access to post-secondary education and training. However, in the federal US where state and local governments are primarily responsible for school education, the Clinton administration has only been able to affect the quality of state education at the margins. For example, Clinton initiated the Goals 2000 policy, which provides competitive federal grants to states to finance educational policies that states define as necessary to improve state education. Later, he proposed additional competitive federal grants to help states improve their weakest schools; and when Republican congressional majorities threatened to abolish Goals 2000, Clinton successfully fought to preserve it until 2000.

To improve educational standards, Clinton has urged states to adopt national testing for both pupils and teachers. As he had done as governor of Arkansas,

Table 3.1 *Clinton's policies*

To provide economic opportunity:	To provide economic security:	To ensure that 'work pays':
expand Head Start for pre-school children from families below poverty line	education as in column 1	increased earned income tax credit (EITC)
	national health insurance (defeated)	increased minimum wage
improve state schools:	health insurance portability	child care subsidies, especially for welfare to work
Goals 2000	allow those who are older than 50 years to buy into Medicare	national health insurance (defeated)
national tests and standards	provide unemployed with health insurance for up to 6 months	health insurance for children
tests to improve teacher quality	Medical and Family Leave Act	extend federal protective regulations to 'workfare'
federal funds to improve teacher quality, to reduce class size and to improve the physical plant of schools	GI Bill for workers who become unemployed (consolidation of existing education and re-training programs into a $2600 grant)	
charter schools and competition in the state sector	introduction of one-stop centres for unemployed	
replace 'social promotion' with after-school and holiday tuition	universal savings accounts for retirement	
reduce the financial barriers to post-secondary education:	defend 'old' Democratic policies:	
tax subsidies for tuition costs	social security pensions	
help with costs in return for national service	Medicare for elderly	
increased Pell scholarships for low income students	Medicaid for those on welfare	
lower interest on student loans	protect Food Stamps	
	protect low income home energy assistance program (LIHEAP)	

Clinton has supported the testing of teachers to ensure that they are qualified to teach; but he has also sought federal funds to help improve teacher quality. Opposing the practice of social promotion (whereby students are automatically promoted to the next grade in order to remain with their age cohort even when they are educationally unprepared), Clinton has urged states and educational districts to provide summer schools and after-school tuition to help weaker students. Furthermore, Clinton has supported the creation of new charter schools in order to improve the quality of state education by introducing competition within the state sector. In addition, Clinton has recommended additional federal funding to improve the physical structure of schools, to hire more teachers in order to reduce class size in the early years of schooling, and to construct more class rooms. His 1999 State of the Union address proposed that the federal government hold states and school districts accountable for their effective use of federal educational funds (Clinton, 1999:4–5). Hence, like a traditional Democrat, he has supported increased federal funds for state schools, which are primarily the responsibility of state and local governments; but like a New Democrat, he has sought to ensure that those federal funds are used effectively at state and local level.

Seeking to construct a broad cross-class coalition, Clinton has identified himself with only one pre-university educational policy which targeted the poor: increased spending on Head Start, a pre-school program which was created during the 1960s' 'war on poverty' and which prepares children from families with incomes below the official poverty line for school. Since Clinton became president, the budget for Head Start has increased from $2.2 billion in fiscal year 1992 to $4.4 billion for fiscal year 1998. Even so, Head Start still covers only 40 per cent of eligible pre-schoolers (Kirchhoff, 1998:1745–6). His cross-class political strategy also explains his opposition to Republican attempts to secure public funding of private schooling via the creation of tax-free educational savings accounts and school vouchers.

Reducing the financial barriers to post-secondary education

Clinton has also sought to reduce the financial barriers to post-secondary education, so that two years of post-secondary education would become as universal as a high school diploma had been for earlier generations of Americans (Clinton, 1997a:5). Although most of his proposed policies primarily benefit the middle class, some benefit a broader cross-section of Americans and others have been specifically targeted at the poor.

The Clinton administration successfully pressed for a tax credit (worth up to $1500) annually for the cost of the first two years of post-secondary tuition. This was clearly targeted at the middle class since only those paying at least $1500 of federal income tax receive the full benefit, while those paying little or no federal income tax receive little or nothing. It has also provided cheaper student loans through legislation that eliminates the middlemen in the granting and administering of federally guaranteed student loans for university.

In 1993, Clinton proposed and Congress legislated a new national service programme which would reward community service by providing its participants not only with a stipend and, when necessary, with health insurance and child care, but also with an education grant worth $4725 annually for up to two years. By ensuring that such community service would be remunerated rather than unpaid, the Clinton administration ensured that working class and lower income Americans were able to participate in the programme, thereby earning a substantial contribution towards the cost of two years of post-secondary education. When, in 1995, the new Republican congressional majorities sought to abolish Clinton's national service policy, Clinton successfully fought to retain it although he had to accept a substantial reduction in its budget which restricted the number of participants. In addition, Clinton successfully supported the expansion of Pell grant scholarships for students from economically disadvantaged backgrounds and an increase in work-study grants.

Despite occasionally calling for the restoration of the old social contract which once compelled employers to share their prosperity with their employees (Clinton, 1995:305; 1996a:5), the Clinton administration has relied exclusively on expanded access to post-secondary education to solve the problems of growing inequality and stagnating or declining wages (Clinton, 1993a:399; 1993b:1; 1994:194; 1995:300, 303). It certainly has eschewed any more radical mechanisms for reducing inequality, including Reich's suggestion to use tax cuts to reward employers who recognise their wider social responsibilities and to penalise with tax increases those that do not (Reich, 1997:293). 'We know', Clinton has argued, 'from the 1990 census that most young people who get at least two years of college or more get a job with a growing income. And young people who have less than two years of college, or who don't even have a high school diploma tend to get a job with a stagnate [sic] or a declining income' (Clinton, 1997c:4). However, even if Clinton succeeds in his declared goal of making two years of post-secondary education the new norm, the data contradict his assumption that greater education will necessarily produce real income gains, much less reduce economic inequality (Mishel *et al.*, 1999).

Economic security

Accepting Reich's (1997:121–2) distinction between the different types of new and old unemployment, Clinton (1994:195) explained the need for more education and training in this way: 'the old unemployment system just sort of kept you going while you waited for your old job to come back. We've got to have a new system to move people into new and better jobs because most of those old jobs just don't come back.' To address this new type of unemployment, Clinton then proposed a GI bill for workers which would consolidate existing retraining and education programmes into 'a simple voucher worth $2600 for unemployed or underemployed workers to use as they please for community college tuition or other training' (1996a:5).

However, for all its rhetoric, the Clinton administration has achieved little new investment in improving the skills of economically dislocated workers. Not least, this was because Robert Reich, the leading advocate of such investment, was quickly marginalised in the first Clinton administration by the key economic decision-makers – Secretary of Treasury Lloyd Bentsen, Office of Management and Budget (OMB) Director Leon Panetta and Federal Reserve Board Chairman Alan Greenspan – all of whom gave priority to reducing the budget deficit, not to increasing public investment in education and training. Furthermore, with the exception of the chairwoman of his Council of Economic Advisers, Laura Tyson, Clinton's economic advisers rejected Reich's idea of public investment and a separate investment budget and especially the need to provide more resources for post-secondary education and skills training for the unemployed and poor (Reich, 1997:89, 146–7). Reich discovered that the Clinton administration was unwilling to tax the economic winners of the past two decades to pay for the necessary education and training which would help welfare recipients and the unemployed obtain decent jobs (Reich, 1997:155–6, 213–14). The one education and training innovation which Reich backed and which was enacted saved money. Responding to the new type of unemployment, this initiative introduced one-stop centres which not only paid unemployment insurance to qualifying workers but simultaneously provided help with re-training and finding a job (Reich, 1997:130–1).

Health security

For Clinton, the national government also has a legitimate and positive role in ensuring the availability of both health care and retirement pensions. Clinton's health security bill, rejected by Congress, would have provided all Americans with high quality health insurance. That bill fitted the New Deal model, although the context of large budget deficits and public opposition to increased taxation precluded Clinton from opting for direct government provision of universal health care. In effect, Clinton's health security bill combined the agenda of economic security pursued by New Deal Democrats with the fiscal prudence of New Democrats (Skocpol, 1997), but eventually to no avail.

After Congress had rejected his health security bill, Clinton manifested his commitment to health security by supporting a number of incremental health care reforms, such as the Kassebaum-Kennedy law for health insurance portability which made it easier for Americans to change jobs without losing their health insurance. Recognising that unemployment threatens Americans with the loss of employer-provided health care, Clinton's acceptance speech to the 1996 Democratic convention, his 1997 State of the Union address and his 1997 budget proposed that the government provide health care for those workers who become temporarily unemployed (Clinton, 1996b:2488; 1997a:7). Similarly, to improve the quality of health care provided by managed care plans, Clinton's

1998 and 1999 State of the Union addresses proposed that Congress enact an enforceable patient's bill of rights (Clinton, 1999:5–6; 1998a:6).

Defend policies providing economic security

Just as New Labour committed additional resources to the National Health Service (NHS), which was the creation of old Labour, Clinton has defended popular 'old' Democratic policies, especially social security pensions, Medicare and Medicaid. His 1999 State of the Union address proposed to use more than three-quarters of the projected budget surplus for social security and Medicare and another 11 per cent to help fund universal savings accounts for retirement security (Clinton, 1999:2–3). Furthermore, after successfully resisting the large cuts in Medicare and Medicaid proposed by congressional Republicans, Clinton later accepted substantial cuts in both health care programs in order to balance the federal budget. Clinton operated here both as a New Deal Democrat defending government-provided economic security and as a New Democrat committed to fiscal prudence. In addition, Clinton defended the low income home energy assistance programme, which subsidises the fuel bills of low income families from the budget cuts of House Republicans. Finally, despite signing the Republicans' 1996 welfare bill, Clinton prevented them from de-nationalising Food Stamps (which subsidise food purchases for those with low incomes), while accepting small cuts in benefits and eligibility.

Making work pay

Clinton and New Labour's Chancellor Gordon Brown share a common desire to make work pay for low income workers, including those forced off welfare. In contrast to the 1996 welfare law which simply used compulsion to obviate the problem of economic disincentives discouraging welfare recipients from moving off welfare into paid work, Clinton has sought to provide an economic carrot to encourage that movement. Despite Clinton's simplistic declaration that 'the best anti-poverty program is still a job'(1996c:2217), he, unlike the Republican authors of the 1996 welfare law (see below), at least tackled some of the major obstacles confronting the working poor: low wages and the expenses of paid employment, especially the high cost of health care and child care.

Increasing the EITC

One of Clinton's greatest successes in making work pay was his qualitative expansion of the earned income tax credit (EITC) which benefits the working poor, not welfare recipients. As evidenced by his introduction of the working family tax credit in the 1999 budget, the British Chancellor Gordon Brown is a fan of the EITC, which rewards paid work by providing low wage workers with a refundable income tax credit. Since the credit is calculated as a percentage of earned income, the value of the credit increases as wages increase until the maximum credit is attained; then the credit gradually decreases until it is finally

Table 3.2 *Clinton's 1993 expansion of the earned income tax credit (EITC)*

		1993 pre-Clinton	Clinton's original EITC proposal	New EITC legislated 1993
Family with 2 or	Income ceiling:	$23070	$30000	$28000
more children	Maximum benefit:	$1513	$3371	$3371
Low income worker,	Income ceiling:	Ineligible	$9000	$9000
no children	Maximum benefit:	Ineligible	$306	$306

phased out. The EITC therefore provides an incentive for paid work since every dollar earned will produce more income for a family. The EITC provides a dollar for dollar reduction in the taxes which eligible low wage earners owe the federal government. If the credit exceeds the worker's tax liability, the government refunds the difference.

Candidate Clinton had originally pledged to expand the EITC so that 'no one with a family who works full time' would be under the poverty line (Cloud, 1993:585; Danziger and Gottschalk, 1995:36). Although large budget deficits and conservative opposition compelled President Clinton to retreat from that pledge, he still proposed to increase the EITC sufficiently to ensure that minimum wage working families with one or two children would earn more than the official poverty line once food stamp benefits were included (Cloud, 1993:583–4). Furthermore, he proposed to extend the EITC to almost all families earning less than median family income – that is, the families which had suffered most from declining or stagnating wages (Mishel *et al.*, 1999). Clinton also intended this expanded eligibility to help neutralise the immediate regressive effects of his proposed energy tax (Cloud, 1993:585–6).

Clinton did not achieve all that he had originally sought, but he more than doubled the maximum EITC benefit for families with at least two children, from $1513 in 1993 to $3371 by 1996 (Table 3.2). In addition, Clinton increased the maximum income that a family could earn before becoming ineligible for the EITC. Pre-Clinton, families with two or more children earning up to $23070 annually were eligible for the EITC. Clinton originally proposed to increase the maximum family income to $30000, but Congress forced him to accept an income ceiling of $28000 (Table 3.2). Also, for the first time, Clinton extended EITC eligibility to low income workers who did not have children. Finally, when the Republican majorities in Congress proposed to cut the EITC and to exclude from eligibility low wage workers without children, Clinton used his veto to defeat them.

Increasing the minimum wage

Despite the Republican majorities in the 104th Congress, Clinton achieved a two-stage increase in the hourly minimum wage from $4.25 to $5.15 (£3.22)

Table 3.3 *Increasing the hourly minimum wage*

Pre-Oct. 1996	Clinton's 1996 two-stage increase		Clinton's 1999 proposal	New Labour's 1999 minimum wage
	1st stage (1 Oct. 1996)	final stage (1 Sep. 1997)		
$4.25 (£2.65)	$4.75 (£2.97)	$5.15 (£3.22)	$6.15 (£3.84)	£3.60 ($5.76)

by September 1997 (Table 3.3). Although UK per capita income is only 76% of US per capita income (Mishel *et al.*, 1999:357), the new US minimum wage is less than the £3.60 (about $5.76) implemented by New Labour (Table 3.3). Clinton's 1999 State of the Union address called for a further two-stage increase in the minimum wage to $6.15 (£3.84) (Clinton, 1999:5).

Similarly, manifesting his commitment to making work pay for those forced off welfare, Clinton used his veto to compel congressional Republicans to include more federal funds for child care in the 1996 welfare law. Furthermore, Clinton proposed to introduce national health insurance, which would have removed the high cost of medical insurance and medical care as a deterrent to paid employment for welfare recipients. Although Congress rejected that legislation in 1994, three years later Clinton compelled congressional Republicans to spend $24 billion over five years to pay for health insurance for up to half of the ten million children who currently lack it. Finally, ignoring the opposition of congressional Republicans, the Clinton administration extended the protection of federal law to 'workfare', especially the minimum wage (Katz, 1997a).

The limits to making work pay

Prioritising moving welfare recipients into work, both Clinton and New Labour see the transformation of the welfare state as an essential part of their political projects. Blair's professed desire to end the 'something for nothing' culture echoes Clinton's formulation of 'two years and out'. Even if unintentionally, the harsh rhetoric of both leaders benefits the conservative attack on welfare and war on the poor. Clinton's support for the Republicans'1996 welfare law identified him with a conservative version of welfare reform.

Having extracted some concessions from the congressional Republican majority, Clinton signed in August 1996 the Republicans' welfare legislation – the Personal Responsibility and Work Opportunity Reconciliation Act (PRWORA) – which cut welfare spending by $54.1 billion through to 2002 and therefore helped shrink the budget deficit. Although Clinton objected to some relatively minor parts of the 1996 welfare law – e.g., the denial of

---

Box 3.1 *Key features of the 1996 welfare law, the Personal Responsibility and Work Opportunity Reconciliation Act (PRWORA)*

- Abolished the right (or entitlement) to welfare
- Individual states determine eligibility
- Maximum 5 years life-time limit on welfare; permit individual states to set lower limit
- Maximum 2 years on welfare without work; permit individual states to set lower limit
- Cut welfare spending and therefore reduced the budget deficit
- Denied welfare to legal immigrants
- Cut Food Stamp benefits (i.e., a federal subsidy for low income families to purchase food)
- Replaced matching federal funds with a federal block grant
- Permitted states to deny welfare to children born to welfare recipients and to unwed parents under 18 years
- Created incentives for states to cut welfare spending
- Assumed that anyone who wants a job can get and keep one

---

benefits to legal immigrants, he endorsed the principal features of the 1996 law (Box 3.1) which accorded with his professed desire to 'end welfare as we know it' (Clinton, 1996c). That law ended the right to welfare and therefore gave individual states the authority to exclude needy families from welfare, simply because the money was not available. It also gave the states the power to determine eligibility, although the states have historically employed a variety of arbitrary criteria – 'suitable home', 'man-in-the-house', and 'availability for work' rules, as well as racial discrimination – to exclude impoverished families from welfare.

Rather than providing welfare recipients with the education and other skills necessary to obtain and keep a job which would provide them with an adequate family income, PRWORA is wedded to the work-first model of getting welfare recipients either into paid work or into job search programmes. The 1996 law 'assumes that anyone on the dole can get and keep a job; it sets a time limit, then leaves recipients to find their way out of the welfare culture on their own. The top priority is steering recipients directly into paid or unpaid jobs, or at least job search and job placement programs. Training is a much lower priority, and long-term training is almost out of the question' (Grunwald, 1997). The original version of Clinton's welfare reform bill was withdrawn and re-written because its attempt to fund welfare to work would have cost $2 billion more than existing welfare spending (Reich, 1999:49; 1997:319). Clinton's success in the 1997 budget negotiations in extracting from congressional Republicans an additional $3 billion to help move welfare recipients into work and his recent proposal for a further $1 billion to extend training for welfare to work do not fundamentally alter PRWORA.

In accordance with candidate Clinton's pledge that the rule for welfare recipients would be 'two years and out', the 1996 law imposed a two year cap on receiving welfare without being required to work and limited most welfare recipients to a lifetime maximum of five years even though 93 per cent of welfare recipients in 1995 were single parent families (Wadden, 1998:203). Hence, the law forces even single parents with young pre-school children to work. Furthermore, the 1996 law also permitted individual states to impose stricter time limits; in less than one year after the passage of the 1996 law, one-third of the states had already done so (Jencks, 1997:2). For example, Massachusetts requires all welfare recipients, including single parents with young children, to begin work within 60 days, not two years. Also, by abolishing any right to welfare and by introducing a federal block grant, the new law created clear political and financial incentives for the states to reduce welfare spending. Finally, reflecting the cultural-religious conservatism of the religious right, the law permits states to deny welfare to children born to welfare recipients and to unwed parents under 18 years.

Unlike Clinton's original welfare reform bill which would have made the government the employer of last resort for welfare recipients compelled to work (Clinton, 1993a:401), the 1996 PRWORA assumes that all who want to work can find employment in the private sector. While the current booming US economy with its low level of unemployment is partly responsible for the reduction in the welfare rolls, a future economic recession would reveal the hollowness of that assumption. Clinton's policies for ensuring that there are jobs for individuals who are forced off welfare evidence his credentials as a New Democrat. To encourage business to invest in areas of high unemployment (so-called empowerment zones) in order to overcome the geographical mismatch between the unemployed and job opportunities, Clinton favours tax incentives and government guaranteed loans. In addition, he uses both tax incentives and moral persuasion (the Welfare to Work Partnership) to induce businesses to employ former welfare recipients (Clinton, 1996a:5; 1997a:3, 8; 1998a:10; 1999:7). Furthermore, under the new 1996 law, some states use welfare funds to subsidise businesses which employ welfare recipients (Katz, 1997b:2605).

Although there might be some ambiguity about whether New Labour gives priority to helping the poor and reducing poverty or to reducing the welfare rolls in order to reduce government expenditure, Clinton's public statements have constantly emphasised welfare reduction, not poverty reduction, as the measure of successful welfare reform (Clinton, 1999:1, 7; 1998a:1, 6; 1998b:4; 1997a:1, 3; 1997b: 2; 1997c:2, 3; 1996b:2485; Democratic Party, 1996:42). Clinton's definition of successful welfare reform implicitly agrees with conservatives that the problem is welfare, not poverty. Furthermore, reducing the welfare rolls helps achieve the neo-liberal objective of reducing and eventually eliminating deficit financing.

Conclusion

Clinton has been more successful in achieving the third way's neo-liberal objectives than its distinctive goal of investing in human capital. For example, his first budget substantially reduced the budget deficit. Then, under pressure from the new Republican congressional majorities elected in November 1994, his 1996 State of the Union address noted that there was now a 'broad bipartisan consensus that permanent deficit spending must come to an end' (Clinton, 1996a:2). Reflecting this ostensible consensus, the 1997 budget agreement between Clinton and congressional Republicans together with a booming US economy, the 1990 deficit reduction act, and the 1993 budget eliminated the budget deficit. Similarly, under Clinton's leadership, Congress enacted the North American Free Trade Agreement (NAFTA) despite the opposition of organised labour – a core Democratic constituency – which feared that Mexico's low wages and lack of environmental protection would hurt American workers.

According to Reich (1999:50), Clinton's attempt to achieve active government was obstructed by two political obstacles that threaten the third way in all countries. First, Clinton never solved the problem of how to pay for the necessary public investment in education and training. Deficit financing or government borrowing was ruled out by the need to reduce the deficit in order to avoid high interest rates that would discourage capitalist investment. Skocpol (1997:174) has concluded that the large budget deficit of approximately $300 billion inherited by Clinton prevented him from achieving significant public investment: 'the Clinton administration's hopes to "invest" in education, national service, and job training were dashed against the rocks of fiscal austerity, as were its plans for welfare reforms that included job training and child care for single mothers as they were pushed off public assistance'. According to Reich (1997:105), Clinton shares some of the blame for this failure since he did not make a sufficient effort to educate the US public about the long-term importance of such public investment.

Second, Clinton found it difficult to fashion a durable supporting coalition because major social interests usually supported only one of the two dimensions of the third way. For example, many large corporations and wealthy individuals favour economic neo-liberalism; but they do not want to have to pay for the necessary training and education. Similarly, while organised labour might support education and training programmes, it did not see them as sufficiently compensating ordinary workers for the increased economic uncertainty produced by expanded free trade and greater labour market flexibility (Reich, 1997:68–9, 131, 137–9). Hence, while Clinton qualifies as a 'third wayer', he has enjoyed only limited success in achieving the public investment which distinguishes the third way from neo-liberalism. It will be interesting to see if New Labour can now fare any better.

References

Clinton, W. J. (1993a) 'Clinton Outlines His Plan to Spur the Economy', *Congressional Quarterly* (20 February), pp. 399–404.

Clinton, W. J. (1993b), 'President Clinton's First Inaugural Address', http://www.usembassy.org.uk/clintn1.htm.

Clinton, W. J. (1994), 'Clinton [State of the Union Speech] Stresses Welfare, Health-Care Reform', *Congressional Quarterly* (29 January), pp. 194–8.

Clinton, W. J. (1995), 'Clinton [State of the Union] Speech Envisions Local Empowerment', *Congressional Quarterly* (28 January), pp. 300–5.

Clinton, W. J. (1996a), 'State of the Union Address: US Is "Making a Difference" for World Peace', http://www.usembassy.org.uk/clintn3.htm.

Clinton, W. J. (1996b), 'Clinton Describes His Path to the 21st Century', *Congressional Quarterly* (31 August), pp. 2485–9.

Clinton, W. J. (1996c), 'Presidential News Conference: Clinton Says Welfare Bill is a "Real Step Forward"', *Congressional Quarterly* (3 August), pp. 2216–18.

Clinton, W. J. (1997a) 'Clinton's State of the Union Address', http://www.usembassy.org.uk/clintn6.htm.

Clinton, W. J. (1997b), 'President Clinton's Inaugural Address', http://www.usembassy.org.uk/clintn6.htm.

Clinton, W. J. (1997c), 'Clinton Democratic National Committee Remarks', http://www.usembassy.org.uk/clintn17.htm.

Clinton, W. J. (1998a), 'Clinton's State of the Union Address', http://www.usembassy.org.uk/clintn55.htm.

Clinton, W. J. (1998b), 'Clinton's Remarks at Democratic Leadership Council "National Conversation"', http://www.usembassy.org.uk/clintn78.htm.

Clinton, W. J. (1999), 'The State of the Union Address', http://www.whitehouse.gov.

Cloud, David S. (1993), 'Clinton Looking to Tax Credit to Rescue Working Poor', *Congressional Quarterly* (13 March), pp. 583–7.

Danziger, S. and Gottschalk, P. (1995), *America Unequal*, Cambridge, Harvard University Press.

Democratic Party (1996), 'Draft Democratic National Platform,' *Congressional Quarterly* (17 August), pp. 35–52.

Grunwald, M. (1997) 'Welfare-to-Work Isn't Cheap: How She Got a Job', *The American Prospect*, 33:25–9.

Jencks, C. (1997), 'The Hidden Paradox of Welfare Reform: Why Single Mothers May Earn More but Do Worse', *The American Prospect*, 32:33–40.

Katz, J. (1997a), 'Worker Protections Remain for Welfare Recipients', *Congressional Quarterly* (2 August), pp. 1847–8.

Katz, J. (1997b), 'Long-Term Challenges Temper Cheers for Welfare Success', *Congressional Quarterly* (25 October), pp. 2603–10.

Kirchhoff, S. (1998), 'Head Start Is Growing, But Is It Improving?', *Congressional Quarterly* (27 June), pp. 1743–6.

Mishel, L., Bernstein, J. and Schmitt, J. (1999), *The State of Working America 1998–99*, Ithaca, N.Y., Cornell University Press.

Reich, R. (1997), *Locked in the Cabinet*, New York, Alfred A. Knopf.

Reich, R. (1999), 'We Are All Third Wayers Now', *The American Prospect*, 43:46–51.

Skocpol, T. (1997), *Boomerang: Health Care Reform and the Turn against Government*, New York, W.W. Norton.

Skowronek, S. (1993), *The Politics Presidents Make*, Cambridge, Mass., Harvard University Press.

Wadden, A. (1998), 'A Liberal in Wolf's Clothing: Nixon's Family Assistance Plan in the Light of 1990s Welfare Reform', *Journal of American Studies*, 32(2):203–18.

4

New Labour and the
'Left that is left' in Western Europe

Jill Lovecy

Introduction

One prominent element in the party's overall transition from 'old' to 'New' Labour, noted in Chapter 1, was its commitment to engaging constructively in what has now become the European Union (EU) (on this see Chapter 17). Under Neil Kinnock, then John Smith and Tony Blair, the party increasingly projected itself as being at ease with things European. This was facilitated during Thatcher's ascendancy by the trade unions' new interest in Europe as a source of employment-related rights, and by the presence of the French social democrat Jacques Delors, a forceful advocate of building Europe's social dimension, at the head of the European Commission from 1985 to 1994. This broad re-orientation underway within the UK labour movement found symbolic expression in the TUC's invitation to Delors to address its 1988 Congress, and in the warmth of his reception there.

Whilst Europe figured positively in New Labour's 1997 manifesto, however, the policies of other west European social-democratic parties did not. There was, it is true, little incentive for New Labour to identify itself with the European Left in the late 1980s and early 1990s. This was a period when most of these parties were engaged in rethinking their policy priorities against a general trend of electoral decline. By the time of Blair's election as party leader in July 1994, only Spain, of the five large EU member-states, was governed from the Left. In contrast, the centre-left sources claimed for New Labour policies across the Atlantic and in other parts of the English-speaking world – however problematic these claims – had the immeasurable advantage of associating the party and its leadership with electoral success and the aura of office.

Nevertheless Blair's triumphant entry into Downing Street on 2 May 1997 was to be dramatically re-cast, within a matter of weeks, in a quite new light: as a decisive turning-point in the political fortunes of the European Left.

On 3 June 1997 New Labour was joined in France by a 'pluralist left' government under the socialist party leader, Lionel Jospin. This was a wholly unexpected turn of events, resulting from President Jacques Chirac's misjudgement

Table 4.1 *Governments led from left-of-centre in EU member-states (as of May 1999)*

Date govt formed	Country	PM & PM's party*	Composition of government
June 1986	Austria	V.Klima[a] SPÖ	coalition + *christian democrats*
Jan. 1993	Denmark	P.N.Rasmussen SD	coalition + *three small centre parties*
Oct. 1993	Greece	C.Simitis[b] PASOK	single-party majority-government
Aug. 1994	Holland	W.Kok PvdA[c]	coalition *radical-centre & neo-liberal right*
Sep. 1994	Sweden	G.Persson[d] SAP	single-party minority-government
April 1995	Finland	P.Lipponen SSDP	coalition + *ex-communists, greens, Swedish minority party & conservatives*
Oct. 1995	Portugal	A.Guterres PS(P)	single-party minority-government
May 1997	**UK**	**Tony Blair (N)LP**	**single party majority-government**
June 1997	France	L. Jospin PS(F)	coalition + *communists, greens & other left*
Oct. 1998	Germany	G. Schröder SPD	coalition + *greens*
Nov. 1998	Italy	M.d'Alema PDS	coalition + *other centre-left, greens & centre*

[a] F. Vranitzky, SPÖ, to Jan. 1997
[b] A. Papandreou, PASOK, to Jan. 1996
[c] Coalition collapsed May 1999, but remained as caretaker government pending new elections
[d] I. Carlsson, SAP, to March 1996
* For a listing of these acronyms and the parties' full titles, see Appendix 2.
Sources: Keesings' Record of World Events 1986–98; West European Politics, election reports, vols 10–22 (1987–99)

in calling early legislative elections. But the west European Left's resurgence as a governing force was to gather pace over the next 18 months, reaching its high point in the autumn of 1998 when the German social democrats finally returned to government (see Table 4.1). By this date, of the EU's five large states only Spain was not governed from the Left. Within a decade of the fall of the Berlin Wall and the demise of the Soviet Union's red empire to the east, the political map of Western Europe had turned unprecedentedly, and almost uniformly, 'pink'. With the addition of Belgium and Luxembourg, where sister parties were in governing coalitions led by their christian-democrat partners, left-of-centre parties were now participating in government in 13 of the EU's 15 states and were leading 11 of them.

The presence in other European governments of a growing number of such parties now served, however, to throw into sharper relief the distinctiveness of New Labour's policy agenda, language and values. Here were parties coming into government pledged, as in France, to halting further privatisation and tackling unemployment by legislating for a 35-hour week; or promising, as in Germany, to repeal recently introduced measures promoting labour-market flexibility and create a neo-corporatist forum between government, employers and the unions in an 'Alliance for Jobs'; or, as in Sweden, committed to sustaining generously redistributive welfare and active labour-market policies with government spending still accounting for nearly 60 per cent of GDP.

The long-standing and pervasive ambiguities that have attached to social democracy and its national variants suggest, however, that it would be unwise simply to juxtapose New Labour, and the identity it now seeks to project, against an otherwise relatively homogeneous family of west European social-democratic parties. Indeed, two other parties, the Spanish PSOE under Felipe Gonzalez and the Dutch PdvA under Wim Kok, did re-invent themselves politically along somewhat similar lines to New Labour in this period. However, these two cases contrast with that of the UK Labour Party in two important respects. Both these parties became advocates of neo-liberal style market disciplines not as parties of opposition but as parties of government. Moreover, in neither of these parties did internal organisational reforms take quite such dramatic forms (Colomé, G. 1998; Wolinetz, 1993; 1995).

Table 4.1 shows that New Labour is set apart from virtually the entire west European Left in its position as a single-party government commanding a clear parliamentary majority. All the other parties – with the sole exception of Greece's PASOK – have, in contrast, been plugged into the politics of *domestic power-sharing* in the contemporary period. This distinction can be summarised in terms of the UK party operating within what has been a highly 'majoritarian' model of democratic government, whereas all the other countries' political systems exhibit significant features of power-diffusion and 'consensualism' (Lijphart, 1984).

What also stands out, perhaps even more strikingly, from this table is the sheer variety of these parties' current political circumstances as parties of government. Here it is worth distinguishing between two separate dimensions to this variety:

- Firstly, in respect of the *forms of power sharing* in which these parties are engaged. For most coalition building is the norm, but in Denmark, Sweden and Portugal (and also in France in the 1988–93 period) left-of-centre parties have chosen instead to form single-party minority governments. Within coalition governments, inter-party negotiations will normally encompass not only the partner parties' cabinet members but also their parliamentary party groups and extra-parliamentary organisations. In the case of minority governments, however, policy bargaining with non-governmental parties may be conducted primarily on a piecemeal basis and within the parliamentary arena (Lovecy, 1991). But for all of these parties inter-party consultations and bargaining with second, third or more parties impact in complex ways on internal party organisation and debate.

- Secondly, in terms of the *extraordinarily diverse assortment of political partners* with which left-of-centre parties in Western Europe have been involved in the contemporary period. These range from the 'pink-red-green' and 'pink-green' combinations of France and Germany; through a variety of more centrist alliances to Finland's 'rainbow' coalition (stretching from the ex-communist left through socialists and greens to conservatives); and to the unprecedented 'purple' coalition formed in Holland. Here, Wim Kok joined with the secular parties of the radical-centre and neo-liberal right, bypassing his erstwhile christian-democratic allies on the centre-right who had participated in every government since 1918 (Wolinetz, 1995:193). This was subsequently mirrored in Belgium following the June 1999 elections when socialists and greens joined a liberal-led coalition, excluding the christian-democrats from government for the first time in 40 years.

In underlining the political heterogeneity of their situations as parties of government, the data presented in Table 4.1 thus reminds us of the widely divergent pathways to power which have been open to these parties at the national level.

The rest of this chapter endeavours to shed light on New Labour's relationship to the changing identity of this broad social-democratic family by examining the embeddedness of its varied national components each within their own, rather differently organised, liberal-democratic states. The primary focus here will not be on their differing policies and programmes, for what we are analysing are parties not policy think-tanks; nor, indeed, political sects. As parties, they seek to mobilise electoral support and position themselves for participation in government and, in doing so, they are each subject to a distinctive mix of domestic, as well as external, pressures and opportunities. And in responding to these, differences in their internal organisational arrangements as parties also matter (Kitschelt, 1994:207–53).

The pressures and opportunities which the parties of the Left face in their domestic environments do not of course derive only from the differing versions of liberal democracy operating in each country (and which they helped to build). The experience of creating and managing mixed economies and welfare states has been crucial to their identities. But here, too, their domestic environments have diverged considerably. Notable differences have centred on the size and status of their public sectors, on the roles played in industrial investment by equity capital and long-term credit respectively (Zysman, 1983; Shonfield, 1965), on the funding principles and management of welfare provision

(Esping-Andersen, 1990) and on the legal framework for industrial relations (Ferner and Hyman, 1992). The Labour Party in the UK has clearly faced a context which, in these respects, stands apart from much of continental Europe – a contrast sometimes characterised in terms of opposing Atlantic and Rhineland models of capitalism (Albert, 1993; see also Lovecy, 2000 on these countries' differing political economies and to the changes they are now under-going in an era of regionalisation and globalisation).

The remainder of this chapter is divided into two main sections. The first looks at the electoral bases of four European parties of the Left (in France, Germany, Italy and Sweden), the differing pathways they have followed into government in the contemporary period and considers the ways in which these have impinged on party reform. A second section then offers a broader histori-cal and comparative canvas against which to set the case of New Labour, by considering the experiences of these four parties in attempting, at varying points during the last forty years, to renew their political identities and reposi-tion themselves within their domestic party-systems.

Patterns of electoral support and pathways to power

During the five years from autumn 1993 to autumn 1998, the parties of the west European Left rode a quite exceptional wave of political success. Of twenty sets of parliamentary elections held in eighteen countries in this period, no less than sixteen resulted in the formation or retention of governments led from left-of-centre. Yet their resurgence as parties of government in this period was not based – in other parts of continental Europe any more than in the UK – on a corresponding electoral resurgence. Most of these parties instead suffered a decline by comparison with their electoral peaks achieved one or two decades previously, or somewhat earlier – the Labour Party's high points being in 1951 and 1966.

As parties committed to humanising capitalism, by developing mechanisms of social solidarity and social justice and seeking in the longer term (and more ambitiously) to replace its social and economic order, all of these parties have faced a number of common challenges in the recent period. These challenges arose notably from the declining electoral weight of the industrial working class and its dispersal within what are now more diversified social formations; and from the shift to media-driven rather than mass party-based electoral cam-paigning. From the 1980s, a rising tide of neo-liberalism directly and vigor-ously contested the values and underlying premises of social democracy, whilst additional electoral competitors emerged in the form of green parties and of a renascent extreme-right.

However, the timing and extent of such trends and their impact on the size and composition of these parties' electoral support have differed significantly. A crucial factor here has been these countries' different electoral systems and their consequences for the structuring of party competition. The use of proportional representation in various forms in most of continental Europe has helped to sustain rather differently structured party systems underpinned by cross-cutting political cleavages, whereas the UK's party system has been largely shaped by the contrasting logic of its winner-takes-all electoral system. But electoral systems are themselves open to change. With the advent of the Fifth Republic, France adopted a modified form of plurality for parliamentary elections in 1958, with a two-ballot system. Combined with the introduction of direct universal suffrage for presidential elections from 1962, again with two ballots, this contributed to the bi-polarisation of the French party system. In Italy, more recently, the 1992 electoral reform for the lower house of the parliament also sought to introduce a bi-polarising logic in order to secure a clearer correlation between electoral choice and the party composition of governments.

Participation in government in the contemporary period has in any case been achieved on the basis of widely varying levels of electoral strength. Table 4.2 ranks 18 left-of-centre parties from the states of the EU and the European Economic Area by electoral strength (see column 3) at the most recent parliamentary elections. Two main groupings of parties can be identified here (with two further parties, in Ireland and Iceland, being marginal players):

• The first encompasses parties securing a major (33–45 per cent) share of the vote. New Labour belongs here, along with eight other parties. Of these only the German, Greek and Portuguese parties, however, along with New Labour, attracted over 40 per cent of the vote.
• The second covers a further seven parties enjoying a more modest level of support (20–25 per cent), with the French PS and the Italian (ex-communist) PDS forming a distinct sub-category. Despite the narrowness of these latter parties' electoral bases, both have constructed electoral alliances securing a share of the vote similar to that of individual parties in the first grouping.

By comparing the data recorded in columns 3 and 4 of Table 4.2, the degree of proportionality between share of votes and share of seats in each country can be seen. New Labour stands out in terms of the disproportionately high share of seats it gained (62.6 per cent based on 43.3 per cent of the vote). But it is joined here not only by PASOK in Greece but also by the PDS in Italy and the French PS, with the latter indeed benefiting from an even higher degree of disproportionality in 1997.

The data presented in this table serves as a reminder that parties commanding limited levels of electoral support can nevertheless aspire to playing a leading role in governing a range of west European states today. To this must be added the corollary that electoral decline has not necessarily served – in the way that it undoubtedly did for the UK Labour Party – as a spur for these other parties to rethink their policy priorities. Equally, it is clear that party leaders seeking to engage directly with such disparately-sized electoral constituencies do face qualitatively different tasks of party and policy management. The recent experiences of four of these parties serve to illustrate these points.

Table 4.2 *Main left-of-centre parties and alliances in 18 west European states ranked by electoral strength at last parliamentary elections (as of May 1999)**

		1 Party/alliance	2 Date of last election	3 % of votes cast	4 % parliamentary seats held
Portugal	PS(P)		Oct. 1995	43.9	48.7
UK	**NL**		**May 1997**	**43.3**	**62.6**
Greece	PASOK		Sep. 1996	41.4	57
Germany	SPD		Sep. 1998	40.9	43.1
Austria	SPÖ		Dec. 1995	38.1	38.8
Spain	PSOE		March 1996	37.5	40.3
Sweden	SAP		Sep. 1998	36.6	37.5
Norway**	DNA		Sep. 1997	35	39.7
Denmark	SD		Sep. 1994	34.6	35.4
Finland	SSDP		March 1995	28.3	31.5
Luxembourg	POSL		June 1994	27.6	28.3
France	PS(F)		May 1995	26.5[a]	45.9[b]
	PS(F) + coalition allies		May 1995	47.8[a]	55.3[b]
Netherlands	PdvA		May 1998	25	30.0
Belgium	PSB +BSP		May 1995	24.5	17.3
Switzerland**	PSS		Oct. 1995	21.8	27
Italy	PDS		April 1996	21.1[b]	23.5
	PDS and coalition allies		April 1996	34.8[b]	45.1
Iceland**	SDP		Aug. 1995	11.4	11.1
Ireland	ILP		June 1997	10.4	10.2

[a] Percentage of votes cast on 1st ballot
[b] Percentage of votes cast for seats allocated by PR
* For a listing of these acronyms and the parties' full titles, see Appendix 2
** Members of the European Economic Area
Sources: Keesings' Record of World Events 1986–99; West European Politics, election reports, vols 10–22 (1987–99); European Journal of Political Research, 4(1):(1998)

Electoral decline and survival in office: the case of the SAP in Sweden
The Swedish party's recent experience is of especial interest because the entrenched hegemony it had previously won in its domestic political system was unequalled in Western Europe. After four decades in office, the SAP was nevertheless relegated to opposition in 1976 when electoral opinion polarised over radical proposals for wage-earner funds (on this, see below). The SAP also lost the next election, in 1979. Over the last two decades, the party has seen its electoral base shrink back, to 36 per cent in 1998, its lowest point since 1921. This shrinkage has especially affected its core industrial working-class base, leaving the SAP increasingly reliant on the support of manual and non-manual public-sector employees and of women. The latter, now the majority of the workforce in the public sector, have been the main beneficiaries of the ambitiously egalitarian

welfare state built up from the 1950s. In 1994, the party temporarily increased its share of the vote (up to 45.4 per cent), only to fall back in 1998 (below its 1991 low point of 37.7 per cent). However, even with its support reduced in this way, the party retained office through a succession of coalition or minority governments from 1982 to 1991, and again following the 1994 and 1998 elections. The policy divisions that beset its three centre-right opponents, especially over the EU, strengthened its position. In these circumstances, and facing competition from a small radical rival (*Venstre*) to its left, the SAP has had strong incentives to try to sustain its stance as the defender of the Swedish welfare state.

Limited electoral support and coalition leadership: the cases of the French PS and the Italian PDS

These parties are the products of two quite contrasting modernising projects, but their current political circumstances, as parties able to mobilise only a limited share of the vote in their own right, deserve consideration here. The French PS entered government under Jospin in 1997 having gained only 26.5 per cent of the vote. This was down from its high point of 38 per cent in 1981, secured in the wake of François Mitterrand's election to the presidency (and which had won the PS an outright parliamentary majority). It was nevertheless a considerable improvement on its performance in 1993, when it fell back to the position it had been in twenty years earlier, with around 20 per cent. In Italy in 1996, the PDS with Achillo Occhetto as its leader, found itself in this same league, with 21.1 per cent. This, too, compared unfavourably with the level of support (27–34 per cent) enjoyed by the Italian Communist Party from the late 1960s into the 1980s but it marked a welcome recovery from the PDS's baptism of fire in 1992, when it had gained a mere 16.1 per cent of the vote. That the leaders of these two parties now head their countries' governments, despite such narrowly based electoral support, is worth underlining. The UK Labour Party, in contrast, contemplated possible nemesis in 1983 when its vote sank to 27.6 per cent and put the third-party Liberal/Social Democratic Alliance, with 25.4 per cent, within overtaking distance. The PS and PDS operate, however, with parliamentary electoral systems (and, indeed, for regional, local and European elections) which offer incentives for smaller parties to stay in the game, maintaining their own separate political identities and organisations. But in the current period both these parties have cemented linkages with much smaller parties to their left and centre in order to take advantage of the substantial incentives which their parliamentary electoral systems also provide – in terms of translating votes into seats – for parties organised in national electoral alliances. However, such alliances, and the electoral systems underpinning them, have provided a particularly complex environment for these parties to pursue policy or organisational reforms.

Exclusion from national government: the case of the German SPD

In contrast, the SPD has in the recent period shared with its UK counterpart the experience of relegation from national office (in its case for 16 years from

1982), whilst nevertheless sustaining a comparatively large electoral base – the SPD's support running between a high of 38.2 per cent in 1983 and a low of 33.5 per cent in 1990. But the SPD's pathway back into national government was quite different from that of New Labour, both because it operates in a federal state with a second tier of elected government at the *Land* level, and because Germany's electoral systems virtually ensure coalition government at both federal and *Land* levels. Smaller parties like the Free Democrats (and more recently the ex-communists in eastern Germany) have thus been able to maintain a parliamentary presence in both federal and *Land* arenas or, like the Greens, have been able to gain entry to them. By limiting the payoffs that could accrue from the SPD fundamentally reforming its programme, these and related institutional factors have also contributed to the SPD's distinctive processes of policy and party management. In particular, a crucial layer of regional leadership, responsive to the party's varying configurations of electoral support and coalition strategies in each *Land*, has been built into the SPD's organisation. Indeed, leading a *Land* government has become a normal qualification for those seeking nomination as its chancellor-candidate. Schröder (candidate in1998) was Prime Minister of Lower-Saxony, Rudolph Scharping (1994) of Rhineland-Palatinate, and Oskar Lafontaine (1990) of Saarland. The presence of this pool of SPD *Land*-premiers certainly facilitated the turnover of chancellor-candidates in the period from 1982 (Schröder being the SPD's fifth challenger to Chancellor Kohl) and limited the capacity of such individuals, with their networks of advisers and party allies, to durably refashion the SPD's policics and alliance strategy.

Programmatic renewal and organisational reform

Institutional and electoral circumstances may have combined in most of western Europe against self-proclaimed party modernisers in the mould of Tony Blair, but the overall centre-of-gravity of west European social democracy nevertheless clearly shifted in the 1980s and 1990s towards a more moderate centre-left stance. This was a period when many of these parties engaged in protracted processes of programmatic renewal, but the results of such rethinking and internal party debate were often inconclusive (Gillespie and Paterson, 1993; Anderson and Camiller, 1994).

In order to set this recent pattern of developments in a broader historical and comparative perspective we will examine here the contrasting trajectories which four of these parties followed in attempting, over the last four decades, to modernise themselves and recast their political identities. In two cases – the SPD in Germany in the late 1950s and the PCI/PDS in Italy in the early 1990s – the leading proponents of these projects understood modernisation to mean *moderation* and an explicit shift towards the centre-ground. In contrast, in both the French PS in the early 1970s and the Swedish SAP later in the same decade, modernisation was conceived – at least, initially – in terms of a *Left radicalisation.* However, whereas in France, Germany and Italy, as in the UK, the trigger for party modernisation came from prolonged exclusion from national government, the SAP's attempted leftward shift emerged, instead, as a response to the mounting problems confronting its own economic strategy in government.

Germany

The SPD's crucial reform, at its 1959 Bad Godesberg conference, was initiated by a younger generation seeking to break through the party's electoral 'glass-ceiling' of 30 per cent of the national vote. By turning the party into a broad-based *Volkspartei* and dropping its symbolically charged commitment to public ownership, they hoped to dislodge the christian-democrat CDU from its dominance over federal government (Braunthal, 1993). This was influentially theorised by Kirchheimer as a new 'catch-all' style of party politics, breaking with mobilisation around class or religious cleavages (Kirchheimer, 1966). He contended, moreover, that re-shaping the programmes of older mass-parties and broadening their electorates would require matching internal organisational reforms, enabling a more personalised style of political leadership to engage with the electorate through the media and reducing the role of party activists in setting policy. This reform trajectory, closely resembling that undertaken recently by New Labour (on this see Chapter 1), was not fully realised by the SPD after 1959, even though it did expand its vote (above 40 per cent) and entered federal government from 1966 to 1982. Its policy-shift remained limited, nevertheless, with the weight of the party's *Land*-level organisations and the requirements of coalition-bargaining helping to sustain marked forms of 'partyness'. This was reinforced after 1974 with the separation of the posts of party chairman and chancellor/chancellor-candidate (until Schröder re-united the two in April 1999).

After 1982, the party's attempts to re-assess its policies and strategy in opposition failed to gain momentum. Such attempts were certainly complicated by the choice of potential alliance options for the SPD, and by the relative moderation of its christian-democrat competitor's policy-stance. However, the party career of a leading figure such as Oskar Lafontaine is also instructive. After 1982, he had emerged as *the* forceful policy moderniser within the SPD's younger generation, provoking its trade union allies with his advocacy of increased labour flexibility. Subsequently, as *Land* prime minister he nevertheless proved adept at defending employment in his region's old industrial base through public subsidies (Padget and Paterson, 1994:112–21). Following his party's defeat in 1990, when he was the SPD's chancellor-candidate, he went on to lead resistance to any re-centring of the SPD, as party chairman counterbalancing Schröder and his New Labour-influenced '*Neue Mitte*'. As a result, party renewal in Germany centred in this period not on the changed identity of the SPD but on the unprecedented alliance it established at the federal level with the Greens, ushering in Europe's first Green foreign minister, and also on the presence in the federal party system after 1989 of the ex-communist PDS, to the SPD's left.

Italy

The Italian Communist Party's reinvention of itself as a moderate social-democratic party of government arguably involved a more far-reaching transformation than that from 'Old' to 'New' Labour – especially since, as the largest party of the Italian Left, it had been excluded from national governments for over forty years. Under Enrico Berlinguer in the 1970s, the party's briefly attempted 'historic compromise' with the christian-democrats had been aimed at re-positioning it as a regime-insider but without directly participating in government. An inconclusive reform debate, triggered by the party's fading electoral fortunes in the 1980s, was transformed in 1989 following the fall of the Berlin Wall when Occhetto, as party leader, proposed that the party should re-found itself. This was finally agreed in 1991. The new name, Party of the Democratic Left (PDS) was designed to exclude any reference to socialism or to labour (Abse, 1994:218) but provoked the breakaway of *Rifondazione Comunista* (RC).

The dropping of democratic centralism meant that programmatic change was certainly accompanied here by fundamental organisational reform (Pamini, 1998), but this did not enable the new PDS to develop a 'catch-all' electoral profile: to the contrary. In any case, its occupation of a social-democratic space was only possible once its smaller socialist rival, the PSI, which Bettino Craxi had converted into a 'presidentialised' vehicle for his own personal ambitions, had, along with the Christian Democrat Party, imploded under the weight of political scandals.

From 1994 these scandals, centring on mafia linkages and corrupt party financing, went on to engulf the new premier, the media-magnate Silvio Berlusconi. It was only at this point that the Olive Tree alliance organised around the PDS was thus finally able to secure a relative parliamentary majority for the Italian Left in 1996, enabling the PDS to enter government. But initially it played a secondary role with Roman Prodi, an unaligned technician, as premier. And indeed rather than sealing the Left's victory, the accession in 1998 of the new PDS leader, d'Alema, to the premiership produced instead a shift into the centre-ground. Whereas Prodi had relied on the RC's parliamentary votes, that linkage was now dropped, support for the governing coalition now incorporating the former christian-democrat prime minister and president, Francesco Cossiga.

France

In contrast, the French case of an attempted Left radicalisation centres on a party which historically lacked a major industrial working-class base (this having been largely won to the French communist party). Moreover, the new PS, founded in 1969–71 to replace the moribund *Section Française de l'Internationale Ouvrière* (SFIO), also faced the distinctive challenge of adapting to the Fifth Republic's highly personalised version of 'catch-all' electoral competition focused on direct elections for the presidency (Cole, 1990). In these circumstances, the new party's commitments to extensive nationalisations and wealth-redistribution helped to underpin the second-ballot alliance it needed with its (electorally stronger) communist rival (the PCF), and to expand its own working-class support at the PCF's expense. Such 'Old' Left policies were also leavened with an array of 'New Left' policies aimed at creating a more participatory democracy, and these proved effective in extending its appeal into the centre-ground and amongst younger voters and women. But this mix of policies and the party's use of proportional representation (PR) for filling its elective bodies made for unstable, and highly opaque, factional politics within the PS. In 1981, both Mitterrand, in his bid for the presidency, and subsequently his party succeeded in winning a substantial share of the working-class vote, but failed to hold on to much of this once they abandoned redistributive policies in government. The President repositioned himself in a moderate left-republicanism, winning re-election in 1988, but as a party of government the PS' vote slid inexorably (Sawicki, 1998).

Once Jacques Delors had ruled himself out as its candidate for the 1995 presidential elections, internal policy debate in the PS again came to be decisively shaped by the requirements of electoral alliances. With Jospin at its head, for the following parliamentary elections (due in 1998) the PS would need electoral pacts not only with the much-reduced PCF but also with the greens and two smaller parties. The renewed priority the party now accorded to tackling unemployment, through legislating for a 35 hour week, and its opposition to further privatisations of utilities, were to provide a crucial platform for this complex electoral alliance-building exercise.

Sweden

This second case of attempted left radicalisation in the 1970s, undertaken by a long-standing party of government with a solid industrial working-class base, centred on establishing an innovative instrument for democratising and socialising the economy: wage-earner funds. A distinctive feature of this case is that this strategy did not originate in either the government's or the party's own policy-processes. Instead, like the solidaristic wage-bargaining strategy which the SAP had pursued in government during the previous two decades, the wage-earner fund proposals were devised by leading economic researchers at the party-linked federation of blue-collar unions, *Landsorganisationen* (LO). As with solidaristic wage-bargaining, the radicalism of this new strategy was complemented by concern to bolster the competitiveness of Swedish capital – in this case by combating the wage-drift which that earlier strategy had generated (Pontusson, 1994:27–33). However, by the time the SAP returned to office in 1982 it had developed its own full-time party-research department and begun to adopt an altogether less radical stance. It introduced only a temporary, much pared-down version of the original project (this legislation being subsequently repealed by Sweden's first conservative-led government in 1992).

The new 'Third Road' strategy it developed in this period was designed to enable the SAP to continue to anchor its identity in redistributive welfare and active labour-market provisions, but prioritised the pursuit of economic efficiency, growth and competitiveness as the necessary pre-conditions for maintaining such policies. This was a key shift, opening up divisions within the SAP as its leadership, in office, went on to become advocates of Swedish entry into the EU and to undertake substantial welfare cutbacks along with income-tax cuts.

Conclusion

This examination of the varying domestic political environments of the west European Left and of the very different timing and extent of these parties' gravitation to date towards a more moderate stance has confirmed key features of New Labour's 'difference'. The particular mix it put together in opposition – pursuing the electoral middle ground, promoting market mechanisms (albeit regulated by appropriate agencies), and radically overhauling its internal structures – has not been fully matched elsewhere. The foregoing discussion has therefore also pointed up the importance of the distinctive institutional environment and political circumstances in the UK during this period that facilitated this modernisation project. New Labour's difference has in turn been reflected in tensions that have arisen over its international initiatives to create 'third way' forums for a wider constituency embracing Clinton's Democrat Party, and also in the EU over its advocacy of 'a culture of enterprise' and labour-market flexibility. Where then should we place New Labour in relation to 'the Left that is left' (Sassoon, 1997:777) in Western Europe? Analyses of New Labour developed by academic and political commentators in the UK suggest three sharply contrasting responses to this question.

A first response has been to characterise New Labour's 'third way' as essentially providing for the 'renewal of social democracy' by 'transcend[ing] both old-style social-democracy and neo-liberalism' (Giddens, 1998:25–6). While identifying this as a 'politics of the radical centre' (Giddens, 1998:44–6, 64–8), Giddens contends that this represents the logical adaptation of social democracy to the social, economic and cultural processes of globalisation. He suggests, therefore, that we should expect other social-democrat parties to follow New Labour's lead, although with appropriate national variations. Yet the foregoing discussion has pointed to formidable obstacles facing any re-alignment of the continental European Centre-Left onto this 'radical-centre'. Indeed, the SPD's attempt to re-invent itself as a 'catch-all' *Volkspartei*, for all its elements of success, testifies to the difficulties which parties seeking to escape from historically-derived identities confront, especially if such changes work against the grain of other institutional dynamics in their domestic environment. At the same time, if New Labour's 'escape' has been made possible by a quite particular mix of circumstances not duplicated elsewhere, then there remains the possibility that changed circumstances in the UK may yet lead to it retreating from this 'radical-centre'.

A second response has been to argue that the centre-ground which New Labour now seeks to occupy, whilst certainly new for the UK, is by no means new for Europe. For with its affirmation of societal interdependence and concern with securing the expression of that interdependence through inclusive political and economic institutions and forms of power-sharing, is this not essentially the territory of continental christian-democracy (Marquand, 1997)? New Labour has certainly promoted its constitutional reform agenda as creating a more inclusive, and responsible, political pluralism. At an early stage the Blair leadership also sought to bring centre-stage a European model of economic management drawn specifically on the traditions of European christian-democracy, in order to give intellectual coherence to its modernisation project for 'Great Britain plc' (Hutton, 1994 and 1998). This was the model of 'stake-holding', derived essentially from Germany's social market economy. However, the adoption of stakeholding as New Labour's 'big idea' proved short-lived. Not least, this was because of the mounting problems that Germany's style of organised capitalism encountered from the early 1990s in the aftermath of reunification (and subsequent evidence that its leading industrial firms and banks were beginning to align themselves more closely on an 'Atlantic' style of capitalism). The difficulties that transposing this approach to the very different institutions of the UK economy would pose were also all too evident: notably for corporate governance and shareholder rights, but also for the forms of labour-market flexibility advocated by New Labour. The latter do not sit easily with the more formal social partnership arrangements that have hitherto enjoyed wide support amongst both christian-democrat and social-democrat parties in much of Western Europe.

A third response has been to locate New Labour squarely outside the twin worlds of social and christian-democracy, by placing it instead within an older, and distinctively British, radical tradition – as a revival of Liberalism or, more specifically, of New Liberalism in the early twentieth century, with its agenda of radical constitutional reform (Gould, 1998; Marr, 1998). There are certainly striking parallels to be drawn between that agenda and New Labour's constitutional ambitions embracing Scottish and Welsh devolution, reform of the House of Lords, the introduction of a Bill of Rights and elements of proportional representation in elections. In terms of the analysis developed here, however, these policies pose something of a paradox. For if New Labour is to prove enduring, it will need to find appropriate underpinnings for this project in its institutional environment – both political and economic. But it is not clear, precisely, that its constitutional agenda will provide these, at least in terms of the structuring of party and electoral competition.

Certainly New Labour's devolution initiatives and the adoption of proportionality for elections to the Scottish Parliament and the Welsh Assembly, from 1999, have introduced the Party in these two regions to the very different dynamics of institutionalised power sharing. Equally, the proportional system used with regional lists for the European elections of 1999 helped stimulate new patterns of electoral behaviour and of partisan identification. Such constitutional and electoral changes may therefore be creating a setting favourable to the forms of political pluralism in which its sister parties of the Second International have learned to operate in continental Europe. Yet the more inclusive and consensual aspects of this setting, it has been suggested here, have both inhibited a decisive shift towards the 'radical-centre' by most of these social-democrat parties whilst also sustaining a space for smaller competitor-parties further to the left, as we have seen in Sweden, France, Italy and Germany. Moreover, as will be seen in subsequent chapters important areas of New Labour's policy-agenda cannot simply be adopted in the UK but need to be matched by decisions processed through the distinctive institutions of the EU arena of governance. Developments at both the national and sub-national levels, in the UK, and at the European level may thus test the New Labour leadership's ambitions to break so decisively with their party's past.

References

Abse, T. (1994), 'Italy: A New Agenda', pp. 189–232 in P. Anderson and P. Camiller (eds), *Mapping the European Left*, London, Verso/*New Left Review*.

Albert, M. (1993), *Capitalism against Capitalism*, London, Whurr.

Anderson, P. and Camiller, P. (eds) (1994), *Mapping the European Left*, London, Verso/*New Left Review*.

Braunthal, G. (1993), *The German Social-Democrats since 1969: A Party in Power and Opposition*, Boulder, Colo. and Oxford, Westview Press.

Cole, A. (1990), *French Political Parties in Transition*, Aldershot, Dartmouth.

Colomé, G. (1998), 'The PSOE: The Establishment of a Governmental Party' in P. Ignazi and C. Ysmal (eds), *The Organisation of Political Parties in Southern Europe*, Westport, Conn., Praeger.

Esping-Andersen, G. (1990), *The Three Worlds of Welfare Capitalism*, Princeton, N.J., Princeton University Press.

Ferner, A. and Hyman, R. (eds) (1992), *Industrial Relations in the New Europe*, Oxford, Blackwell.

Giddens, A. (1998), *The Third Way: The Renewal of Social Democracy*, London: Polity Press.

Gillespie, R. and Paterson, W. (eds) (1993), 'Rethinking Social Democracy in Western Europe', special issue of *West European Politics*, 16(1).

Gould, P. (1998), *The Unfinished Revolution: How the Modernisers Saved the Labour Party*, London, Little Brown.

Hutton, W. (1994), *The State We're In*, London, Jonathan Cape.

Hutton, W. (1998), *The Stakeholding Society: Writings on Politics and Economics*, London, Polity Press.

Keesings' Record of World Events.

Kirchheimer O. (1966), 'The Transformation of Western European Party Systems' in J. Lapalombara and M. Weiner (eds), *Political Parties and Political Development*, Princeton, Princeton University Press.

Kitschelt, H. (1994), *The Transformation of European Democracy*, Cambridge, Cambridge University Press.

Lijphardt, A. (1984), *Democracies: Patterns of Majoritarian and Consensus Government in 21 Countries*, New Haven, Conn.,Yale University Press.

Lovecy J. (1991), 'Une majorité à géométrie variable. Government, Parliament and the Parties, June 1988–June 1990', *Modern and Contemporary France*, 46 (July):49–62.

Lovecy, J. (2000), 'National Varieties of Capitalism and the "Left that is Left" in W. Europe', Department of Government, University of Manchester, Working Paper.

Marquand, D. (1997), 'Blair's birthday. What is There to Celebrate?' *Prospect* (May).

Marr, A. (1998), 'Blair's Big Secret: He's a Liberal', *Observer* (26 July).

Padget, S. and Paterson, W. (1994), 'Germany: Stagnation of the Left' in P. Anderson and P. Camiller (eds), *Mapping the European Left*, London, Verso/New Left Review.

Pamini, M. (1998), 'From Militants to Voters: From the PCI to the PDS' in P. Ignazi and C. Ysmal (eds), *The Organisation of Political Parties in Southern Europe*, Westport, Conn., Praeger.

Pontusson, J. (1994), 'Sweden: After the Golden Age' in P. Anderson and P. Camiller (eds), *Mapping the European Left*, London, Verso/New Left Review.

Sassoon, D. (1997), *One Hundred Years of Socialism. The West European Left in the Twentieth Century*, London, Fontana.

Sawicki, F. (1998), 'The Parti Socialiste: From a Party of Activists to a Party of Government' in P. Ignazi and C. Ysmal (eds), *The Organisation of Political Parties in Southern Europe*, Westport, Conn., Praeger.

Shonfield, A. (1965), *Modern Capitalism: The Changing Balance of Public and Private Power*, London, Oxford University Press.

Wolinetz, S. (1993), 'Reconstructing Dutch Social Democracy', *West European Politics*, 16(1):97–111.

Wolinetz, S. (1995), 'The Dutch Parliamentary Elections of 1994', *West European Politics*, 18(1):188–92.

Zysman, J. (1983), *Government Markets and Growth. Financial Systems and the Politics of Industrial Change*, Oxford, Robertson.

5

New Labour and the machinery of government

Martin Burch and Ian Holliday

Machinery of government questions ought to be an essential concern for any party seriously seeking office. If the machine cannot be made to work, policies cannot be effectively delivered. Three key aspects of the government machine are analysed here: the central executive, the rest of central government, and local government. In each area the chapter examines Labour's promises and performance.

With regard to central government, very few promises were made in opposition and Labour appeared to have few detailed plans for change beyond some experiments with the task force approach to government. In this, it had a good deal in common with many recent governments (of which Heath's in 1970 is the only significant exception). In fact, a lot had been planned for the central executive, and some of it found its way into the public domain through leaks to the press and in the book written by Peter Mandelson and Roger Liddle, *The Blair Revolution: Can New Labour Deliver?* This outlined proposals for a non-ministerial political manager, a strengthened policy unit in the Prime Minister's Office and for closer integration of this office with the Cabinet Office to drive the government's strategy forward (Mandelson and Liddle, 1996:241–2). All this thinking was unofficial and centred on the leader's group of advisers. None of it was mentioned in the manifesto, which made only passing reference to central government as unnecessarily secretive, 'centralised, inefficient and bureaucratic' (Labour Party, 1997:32). Indeed, other than the promise of a Freedom of Information Act (dealt with in Chapter 6), the manifesto contained no concrete proposals.

More was said and promised on local government. The diagnosis was that local authorities had become too constrained by central government and needed to be made more accountable to local people. Labour went into the general election campaign with a lengthy list of commitments which can be organised under the themes of democratisation, finance, standards and partnership (see Box 5.1).

With regard to machinery of government, Labour's official position on assuming office did not mark a significant break with that of its Conservative

---

Box 5.1   *Labour's manifesto and local government*

Democratisation
- Some councillors to be elected annually
- Pilot of elected mayors with executive powers in cities

Finance
- Abolition of 'crude and universal' council tax capping, but reserve powers to be retained to control excessive rises
- Fairer distribution of government grant
- Business rate 'should' be set locally, but no change without full consultation with business
- Capital receipts from council houses sales to be reinvested in housing schemes

Standards
- Compulsory competitive tendering (CCT) to go, but councils to seek 'best value'
- Councils to pursue local target plans for service improvement
- Audit Commission to be given more powers to monitor performance and efficiency
- Where necessary, government to send in management team with powers to remedy failure
- Local education authorities (LEAs) to devolve more power and monies to school heads and governors
- LEAs that are failing to be suspended with central management team sent in

Partnership
- Councils to have a duty to promote the economic, social and environmental well-being of their area
- Councils to be given powers to develop local partnerships with voluntary organisations and business

---

predecessor. The restructuring of central government into executive agencies under the Next Steps programme had been accepted in opposition, as had the move towards the application of more effective management techniques and efficiency drives (Theakston, 1997). Concerning the functions and finance of local government, Labour's policy was also in line with that of its predecessors. True, local authorities were to be treated a little more considerately, but they were not promised extra money, or any return of the powers taken from them. Labour's stance on democratisation and standards was more distinctive, especially in the commitment to abolish compulsive competitive tendering (CCT) and replace it with 'best value' (though it was not clear what that meant). The theme of partnership was also new and drew on the experience of Labour councils in the major conurbations.

The real difference in these linked areas was with old Labour in the local government sphere. New Labour's implied position on central government was distinct in the sense that the operation of central government had changed quite radically since the late 1970s, but even this had built on trends which were very evident when Labour was last in office. Old Labour saw a substantial role for local government as a major provider of services and a principal supplier of public goods. By contrast, New Labour sees no future in the old model of councils trying, as Deputy Prime Minister John Prescott put it, to 'plan and run most services' (DETR, 1998:1). To Blairites, local government is only one of a number of agents operating in the local domain.

In government, New Labour developed a series of machinery of government themes. Some were floated in ministerial speeches, others in speeches given by top civil servants, others in the language of government bills, white papers and press releases. A key early speech was delivered by Peter Mandelson (then the Minister without Portfolio) in September 1997 (Mandelson, 1997). Far more important, however, was a House of Commons statement made by Tony Blair in July 1998 (Blair, 1998a). This drew on the themes of a review which the Cabinet Secretary, Sir Richard Wilson, had been commissioned to undertake in January 1998. Completed by April 1998, this review pulled together many of the emergent themes and proved to be a critical reference point for subsequent reform. The three developing elements of the 'third way' for machinery of government issues were:

1 the notion of 'joined-up government' (a much-used sound bite), implying a seamless web of public services;
2 public-private partnerships to generate effective service delivery; and
3 an emphasis on actual outcomes as they affect the citizen (and therefore effective implementation), rather than on traditional outputs such as new legislation or ministerial directives.

Labour also sees itself as a government in office to fulfil clear commitments as laid down in the manifesto, with progress reported in an Annual Report published at the end of each parliamentary session (Cabinet Office, 1998a).

The central executive

The central executive comprises a small set of organisations that seek to co-ordinate and direct government policy. The Prime Minister's and Cabinet Offices are at the centre of the centre. For taxation and public expenditure, the Treasury is key. Other organisations dealing with political support and legal matters also play an important role. In government, Labour has taken steps to alter and augment key elements within the central executive, notably the Cabinet Office. Like its Conservative and Labour predecessors it has attempted to enhance capability at the centre but has done so in a much more systematic and substantial way. This has been carried out in a series of little publicised innovations. Indeed Blair has announced 're-inventing government' to be a key part of Labour's reform agenda (Blair, 1998b). Arguably, the cumulative effect of these changes has been to create an executive office in all but name (Burch and Holliday, 1999).

When Labour came to power, the Prime Minister's Office had four main sections: the Private Office, the Political Office, the Press Office and the Policy Unit. Under Blair, changes have been made to most of these sections. The Private Office now has attached to it a special assistant for presentation and planning, Anji Hunter, and two part-time assistants to the Prime Minister's wife. The Press Office has been slightly expanded to about 12 people and is headed by the controversial Alastair Campbell, who transferred directly to Number 10 from the Leader's Office in Opposition and is employed on a special contract as a temporary civil servant. The Policy Unit, headed by David Miliband, has been expanded to around 13 desk officers and five support staff. It now has a higher profile in Number 10, and has also built links with the Cabinet Office. In addition to these changes a fifth section, the Strategic Communications Unit, has been created in Number 10 with a staff of six. Its job is to generate a coherent and unified presentation of government policy by co-ordinating departmental announcements and ensuring that they are 'on message'. It also attends to the timing of government press releases and statements in order to eliminate clashes and ensure a smooth and effective take up in the media. Over and above each of these sections, Blair has appointed a Chief of Staff, Jonathan Powell, with a desk in the Private Office, to pull together the work of the Prime Minister's Office and to co-ordinate it with that of the Cabinet Office. Like Campbell, Powell took his position from Opposition into government and is employed as a temporary civil servant. Apart from a failed experiment along these lines in Thatcher's first term, covering the political side of the office, the post of Chief of Staff counts as a Labour innovation. Taken together, these changes amount to a clear but not dramatic strengthening of the Prime Minister's Office.

From the early 1990s onwards, the Cabinet Office had two main sections: the Cabinet Secretariat and the Office of Public Service (OPS). These have been integrated under Labour into a single Cabinet Office with a management committee under the chair of the Cabinet Secretary and Head of the Home Civil Service, Sir Richard Wilson. The aim is to ensure, in his words, that 'management and policy sit side by side' (Wilson, 1998:5). The traditional work of the Cabinet Secretariat – servicing Cabinet and its committees – has not changed significantly, but it has been augmented by the creation of new sections and units at the core of the Office to deal with specific areas of business and policy issues. In May 1997, the Secretariat developed a new pro-active section to manage Labour's constitutional agenda and in December 1997 a special unit was created to deal with social exclusion in an attempt to tackle this problem across departmental boundaries. In part, this served as the prototype for the further changes developed in the wake of the Wilson report. These changes have resulted in the creation of a new Central Secretariat, in addition to the existing ones, and the creation or placing at the core of the Office three further units which, like the Social Exclusion Unit, are intended to tackle problems that cross departmental boundaries. Cabinet Office units have been created before – devolution in the 1970s, inner city and urban policy in the 1980s – but the new units break new ground in the extent of their intervention and in their use of outsiders to work alongside civil servants. The nature of these changes at the very core of the Cabinet Office are outlined in detail in Box 5.2.

Closer integration of the two parts of the Cabinet Office has been followed by a reorganisation of the functions previously contained within OPS, so as to highlight public service delivery and the standards and training of civil servants. Two main innovations were announced in July 1998 concerning these matters. One was a Centre for Management and Policy Studies to incorporate the Civil Service College and ensure that best practice makes its way into the civil service from business and elsewhere. The other was a Management Board for the Civil Service, chaired by the Cabinet Secretary and bringing together permanent secretaries from some government departments. The July changes also saw the relocation of the Head of the Government Information and Communication Services to the Cabinet Office. Like the Prime Minister's Office, the Cabinet Office has been strengthened under Blair.

All these changes were accompanied by alterations in the ministerial team. In particular, in July 1998 a Minister for the Cabinet Office was created with a seat in the Cabinet and responsibility for the effective co-ordination and presentation of the government's policies. Jack Cunningham was initially appointed to this post, and was immediately dubbed the 'Cabinet Enforcer' by the media. He was replaced by Mo Mowlam in October 1999. Notably, the lines of responsibility for core parts of the Cabinet Office still remained with the Prime Minister via the Cabinet Secretary. Also brought more closely within the ambit of the Cabinet Office were those individuals and organisations responsible for organising the government's parliamentary business, notably the Leaders of the Commons and Lords (Margaret Beckett and Baroness Jay) and their staff and the offices of the government whips in both Houses. For the first time this formally recognised the full range of management tasks which have been increasingly centred on the central executive (Burch and Holliday, 1996:81–106).

The full import of the change in the central executive can only be grasped by analysing the Prime Minister's and Cabinet Offices together. Building again on a clear trend, the Blair government has sought to integrate the work they do. Powell's co-ordinating role as Chief of Staff in Number 10 is one element in this attempt. A weekly planning meeting chaired by the Prime Minister and attended by the Minister for the Cabinet Office, the Cabinet Secretary, the heads of the Cabinet Secretariats, the Chief of Staff and the Head of the Policy Unit is a second. A third is increasingly close links between the Cabinet Secretariats

---

Box 5.2   *Innovations at the core of the Cabinet Office
since May 1997*

Constitution secretariat
- Established in May 1997
- Drives and co-ordinates the constitutional reform programme; services the relevant Cabinet committees and machinery
- Staffed by civil servants
- Reports to the PM via the Cabinet Secretary

Central secretariat
- Established in Autumn 1998
- Advises on ministerial responsibilities and accountability; the machinery of government; propriety and ethics issues in relation to government personnel; and public appointments and public bodies. Services the Cabinet Office's Management Board
- Staffed by civil servants
- Reports to the Cabinet Secretary and through him to the PM

Social exclusion unit
- Established in December 1997
- Co-ordinates and assists government action on social exclusion through (a) improving knowledge in government about why social exclusion takes place and (b) promoting solutions and encouraging co-operation across government

---

and officials in Number 10, notably in the Policy Unit. A fourth, more important, element is the restructuring of the two offices that took place following the review by the Cabinet Secretary and the Prime Minster's July 1998 statement.

Alongside these changes, the other major innovation at the heart of government has been in central planning and monitoring of public expenditure. The Comprehensive Spending Review (CSR) was key to this. Conducted during the first year in power, the outcome was announced by Chancellor Gordon Brown in July 1998. The key procedural shift was the requirement that departments justify their expenditure claims over a three-year period before a Cabinet committee chaired by the Chancellor. The position of the Treasury at the heart of the tax and spend process has potentially been enhanced by the shift to a clearer monitoring system (Burns, 1997).

These new mechanisms for central oversight are the main changes in the central executive, but there are others that point in a slightly different direction. The *Modernising Government* White Paper, published in March 1999, sought to further the pursuit of joined-up, customer-focused, efficient government by

- Staffed by civil servants and personnel seconded from local authorities, public agencies, voluntary bodies and business
- Reports to the PM through the Cabinet Secretary

Performance and innovation unit
- Established in October 1998
- Examines medium- to long-term public policy challenges that cut across the public sector. Promotes innovation in policy and service delivery and 'joined-up' policy making throughout Whitehall. Works through doing short studies on relevant topics
- Staffed by civil servants and seconded personnel from local authorities, public agencies, voluntary bodies and business
- Reports to the PM through the Cabinet Secretary

Women's unit
- Established in 1997; transferred to the Cabinet Office in July 1998
- Co-ordinates work across departments to promote the interests of women by working on a range of specific issues
- Staffed by civil servants with some outside advice
- Reports to Leader of the Lords, who is Minister for Women

UK anti-drugs coordination unit
- Established in 1997; transferred to the Cabinet Office in July 1998
- Co-ordinates the Government's anti-drugs strategy.
- Staffed by civil servants and others from local government and public agencies
- Reports to the Minister for the Cabinet Office

eliminating barriers within the state, publicising best practice, increasing training programmes for ministers and officials, and cutting regulation. Among its specific commitments were a pledge that by the end of the year 2000 NHS Direct will take phone calls 24 hours a day, seven days a week, and that by 2008 all basic dealings with government will be deliverable electronically (Cabinet Office, 1999a). More generally, the central state is becoming increasingly open and communicative. In large part this shift has been driven by technological change, and in particular the invention of the Internet. But there is also a changing culture at the centre. More of what was once considered highly sensitive information is now released, including the remits and memberships of ministerial Cabinet committees, various codes and guidelines governing the operation of the central executive (for example, the *Ministerial Code*), and details about how business is planned and legislation drawn together (Cabinet Office, 1996; 1997; 1998b and 1999b). This change was already visible under the Conservatives, but has become more noticeable and systematised under Labour.

The rest of central government

Change in the structure of government departments is more notable for what has not happened under Labour than for what has. A Department for Europe, an idea floated in some parts of the press, has not been created. More significantly, no Ministry for Women has been established. Instead, in May 1997 Labour formed the monster Department of the Environment, Transport and the Regions (DETR), and split the Department for International Development (DfID) out of the Foreign and Commonwealth Office (FCO). It also took powers to set interest rates from the Treasury and located them in the Bank of England. Creation of the DETR had some administrative rationale, but was also a means of providing Deputy Prime Minister John Prescott with a substantial ministry. Creation of the DfID honoured one of Labour's long-standing commitments. Neither marked a major change in the shape of Whitehall. Operational autonomy for the Bank of England was more significant. However, perhaps the greatest change in the structure of government departments has been the result of devolution to Scotland, Wales and Northern Ireland. In July 1999 the three territorial offices ceased to exist as fully-fledged departments and the positions of the three secretaries of state were dramatically altered as administrative competencies were transferred to the devolved executives and assemblies.

Far more innovative, and indicative of Labour's approach to machinery of government questions, were the many task forces put in place almost as soon as it had been elected. Located within central government but staffed at least partly by outsiders, task forces were given a specific brief and required to come up with options for change within a clear time-scale. So amorphous is the central concept of task force that it is impossible to say with any precision exactly how many the Blair Government has created. Barker (1998) notes that the three terms 'review', 'task force' and 'advisory group' are all used by government departments, and that no clear analytical divide can be made between them. Putting all three together, Labour had created 227 new teams within its first year or so in office, of which 132 were formally known as reviews, 61 were called groups, and 34 were task forces. The greatest number were concentrated in the Home Office (32), the Scottish Office (29) and the Department of Health (24) (Barker, 1998:Appendix). All these numbers actually tell us far less than we would like to know. However, the really key points are clear: that the New Labour Government is (i) not averse (indeed keen) to bring in outside experts and (ii) no respecter of departmental boundaries when it comes to problem solving. Indeed, the task force approach is an excellent fit with Labour's general theme of a partnership approach to government and with its philosophy of assembling individuals with hands-on experience to focus on specific problems.

In dealing with the civil service, Labour has made no real departure from the Conservatives' agenda. Business methods remain key. The Next Steps reforms with their creation of executive agencies have been picked up in their entirety.

Involving business in the challenges of government is one of the purposes of task forces and learning from business is an objective to which the Cabinet Office changes of July 1998 are intended to contribute. In particular, the Central IT Unit has two main objectives: to develop unified IT systems within government; and to extend electronic delivery of government services (with a target of 25 per cent of all public dealings with government to be capable of electronic delivery by 2002). The Modernising Public Services Group, incorporating the Effective Performance Division and the Service First Unit, builds on the Major Government's Citizen's Charter initiative. Its main innovation to date is the People's Panel, a set of 5000 individuals randomly selected and available to all publicly funded bodies wanting to survey public views of service delivery. Full survey results are published on the Cabinet Office website, with summaries distributed to anyone who expresses an interest. These changes are essentially incremental. The belief that government should relate to its citizens in much the same way as J. Sainsbury and Tesco relate to their customers is common to the Labour and Conservative parties in the late 1990s.

Outside the Cabinet Office, the Blair administration has made very few substantial structural changes to British central government. However, to see this as evidence of continuity is to miss the important point that the leaders of the Blair 'revolution' are concerned not to let structural issues get in the way of an effective central state. For them, structural boundaries are there to be crossed in the search for appropriate solutions to perceived problems. This means bringing outsiders in just as much as it means pulling together cross-Whitehall teams. Whether such a fluid approach will succeed remains to be seen. For all sorts of reasons – institutional, cultural, personal – established structures have a tendency to reassert themselves.

Local government

In the local government sphere initiatives were taken soon after the Blair government was elected to office. Its general approach has been two-pronged: to establish new consultative machinery between central and local government; and to use this and a wider consultation exercise to develop proposals for reform leading to legislation in 1999 and subsequent years. The central theme of local government reform quickly became 'better value'.

Consultation began in June 1997 with the establishment of a new Central-Local Partnership meeting chaired by the Deputy Prime Minister. This brought together Cabinet and other key ministers, plus leading members of the Local Government Association. This is the forum in which major, Whitehall-wide issues affecting local government are discussed. In addition there are less formal meetings between ministers and councillors to consider specific service and finance issues. These new arrangements replaced the existing Consultative Council on Local Government Finance and the Housing Consultative Council. Similar consultation arrangements were set up in Scotland and Wales. In

September 1997, the Government created a Business Forum to advise on local government finance and especially the localisation of business rates. This brings together ministers and representatives of both large and small business associations.

These initiatives were paralleled by a rapid development of policy proposals. In June 1997 the Government announced a number of pilot schemes intended to develop the idea of best value. In July it announced a review of the local government finance system. In October the framework for spending the money released under the capital receipts initiative was revealed, with £174 million to be made available in 1997–98 and £610 million in 1998–99. These were early tranches from the £5 billion of accumulated funds that local authorities had built up through the sale of assets (such as council houses, land and redundant buildings). Under the previous government, these could only be used to pay off debt. Measures were also taken to encourage and develop local government Private Finance Initiative (PFI) projects. By February 1998, 40 of these had been approved. The initial process of policy review, however, began to come to fruition in February and March 1998, when a series of six consultative papers under the general title *Modernising Local Government* was published. These covered local democracy and community leadership, best value, local financial accountability, business rates, capital finance and ethical standards. The White Paper *Modern Local Government* followed them, in July 1998. This declared that 'the old culture of paternalism and inwardness needs to be swept away' (DETR, 1998:para. 3) and contained a series of detailed proposals designed to carry out Labour's manifesto commitments. A Local Government Bill was published in December 1998 to take many of these proposals forward, and was duly enacted in July 1999. The main focus of the Act was on local government finance, rather than on the executive arrangements of local councils and the conduct of councillors and officers. These latter projects are taken up in subsequent legislation, as outlined in a draft Bill on the organisation and standards of local government published in March 1999 (DETR, 1999).

In the local government domain, action on localising business rates and council tax capping was less radical than the manifesto implied. The replacement of CCT by best value could certainly be said to involve a good deal of conjuring with words. In Boxes 5.3 and 5.4 we outline the Blair Government's main local government initiatives according to whether they involved significant or marginal change from the situation prior to May 1997.

When put together, these local government reforms are both centralising and decentralising. The shift from CCT to best value clearly releases local councils from some Conservative-imposed constraints. However, best value itself is not exactly a permissive regime. As developed in the 1998 White Paper, it has four main strands:

1 service targets, focused on the 3Es (economy, efficiency and effectiveness) which Thatcherite Conservatism first developed;

Box 5.3 *Labour's proposals for local government –
significant change*

Democratisation
- Councils to review their political management arrangements and draw
  up a plan, with timetable, to introduce one of three new models:
  1 directly-elected executive mayor with cabinet; mayor to appoint
    cabinet from among councillors
  2 cabinet with leader; leader to be elected by council; cabinet to be made
    up of councillors appointed by leader or elected by council;
  3 directly-elected mayor with full-time council manager appointed by
    council (proposals for directly-elected mayor require endorsement in
    local referendum)
- Councils able to hold local referendums and to make it easier to vote (e.g.
  electronic voting, mobile polling stations and voting on different days)

Finance
- Aggregate grant provision to be determined on a three-year basis; review
  of the grant allocation system
- Local government capital finance to be simplified with incentives for
  councils to make better use of capital assets
- Abolition of requirement to set aside for debt repayment receipts from
  asset sales (other than council houses)

Standards
- Beacon councils – those in touch with local people, with strong business
  links, with modern management structures and delivering best value –
  to be designated centres of excellence and given increased scope to act
- New Code of Conduct, based on national model, to cover councillors and
  council employees; backed by an independent Standards Board, with
  powers to suspend or disqualify councillors

Partnership
- Successful councils to be enabled to do more for their communities and
  to test new approaches to public service.

2 annual local performance plans which must both survey past performance
  and detail future plans;
3 new external audit and inspection requirements; and
4 consultation with the public.

Similarly, the abolition of council tax capping has been replaced by important
reserve powers vested in the Secretary of State for English councils, and in
each of the three devolved assemblies for councils in the rest of the UK.

Box 5.4   *Labour's proposals for local government –
marginal change*

Democratisation
* More frequent local elections

Finance
* 'Crude and universal' council tax capping to end; government to retain
  reserve power to control 'excessive' increases
* Councils to involve business in local tax and spending decisions
* National business rate to be retained, but councils able, within limits of
  1 per cent of national rate within any one year up to maximum of 5 per
  cent over time, to vary rate up or down; use of income so raised to be
  agreed with local business; beacon councils able to vary rate by a higher
  percentage

Standards
* CCT to go
* New national performance indicators for efficiency, cost and quality;
  councils to set and publish own local targets against them
* Councils to prepare annual performance plans and to undertake 5-year
  performance reviews of all services; reviews to:
  – make comparisons with others' performance;
  – consult local taxpayers, including business, on how service can be
    improved;
  – embrace 'fair competition' to secure efficient services
* New Best Value Inspectorate to provide regular inspection of all local services; government to act swiftly if councils fail to tackle serious performance failures

Partnership
* Strengthening of councils' powers to work in partnership with other
  public, private and voluntary organisations in order to promote the well-
  being of their area.

Nevertheless, after 20 years of local government marginalisation, the Blair
Government has made some moves to reverse the trend. Arguably, more
money is now being awarded to local councils. Certainly ministers say this is
the case, though the figures are more ambiguous than they concede. Best
value may not be a complete break with CCT, but it is undoubtedly less con-
straining on local councils. Although some capping powers have been
retained, they do not appear to be as draconian as under the Conservatives.
Looking to the future, beacon councils could one day be given important dis-
cretionary powers.

Evaluation and interpretation

Labour has made clear progress in putting its manifesto commitments on machinery of government into practice. In fact, this is an area in which much activity has taken place that was not specifically mentioned in the election programme. As the most specific commitments were made on local government, this is the easiest place to evaluate the match between promise and performance. There has been some dilution of the proposal to localise the setting of the business rate, in direct response to business opinion articulated through the government's Business Forum. Moreover as 'best value' has been fleshed out in detail it has become clear that, while it involves a wider programme of measures, it shares some of the characteristics of CCT which, officially, is to be ended. The Code of Conduct is a new initiative, which has emerged since the election as a result of controversies concerning the activities of some Labour councillors. What is especially revealing about the 1998 proposals is the central emphasis on standards. Clearly evident here is New Labour's concern with framework setting and regulation from the centre. A mix of league tables, performance measures and targets, punishment and reward, and oversight and monitoring bodies – all backed by the threat of direct intervention – is becoming a key characteristic of Labour's approach to service delivery.

Evaluation is harder when it comes to central government, though it is important to note that Labour has not changed markedly what was bequeathed to it. Nevertheless, the three themes we identified at the beginning – joined-up government, public-private partnerships, and outcomes not output – have given New Labour a distinctive approach. Compared with the outgoing Major Government, which was moving partly in this direction, there is greater emphasis on openness and making services user-friendly. Changes at the very heart of government also build on past trends, but since May 1997 the extent of integration between the Prime Minister's Office and the Cabinet Office has been truly significant (Burch and Holliday, 1999). The July 1998 changes prompted by the Wilson review are genuinely important, and indicate the growing role of 'the Centre' in driving the Labour programme forward.

How to explain this? Firstly, Labour's approach to machinery of government partly feeds off its campaign strategy organisation, which comprised a restructuring of the party in a modern media context. In particular, there has been an enhancement of central oversight mechanisms so as to ensure that the party speaks with one voice. This Millbank Tower (the location of Labour's media unit) dimension generates a very strong divide between old and New Labour. Secondly, leading figures' experience of entering government without prior direct knowledge made them critically and acutely aware of the limitations of the ways in which the central executive worked. Considerable resources and lines of communication were concentrated on the Centre, but were not fully galvanised and directed to achieving the government's objectives in terms of actual delivery of outcomes. They also identified departmentalism, or the 'silo' approach to government, as a serious problem. What was needed was a machine that was more integrated at the centre, more 'joined up' at all levels, and more responsive throughout. Beyond this, the role of the onward march of technology must not be overlooked. Some of the changes made by Labour have happened chiefly because they could; the entire IT strategy is the best instance of this.

Finally, it is impossible to ignore the role of personality in shaping government strategy at the centre. New Labour has a strong Prime Minister and also a strong Chancellor. The power balance between Blair and Brown is an important feature of the administrative politics of the Labour Government; it has served to enhance the position of an already powerful Treasury. In addition, it has been one of the factors prompting strengthening of Number 10 and the Cabinet Office.

We opened by saying that machinery of government questions ought to concern any governing party. Three characteristic aspects of New Labour are its interest in structural and operational questions, its penchant for tight organisation with a strong steer from the centre, and its concern to deliver on promises made. Changes in the machinery of government reflect these characteristics. What has emerged is a more streamlined central executive with the power potential of the key actors within it greatly enhanced. The extent to which and the ways in which that power is actually exercised is bound critically to shape the delivery of Labour's programme.

References

Barker, A. (1998), 'The Labour Government's Policy "Reviews" and "Task Forces": An Initial Listing and Analysis', *Essex Papers in Politics and Government*, 126.

Blair, T. (1998a), Statement to the House of Commons, *Hansard*, 1997–98 session (28 July), cols 132–4.

Blair, T. (1998b), 'Modernising Central Government', Speech to the First Senior Civil Service Conference, 13 October.

Burch, M. and Holliday, I. (1996), *The British Cabinet System* (London: Prentice Hall).

Burch, M. and Holliday, I. (1999) 'The Prime Minister's and Cabinet Offices: An Executive Office in All But Name', *Parliamentary Affairs*, 52:32–45.

Burns, Sir T. (1997) 'Preparing the Treasury for the Election', *Public Policy and Administration*, 13:1–12.

Cabinet Office (1996), *Guide to Legislative Procedures*, mimeo, London, Cabinet Office.

Cabinet Office (1997), *Ministerial Code: A Code of Conduct and Guidance on Procedures for Ministers*, London, Cabinet Office.

Cabinet Office (1998a), *The Government's Annual Report*, London, Cabinet Office.

Cabinet Office (1998b), *Finding Your Way Round Whitehall and Beyond: A Guide for Senior Civil Servants*, mimeo, London, Cabinet Office.

Cabinet Office (1999a), *Modernising Government*, Cm 4310, London, Stationery Office.

Cabinet Office (1999b), 'The Structure and Responsibilities of the Cabinet Office', *Minutes of Evidence*, Select Committee on Public Administration, HC Paper 82, 1998–99 session.

DETR (Department of the Environment, Transport and the Regions) (1998), *Modern Local Government: In Touch with the People*, Cm 4014, London, Stationery Office.

DETR (1999), *Local Leadership: Local Choice*, Cm 4298, London: Stationery Office.

Labour Party (1997), *New Labour: Because Britain Deserves Better*, London, Labour Party.

Mandelson, P. (1997), 'Coordinating Government Policy', Speech to University of Birmingham Conference, 16 September.

Mandelson, P. and Liddle, R. (1996), *The Blair Revolution: Can New Labour Deliver?* London, Faber and Faber.

Theakston, K. (1997), 'New Labour, New Whitehall?', *Public Policy and Administration*, 13:13–34.

Wilson, Sir R. (1998) 'Modernising Central Government: The Role of the Civil Service', Speech to the first Senior Civil Service Conference, 13 October.

6

New Labour and the constitution

Martin Burch and Ian Holliday

Constitutional reform was one of the few areas in which Labour made radical manifesto promises distinguishing it from its Conservative opponents and its old Labour inheritance. The Conservatives in 1997 stuck to the formula that had served them well in 1992, when John Major's dramatic warning about the dangers devolution posed to the UK – 'Wake up, my fellow countrymen. Wake up *now* before it is too late' (Baker, 1993:37) – was thought to have helped tip a close election. Old Labour in government, led by Wilson and Callaghan, never offered much in the sphere of constitutional reform, was rarely committed to change, and saw the few measures pursued in the 1960s and 1970s – reform of the House of Lords and some devolution to Scotland and Wales – come to nothing. New Labour's constitutional programme, which built on the agenda developed towards the end of the Kinnock era, was in fact the most radical put forward by a major party for more than 80 years.

The contribution of the Blair leadership to development of that programme was twofold. On the one hand it organised the various elements into priorities, both to minimise any detrimental electoral consequences and to generate a clear strategy and timetable for implementation. On the other, it placed Labour's constitutional programme in the context of a wider modernisation of British politics inspired by notions of democracy, decentralisation, accountability, community and co-operation. Not all these notions are compatible.

The constitutional agenda featured among Labour's ten manifesto commitments, but it did not have a place among its five election pledges. The constitution, though important, did not therefore rank alongside education, health, welfare to work, crime and a low-tax economy in Labour's list of priorities. The constitutional measures listed in the manifesto (Labour Party, 1997:32–5) were:

- Removal of the right of hereditary peers to sit and vote in the House of Lords, and greater party political balance among life peers
- Modernisation of the House of Commons

- A referendum on the voting system for the House of Commons
- A Freedom of Information Act
- Devolution of power to Scotland and Wales
- An elected mayor and assembly, and a regional development agency (RDA) in London
- RDAs and appointed regional chambers in England and legislation 'to allow the people, region by region, to decide in a referendum whether they want directly elected regional government'
- Incorporation of the European Convention on Human Rights (ECHR) into UK law.

The significance of Labour's agenda is that its reform proposals challenged many of the most fundamental aspects of the British polity. That polity has three inter-linked components:

1 A centralised metropolitan state (reinforced by metropolitan dominance in the economic, social and cultural spheres)
2 Government by an elite focused on an enclosed and exclusive central bureaucracy
3 A tendency towards what Lord Hailsham (1978) has referred to as an elective dictatorship through the operation of a majoritarian electoral system, consequent executive dominance of the legislature and limited formal constraints on the exercise of power.

The constitutional agenda promoted by Labour in 1997 addressed each of these components through:

- Devolution to Scotland and Wales and regional reform in England
- Freedom of information legislation
- Electoral and parliamentary reform and civil liberties legislation.

This chapter concentrates on analysing developments in these three critical areas. The central task of each section is not merely to monitor change, but also to assess the extent to which it is likely to transform the British polity.

One general point to be made at the start is that the key machinery used for thinking through constitutional issues was a set of six Cabinet committees (chairs are given in brackets):

1 CRP (Prime Minister): strategic issues relating to the constitutional reform programme
2 DP (Lord Chancellor): devolution policy (formerly DSWR (Lord Chancellor)): devolution to Scotland, Wales and the English regions)
3 CRP(EC) (Lord Chancellor): incorporation of ECHR into UK law
4 CRP(HL) (Lord Chancellor): House of Lords reform
5 CRP(FOI) (Lord Chancellor): freedom of information issues
6 JCC (Prime Minister): issues of joint interest to the Government and the Liberal Democratic Party.

Table 6.1 *Results of elections to the Scottish Parliament and Welsh Assembly, May 1999*

	Scotland			Wales		
	1st vote (%)	2nd vote (%)	Seats	1st vote (%)	2nd vote (%)	Seats
Labour	38.8	33.8	56	37.6	53.4	28
SNP/Plaid Cymru	28.7	27.0	35	28.4	30.5	17
Conservative	15.6	15.4	18	15.9	16.5	9
Liberal Democrats	14.2	12.5	17	13.4	12.6	6
Other	2.7	11.4	3	4.7	5.1	0
Turnout	58%			45%		

Source: Economist, 15 May 1999:31–5.

As can be seen from this list, the role of the Lord Chancellor, Lord Irvine of Lairg, has been critical in developing Labour's constitutional agenda in government. Also worth noting is the JCC, which brings Liberal Democrats into the Cabinet system and may point towards a future governing coalition on the centre-left of British politics. In terms of actually taking reform forward, the JCC has, however, been the least significant of these six committees.

Devolution to Scotland and Wales and regional reform in England

The Blair Government moved quickly to fulfil its election promises on devolution, with DSWR being the key Cabinet committee. In July 1997 the White Papers *Scotland's Parliament* and *A Voice for Wales* were published by the respective territorial ministries (Scottish Office, 1997; Welsh Office, 1997). It was on the basis of these proposals that the people of Scotland and Wales voted in referenda, held on 11 and 18 September 1997 respectively. In Scotland two referenda were held, on the principle of a parliament and on its limited tax-raising powers. The votes in favour were 74–26 and 64–36 and there was a turnout of 62 per cent. In Wales the single referendum on the principle of an assembly was passed by the slenderest of margins (50.3 per cent to 49.7 per cent) and turnout was only just over 50 per cent. Only one in four Welsh people voted for the Assembly. These proposals also formed the basis for the legislation which made its way through Parliament in 1997–98 and secured the royal assent on 31 July 1998. The only significant change was introduction of a cabinet form of executive in Wales more in line with the Scottish model. The first elections to the Scottish Parliament and Welsh Assembly were held in May 1999 (for the results, see Table 6.1), with both bodies convening in July 1999.

In this sphere Labour can certainly be said to have delivered on its commitments. The new structures that have been created follow the Labour manifesto in providing distinct and varied approaches to devolution. The key difference is

Box 6.1 *Structures and powers of the Scottish Parliament and Welsh Assembly*

Scottish Parliament	Welsh Assembly
• 129 members elected by Additional Member System of voting: 73 constituency + 56 party list	• 60 members elected by Additional Member System of voting: 40 constituency + 20 party list
• 4-year term – Early dissolution poss.	• Fixed 4-year term – Early diss. not poss.
• Cabinet headed by first minister	• Cabinet headed by first secretary
• Legislative powers	• No legislative powers
• Tax-varying powers of ±3p	• No tax-varying powers
• Westminster's reserve powers defined; all others devolved	• Specific powers devolved
• Legislative and executive powers in all but: – UK constitution – Foreign affairs – Defence/national security – Macro-economic/fiscal – Employment – Social security – Transport safety/regulation	• Executive powers only to cover: – Education and training – Health and social services – Local government and housing – Agriculture – Transport – Industry and economic development – Environment
• Secretary of State to retain seat in Cabinet	• Secretary of State to retain seat in Cabinet
• Scottish ministers may participate in EU Council of Ministers meetings	• Only Secretary of State may participate in EU Council of Ministers meetings

that the Scottish Parliament has legislative powers and extensive executive powers, whereas the Welsh Assembly does not have legislative powers but has executive powers covering the range of policy areas previously vested in the Welsh Office. The structures and powers of the two devolved bodies are given in Box 6.1.

Devolution to Scotland and Wales was accompanied by the election of a devolved assembly in Northern Ireland following the 'Good Friday' peace agreement in 1998, though transfer of full executive powers awaited the agreement of the parties involved to form a government. Taken together the creation of the three devolved parliaments marked a radical change in the structure of government in the UK and raised the question of how the new governments would relate to Whitehall and Westminster. In order to ensure that relationships would be smooth and workable, civil servants in London and the devolved capitals drew up in the period prior to the elections a series of draft administrative concordats covering the way in which business should be conducted. These were submitted to the elected governments following the transfer of functions in July 1999. Co-ordination machinery has also been established to cover both relations within the UK and in the islands of Britain and Ireland more broadly. A joint ministerial committee brings together ministers from the UK and the devolved governments to consider reserved matters that impinge on devolved responsibilities. Committees of officials and a joint secretariat support this consultative body. To cover the wider, cross-islands dimension, a British-Irish council has been established bringing together representatives of the UK and Irish governments along with those from the Scottish, Welsh and Northern Ireland administrations. Potentially, these moves have enormous significance and were not foreseen in Labour's manifesto or its preparations for office.

Regional reform in England was split into two separate projects, again in line with Labour's manifesto commitments. For the English regions outside London, the December 1997 White Paper *Building Partnerships for Prosperity* proposed nine RDAs, led by business but drawing in other regional interests (DETR, 1997). The RDAs' central task was to develop and implement a regional economic strategy, on the basis of which they were to advise government. They were also to be the lead regional bodies for co-ordinating inward investment, raising people's skills, improving the competitiveness of business, and social and physical regeneration. In addition, consultative regional chambers, which might one day form the basis for elected assemblies, were planned. Following the passage of the necessary legislation, in July 1998 chairmen-designate of the RDAs were announced, and they and some of the consultative regional chambers came fully into operation from April 1999 onwards. The maximum annual budgets of the RDAs are about £200 million.

The powers and resources of the RDAs are much more limited than those implied in the White Paper and are in keeping with the Government's cautious approach to English regional devolution outside of the metropolis. In London, a very different approach was taken. Here the March 1998 DETR White Paper *A Mayor and Assembly for London* set out the Government's plans for a powerful directly-elected mayor and 25–member assembly, which would together constitute the Greater London Authority (GLA) with an annual budget of at least £3.25 billion (DETR, 1998). The GLA is to be strategic, covering the 32 London boroughs and the City of London. Of the two new institutions, the key one is to be the mayor, reflecting Labour's commitment to reinvigorating city government through clear, though accountable, leadership. The main powers devolved to this person are in the spheres of transport, economic development, the environment, planning, police, fire and culture. The role of the assembly will be essentially to hold the mayor to account. Londoners voted on these proposals in a referendum held on 7 May 1998. On a turnout of only 34.6 per cent, they voted 72–28 in favour of the changes. As in Wales, only one in four people actually voted for the new arrangements. The first elections, originally planned for 1999, are now to take place in May 2000 with the mayor and assembly in operation by July of that year.

Freedom of information

A Freedom of Information Bill was not included in the programme for Labour's first parliamentary session, though in the Queen's Speech the Government did commit itself to producing a White Paper. This task fell to David Clark, Chancellor of the Duchy of Lancaster and Public Service Minister. He established a Freedom of Information Unit within the Office of Public Service (OPS) and employed James Cornford, former chair of the Campaign for Freedom of Information as his special adviser. Policy development was overseen by CRP(FOI), on which every Cabinet minister, bar the Prime Minister and Deputy Prime Minister, had a seat. It was serviced by an official committee, CRP(FOI)(O), with a parallel membership. The failure to include a bill in the first session was seen by freedom of information campaigners as a setback. The official reasons given were that Labour's devolution proposals for Scotland, Wales and London left little room in the parliamentary timetable for a further, substantial constitutional bill. Officials also felt that the bill drafted by Labour in opposition was too rudimentary to proceed to legislation. In fact, that draft was quite detailed, being based on a previously considered private member's bill and an outline bill promoted by the Campaign for Freedom of Information. Some found the delay worrying given Labour's previous failed attempt to introduce legislation under the Wilson and Callaghan governments of the 1970s (Burch and Holliday, 1996:165–71; Kellner and Crowther-Hunt, 1980).

Clark's team worked with good effect over the seven months to December 1997, when a White Paper, *Your Right to Know*, was published (Cabinet Office, 1997). This revealed a far more radical approach than most commentators had expected (Box 6.2). As planned, a process of public consultation followed, along with an examination of the proposals by the Commons select committee on public administration. In the July 1998 ministerial reshuffle, Clark was removed from his post following a lengthy whispering campaign against him. Soon afterwards, responsibility for freedom of information was moved from OPS to the Home Office.

A draft Freedom of Information Bill was finally published by Home Secretary, Jack Straw, in May 1999, and put out for consultation for a six-month period (including a six-week stint in Parliament). Among the many departures made from the line established by Clark's White Paper, three were particularly significant. Exemptions preventing release of information in 22 areas of public life, including policy making, commercial secrecy, the economy, international relations and health and safety featured at the heart of the draft bill. The powers of the Information Commissioner were effectively undermined by clauses

---

Box 6.2 *The Freedom of Information White Paper*

- FOI Act to give everyone a legal right to see records or information held by government
- FOI to apply to the whole public sector, to private-sector organisations working for government and to privatised utilities; sole exceptions are MI5, MI6, GCHQ and the Special Forces (SAS and SBS)
  - ✓ All information to be available except that concerning:
  - ☐ sensitive security and intelligence matters
  - ☐ personnel files of government employees
  - ☐ material that could undermine crime prevention or prosecutions
      Or that which would clearly cause 'substantial harm' to:
  - ☐ national security, defence and international relations
  - ☐ internal discussion of government policy
  - ☐ law enforcement (e.g. information encouraging tax evasion)
  - ☐ personal privacy
  - ☐ business activities such as trade secrets
  - ☐ the safety of individuals, the public or the environment
  - ☐ personal references given in confidence
- More government information to be published as a matter of course on:
  - ✓ facts and analyses used by government when making policy
  - ✓ guidance on dealing with the public
  - ✓ reasons for government decisions
  - ✓ costs, targets, performance and complaints procedures
- Public to seek information by contacting the organisation concerned; a small fee (about £10) to be charged to cover administration costs
- Independent Information Commissioner to be appointed to consider appeals against refusal of requests for information and complaints about delays and excessive charges

---

preventing him or her from overruling a public authority and ordering disclosure of information on public information grounds (*Guardian*, 22 June 1999, p. 9). The Clark commitment to public access to information unless it caused 'substantial harm' was replaced by the much weaker test of 'prejudice'. Unsurprisingly, this unimpressive set of proposals provoked a storm of political protest on the Labour backbenches, in opposition parties and among interest groups committed to freedom of information. Amendments to the draft bill are almost certain to take place before it is formally introduced in the 1999–2000 session of Parliament.

By proposing a legal right to see information, Clark's White Paper broke new ground in challenging the tradition of secrecy that has characterised British government. However, much depended on how the exemptions were defined, and on the powers given to the Information Commissioner. As Clark stated at the launch of his White Paper, the proposals 'if fully implemented, would transform this country from one of the most closed democracies to one of the most open' (Cabinet Office, 1997). This was very true, but the 'if' was big. Once the Home Office had become the lead department, a degree of backtracking took place, resulting in publication of a draft bill that was a significant disappointment to many interested parties.

Electoral and parliamentary reform and civil liberties legislation

Labour's first substantial move in this sphere was civil rights legislation, with the lead forum for policy development being CRP(EC). The October 1997 Home Office White Paper, *Rights Brought Home*, outlined the means by which the ECHR would be incorporated into UK law, and thereby made actionable in UK courts (Home Office, 1998). The Human Rights Bill duly made a largely uncontroversial passage through Parliament, with the ensuing Act being placed on the statute book in November 1998. Initially intended to come into effect in January 2000, the Act will not now have effect until October 2000, to allow the British public sector time to prepare itself for the changed operating environment it creates. The key shift is from the prohibitions (negative rights) of Britain's common law tradition to a set of positive rights running from the right to life to various freedoms of thought, expression, association and so on. Even though implementation is being delayed, a rush of litigation is expected as vast areas of the state, from judges and top civil servants down to the lowliest local government official, are for the first time exposed to rights-based legal challenges from citizens. In addition, ministers will henceforth have a duty to certify that proposed legislation is compatible with the ECHR. Courts will not have the power to strike down Acts which do not comply with its provisions, but they will be able to declare them incompatible and impose something of a moral obligation on the government to change the law. This is a major reform which will alter the nature of the UK state by shifting some power from the legislature to the judiciary, and also have an impact on the lives of many UK citizens.

As promised in the Labour manifesto, the first step taken towards possible reform of the electoral system was appointment of an independent commission to consider the options. This five-person body, created in December 1997, was headed by Lord Jenkins of Hillhead, formerly Labour Home Secretary and Chancellor, President of the European Commission, Leader of the Social Democratic Party and at the time of his appointment Leader of the Liberal Democrats in the House of Lords. Its brief was to assess voting systems for the House of Commons using four criteria: broad proportionality; stable government; voter choice; and maintenance of a link between MPs and geographical constituencies. The commission reported in October 1998, recommending that the UK adopt a system called Alternative Vote Top-Up. Under this system UK parliamentary boundaries would be redrawn to cut the number of constituencies from the current 659 to between 530 and 560. Voters would then get two votes, one for their constituency MP and a second for the top-up MPs to be elected in their region. The first vote would be cast on an alternative vote system, whereby individuals rank party candidates in order of preference (1,2,3, etc.) and at the count votes are successively redistributed from the least-popular candidate until one candidate has secured 50 per cent of votes cast. The second vote would operate on a cross-in-a-box basis, whereby voters select their favoured party or candidate from that party. The parties that gain top-up seats would be decided on the basis of a group of around seven constituencies. Jenkins' solution was an ingenious way of making the British electoral system more proportional while also retaining the constituency link and generating single-party government in years like 1983, 1987 and 1997. In years like 1992 it would generate coalition government. There was, however, limited Labour Party enthusiasm for change, and the Prime Minister and Home Secretary were prepared to sit on the issue by announcing a lengthy consultation exercise. There is little chance that Labour will deliver on its manifesto promise of a referendum on the voting system for the House of Commons during this Parliament, even though it has introduced proportional representation for elections to the devolved assemblies and the European Parliament.

With regard to Parliament itself, the main task was held to be reform of the House of Lords. The relevant Cabinet committee was CRP(HL), which began work in January 1998. Its first initiative was to seek to expel the hereditary peers from the Lords, thereby meeting Labour's core manifesto commitment. The Lords by early 1999 had 759 hereditaries sitting alongside 510 life peers and 26 bishops and archbishops (making a total of 1295 members). Legislation flagged in the Queen's Speech of November 1998 was introduced to Parliament in January 1999 and came into effect in autumn 1999. One amendment made to it during its passage through Parliament was a temporary stay of execution for 91 hereditaries, following a secret deal hatched by Lord Weatherill, leader of the crossbench peers in the Lords, Lord Cranbourne, leader of the Conservative majority, and members of the Labour Cabinet. The fact that this deal was kept secret even from William Hague, Conservative Leader in the Commons and the country, meant that Cranbourne was sacked from his post. The deal itself, however, survived as a means of retaining some of the more active and expert hereditaries in the transition period.

At the same time as it introduced its short bill for removal of the hereditaries, the Government published a White Paper, *Modernising Parliament: Reforming the House of Lords* (Cabinet Office, 1999), setting out its view of what might replace the Lords in the long term. This was a very unspecific document intended mainly to give a steer to the ten-member royal commission established, in February 1999, under the chairmanship of former Conservative minister Lord Wakeham. The brief of the Wakeham Commission was to come up with options for change by the end of 1999 (Royal Commission on the Reform of the House of Lords, 1999). The steer provided by the White Paper was in favour of:

- a combination of nominated and indirectly elected members;
- at least some of the indirectly elected members coming from the devolved assemblies; and
- reduced powers for the new second chamber through loss of the Lords' ability to delay some legislation by up to a year and to strike down secondary legislation.

In the Commons an early reform, mentioned rather ambiguously in the manifesto, was a switch from two 15–minute sessions of Prime Minister's questions on Tuesdays and Thursdays, to one 30–minute session on Wednesdays. The select committee on modernisation, chaired by Labour's Leader of the House, made a series of minor proposals. Most important in Labour's first year was a reform to allow greater consultation before and after bills are published, though this was mainly to be at the discretion of the government's business managers. The draft Freedom of Information Bill published in May 1999 was an instance of this new practice. The select committee on procedure also began to look at the central issue of the impact on Parliament of devolution and electoral reform. Given the potential magnitude of those impacts, its approach was surprisingly dilatory. However, in May 1999 the committee published an initial report on the procedural consequences of devolution, recommending abolition of the Scottish, Welsh and Northern Irish Grand Committees, restriction of questions to the Scottish and Welsh Secretaries to matters relating to their reduced responsibilities, and a new procedure for bills relating exclusively to one part of the UK (Procedure Committee, 1999).

As important as any of this has been Labour's general approach to Parliament. In the *Times* in 1998 Peter Riddell wrote articles attacking ministers for their neglect of this institution. Blair, it was reported after one year in office, had attended only 5 per cent of all divisions, a record low for a premier. He was also seen only rarely in the Commons. For Labour, Riddell concluded, Parliament was just one means of communication alongside focus groups, road shows and citizens' juries. On big issues, referenda were the chosen mechanism. His conclusion was that 'in practice, as opposed to constitutional theory, a separation of powers is developing' (Riddell, 1998).

Evaluation and interpretation

On the constitution, Labour has carried forward its manifesto commitments and in some cases, notably Scotland, developed them further and more quickly than was expected. Some matters remain to be brought to resolution, notably House of Lords reform, electoral reform and freedom of information. There is also the tricky question of England, both its internal structure and how it relates to the new structures in Wales, Scotland and Northern Ireland. Indeed, Labour's piecemeal pursuit of constitutional reform has raised questions about the overall nature of the settlement itself. Interestingly, the reform process is beginning to generate its own set of policy problems that will in time require policy solution. Nevertheless this is one area where Labour came in with a radical agenda which it has so far only partially carried through. These are early days and the reforms are still being implemented, but at least in some areas progress has been substantial.

To what extent are Labour's reforms likely to have a truly radical impact? Could they undermine those fundamental aspects of the British polity mentioned at the beginning of this chapter? Change may be said to be radical when it has one or more of the following dimensions: it is big, or involves a revision of underlying principles, or a shift in trend. Judged by these criteria, Labour's constitutional reform programme certainly implies radical change to some of the fundamentals of UK politics. However, this judgement cannot be applied uniformly to all aspects of the programme. Moreover, there remains the moot point concerning practical outcomes once the legislation is implemented. The proposals for Scotland and Wales do imply fundamental change on all criteria. These are large changes which affect the underlying principles of the UK state and mark a significant break with past patterns and trends. Incorporation of the ECHR into UK law, though a smaller change, has enormous potential significance as it enshrines, for the first time, the concept of human rights, as opposed to liberties, in the fabric of national law. Reform of the House of Lords and freedom of information are potentially equally challenging; though here everything depends on the extent and form in which they are ultimately carried through. Less predictable is the impact of voting reform should it take place in the next Parliament. Creation of an elected regional authority and mayor for London can be seen mainly as a reversion to the *status quo ante* the mid-1980s. The nature of the proposal and the context are, however, different. In the early 1980s, powerful metropolitan authorities covered the major conurbations of England. These have not been resurrected, and the RDAs that have been created lack funds and powers and have had no significant power devolved to them from the London centre. Curiously, the outcome of Labour's constitutional reform programme could be a more decentralised UK, but a more centralised and metropolitan England.

If we return to the three underlying principles of the British polity identified at the start of this chapter, what we find is that the majoritarian electoral system is still in place for Westminster, executive dominance has not only not been challenged but may even have been enhanced since May 1997 (on this, see Chapter 5), and a Freedom of Information Act has still not been enacted so as to open up the traditionally exclusive nature of the bureaucracy. These are important gaps in the programme of constitutional change enacted in the early Blair years. Other reforms, notably devolution and incorporation of the ECHR into UK law, are, however, changing the nature of British politics, to such an extent that parts of standard textbooks now need to be substantially rewritten. Moreover, the knock-on impacts of those reforms that have been carried through are likely to have significant consequences, the exact outcome of which is difficult to foresee.

References

Baker, K. (ed.) (1993), *The Faber Book of Conservatism*, London, Faber and Faber.

Burch, M. and Holliday, I. (1996), *The British Cabinet System*, Hemel Hempstead, Prentice Hall/Harvester Wheatsheaf.

Cabinet Office (1997), *Your Right to Know: Freedom of Information*, Cm 3818, London, Stationery Office.

Cabinet Office (1999), *Modernising Parliament: Reforming the House of Lords*, Cm 4183, London, Stationery Office.

DETR (Department of the Environment, Transport and the Regions) (1997), *Building Partnerships for Prosperity: Sustainable Growth, Competitiveness and Employment in the English Regions*, Cm 3814, London, Stationery Office.

DETR (1998), *A Mayor and Assembly for London: The Government's Proposals for Modernising the Governance of London*, Cm 3897, London, Stationery Office.

Hailsham, Lord (1978), *The Dilemma of Democracy*, London, Collins.

Home Office (1998), *Rights Brought Home: The Human Rights Bill*, Cm 3782, London, Stationery Office.

Kellner, P. and Crowther-Hunt, Lord (1980), *The Civil Servants: An Inquiry into Britain's Ruling Class*, London, Macdonald.

Labour Party (1997), *New Labour: Because Britain Deserves Better*, London, Labour Party.

Procedure Committee (1999), *Report on the Procedural Consequences of Devolution*, HC Paper 185, 1998–99 session.

Riddell, P. (1998), 'Does Anybody Listen to MPs?', *Times*, 23 March.

Royal Commission on the Reform of the House of Lords (1999), *Reform of the House of Lords: A Consultation Paper*, London, Royal Commission on the Reform of the House of Lords.

Scottish Office (1997), *Scotland's Parliament*, Cm 3658, London, Stationery Office.

Welsh Office (1997), *A Voice for Wales: The Government's Proposals for a Welsh Assembly*, Cm 3718, London, Stationery Office.

7

New Labour and Northern Ireland

Nick Randall

Northern Ireland policies have generally assumed a very low priority in the Labour Party's electoral and ideological prospectus. Indeed, for long periods it has seemed 'Labour's policy towards Northern Ireland has not been so much inadequate as non-existent' (Jones and Keating, 1985:167). Such inattention has been the product of several factors. With the party refusing to organise and recruit in Northern Ireland there has been little incentive to develop detailed policies for the province, a factor further reinforced by the general indifference of the mainland electorate. However, this neglect has also been attributable to the general desire of all British political parties to avoid entangling themselves in the affairs of the province and the primacy of addressing the instrumental material needs of the working class in the Labourist paradigm.

Labour governments have been forced, however, to grapple with the Northern Ireland problem and their record establishes a clear pattern of sympathy for, and accommodation with, Unionism (Barton, 1992; Bell, 1982). But in 1981, the party dramatically revised its policy, accepting a commitment to Irish unity by agreement and consent. This policy nevertheless proved problematic since it called for active campaigning to win the consent of the majority, but also accepted that Northern Ireland could not be forced out of the UK. Over the following years, the party undertook a number of policy shifts to give these contradictory commitments substance. Initially, consent was to be engineered by the creation of a united working class in Northern Ireland through radical socialist policies. By the mid-1980s, this had been abandoned in favour of measures of harmonisation and reform to secure a united Ireland. Although such policies endured, by the 1992 election the party nevertheless stressed that Irish unity was to be understood only as a very long-term aspiration. (Bew and Dixon, 1994).

Under Tony Blair and Mo Mowlam the party has repositioned itself firmly within the bi-partisan consensus on Northern Ireland by supporting the initiatives of the Conservative government, by de-emphasising the policy of unity and by positioning the party closer to Unionism. Thus, the 1997 manifesto

---

Box 7.1   *Labour's Northern Ireland policies in the 1997 manifesto*

- Stresses the party's bi-partisanship during the peace process
- Promises 'as great a priority attached to seeing that process through with Labour as under the Conservatives'
- A commitment to 'reconciliation between the two traditions and to a new political settlement which can command the support of both'
- Acceptance of the principle of consent
- Pledges 'effective measures to combat the terrorist threat'
- Action to guarantee human rights, strengthen confidence in policing and to combat discrimination at work
- Measures to reduce tensions over parades
- Action to 'foster economic progress and competitiveness in Northern Ireland, so as to reduce unemployment'

Source: Labour Party, 1997.

---

emphasises the principle of consent and seeks reconciliation between the two traditions in Northern Ireland rather than reunification. The magnitude of change was particularly apparent on Tony Blair's visit to Belfast on 15 May 1997, where he professed 'I believe in the United Kingdom. I value the Union' and suggested that 'none of us in this hall today, even the youngest is likely to see Northern Ireland as anything but a part of the United Kingdom'. Accordingly, Blair concluded, 'Unionists have nothing to fear from a New Labour government . . . The government will not be persuaders for unity' (Blair, 1997). In this area, as elsewhere in the party's revised ideology, New Labour offered not so much a novel departure, but in many ways a restoration of attitudes held prior to the rise of the Labour left in the 1980s. Box 7.1 sets out the commitments of Labour's 1997 manifesto on Northern Ireland and this chapter will examine action on these commitments beginning with Labour's stewardship of the peace process.

New Labour and the peace process

The talks process which the Blair Government inherited on entering office had begun on 10 June 1996, following the Forum election of 30 May 1996. However, the talks had failed to progress beyond procedural issues by March 1997 when they were suspended to allow the parties to contest the general election. At this juncture the peace process appeared to be moribund, the victim of the Major Government's repeated redefinition of the conditions for inclusive negotiations. Immediately after the election, the new Northern Ireland secretary, Mo Mowlam, in line with an election campaign pledge, proposed that Sinn

Fein could enter the talks due to restart in September if there was an Irish Republican Army (IRA) cease-fire. Mowlam offered Sinn Fein a series of official meetings in advance of a cease-fire. The murder of two Royal Ulster Constabulary (RUC) officers in Lurgan on 16 June brought pressure to suspend these contacts, but meetings continued and at the end of June a British government *aide memoire* offered Sinn Fein a place at the talks within six weeks of an IRA cease-fire.

However, as violent nationalist protests flared throughout Northern Ireland after the Orange Order were allowed to march down the predominantly Catholic Garvaghy Road, inclusive talks seemed a distant prospect. The situation was rescued by an unlikely source on 10 July with the Orange Order's historic decision to voluntarily re-route four controversial parades. This was followed on 19 July by the IRA's announcement of a restoration of its cease-fire and on 14 September Sinn Fein entered the talks, affirming its commitment to the Mitchell Principles of democracy and non-violence. At the end of September, Mowlam was able to announce the start of substantive negotiations, albeit in the absence of the Democratic Unionist Party (DUP) and UK Unionist Party which boycotted the talks.

The talks were soon thrown into fresh doubt by the decision of the Irish Government to release nine IRA prisoners on 19 December. Furious at what it saw as too many concessions to Sinn Fein, particularly on prisoner releases, the Progressive Unionist Party (PUP) threatened to quit the talks unless action was taken to release Loyalist prisoners while critics in the Ulster Unionist Party (UUP) urged Trimble to reconsider their party's position. Unrest was also increasingly evident amongst Loyalist paramilitaries and escalated dramatically on 27 December when the leader of the Loyalist Volunteer Force (LVF), Billy Wright, was murdered inside the Maze prison by the Irish National Liberation Army (INLA). This sparked a series of killings across Northern Ireland and led Loyalist prisoners in the Maze to withdraw their support for the peace process. It took a visit by Mowlam to the 274 Loyalist prisoners in the Maze to convince them to reverse their decision and to allow the talks to resume with both the Ulster Democratic Party (UDP) and PUP present.

A fresh crisis emerged on 22 January when the RUC Chief Constable declared the involvement of a Protestant paramilitary group, the Ulster Freedom Fighters (UFF), in three recent killings. Although the UFF announced a restored cease-fire the next day, the UDP left the talks on 26 January in anticipation of inevitable exclusion by virtue of its connections with the UFF. The UDP were allowed to return on 23 February after this fresh cease-fire had been shown to hold. Three days earlier, however, the talks had been convulsed again after the two governments concluded that the IRA were involved in the death of a suspected drugs dealer and a member of another Protestant paramilitary organisation, the Ulster Defence Force (UDF). Sinn Fein was also allowed to re-enter the talks on 9 March after evidence that the IRA cease-fire was being observed.

Two days before the deadline of 9 April the talks' chairman Senator Mitchell finally presented the parties with a draft document outlining a proposed agreement. However, Unionists were unimpressed and Trimble wrote to Blair in the belief that 'This document is not something the UUP could recommend to the greater number of people in Northern Ireland for approval' (*Guardian*, 8 April 1998). The UUP complained that the issue of consent was not adequately conveyed and that the North-South bodies would lack accountability to the Northern Ireland Assembly. Over the following days, a frantic series of negotiations was undertaken between the parties and Blair and Ahern. But as the deadline approached on early Friday, the UUP delegation expressed deep reservations on the draft of the final text and the talks seemed to be on the verge of collapse. Blair intervened; sending Trimble a letter asserting the British government's belief that decommissioning should begin in June and that those connected to paramilitary organisations which refused to decommission should be barred from ministerial office. This intervention swayed Trimble (but not all of his delegation) and at 5.26 p.m. on 10 April the talks adjourned and an agreement was secured.

The Good Friday agreement: 'Sunningdale for slow learners'?

The key features of the agreement reached between the parties on 10 April 1998 are:

- *A recognition that 'the present wish of a majority of the people of Northern Ireland, freely exercised and legitimate is to maintain the Union'* (Northern Ireland Office, 1998:2). Northern Ireland will continue to be a part of the United Kingdom as long as the majority wishes it to remain so.
- *Amendment of Articles 2 and 3 of the Irish constitution* to remove its territorial claim over Northern Ireland.
- *A 108-member Assembly in Northern Ireland* elected by Single Transferable Vote and 'subject to safeguards to protect the rights and interests of all sides of the community'(Northern Ireland Office, 1998:5). The Assembly will exercise full legislative and executive authority for the areas under the responsibility of the six Northern Ireland Office departments. As safeguards, the allocation of Committee Chairs, Ministers and Committee membership will be made in proportion to party strengths. Key decisions will be taken on a cross-community basis, either by parallel consent (a majority of members of the Assembly and a majority of the nationalist and unionist delegations voting in favour), or a weighted majority of 60 per cent of members including at least 40 per cent of the nationalist and unionist delegations. Executive authority in the new Assembly will be discharged by a First Minister, a Deputy First Minister and up to ten ministers, who together will form an executive. The Secretary of State for Northern Ireland will remain responsible for Northern Ireland Office matters not devolved to the Assembly.

- *A North–South Ministerial Council* designed to 'develop consultation, co-operation and action within the island of Ireland' (Northern Ireland Office, 1998:11), mutually inter-dependent with the Northern Ireland Assembly.
- *A British-Irish Council* incorporating the British and Irish governments and representatives of the devolved institutions in Northern Ireland, Scotland and Wales, meeting twice a year to discuss issues such as transport, agriculture, environment, health and Europe.
- *A British-Irish Intergovernmental Conference* to replace the Anglo-Irish Intergovernmental Council and Intergovernmental Conference designed to facilitate co-operation on non-devolved matters.

The agreement also includes a range of measures on human rights, equality issues and prisoner releases. These will be examined below. For the moment, we shall consider the novelty of the agreement.

Despite New Labour's fascination with the modern and new, the Good Friday agreement contains little that is novel. Many commentators have remarked upon the similarities between the 1998 agreement and that fashioned in 1973. Indeed, the SDLP's Seamus Mallon has described the Good Friday agreement as 'Sunningdale for slow learners'. In many respects this is the case, although the North-South Ministerial Council is significantly reduced from that agreed at Sunningdale. What is novel is the balance of forces which gave the 1998 agreement greater prospects for success than the Sunningdale agreement. Unlike the Sunningdale agreement, it enjoys the support of a broader coalition of forces with all parties in the talks having accepted the agreement.

The immediate threat to the Good Friday agreement, as Sunningdale had shown, came from the reaction of the UUP. In the event, it is clear that the then leader of the UUP, Brian Faulkner, accepted an agreement in 1973 which he could not sell to his own party. Trimble's parliamentary colleagues were also deeply divided on whether to accept the 1998 agreement and the support of the extra-parliamentary UUP was by no means certain. Therefore, the 72 per cent of the votes that Trimble received from delegates at the UUP ruling council proved essential to the short-term viability of the agreement. Equally significant, the agreement was endorsed by the paramilitary Ulster Defence Association (UDA) and UFF, both of which are linked to the UDP. For Sinn Fein the decision whether to accept the agreement and abandon abstentionism in Stormont politics was a historic one. A decision was deferred until a special conference on 10 May, but in the event 319 of the 350 delegates backed the change in policy and accepted the agreement.

A further distinction is the much firmer and broader democratic legitimacy the contemporary settlement enjoys following the referendum on 23 May and the subsequent elections to the Assembly. Trimble set 70 per cent support in the referendum as the signal of the Unionist community's assent, but at several stages this looked under threat, not least after the British government paroled four IRA prisoners to present the case for a yes vote at the Sinn Fein special conference. The campaign was also dogged by disputes over decommissioning and an insistent backdrop of successful and unsuccessful acts of violence by dissident Republicans. Nevertheless, the agreement was ratified on both sides of the border with 71.1 per cent voting for the agreement in Northern Ireland, although it is estimated that only 55 per cent of Unionists backed the deal. Elections to the new Assembly followed on 25 June and provided dissident Unionists with a further opportunity to frustrate the agreement. However, the DUP and UK Unionists gained only 27 seats rather than the 30 they required to prevent Trimble securing the 40 per cent of the Unionist bloc necessary under the sufficiency of consensus mechanisms of the new Assembly.

A triumph for New Labour?

A *Guardian* and *Irish Times* opinion poll conducted soon after the agreement asked who deserved most credit for securing the agreement (*Guardian*, 16 April 1998). Voters in both Northern Ireland and the British mainland believed that figures in the Labour Government were among the chief architects of the agreement. There is undoubtedly some justice in this general assessment, since there are several areas where the Labour Government's actions and attributes proved significant in securing a settlement:

- *Labour's landslide victory in May 1997* meant that Labour did not need to depend on the Unionists for parliamentary support and removed their power to extract concessions by threatening the survival of the government as they had done in the previous parliament. This provided Labour with a freedom of manoeuvre that the Conservatives had not enjoyed since 1992. However, any settlement would still require the support of the Ulster Unionists to succeed and freedom of manoeuvre was of little value if the new government lacked the political will and other resources to tackle the Northern Ireland problem.
- *The new government enjoyed a reservoir of good will* since it was untarnished by previous failed attempts to secure an agreement. This was particularly significant in the calculations of the Republican movement which had come to distrust the Conservative Government after it had stalled on Sinn Fein's entry into substantive negotiations following the 1994 cease-fire. Indeed, a restoration of the IRA cease-fire was purposely delayed until after the election in the hope that Major would be defeated. This was coupled with fortuitous political developments in the Irish Republic where the replacement of John Bruton by Bertie Ahern as Taoiseach (the Irish Republic's equivalent of a prime minister) within a month of Labour's election victory removed a figure seen by Republicans as overly sensitive to Unionist anxieties.
- *The new government made the peace process a priority.* Goodwill can quickly evaporate in the context of Northern Irish politics but the Labour Government

made it clear that Northern Ireland was a priority issue and acted to try and maintain the momentum of the peace process. This was demonstrated by Blair's choice of Northern Ireland as the location for his first visit anywhere as Prime Minister and the selection of the Taoiseach for his first meeting with the leader of a foreign government.

- *The injection of a new flexibility into the peace process.* The new government maintained the momentum of talks by a more flexible approach than that of its predecessor. Where Major had stalled on the entry of Sinn Fein into substantive negotiations, New Labour moved quickly to accept Sinn Fein into the talks process and kept the issue of decommissioning deliberately vague. The Labour Government also undertook a more active strategy of confidence-raising measures than that contemplated by the previous government. For example, the Conservatives had refused to allow IRA prisoners on the mainland to be transferred to jails in Northern Ireland and rejected a new inquiry into Bloody Sunday. The Labour Government in contrast showed much more flexibility on these issues. Indeed, it is doubtful whether a Conservative government could have accepted the Good Friday agreement, given the opposition expressed by a number of past and present Conservative MPs and vividly demonstrated when the Conservatives voted against the programme of accelerated releases of convicted terrorists in June 1998. Accordingly, any agreement secured by the Conservatives would have lacked this important concession to Republicanism.
- *The election of a 'New Labour' government.* Although it is likely that a Labour government elected in 1992 would have proved as supportive of the Union as previous Labour governments, it would nevertheless have faced deep suspicion from the Unionists because of its commitment to Irish unity. Since the party has abandoned this goal and become increasingly supportive of the Union, it has more readily secured the trust of the Ulster Unionists. Indeed, it appears Blair gave Trimble crucial psychological backing and this proved instrumental both in getting Trimble into talks with Sinn Fein and in convincing him to accept the agreement.

The Good Friday agreement was, nonetheless, the product of a complex interaction of forces, many of which predate the election of the Labour Government and the dynamics of many of which the Labour Government could not control. Chief among these were:

- *The cumulative achievements of a decade-long peace process.* A series of initiatives, including the Anglo-Irish Agreement, the Hume–Adams talks of 1988, the opening of secret lines of communication between the British government and the Republicans in 1990, and the Downing Street agreement, played a crucial role in developing the peace process. Even the Brooke and Mayhew talks, although they substantively failed to reach a solution, nevertheless contributed by familiarising the participants with democratic negotiation.

- *Ideological change in the Republican movement.* We can now see that the by-election victory in 1981of the hunger striker Bobby Sands was the beginning of a more overt involvement in the political process by Sinn Fein, with the mass campaigns in support of the hunger strikers demonstrating the possibility of a broad-based Republican movement. This was coupled with an increasing recognition that a British withdrawal was not imminent and that 'one last push' would not secure a united Ireland. These imperatives, coupled with war weariness and increasing loyalist attacks upon Republicans, prompted ideological changes. In 1986, Sinn Fein implicitly recognised the legitimacy of the 26-county Irish Republic when it voted by a three-to-one majority to abandon abstentionism in the South. Equally, Sinn Fein policy documents in the 1990s introduced pluralistic notions of identity and parity of esteem and acknowledged that an immediate British withdrawal was unfeasible. Despite a schizophrenic public posture designed to maintain the unity of the movement, the implicit and explicit repudiation of Republican nostrums continued after the 1997 election. For example, Adams became the first Sinn Fein leader to visit Downing Street since Michael Collins in 1921 and, as we noted above, the party accepted partition and the end of abstentionism in the North in May 1998. Although the Sinn Fein leadership characterises the Good Friday agreement as a transitional arrangement leading to a united Ireland, it is hard to resist Ryan's conclusion that Sinn Fein now seeks to represent the Catholic community in Northern Ireland while the aspiration of a united Ireland has become reliant on 'a concatenation of circumstances which must be beyond the hopes of even the most unreasonable optimist' (Ryan, 1997:80).
- *Changes within Unionism.* Electorally and demographically the hegemony of Unionism in the province shows signs of slipping and has contributed to political realignments within Unionism. The UDP and PUP have increasingly begun to attract the support of urban working class Protestant voters from the UUP and DUP. Both groups have contributed a more flexible voice in the peace process than the DUP and have shown an unusual degree of self-criticism and reflection. Despite his hard-line credentials, Trimble has also engineered a change of attitudes, giving indications of seeking a more progressive Unionism, in which, in particular, the UUP's link with the Orange Order appears under threat.
- *External factors.* As Roger MacGinty has argued, 'it is clear that the American influence on the peace process, both from influential Irish-Americans and the Clinton administration has been profound' (MacGinty, 1997:243). Recent years have seen the emergence of a new Irish-American lobby in the boardrooms of corporate America, which has pressured the Clinton administration to take an active interest in Northern Ireland. In turn, the Clinton administration has helped strengthen Gerry Adams' position, for example by offering him the respectability of a visa. Moreover, as Michael Cox has persuasively argued, the end of the Cold War and the resolution of other seemingly

irresolvable conflicts elsewhere in the world had an important impact, particularly on the Republican movement, but also in allowing Britain to renounce any strategic interest in Northern Ireland (Cox, 1998).

The peace process since the agreement

The Good Friday agreement was arguably the major achievement of Labour's first year in office. However, in its second year progress on consolidating and implementing that achievement was beset by a number of problems.

The issue of parades has escalated in recent years, with particular attention focusing on the Drumcree parade each July. Labour was unable to legislate on the recommendation of the North Review for an independent body to facilitate mediation and to issue determinations on parades in time for the 1997 marching season. Serious rioting followed the decision to allow the Drumcree march to proceed. The new Parades Commission was in place in 1998, but its attempts to mediate at Drumcree failed and the parade was re-routed away from the predominantly Catholic Garvaghy Road. The Orange Order stood their ground at the barricades erected by the security forces, widespread Loyalist violence ensued and the viability of the Good Friday agreement appeared under threat. But a grim turn of events defused the crisis. On 12 July 1998, three Catholic children were killed in a Loyalist fire bombing and in the widespread condemnation that followed the number of protesters dwindled to a token presence.

Equally, via the same dreadful logic, the Omagh bombing of 15 August 1998, carried out by the Real IRA, temporarily bolstered the peace process. The bomb, which killed 29 and injured 220, represented the largest loss of life in a single incident in Northern Ireland. It prompted both the INLA and Real IRA to declare cease-fires and for the first time Sinn Fein used the word 'condemnation' in connection with Republican violence.

As the Northern Ireland Assembly opened on 15 September, another obstacle loomed. The Good Friday settlement required agreement upon the areas of responsibility of the North-South Ministerial Council by 31 October. This deadline subsequently passed and it was only on 18 December 1998 that six cross-border bodies and ten Northern Ireland ministries were agreed upon.

Against a background of continuing violence – which saw one of the most violent periods of paramilitary summary justice and a number of murders, most notably those of the ex-IRA informer Eamon Collins and the human rights lawyer Rosemary Nelson – it was decommissioning which proved the most intractable obstacle to the formation of the executive and the transfer of powers to the new Assembly. Despite British and Irish support for decommissioning parallel to the negotiations and the establishment of an International Commission on Decommissioning in September 1997, there was no progress on this objective during the negotiations. The Good Friday agreement subsequently called upon participants to reaffirm their commitment to the total disarmament of all paramilitary organisations and to use their influence to achieve this goal within two years. However, as noted above, the Prime Minister wrote to David Trimble pledging to disbar from ministerial office those associated with paramilitary organisations refusing to decommission. Trimble has consistently referred to the spirit of the agreement and Blair's letter in support of his demand that progress must be made on decommissioning before Sinn Fein take their two ministerial posts in the executive. In turn, Sinn Fein has insisted that this issue should not delay the formation of the executive, arguing that Blair's letter is not part of the agreement and that the agreement does not specify when decommissioning should begin.

Despite hours of meetings and the Loyalist Volunteer Force's (LVF) decommissioning of some of its weapons in December 1998, these positions have so far proved irreconcilable. On 8 March 1999, Good Friday was again designated as the deadline for agreement between the parties on decommissioning and the establishment of the executive. Again, this proved elusive. Instead, the two governments issued the Hillsborough declaration which proposed that a shadow executive be formed and that within a month 'a collective act of reconciliation . . . take place which will see arms put beyond use on a voluntary basis' (Blair, 1999). This would then trigger the transfer of power to the new institutions. However, the Hillsborough declaration failed to satisfy the parties and a fresh deadline for agreement was set for 30 June. Despite an eleventh-hour Sinn Fein statement that it was confident it could persuade the IRA to decommission by May 2000, described by Tony Blair as a 'seismic shift', and a reciprocal statement of confidence in Sinn Fein's negotiating skills from the IRA, the Ulster Unionists demanded stronger assurances on decommissioning and the 30 June deadline passed without agreement. As the talks ground to a halt on 2 July the two governments again took the initiative, issuing another joint declaration: 'The Way Forward'. This proposed that an executive be formed on 15 July after a devolution order had been passed at Westminster. Decommissioning would be expected to begin immediately and a 'fail-safe clause' required that any failure to meet decommissioning commitments would lead to the suspension of the institutions established by the Good Friday agreement (Northern Ireland Information Service, 1999a).

The fate of these proposals was effectively decided on 14 July 1999, when the UUP executive reaffirmed its demand for prior decommissioning in a meeting lasting just 15 minutes. The UUP then failed to attend the Assembly meeting called to nominate the executive on the following day. As a consequence no executive was formed, Seamus Mallon resigned his position as Deputy First Minister and the Good Friday agreement was placed into review over the coming summer months.

The New Labour Government and social and economic policy in Northern Ireland

As Seamus Dunn has recognised, 'The range of problems that contribute to the conflict is very large and complex, and political accommodations, although they are a very good start, will not deal with all the issues' (Dunn, 1995:3). This is an analysis shared by the New Labour Government and one entrenched in the Good Friday agreement. Indeed, since coming to office Labour has signalled that action on social and economic inequalities, issues of cultural identity and problems of security are essential alongside any constitutional settlement. It is to these issues which we will now turn our attention.

Economic policy

Since taking office, the Northern Ireland ministerial team has continually reiterated its belief that the economic revival that New Labour seeks to engineer on the British mainland must also encompass the Northern Ireland economy. Indeed, political stability in the province and economic prosperity are seen by Labour as inextricably linked. In many ways, the recent performance of the Northern Ireland economy gives grounds for optimism. Throughout the 1990s, Northern Ireland has enjoyed faster economic growth than any other region of the UK while manufacturing output has grown twice as fast as the UK average in the last five years.

Yet chronic economic weaknesses persist and a high degree of deprivation remains evident. Although the gap has narrowed, Northern Ireland's GDP remains significantly below that of other regions of the UK at around 80 per cent of the UK average (Department of Economic Development (Northern Ireland), 1999a:70). In 1998, the average weekly wage in Northern Ireland stood at £333, one of the lowest average gross weekly household incomes in any of the regions of the UK (Department of Economic Development (Northern Ireland), 1999b).

Although unemployment has fallen significantly, such that by the second quarter of 1999 the ILO unemployment rate stood at 7.2 per cent and was lower than rates in Merseyside, the North East, London, Scotland and Wales, it was still higher than the UK average of 6.0 per cent (Department of Economic Development, 1999b). Moreover, despite convergence over the last decade, Northern Ireland continues to experience one of the highest rates of long-term unemployment in the UK. In the fourth quarter of 1998, those unemployed for more than one year represented 46.9 per cent of the unemployed compared with 28.3 per cent for the UK as a whole (Department of Economic Development, 1999a:71).

Although economic differentials between the two communities have been eroded over the period of direct rule, particularly in employment, these economic shortcomings continue to be unequally borne by the two communities. Catholics are substantially more likely to be unemployed than Protestants and almost two-thirds of the long-term unemployed come from the Catholic community. Correspondingly, Catholics are twice as likely to be in receipt of income support and family credit and the income levels of Catholic households tend to be lower than those of Protestants.

As in Britain as a whole, the Labour Government is seeking to resolve these problems through supply-side labour market policies. The Labour Government has committed £140 million over the lifetime of the Parliament to apply the Government's New Deal to Northern Ireland. By mid-March 1999 10,000 had signed up for the New Deal and over 2,000 had found work (Northern Ireland Information Service, 1999b). These measures were supplemented in May 1998 with the announcement of £315 million of extra investment in Northern Ireland by the British government, comprising a £150 million Investment Fund, a £65 million Employment and Skills Fund, a £100 million Enterprise Fund and special incentives allowing new investment in plant and machinery to be offset against tax.

However, the Government has also emphasised inward investment's contribution to Northern Ireland's economic regeneration. For example, speaking to the CBI, Mo Mowlam (1997) asserted that: 'Increasing inward investment is crucial.' The province has had an impressive record in attracting such investment, but each new deal takes eighteen months to two years to negotiate and it can be many years before the job targets materialise. Furthermore, such jobs as are created tend to be part-time or short-term. Finally, Northern Ireland is no doubt attractive to such inward investors because its labour costs are significantly below those found elsewhere in the UK and are amongst the lowest in Europe. Such characteristics certainly do not augur well for the Labour Government's oft-cited aim of creating a dynamic high skill, high wage and high value added economy in Northern Ireland. Nor does the vulnerability and dependence which such investment brings give grounds for encouragement, given the economic turmoil which we have witnessed recently around the world (see Shirlow, 1997).

Human rights and combating discrimination

Speaking in March 1998, Mo Mowlam argued: 'Rights and equality issues were there at the beginning of the dispute we see today and I don't believe that any lasting settlement can be achieved without those issues being addressed too' (Mowlam, 1998). Elements of New Labour's broader agenda have particular cogency in addressing these concerns. This particularly applies to the incorporation of the European Charter on Human Rights into British law and with which legislation passed by the Assembly will have to comply. However, this is only one element of New Labour's policies to guarantee human, political and civil rights and to secure equality of opportunity.

Accordingly, the Good Friday agreement expresses the hope that the Assembly will draft an indigenous Bill of Rights, and a Northern Ireland Human Rights Commission, to extend and enhance the role of the Standing Advisory Commission on Human Rights, has already been established. A new statutory Equality Commission to replace the Fair Employment Commission, Equal Opportunities Commission, Commission for Racial Equality and the Disability Council in Northern Ireland has also been legislated for. Likewise, the Fair Employment Act of 1989 has been strengthened and the public sector is to be assigned a statutory requirement to promote equality of opportunity, replacing the Policy Appraisal and Fair Treatment (PAFT) guidelines introduced by the Conservatives.

Education

In education, the concerns that New Labour had raised during its latter years in opposition regarding underachievement and standards seem less urgent in the case of Northern Ireland. The Northern Ireland education system achieves standards that in many respects outclass those of the mainland. Similarly, Northern Ireland's schools enjoy a much more favourable pupil–teacher ratio than elsewhere in the UK. However, the same insistence on the need to improve standards has nevertheless been carried to Northern Ireland, with a School Improvement Programme of professional and financial support for improvement in 80 underachieving schools and 50 pilot literacy and numeracy summer schemes.

As with its predecessor, the Labour Government is convinced of the potential of the education system in tackling sectarianism. Under Labour, the movement of existing schools to integrated status has continued. Moreover, as part of the Good Friday agreement the Department of Education in Northern Ireland has been given an additional responsibility to encourage Irish-medium schools. A further development which is also likely to have an impact on educational differentials is the decision to establish a common and equitable basis of funding between the variety of schools in Northern Ireland, which will address the higher level of per capita funding in Protestant schools.

Security issues

We considered developments concerning decommissioning and parades above, but prisoner issues were a key element of the confidence-building measures undertaken by the British government during the peace process. Action on prisoner releases has formed one of the most contentious elements of the Good Friday agreement. Both governments have begun an accelerated programme of releases of convicted members of paramilitary organisations that have established a complete or unequivocal cease-fire. At the time of writing, close to 250 paramilitary prisoners have been released.

In regard to policing, the new government has shown a greater willingness to address the defects of the RUC than the previous government, which, in its 1996 White Paper on the RUC merely reaffirmed the status quo. Since coming into office, the Labour Government has removed references to the Crown in the RUC's oath of allegiance and has created a Police Ombudsman to handle police complaints. However, more thoroughgoing reform has been left to the Independent Commission on Policing chaired by Chris Patten, which reported in September 1999. Clearly, the Commission faced difficult decisions, not least because Unionists see the maintenance of the existing institutional arrangements in the RUC as essential while most nationalists have traditionally seen the same institutions as evidence of the sectarian nature of the state. Accordingly, the aspiration of the Good Friday agreement for a 'police service capable of attracting and sustaining support from the community as a whole' (Northern Ireland Office, 1998:22) will be difficult to engineer. Should the cease-fires hold, there will inevitably be pressure, as the Good Friday agreement itself seeks, for the normalisation of security arrangements. This will clearly have an impact on the size of the RUC, which employs close to 8500 full-time officers. Such pressures are likely to raise contentious issues when coupled with the demand for a more representative police force. As Hillyard has noted, the RUC provides important employment opportunities for one section of the community 'and this will pose a major structural problem following any settlement, due to the need for a drastic reduction in the number of security personnel' (Hillyard, 1997:105). In this context it seems difficult to see how the conflicting objectives and concerns of the two communities can be resolved entirely to the satisfaction of either.

It is not surprising therefore that the recommendations of the Patten Report were eagerly awaited. The report proposed renaming the RUC as the Northern Ireland Police Service, suggested that the badge and other symbols of the service be replaced, and that the Union Flag be no longer flown from police buildings. It demanded renewed efforts to increase the proportion of Catholics in the service to 30 per cent of the force in ten years. Finally, should the ceasefires hold, it proposed that the manpower of the force be cut to 7500 full-time officers over ten years (Independent Commission on Policing for Northern Ireland, 1999). While these recommendations were wholeheartedly endorsed by the SDLP, Sinn Fein refused to be rushed into a response. In contrast, the UUP did not need time to consider its attitude, rejecting the report immediately, describing it as deeply flawed and gratuitously insulting.

Conclusion

In 1979, after the fall of the previous Labour government, Gerry Fitt suggested that 'When we look back in history, we see clearly that Labour governments are not the best governments to grapple with the Irish problem' (quoted in Bell, 1982:135). The first two years in office of the Labour government elected in 1997 suggest that future historians may have to reappraise this judgement.

Labour has made substantial progress in implementing its manifesto pledges on Northern Ireland. In its first year the Blair Government lived up to its self-proclaimed New Labour credentials by succeeding where both Labour and Conservative governments failed in the past: securing inclusive all-party talks, maintaining the momentum of those negotiations and achieving a settlement which attracted widespread consent. There have been six previous attempts at a political solution in Northern Ireland from 1972 and all have failed. Northern Ireland's politics pose particular risks for those who attempt to employ political science in a predictive capacity. But as Labour enters its third year in government it seems uncertain whether an agreement can be reached which will allow the Good Friday agreement to escape joining that catalogue of failures. Whatever hopes had been raised by the peaceful conduct of the Orange Order at Drumcree and Ormeau in July 1999 were quickly dissipated by the failure of 'The Way Forward'. At the time of writing, the peace process is at standstill, the victim of the continued impasse over decommissioning and the coming months seem to promise only continued uncertainty.

While the Labour Government deserves credit for bringing the process this far, its development and ultimate fate is also the product of dynamics and processes over which the Government has exercised little control. Whatever the final outcome of the Good Friday agreement, the future stabilisation of the province will depend on equally complex dynamics. But the Government's social and economic policies will nevertheless play an important role. Here, as in its approach to a constitutional settlement, the Government has attempted to break with the tendency of 'old Labour' governments to address principally the concerns of the Unionist community. Certainly, the Government has undertaken significant measures to meet the equality agenda of the nationalist community, but tough decisions remain, not least over the future of policing in the province. Likewise, it remains to be seen whether the economic bases of sectarianism are eroded. As in Britain as a whole, such an economic revival in which all may share may prove to be one of the most formidable tasks for the New Labour Government.

References

Barton, B. (1992), 'Relations Between Westminster and Stormont During the Attlee Premiership', *Irish Political Studies*, 7:1–20.

Bell, G. (1982) *Troublesome Business – The Labour Party and the Irish Question*, London, Pluto Press.

Bew, P. and Dixon, P. (1994), 'Labour Party Policy and Northern Ireland' in B. Barton and P. Roche (eds), *The Northern Ireland Question: Perspectives and Policies*, Aldershot, Avebury.

Blair, T. (1997), *Speech by the Prime Minister at the Royal Ulster Agricultural Show Belfast* (16 May), Belfast, Northern Ireland Information Service.

Blair, T. (1999), *Remarks by the Prime Minister, the Right Honourable Tony Blair MP on Behalf of the UK and Irish Governments at a Press Conference with the Taoiseach, Bertie Ahern, TD Hillsborough Castle, Co. Down* (1 April 1999), Belfast, Northern Ireland Information Service.

Cox, M. (1998), 'Thinking "Globally" About Peace in Northern Ireland', *Politics*, 18(1): 57–63.

Department of Economic Development (Northern Ireland) (1999a), *Strategy 2010. Report by the Economic Strategy Review Steering Group*, London, HMSO.

Department of Economic Development (Northern Ireland) (1999b) *Labour Force Survey March-May 1999*. Belfast, Department of Economic Development.

Dunn, S. (1995), *Facets of the Conflict in Northern Ireland*, Houndmills, St. Martin's Press.

Hillyard, P. (1997), 'Security Strategies in Northern Ireland: Consolidation or Reform?'

in C. Gilligan and J. Tonge (eds), *Peace or War? Understanding the Peace Process in Northern Ireland*, Aldershot, Ashgate.

Independent Commission on Policing for Northern Ireland (1999), *A New Beginning: Policing in Northern Ireland. The Report of the Independent Commission on Policing for Northern Ireland*, London, The Stationery Office.

Jones, B. and Keating, M. (1985), *Labour and the British State*, Oxford, Clarendon Press.

Labour Party (1997) *New Labour: Because Britain Deserves Better*, London, Labour Party.

MacGinty, R. (1997), 'Bill Clinton and the Northern Ireland Peace Process', *Aussenpolitik*, 48(3):237–44.

Mowlam, M. (1997), *Address by the Secretary of State, the Rt. Hon Dr Mo Mowlam MP at the Annual Lunch of the Confederation of British Industry (Northern Ireland) at the Culloden Hotel Belfast* (17 September 1997), Belfast, Northern Ireland Information Service.

Mowlam, M. (1998), *Rights and Equalities in Northern Ireland. Speech to the Carnegie Council on Ethics and International Affairs, New York* (18 March), Belfast, Northern Ireland Information Service.

Northern Ireland Information Service (1999a), *The Way Forward. A Joint Statement By The British And Irish Governments* (2 July 1999), Belfast.

Northern Ireland Information Service (1999b), *New Deal Delivers 350 Jobs in Belfast* (15 March), Belfast.

Northern Ireland Office (1998), *The Belfast Agreement: An Agreement Reached at the Multi-Party Talks on Northern Ireland*, Cm 3883, London, HMSO.

Ryan, M. (1997), 'From the Centre to the Margins: The Slow Death of Irish Republicanism' in C. Gilligan and J. Tonge (eds), *Peace or War? Understanding the Peace Process in Northern Ireland*, Aldershot, Ashgate.

Shirlow, P. (1997), 'The Economics of the Peace Process' in C. Gilligan and J. Tonge (eds), *Peace or War? Understanding the Peace Process in Northern Ireland*, Aldershot, Ashgate.

8

The economic policy of New Labour

Michael Moran and Elizabeth Alexander

The most striking feature of the economic policy fashioned by the Labour Party to fight the 1997 general election is well known: it largely accepted the great changes in both the conduct of economic management, and in the structure of the economy, introduced by the Conservatives after 1979. This chapter describes how Labour adapted itself to the Thatcher reforms, examines what it actually committed itself to in 1997, traces what it did in office and concludes by examining how far Labour had, after its first two years in office, fashioned a distinctive strategy.

Labour and the economic statecraft of Thatcherism

The language of *statecraft* is an illuminating way to compare the economic choices that political leaders make. *Statecraft* is what elites do, in particular what they do to get their hands on the institutions of the state, and what they do, once in office, with the resources of the state (on the idea of statecraft, see Bulpitt, 1986). It is illuminating because, whilst recognising that the actions of leaders are constrained by history, institutions and interests, it nevertheless also recognises that what happens is the result of choice by individuals with strategic objectives: in short, it allows for human agency in political life.

In Britain economic statecraft is dominated by two linked objectives. First, elections have to be won and, once victory is won, work has to start immediately on winning the next election. In the minds of political leaders electioneering never ceases. This is for a good reason: since at least the end of the First World War the two main political parties (and almost everybody else) have accepted that office can only be achieved by winning free elections under a first-past-the-post electoral system. Second, the economy has to be managed in a way consistent with winning elections. There is overwhelming evidence from electoral research that voters' choices are conditioned heavily by their perception of economic conditions and by their view of the ability of competing parties to manage those conditions. An economic statecraft has to be fashioned that appeals to enough of these voters to enable the creation of a winning coalition.

As the unbroken 18 years of Conservative rule to 1997 showed, the economic statecraft of Labour's main opponents was highly successful. It had three main elements.

- First, it created winning coalitions by exploiting features of the first-past-the-post electoral system to target groups of voters: notably, those in the south east of England and, beyond that, selected strata of skilled manual and routine non-manual workers. It targeted the latter by promising to lighten the burden of income tax on these groups. It reinforced this by using both the resources of the state and allies in the mass media, to manipulate economic perceptions, particularly at critical electoral moments (Sanders *et al.*, 1987).
- Second, it greatly diminished the influence of a wide range of institutions that had impeded free market forces, in the process reshaping the interests of actors in markets. The best-known examples include: diminishing trade union influence over labour markets by legal reforms and by direct confrontations with particularly powerful unions, such as the miners; transforming housing markets by transferring a large part of the local authority housing stock to private hands; and privatising the great utilities, thus simultaneously opening up whole swathes of the industrial economy to global market forces.
- Third, it consciously used state power to support a prosperous economy in the Southeast, the electoral heartland of Thatcherism. It used state patronage to put public resources into the Southeast. For instance, Mohan (1995:86–91) has shown that one of the driving forces in health reform in the late 1980s was the desire to protect privileged resource allocation for the Conservative heartland in the Home Counties. It used state power to help displace uncompetitive domestic economic elites, allowing integration with more dynamic global economic forces. That is what produced the reforms in the City of London which deregulated financial markets and helped create the great booming commercial economy surrounding the financial institutions of the City of London in the 1980s (Moran, 1991).

By the time Tony Blair became leader of the Labour Party in July 1994, Labour had already acquiesced in all these three elements of Thatcherite statecraft. Labour found it particularly easy to accept parts of the third element of Thatcherism, that involving deregulation to create a booming City economy. It found it easy because it was one the original architects of the key policy changes. The critical event that allowed financial deregulation was the abolition of exchange controls, and although the actual decision was taken in the early months of the first Thatcher Government (November 1979), the preparatory work was done under the last Labour Chancellor, Denis Healey. The critical period in accepting the Conservative reshaping of labour and housing markets, and the privatisation of utilities, was 1985–89, notably the two years after the 1987 general election defeat, which saw a full-scale policy review. By 1989, the Party had done the difficult job of disentangling itself from earlier commitments to re-nationalise the privatised utilities. As early as 1986, Neil Kinnock, as Party leader, had commended to Conference a document on *Social Ownership* that rejected 'old style' nationalisation (Jones, 1996:118). The 1989 policy document, which summarised the results of the two-year policy review, still offered social ownership as an alternative to nationalisation or privatisation, but it was in fact privatisation by another name: it added only marginal measures, like encouraging Employee Share Ownership, to what the Conservatives had already done (Shaw, 1994:87).

Labour's most difficult adaptation was to the first component of Thatcherite statecraft, notably that concerning taxation. Objectively, the Conservatives were on weak ground, because while they had sharply cut rates of taxation for the highest earners, they had failed to deliver a lighter tax burden for the key groups of targeted voters. Indeed, after the general election of 1992 the tax burden rose. Labour's problem partly lay in the fact that a powerful and hostile tabloid press reinforced the popular perception of the Conservatives as the more economically competent and prudent party; and it partly lay in the fact that the Party found difficulty in simultaneously presenting itself as a low taxation party and in catering to the spending demands of other parts of its electoral constituency, such as public sector workers. The first problem was solved for the Party soon after the 1992 election: the catastrophe of 'Black Wednesday' (when the Government was humiliatingly obliged to withdraw from the European Exchange Rate Mechanism in September 1992) destroyed the Conservatives' reputation for superior economic competence. On taxation, the second Major administration created a window of opportunity for Labour after 1992. Forced by economic circumstances to raise taxes, the Conservatives found that they had destroyed their reputation in the eyes of voters as the low tax party. After 1992 polls showed that the Conservatives had lost their lead to Labour as the party of economic competence and low taxation (on this see Chapter 2).

The statecraft of 'New Labour'

By the time Tony Blair became leader, the Labour Party had accepted the Thatcher revolution. But a big problem remained: how to fashion an economic policy that would convince the electors that Labour could improve on Thatcherism. In part the solution lay in symbolic change, notably in the new Clause 4 which Blair persuaded the party to create in place of the old socialist sounding Clause 4. The new clause commended 'the enterprise of the market and the rigour of competition' (on this see Chapter 1). Even in the realm of symbolism, however, much had already been done before Blair's election to the leadership. For example, Kinnock had already announced the discovery of a 'third way' between capitalism and socialism in a Fabian pamphlet in 1985

Box 8.1 *The essence of Labour's economic statecraft in 1997*

The headline pledges
- No increase in basic or top rates of income tax

- Get 250,000 young unemployed people off benefit and into work

The manifesto pledges
- Match the inherited target for low and stable inflation of 2.5 per cent or less
- No rise in basic or top tax rates throughout life of Parliament
- 'Long term objective' of starting rate of income tax of 10 pence in pound
- For first two years of government, work within departmental ceilings for spending already announced
- Conduct a central and departmental (i.e. comprehensive) spending review immediately on assuming office

---

(Jones, 1996:115.) In part the solution was institutional, notably through imposing more central control over policy. From the moment of his election as leader, Blair and his chief ally, the Shadow Chancellor Gordon Brown, overwhelmingly controlled Labour's economic policy. The latter 'imposed an iron grip on the spending plans of Shadow Cabinet colleagues' (Butler and Kavanagh, 1997:52). In May 1995, he ruled out any increase in public borrowing and promised more independence to the Bank of England. He ensured that the party made few explicit spending pledges and costed any outlays against identifiable savings elsewhere. Tactically, the aim was to say as little as possible about economic policy in order to avoid giving hostages to fortune. Of the five headline pledges which accompanied the publication of *The Road to the Manifesto* in 1996 (a draft for the election manifesto), only one concerned a central instrument of economic policy and that involved a pledge to do nothing: there was to be no rise in income tax rates (Butler and Kavanagh, 1997:53–4.)

Labour's manifesto for the 1997 election persisted with this tactic of accepting the constraints on policy created by the Conservatives. It pledged to honour the spending limits for the next two years outlined in his last budget by Kenneth Clarke and thus to fund any fresh spending from savings identified within the envelope of those plans. Box 8.1 draws on the 1997 manifesto to do two things: it highlights the 'headline pledges' on economic policy offered in Labour's summary ten point 'contract with the people'; and it summarises the pledges on economic policy in the body of the general election manifesto itself. The manifesto is revealing because it represents a distillation of what the

Labour leadership, on the eve of achieving power, thought necessary to realise the twin aims of economic statecraft: fashioning a policy to win the next election, and managing the economy in such a way as to win successive elections.

As far as solving the first problem of economic statecraft is concerned – creating a winning electoral coalition – Labour had a consistent strategy from the middle of the 1980s. Substantively, this was to accept the Thatcher revolution; symbolically, to confirm this acceptance by such devices as abandoning 'old style nationalisation', discovering a third way between socialism and capitalism, and rewriting Clause 4; and, tactically, to minimise the number of costable commitments made by the Party in opposition. The Blair–Brown partnership made a dazzling tactical contribution to the realisation of these aims after Mr Blair's election to the Party leadership in 1994, but the hard work of digging the Party out of the hole of opposition to the Thatcher Revolution was done under Neil Kinnock's leadership. As the extraordinary landslide victory of 1997 shows, the Party triumphantly solved the first problem of statecraft: how to create a winning electoral coalition. Policy since then has necessarily had to address the second problem: how to manage the economy so as to keep that electoral coalition together.

Labour's statecraft in office

The economic policy formulated by a political party in opposition is obviously a product of many forces. Entering government with a large majority, as Labour did in 1997, changes the balance of those forces, releasing the Party's leaders from some constraints but imposing others. Even the huge size of Labour's parliamentary majority after May 1997 did not, however, release Labour from the imperative which must govern the actions of all politicians who aspire to success under the British 'rules of the game': creating and maintaining a winning electoral coalition.

What Labour did may usefully be examined under a number of summary headings. All governments have various *instruments* of economic policy at their disposal that they can use to influence the economy; we should first look at the important choices that Labour made about these instruments. Then it is useful to picture economic management as being about the attempt to control the economy at three levels: at the *macro* level, that is at the level of the whole economy; at the *meso* level, that is the level of particular sectors of the economy; and at the *micro* level, that is at the level of the immediate economic decision takers in the economy – be they firms, workers or consumers.

The instruments of policy

One of the striking features of Labour's economic strategy was the way it narrowed the range of instruments available to the Party in government. Promising so exactly in the election manifesto not to raise the top or the basic rate of personal taxation and not to exceed the planned public expenditure totals laid down in the Conservatives' existing plans for two years, removed from the hands of government instruments which have traditionally been important in manipulating the total level of economic activity. It also diminished, of course, the capacity of Labour to redistribute wealth, since taxation in particular has been an important instrument of redistribution. For instance, the budget of the Conservative Chancellor Nigel Lawson in 1988 had, by abolishing all tax rates above 40 per cent, famously redistributed resources in favour of the rich. A Chancellor who declines to change tax rates greatly reduces his ability to transfer resources between the rich and poor although, as we shall see, this did not totally prevent Mr Brown from achieving some modest redistribution.

Labour had good immediate electoral reasons for accepting these constraints. The leadership believed that it lost the 1992 general election because it was typecast in the public mind as the 'tax and spend' Party; and it believed that tax rises forced on the Conservatives after the 1992 general election made the Conservatives highly vulnerable to attack from a party of 'prudence'. But Labour's most dramatic renunciation of an instrument of economic control actually occurred after the election, its decisiveness took most outside observers by surprise, and it had only an indirect connection with electoral calculations. Within a few days of winning office, the Chancellor announced important changes that greatly increased the independent capacity of the Bank of England to control interest rates. Although in opposition both Mr Brown and Mr Blair had spoken of creating a more independent central bank, the speed and radicalism of the change were nevertheless unexpected. Since the 1930s, the control of interest rates has been one of the main ways by which politicians have tried to influence the economy and thus to ensure electoral success. Now, almost the first act of the new Chancellor was to remove this instrument from his control. The new arrangements:

- set an inflation target to be achieved by the Bank of England;
- gave the Bank control over short term interest rates subject only to achieving the inflation target;
- created a new Monetary Policy Committee within the Bank (the majority of members appointed by the Chancellor) to make decisions about interest rates.

The most important reason for this further narrowing of the range of instruments at Labour's disposal seems to have been a desire to manage more effectively what had been a serious problem for previous Labour administrations: the financial markets. The calculation was that entrusting central bankers rather than Labour politicians with responsibility for setting interest rates would reassure the markets, thus fostering confidence for the pursuit of the Government's economic objectives. While in the intervening period the Monetary Policy Committee has been subject to some strong public hints (and probably to stronger private lobbying) about the decisions it should take, it has nevertheless remained a truly independent arbitrator of interest rate policy.

Macro-economic policy

Because Labour had pledged not to exceed the Conservative's total spending commitments for the first two years of the new government's life, nor to raise either the top or basic rates of personal taxation for the whole five-year life of the Parliament, its freedom of manoeuvre in respect of public spending was highly limited. The Comprehensive Spending Review which was conducted in the first year of the life of the new Government (reported, July 1998), was designed to do two things: to fashion a distinctive Labour mechanism for controlling and planning expenditure; and to map out a strategy for public spending growth in the years after 1999, including the crucial period leading up to the next election.

On the former, the result of the review has been the attempt to move to a three-year planning cycle from 1999, to link planned expenditures to commitments on performance indicators made by spending departments, and to impose continuous scrutiny of these commitments by the Treasury. These changes reflect the unusual authority of Gordon Brown as Chancellor and the attempt to convert this authority into more powerful central (Treasury) control of the spending process. How far these new control mechanisms do amount to a distinctive, more effective means of centrally controlling public spending awaits the test of time.

Given the commitment not to raise levels of personal taxation, Labour's freedom to reshape the substance of spending priorities in the Comprehensive Spending Review was limited. The outcome of the review showed some of the constraints under which the Government operates. There were no large shifts in spending priorities – in other words, no big losers in the review – demonstrating the familiar capacity of individual departments and their clients to protect their programmes. There were substantial 'headline' increases for two programmes, health and education. Labour has a strong emotional commitment to both programmes, a commitment reinforced by the fact that workers in health and education are both strong client groups of the Party. But, two features of these planned increases should be noted. First, while they represent significant increases over spending since the middle of the 1990s, the planned levels are by no means unprecedented. Indeed, as a share of national income, health and education spending are not planned to exceed that seen in the early years of the Major Government (Dilnot and Emmerson, 1998).

Second, these increases were in part funded by tax increases not covered by the pledges in the manifesto, such as increases in excise duties, in part from the continued sale of state assets, and in part from the assumed proceeds of continuing economic growth. This last point emphasises how far, New Labour having ruled out many of the conventional instruments of macro-economic management, the Government's strategy is now tied to success in achieving economic

Table 8.1 *Treasury forecasts of economic growth, 1998–2001*

	1998	*1999*	*2000*	*2001*
GDP growth (%)	2.25	1 to 1.5	2.25 to 2.75	2.75 to 3.25

Source: Financial Times, 10 March 1999

growth. That is a clear consequence of giving up many of the instruments which traditionally allowed the state to redistribute resources between social groups, since if the cake is not to be sliced in a radically different way, delivering the promised increases depends on increasing its size.

The reliance on continued economic growth as a means of avoiding difficult redistributive issues has been one of the most problematic features of macro-economic policy in the first two years of the life of the Government. Almost from the moment of assuming office, the East Asian economic crisis and the wider international recession that it prompted overshadowed Labour's conduct of policy. Achieving the Government's ambitions crucially depends on achieving growth targets, but the history of those targets since Labour's assumption of office has a distinctive and, for supporters of the Government, a troubling feature: initially optimistic targets have been revised downwards in the light of the international recession, but the optimism is then restored in projections of growth safely in the more distant future. The longer the Government looks into the distance the more rosy does its vision become. Table 8.1 shows what the Government thought of growth prospects in March 1999 (the projections underlie the plans announced in the budget of that month).

Although New Labour has no great redistributive ambitions it would be wrong to suggest that it has none at all. The Brown Chancellorship has put a stop to the established redistributive policies of the Conservatives. Although high-income groups have not been seriously hit by any of Mr Brown's measures, they have certainly not been beneficiaries. One considerable achievement of the Brown Chancellorship so far, therefore, is to put a halt to the redistribution that for almost two decades was widening economic inequality in the United Kingdom. Any assessment of the Chancellor's impact on income and wealth redistribution needs to be made in the light of the regressive redistributions which we could have expected to continue had the Conservatives won the 1997 election. But there is also a more positive achievement: the Chancellor has made a modest redistribution of resources to some of the very poorest in the community. A range of measures (including a new lower tax rate of 10 per cent on the first £1500 of income) has achieved this. By one authoritative estimate, Mr Brown's budgets have pushed up the incomes of the poorest 20 per cent of households with children by around 15 per cent; by contrast, the incomes of the richest 10 per cent rose by 1 per cent (Browne, 1999). Figure 8.1 summarises the impact of all the Brown budgets for the range of households, from the poorest to the richest (arranged in ten categories, from

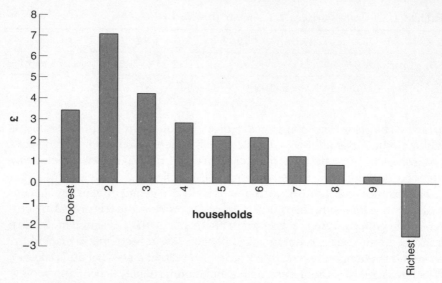

Figure 8.1 *The redistributive effect of Chancellor Brown's budgets*
Source: Browne, 1999

the 'poorest' to the 'richest' decile). The vertical axis measures the effects in pounds.

This picture of modest redistribution nevertheless needs to be interpreted with caution. Labour's commitment not to raise taxes extended only to the taxation of personal incomes. The Chancellor, like all his predecessors, has levied increased consumption taxes (on, for instance, tobacco and fuel). The class connection between consumption and taxation means consumption taxes have partly wiped out the gains on income tax. It is well known, for example, that taxes on cigarettes disproportionately affect the poorest in the community. About the only consistent pattern to emerge from the budgets is that the *employed* poor have gained.

Budgets are central to electoral strategy, but are often quite peripheral to important issues of economic management. The feature that makes them so important electorally is, paradoxically, the very same that can make them marginal to economic management: they attract tremendous media attention. For Chancellors they represent a great political opportunity to sell the government's policies to the electorate. But this very intense media attention also carries the considerable danger of exposing the contradictions in policy and the divisions within government. Chancellors therefore naturally do not use budgets to try to settle issues that divide the Government. A focus on budgets risks missing the fact that important policy issues are often settled by silence, or by a decision not to decide. The single most important macro-economic issue facing the Government after 1997 was indeed settled in this way. The issue concerned the question of the UK's participation in the new currency system created in the European Union, introduced at the start of 1999. It would be difficult to think of a more momentous issue for the conduct of macro-economic policy. Entry into a currency union would shift the most important powers of macro-economic policy to a European level and, in particular, to the new European Central Bank.

There is little doubt that both the Chancellor and the Prime Minister are intellectually convinced of the case for British participation, but a decision has been postponed to beyond the next general election, almost certainly after a referendum. The reasons are twofold. One has to do with party management. Although Labour has not experienced the sort of feuding over the European issue that has so divided the Conservative Party, there remain at all levels of the Party numerous Euro-sceptics. The second has to do with electoral strategy. With a public opinion which has shown a persistent, if shallow, 'Euroscepticism', with a large part of the tabloid press hostile to European currency unification, and with Conservative opponents committed to a policy of declining to join the Euro for perhaps a decade, there are serious electoral risks in joining. The strategy is, then, to 'wait and see' if the Euro prospers; to get to the safety of a second general election victory; and then to hold a referendum on membership. Thus the most important economic issue facing New Labour has been 'decided' by a negative decision and that negative decision has been shaped by issues of party management and electoral strategy.

Meso-economic policy

In the 1980s one of the most important theorists in the Labour Party argued that control of the meso economy was central to effective intervention (Holland, 1987a, 1987b). This account argued that a modern capitalist economy was dominated by a small number of huge enterprises that often monopolised whole sectors. The solution advocated involved increased public control (and some public ownership) at this meso level. The influence of these arguments can be seen in the Alternative Economic Strategy that Labour offered in the 1983 general election. Labour's great defeat in 1983, as we have seen, caused a wholesale rethink of economic policy, pushing it away from this sort of interventionism. Ironically, the Conservatives' success at privatisation made the problem of controlling the meso economy even more acute, for it created a set of big new private enterprises, often occupying monopoly positions. New Labour's policy for the meso economy has been dominated by the question of how to cope with this powerful privatised sector. The Party moved through a number of stages from a manifesto commitment to renationalise privatised enterprises in 1983, to a policy in 1997 that actually committed the government to extend asset sales. Unfortunately, that process of gradual acceptance of the Conservatives' measures left the Party with little scope for new thinking about regulation; and it was further constrained by the way the new regulatory agencies established by the Conservatives to oversee the privatised utilities soon became themselves major institutional interests, elaborating their regulatory regimes and establishing themselves as serious political actors (Prosser, 1997). Labour did promise in opposition to impose a 'windfall tax' on the privatised utilities and swiftly did so in government. However, this is best interpreted as a short-term exploitation of the unpopularity of some of the utilities and a short-term solution to the problem of raising money for the Party's job creation programme for young people, rather than as the reflection of some distinct regulatory strategy. On the wider long term issue of what such a strategy should be, the general election manifesto opted to try to balance all the competing interests:

> In the utility industries we will promote competition wherever possible. Where competition is not an effective discipline, for example in the water industry . . . we will pursue tough, efficient regulation in the interests of customers, and, in the case of water, in the interests of the environment as well. We recognise the need for open and predictable regulation which is fair both to consumers and to shareholders and at the same time provides incentives for managers to innovate and improve efficiency. (Labour Party, 1997)

Shortly after the general election victory, the then Secretary of State for Industry, Margaret Beckett, set up an inter-departmental review of regulation. As one might expect given Labour's position at the General Election, this review (the report of which was published as a Green Paper in March 1998) left untouched both the main structure of the regulatory system and the financial principles guiding regulatory policy. It made only some proposals for marginal changes in structure and policy – for instance, new social and environmental guidelines and more disclosure of information by regulated companies.

Micro-economic policy

Although the macro and meso economic policies pursued by New Labour are shaped by the usual range of factors that mould the economic policy of any government – the need to conciliate interests inside and outside the governing party, the pressure of short-run economic forces, and above all the demands of electoral strategy – it would be wrong to imply that longer run strategic considerations are irrelevant. In opposition, Labour, forced to abandon much of its traditional approach to economic management and to accept the constraints imposed by the 18 years of Conservative rule, was obliged to admit that the sort of 'heroic' policies offered in the past (the National Plan of the 1960s, the Alternative Economic Strategy of the 1980s) were no longer viable. Instead, it turned to micro-economic policy, and in particular to influencing the supply side of the economy. The connection with macro policy, however, is that it was accepted that supply side policies that attempted to influence the decisions of individual firms and workers were most likely to be effective if the wider economy had price stability, and if macro-economic policies were not subjected to sudden shocks and reversals. These considerations, perhaps more than any other, lay behind the decision to give the Bank of England more operational independence and to entrust control over interest rate policy (subject to an inflation target) to its Monetary Policy Committee. Macro-economic stability is assumed to be a pre-condition for effective micro-economic intervention.

What positive role has New Labour assigned to micro-economic policy? In opposition the Shadow Chancellor became briefly a figure of fun (and entered the standard dictionary of political quotations) for a speech delivered in September 1994 which referred approvingly to 'post-classical endogenous growth theory' (see Jay, 1997:58). Nevertheless, while the economic jargon was, wisely, soon abandoned, the phrase did indeed sum up a picture of the economy that has guided much of the economic programme of New Labour. Like virtually every other post-war government, Blair's has taken the task of raising the chronically low rate of British economic growth as its most important objective. But the Party, having abandoned the various 'heroic' approaches to economic management associated with old Labour, is now guided by the belief that growth flows (or is hindered) by a range of factors on the 'supply side' of the economy. Growth is thus in part a function of the degree to which policies and institutions foster technological innovation, since on this view technological innovation is one of the most important influences on economic growth. In part it is also a function of the skill mix in the labour force, the extent to which institutions and policies promote enterprise by individual entrepreneurs and the extent to which policies promote appropriate levels of investment. While New Labour has abandoned the heroic 'planning' mode of the Labour governments of the 1960s, or the attempt to create comprehensive national pacts with the representatives of capital and labour associated with the policies of the 1970s, in its own way this modern approach is also heroic, since it involves the systematic attempt to shape the millions of decisions that are taken by workers, managers and entrepreneurs.

One of the advantages of this approach, from the point of view of the electoral dimension of economic statecraft, is that it allows New Labour continually to announce packages of measures addressed to different parts of the supply side: investment, technological innovation and skill mix. All modern governments are alert to the possibilities of putting political 'spin' on measures, especially when they involve commitments of public funds. Having drawn lessons from the disastrous public presentation of policies during much of the 1980s, Labour is perhaps more sensitive than any of its predecessors to both the dangers and the opportunities in the presentation of policies.

It would be wrong to imply that the commitment to intervention on the supply side at the micro-economic level is only a matter of electoral calculation. There is a real intellectual commitment, in part forced on the Party by the abandonment of the old 'heroic' policies. New Labour's approach has two distinctive, linked, features: a central concern with labour supply, both in quantity and quality; and a concern to integrate this part of micro-economic policy with other policy domains, notably education and social policy. Tony Blair's incantation that Labour's priorities were 'education, education, education' grew from the conviction that higher levels of skill, and the right mix of skills, were the keys to labour supply. One of Labour's ten 'headline' pledges in the 'contract with the people', that formed part of the 1997 manifesto, was to 'get 250,000 young unemployed off benefit and into work' through a mix of job creation and training schemes. This 'New Deal' had, by the beginning of 1999, over 100,000 under-25s in work or training. Since the objectives of the scheme are addressed to long-term problems of employment and skill mix, we cannot sensibly attempt an evaluation of this key part of New Labour's programme at this stage, just as the economic impact of wider education policies, if beneficial, can only be felt over the long term. The New Deal is, however, marked by two obvious controversies. The first is how far the measure is truly adding to employment possibilities in the economy. The second is the relationship between the scheme and the social policies designed by New Labour to address questions of unemployment (on this, see Chapter 12).

Conclusion

The economic policy of New Labour marks a clear break, both in style and substance, with the economic policies of previous Labour governments. Past Labour administrations have had a 'heroic' approach to the economy: that is, they attempted to realise visions of wholesale economic change. New Labour has abandoned this heroic approach. In both style and substance it has accepted the Thatcher revolution. It shares with its Conservative predecessors the belief that government can primarily exercise an enabling influence, creating the conditions for economic prosperity that can only be directly delivered by individual economic agents. But it marks a break with its Conservative predecessors in two respects. First, it does not share the view that the effective functioning of markets demands ever more inequality, has put a stop to the regressive redistributions of the Conservative years, and has even begun a modest programme of egalitarian redistribution. Second, it has a more activist approach to micro-economic intervention, especially in the interests of improving the skills of the British work force. Whether this distinctiveness will be enough to realise the aims of economic statecraft, only time will tell.

References

Browne, A. (1999), 'Is Britain Now A Fairer country?', *Observer* (14 March).

Bulpitt, J. (1986), 'The Discipline of the New Democracy: Mrs Thatcher's Domestic Statecraft', *Political Studies*, 34(1):19–39.

Butler, D. and D. Kavanagh (1997), *The British General Election of 1997*, London, Macmillan.

Dilnot, A. and C. Emmerson (1998), 'Some Win Prizes in Game which Harbours Risks', *Financial Times* (15 July).

Holland, S. (1987a), *The Global Economy from Meso to Macroeconomics*, London, Weidenfeld and Nicolson.

Holland, S. (1987b), The *Market Economy from Micro to Mesoeconomics*, London, Weidenfeld and Nicolson.

Jay, A. (1997), *The Oxford Dictionary of Political Quotations*, Oxford, Oxford University Press.

Jones, T. (1996), *Remaking the Labour Party*, London, Routledge.

Labour Party (1997), *New Labour: Because Britain Deserves Better*, London, Labour Party.

Mohan, J. (1995), *A National Health Service? The Restructuring of Health Care in Britain Since 1979*, Basingstoke, Macmillan.

Moran, M. (1991), *The Politics of the Financial Services Revolution*, London, Macmillan.

Prosser, T. (1997), *Law and the Regulators*, Oxford, Clarendon Press.

Sanders, D., H. Ward and D. Marsh (1987), 'Government Popularity and the Falklands War', *British Journal of Political Science*, 17(1):281–313.

Shaw, E. (1994), *The Labour Party Since 1979*, London, Routledge.

9

New Labour's industrial and employment policy

David Coates

The possession by New Labour of a set of policies capable of strengthening the UK economy was central to its electoral appeal. The Labour Party after 1979 had been electorally vulnerable in this area above all others. New Labour in opposition was well aware of how vital it was to persuade voters that the Party had settled on a set of proposals that were, at one and the same time, economically credible and qualitatively different from those of both old Labour and the Conservatives. Prior to the election, New Labour set about winning public credibility for its policies on industry and employment by developing a new vocabulary in which to describe its broad economic goals, laying down a set of general promises and overall objectives and listing a series of discrete commitments. The relationship of promise to performance for New Labour in this area of policy can therefore best be judged by charting the implementation of promises, the achievement of broad objectives and the creation of an economy commensurate with this new vocabulary.

Policy commitments

New Labour put down at least two broad benchmarks when laying out its industrial and employment policy prior to the 1997 election. In *New Labour: New Life for Britain*, published in 1996, it said that it wanted to create a *stakeholder* economy, as part of 'a genuine one nation, stakeholder society', an economy, that is, which would be 'run for the many and not for the few' (Labour Party, 1996:8, 9, 17). 'Stakeholding' was canvassed in 1996, particularly in speeches and Party publications, as the Party's new big idea.

Although its meaning was never spelled out in detail by any leading Party figure, its use initially seemed to commit the party to a more egalitarian distribution of power within the economy, or at least to changes in forms of corporate governance that would strengthen the position of consumers, workers and suppliers relative to shareholders (see for example Marquand, 1995; Leadbeater and Mulgan, 1996). In a much-quoted address in Singapore in

1996, Tony Blair argued that 'the implications of creating a stakeholder economy are profound. They mean a commitment by government to tackle long term and structural unemployment.' He said that they also mean 'the right relationship of trust between business and government', the 'encourage-ment of self-employed and small business', and the creation of an economy in which everyone 'feels part of the same team, trusts it and has a stake in its success and future' (Blair, 1996). Consequently, there was much discussion of the degree to which the realisation of stakeholding's 'profound implications' required an extensive and radical legislative programme; and in that discussion it is noticeable that Shadow Ministers quickly distanced themselves and the Party from stakeholding's more radical advocates (on this, see Darling, 1997:16).

By the time of the election, though the term was still used in the Party's general publicity material, it had vanished from economic sections of the man-ifesto. The manifesto spoke instead of promoting 'personal prosperity for all', and restricted itself to recording the Party's preference for 'partnership not conflict between employers and employees', and for 'spreading ownership and encouraging more employees to become owners through Employee Share Ownership Plans and co-operatives' (Labour Party, 1997:3, 17). Thus, New Labour went into the general election with the precise meaning and significance of its brief adoption of the rhetoric of stakeholding still unclear and with a question mark over whether stakeholding would continue to be one of the defining benchmarks of its industrial and employment policy.

Where the manifesto was clearer was on New Labour's commitment to the achievement of a 'third way' in industrial and employment policy – that was 'neither old left nor new right', that did not choose (as they had) 'between state control of the economy and letting the market do it all' or between 'head on conflict between bosses and workers and denying employees any rights at all' (Labour Party, 1996:5). New Labour claimed, prior to the election, that 'the political agenda of Britain simply did not need to be like this'. It did not have to be dominated, as in the past, by 'the bitter political struggles of left and right . . . public versus private, bosses versus workers, middle class versus working class' (Blair, 1997a: 2). 'The old left', Tony Blair told the electorate in his intro-duction to the 1997 manifesto, 'would have sought state control of industry. The Conservative right is content to leave all to the market' (Labour Party, 1997). New Labour, however, rejected both approaches. It certainly left behind any Old-Left enthusiasm for public ownership and any whole-scale disman-tling of the Conservatives' industrial relations 'reforms', of the kind promised by earlier Labour Party leaderships. Instead, it offered the electorate its 'third way', built on a set of 'basic minimum rights for the individual at the work-place' and on 'government and industry working together'. It was a third way aimed 'at enhancing the dynamism of the market, not undermining it' in order to 'raise the trend rate of growth by strengthening our wealth-creating base'. (Blair, 1997a: 3, 10). The precise content of this 'third way' was also unclear on election day, but unlike stakeholding, its development as a concept would preoccupy intellectuals and ministers on a number of occasions in Labour's first years in office.

As the election loomed, and in keeping with its tentative exploration of stakeholding and third way alternatives to previous policy packages, New Labour made a number of general statements about the relationship it would establish as a government with the business community, the trade unions and the labour force:

- To the business community it offered 'partnership' to help businesses grow, and in particular 'to develop the small and medium size business sector'. It promised 'tough rules for the non-payment of small business debt', and an improved 'Business Links network to give specialised support to small and medium size firms'. It promised to 'put together the best combination of public and private finance to renew infrastructure', and – in its 1996 documents – even to create 'a publicly owned, publicly accountable railway system as economic circumstances and the priorities of transport policy allow'. It promised to promote British science, R&D and innovation. It promised a set of Regional Development Agencies. It promised new policies to promote competition and protect the consumer. Instead of what it termed Conservative *laissez-faire*, it offered 'a co-operative approach' as 'the new Labour approach to industrial policy' (Labour Party, 1996:13–14).
- To the trade unions New Labour declined to offer any total demolition of the industrial relations legislation of the 1980s. There was to be no 'return to flying pickets, secondary action, strikes with no ballots or the trade union law of the 1970s' (Blair, 1997a:3). Instead New Labour offered 'a fair deal at work', 'modern workplaces with proper standards', a set of 'proper minimum rights for the individual worker' built on a national minimum wage, freedom to join or not join a trade union, and rights of union recognition where a majority ballot is in favour. New Labour also promised to sign up to the European Social Chapter, on the argument that 'basic common terms of employment are entirely compatible with a well-functioning and competitive labour market' (Labour Party, 1996: 5, 14–15).
- To the labour force New Labour made the promise of policy to end youth and long-term unemployment and to reskill the work force to face the employment challenges of a globalised economy. It was convinced, its 1996 documents said, that 'money is being wasted on the bills of failure – unemployment and social decay – instead of being spent on education and investment for the future'. It promised to take '250,000 under-25 year-olds off benefit and into work by using money from a windfall levy on the privatised utilities', to give employers incentives to employ those out of work for more than two years, to reset the training system to 'place demand for skills in the hands of the individual' through individual learning accounts and to create a University for Industry (Labour Party, 1996:5, 16). Its goal, as

expressed in its 1997 Manifesto, was 'educational and employment opportunities for all' (Labour Party, 1997:11).

These general statements of purpose and intent then crystallised into a list of discrete promises in the 1997 Labour Party Manifesto. They can be summarised in three policy clusters.

Business

New Labour promised to:

- reform Britain's competition laws, and pursue tough, efficient regulation where competition cannot act as an effective discipline;
- reinvigorate the Private Finance Initiative, and give self-financing commercial organisations within the public sector more commercial freedom;
- support small businesses by reducing bureaucracy, provide for statutory interest on late payments, improve support for high-tech start ups, improve the Business Links network, and help small firms to sell abroad;
- establish one-stop Regional Development Agencies;
- strengthen the UK's capacity in science, technology and design;
- promote new green technologies and businesses.

Trade unions and worker rights

New Labour promised to:

- leave the key elements of the trade union legislation of the 1980s intact;
- establish minimum standards for the individual at work, including a 'sensibly set national minimum wage' whose level would be set with the advice of an independent Low Pay Commission with members who would include 'representatives of employers, including small business, and employees';
- give people the right to join or not join a trade union;
- grant union recognition where a majority of the relevant work force vote in a ballot for the union to represent them;
- support the Social Chapter, while deploying 'our influence in Europe to ensure that it develops so as to promote employability and competitiveness, not inflexibility' (Labour Party, 1997:17);
- encourage Employee Share Ownership Plans (ESOPs) and co-operatives.

Employment and training

Here, New Labour promised to:

- introduce a budget within two months to begin getting young people and the long-term unemployed back to work;
- give 250,000 under-25s opportunities for work, education and training, through four options (each involving day-release education or training leading to a qualification);
- provide high-quality education and training to all 16–17 year olds;

- give a £75 subsidy/worker for six months to employers willing to take on the long-term unemployed;
- initiate help to lone parents to return to paid employment when their youngest child is of school age;
- offer individual learning accounts to enable individuals to invest in their own training, with a government input of £150 into each account;
- create a new University for Industry, to extend lifelong learning.

Policy initiatives

In charting the manner and degree to which that broad set of promises are now in the process of being implemented, we need to bear in mind the range of Ministries involved in that exercise. For at least the first two of these clusters of policy commitments, the key ministry remains the Department of Trade and Industry (DTI). Since May 1997 the DTI has been run by a series of Secretaries of State (Beckett, Mandelson and Byers), with deputies responsible for trade and competitiveness in Europe, industry, energy, science and technology, competitiveness (and labour law), consumer affairs and the small business sector. But, at least four other ministries impinge on the DTI's territory. The *Treasury* does, both through its general role and through the centrality of the 'welfare-to-work' initiative to the Chancellor's employment strategy. The *Ministry of Defence* (MoD) does, through the heavy dependence of the economy's science base on military–industrial production. The *Departments of Environment and Transport* do, through John Prescott's policies on road and rail renewal. Most potently of all, the *Department for Education and Employment* (DfEE) does, through its responsibilities for employment and training. The DTI's trade policy has also to co-ordinate with the ethical foreign policy stance of the *Foreign and Commonwealth Office* (FCO) and its regional policy with the concerns of both the *Welsh* and the *Scottish Office*. Policy watching requires, therefore, a wide lens.

What is already clear, however, is the seriousness of the departments' collective attempt to pursue the full run of the discrete promises made. By the end of the Government's second year in office, a number of both the minor and major elements in the manifesto list were either still in the process of formation or had yet to emerge. The University for Industry, for example, was still being designed and we had yet to see ESOPs and co-operatives emerge as important government concerns. Nonetheless, by then New Labour had already moved on the bulk of its election promises on industry and employment, as follows.

Business

From the very outset, the Government made clear its determination to build a partnership relationship with the business community, one based on exhortation and consultation rather than on either direction or heavy subsidisation. This determination was clear in Margaret Beckett's opening speeches as Secretary of State for Industry. It was signalled by the appointment of David

Simon (the chairman of BP) as Minister for Trade and Competitiveness in Europe. It was implicit in the caution with which the DTI approached the issue of corporate governance reform and it was evident in both the DTI's policy on competitiveness and the Deputy Prime Minister's extensive use of joint ventures with private capital in key parts of his transport policy.

So, Margaret Beckett immediately wrote to hundreds of companies and business organisations telling them that, under New Labour, she wanted 'the DTI to build a real partnership with every part of industry, so that business can thrive and prosper' (see Box 9.1). It was a message about government–business co-operation and 'third ways' that she and other Ministers then regularly announced in speeches in the City, to the CBI and Institute of Directors and in a number of European fora. The government–business relationship should, as Margaret Beckett put it in May 1988, 'rest on three pillars: strong markets, modern companies and encouraging enterprise' (Beckett, 1998). In particular, it should seek 'to revitalise our manufacturing base by encouraging high-tech industries, boosting exports and "benchmarking" British companies against overseas competitors' (Beckett, 1997). Though the DTI experienced an unusually rapid turnover of senior figures in the first 18 months of the new government and was at its most politically potent only during the brief tenure of Peter Mandelson, in practice its policy priorities remained consistent and explicit, as each new Secretary of State quickly made clear. The world as seen from the DTI did not change with its Secretaries of State for Trade and Industry. It remained a world in which, as Stephen Byers said in his first major speech, 'wealth creation is now more important than wealth distribution', and one, moreover, in which 'government should not hinder' entrepreneurs but rather 'work to ensure the market functions properly and contributes to creating a strong, just and fair society' (Byers, 1999:9)

The main product of that policy consistency and associated worldview was the 1998 White Paper *Our Competitive Future: Building the Knowledge Driven Economy*. It was a White Paper keen to establish the importance, for the future competitiveness of UK-based companies, of a fusion between entrepreneurship and innovation and of people and skills. Putting particular emphasis on the future importance of digital technologies, it committed the Government to policies designed to encourage collaboration between and within companies, to the dissemination of best practice, to the consolidation of strong regional clusters, to the strengthening of competitive processes, and to the general raising of labour skills. In the process, the White Paper also committed the DTI to a new set of roles: triggering innovation in the public sector, 'champion[ing] business needs in government' (DTI, 1998:61), aiding the Small and Medium Enterprise sector, and driving forward the entire enterprise and productivity agenda of the Government as a whole (see Box 9.2).

While maintaining a critical stance towards existing legislation on corporate governance (particularly in relation to the pre-eminence of shareholders, and the excessive salaries awarded to senior directors), the DTI settled for a drawn-out

Box 9.1 *Margaret Beckett's message to businesses large and small, business support organisations and to trade unions, 3 May 1997*

I want the DTI to build a real partnership with every part of industry, so our businesses can prosper and thrive. This means building a high investment, high skill, sustainable economy through open and competitive markets at home and abroad.

Before we came to power we consulted extensively with all sectors of the business community. Now that we are in government we shall build on that consultation, working closely with Britain's entrepreneurs.

We aim to make our manufacturing and service industries competitive so that we are among the best in the world in the 21st century.

In the world, we are particularly keen to work in partnership with Britain's exporters and to expand the number of companies, small and large, who are exporting.

In Europe, we need to give Britain new leadership and to drive for the early completion of the Single Market.

At home, where small and growing firms are the bedrock of a successful enterprise economy, we shall improve the quality of our support in the regions.

Our regulations will be simple, helpful and fair. We have already started discussions with organisations representing small business and with some local authorities about cutting red tape and encouraging enterprise.

In our high skill economy, I want us to have the benefits of stable and co-operative relations between employees and employers. The Social Chapter and the national minimum wage are tools we should use to help us achieve this.

I have a vital responsibility to develop our science base and exploit innovation to boost business in the UK.

Under my leadership, the DTI will seek to create a dynamic and supportive environment in which entrepreneurs with good business ideas and well run established businesses can look to the future with confidence.

Britain is a great place to do business and the best base from which to compete internationally.

Margaret Beckett

period of consultation on the modernisation of company law (a White Paper only in the year 2001) and a preference for voluntary codes rather than law. At the same time, a new Competition Bill was announced in the first Queen's Speech, making the abuse of market power by cartels illegal, strengthening powers of investigation and increasing penalties. A green paper on the enhanced regula-

---

Box 9.2   *The Government's Competitiveness White Paper*

The Government's White Paper sets out the role it and business need to play in improving the UK's competitiveness. Our aim is to close the performance gap between the UK and other major trading nations. This is a job for business but Government must create the right environment for business success by providing an economic framework which is stable and enterprising. The Government will put in place policies and programmes to help business innovate and succeed as we all face the challenge of the knowledge-driven economy . . .

Government's role is to:
- invest in *capabilities* to promote enterprise and stimulate innovation;
- catalyse *collaboration* to help business win competitive advantage;
- promote *competition* by opening and modernising markets.

Source: Our Competitive Future: Building the Knowledge Driven Economy, Cm 4176, December 1998, pp. 6–7.

---

tion of certain of the privatised utilities was issued in March 1998 and legislation followed. The Mergers and Monopolies Commission (MMC) and the Office of Fair Trading (OFT) were not merged, as proposed in opposition; nor did the DTI set out new and more demanding criteria for permitted mergers, as had been foreshadowed prior to 1997. Instead, the new legislation simply replaced the MMC with a new Competition Commission charged to block anti-competitive agreements between companies, with the OFT given greater powers to enforce the new competition rules.

The DTI did not, of course, preside over any new public ownership, as had Labour industry ministries in the past. On the contrary, New Labour shed public assets in air traffic control, student loans, and defence evaluation and research. Instead, the Government reviewed and relaunched its predecessor's Private Finance Initiative. In New Labour's first 18 months in office, a series of major public/private partnership deals were announced (particularly in the transport and health sectors, and in local government). At the local level, close government–industry collaboration was strengthened by the creation of a series of Regional Development Agencies. More generally, Gordon Brown's second budget introduced tax credits on investment in research and development by small and medium size companies, as just one of a string of discrete policy and funding initiatives adopted to strengthen this sector. Other policy innovations here included legislation to entitle small firms to charge interest on late payment of commercial debt, DTI support for the business 'angels' network feeding investment funds to small firms, and the creation of a Small Business Service. In its first two years under New Labour tutelage, the Department also proliferated a series of task forces: charged with tackling such things as excessive red tape and skills shortages. In a move reminiscent of 'Old Labour' industry ministries, on at least one occasion it even provided public funds to persuade a leading overseas car company (in this case BMW) to maintain its UK manufacturing capability.

Trade union and worker rights

Policy here has also matched promises made both in the detail of legislation and in the spirit of that detail. Policy has consistently focused on the provision of individual rather than collective rights, and has been designed throughout to ensure that the provision of minimum employment rights does not undermine the achievement of labour market flexibility and economic competitiveness. The new Government immediately went on the ideological offensive in Europe, calling for greater labour market flexibility and opposing French plans for EU-financed job creation. The Government also implemented the European Working Time Directive and issued a White Paper on employment law (*Fairness at Work*), while pushing for widespread exemptions to the Directive and indicating that the new employment law was a one-off resetting of the legal framework around industrial relations, which, once established, would not be extended further.

The ban on trade union membership at GCHQ was lifted within two weeks of Labour taking power. In the same month, the TUC met the Prime Minister privately in Number 10 for the first time in a decade. But, from the outset, Tony Blair was keen to emphasise New Labour's 'fairness not favours' approach to the unions and to issues of labour market regulation. The TUC was told in September 1997 that there would be no going 'back to the days of industrial warfare, strikes without ballots, mass and flying pickets, secondary action and all the rest' (Blair, 1997b). Nor would there be any return to highly regulated labour markets. As Tony Blair put it in introducing *Fairness at Work*, 'even after the changes we propose, Britain will have the most lightly regulated labour market of any leading economy in the world' (Blair, 1998).

A Low Pay Commission was immediately established. It survived a bruising public clash between Beckett and Mandleson (later to replace her at the DTI) on whether exemptions to a National Minimum Wage were desirable/feasible, and eventually recommended a figure of £3.60/week (with a lower rate for younger workers). This figure was below that sought by the TUC, just 20p more than the 1992 Labour election promise, and nowhere near the '50 per cent of men's median earnings' which had been the Party's original position. It was, however, broadly acceptable to the CBI. The machinery for the establishment of a national minimum wage (including a statutory base for the Low Pay Commission) was introduced in November 1998; and the new single national rate (with no variation by region, sector, occupation or size of firm) was introduced on 1 April 1999.

As already noted, the Government immediately signed up to the Social Chapter, accepting its parental leave and works councils clauses and later (September 1998) brought the European Working Time Directive into UK law.

Box 9.3   *Key proposals in the Employment Relations Bill*

Measures to help parents combine home and work responsibilities
- Increasing maternity leave for all employees to 18 weeks
- 40 weeks maternity leave after one year rather than two
- 3 months unpaid parental leave, including for adoptive parents
- The right to take time off for domestic emergencies
- Tackling discrimination against part-time workers

Minimum standards for all individuals at work
- Raising the limit on compensatory awards for unfair dismissal to £50,000
- Extending protection against dismissal for those taking lawful industrial action
- Prohibiting unfair dismissal waivers in fixed-term contracts
- The right for workers to be accompanied at disciplinary/grievance hearings
- Prohibiting 'blacklisting' or other discrimination because of union membership
- A statutory procedure for individuals to obtain recognition for trade unions, where there is clear support for this
- Legislation to improve the regulation of employment agencies, and to better protect the interests of those using them

Source: http://www.coi.gov.uk/coi/depts/DTI/coi563f.ok.

This provided for all those workers not excluded from its provision a maximum 48-hour week and a minimum of three weeks of paid annual leave, rising to four in 1999. In May 1998 the DTI published its *Fairness at Work* White Paper, outlining a new set of employment laws, which it then brought forward early in 1999 as the Employment Relations Bill (see Box 9.3). The White Paper proposals included new individual rights for workers, including:

- a reduction in the legally required qualifying period for an employee from unfair dismissal from two years to one;
- the removal of any maximum limits on damages that an Industrial Tribunal could award for unfair dismissal; and
- the right for union members to be accompanied by a union representative of their choice during grievance and disciplinary procedures.

The White Paper also included new collective rights, including automatic union recognition when more than 50 per cent of the bargaining unit were unionised, or if – when balloted – 40 per cent of employees voted for recognition. The White Paper also proposed to make it illegal for an employer to discriminate against an employee on the grounds of either union membership or non-membership. Certain of these rights (particularly those around union recognition and unfair dismissal) were much resisted by employers' organisations and subjected to detailed changes as the Bill moved through its legislative stages in 1999.

Employment and training

Here both the Treasury and the DfEE took the initiative early. As promised, the Chancellor announced his £3.5 billion welfare-to-work proposals (his *New Deal*) in July 1997. Designed to get 250,000 young people back into work, these offered four different education or training options for the young unemployed and associated job counselling. The scheme was piloted between January and March 1998, and fully implemented thereafter. Its provisions were subsequently extended to the long-term unemployed over 25 (as well as to their spouses or partners) and to employers in the public, private and voluntary sectors. This was accompanied by changes to the rules governing benefits for 18–24 year olds under the Jobseeker's Allowance. The New Deal also included a six-month £75 per week job subsidy scheme for the long-term unemployed, and a £200 million initiative to find jobs for a million single parents (by advice, training and day and after-school child-care schemes).

The DfEE provided £58 million to start up a series of Employment Zones designed to tackle long-term unemployment black spots. The Treasury simultaneously issued a green paper, *Employment Opportunity for All*, which committed the Government to achieving macro-economic stability, a flexible and adaptable labour market underpinned by minimum standards, skilled and adaptable people, policies which encourage people to move from welfare to work, and a tax and benefit system that makes work pay.

A further DfEE initiative was the publication of a green paper on lifelong learning (February 1998) which committed the Government to investing £150 million in one million individual learning accounts and reconfirmed New Labour's commitment to a University for Industry. The Department also provided £15 million to 'kick start' the launch of the University, planned for the year 2000, announced a new £2 million fund to support trade union education: pledged £143 million to widen participation in higher education; and won £160 million from the European Social Fund to support lifelong learning and skills upgrading. Early in 1999, the DfEE also announced a £112 million scheme, beginning in April 2000, to give 'personal job accounts' to the long-term unemployed. This scheme is to pool existing benefit, training and job search funds in an attempt to help unemployed adults to set up small businesses, improve their skills or acquire extra assistance in their search for suitable work.

Policy effects

Two preliminary conclusions seem appropriate at this stage of New Labour's implementation of its industrial and employment policies: a conclusion relating to their novelty and character, and a conclusion relating to their effectiveness.

Novelty and character of the policy initiatives

On their novelty and character much has already been written and claimed. The industrial and employment policies of the New Labour Government have been – and continue to be – presented as clear evidence of the emerging 'third way' in British politics (on this, see Driver and Martell, 1998; Giddens, 1998). Initially presented (by leading Labour Party figures and sympathetic commentators) as a middle way between Thatcherite market-driven policies and the state-driven policies of previous Labour governments, the portfolio of DTI policies are invariably now defended by ministers as a *balanced* intervention advancing the needs of both employers and workers, and are regularly wrapped in the rhetoric of *partnership* and *justice*. Yet in practice, if partnership is the real watchword here and if balance is genuinely intended, then it is not a partnership of equals that is being advocated; nor is it a balance between Capital and Labour that is being created. On the contrary, the DTI has aligned itself (and the Government) just as near to the institutions and organisations of private business as the rhetoric of partnership allows. It has, for example, moved quickly to ease labour regulations wherever the outcry by employers against their introduction has been particularly strident. This was especially evident in the speed and character of the DTI's reaction to the detail of the Working Time Directive: excluding as it did vast categories of labour, and moving swiftly to deny the applicability of its holiday requirements to such part-time and vulnerable workers as paper boys (*Financial Times*, 11 February 1999, p. 1).

Moreover, Ministers, from Tony Blair downward, have persistently lectured trade unions on the need to subordinate their demands to the imperatives of economic modernisation in the private sector. They have welcomed 'workplace partnerships' (*Financial Times*, 24 April 1999, p. 36) only with unions so inclined and have taken every opportunity (as did their Conservative predecessors) to emphasise the Government's prior commitment to the creation of wealth rather than to its distribution. Of course, it is true that this Labour Government has been (and remains) more active in the pursuit of some parts of its industrial and employment policies (particularly those directed at labour re-skilling) than was its Conservative predecessor. But, even here (on what is arguably its central industrial policy area), New Labour is still as reluctant as were the Tories to introduce any compulsory levy on firms. The Government prefers a policy of exhortation and voluntarism of a kind far less radical than that advocated by Labour in the 1980s (on this, see King and Wickham-Jones, 1999).

This marginal discontinuity in policy from both the Conservatives and from Old Labour is hardly enough to sustain the wildest of the 'third way' claims. New Labour certainly has self-confidence about its policies, and a propensity to package them in a 'third way' wrapper, which its Thatcherite predecessors latterly had lost. Take away the wrapper, and the underlying product looks remarkably similar in direction and detail to that pursued by the Heseltine DTI. New Labour's 'third way' in industrial and employment policy may be new when measured against the industrial and employment policies of the early Thatcher governments, but it looks remarkably similar to the industrial and employment policies of the later Major ones. To that degree at least, New Labour's 'third way' may not be quite as novel as some of its proponents would have us believe.

Effectiveness

These are early days, of course, and the policy difference between the Major and Blair governments may yet intensify, particularly if the employment-creating initiatives of the DfEE (and the Treasury) do begin to bear significant fruit. In the end, the appropriate test both of their novelty and of their effectiveness will be whether, in Tony Blair's words, New Labour's third way economics do 'raise the trend rate of growth by strengthening our wealth-creating base'. All that can be said now is that such a strengthening has not yet materialised, nor are there many signs of its coming. After two years of New Labour government, the UK manufacturing sector is still in recession and the UK balance of trade deficit is still at record heights. Though in work to a degree not matched by labour forces elsewhere in Western Europe, the UK labour force is still, by comparison to them, earning low wages and working long hours. The rhetoric of policy may have moved in new ways, and its presentation by ministers may have acquired a new professionalism and a new energy. But in the world of industry and finance, to which that new policy is primarily addressed, old ways remain firmly in place. New Labour's rhetoric has not yet dented the entrenched triad of net capital export, low manufacturing investment and high dividend payouts which combined to rob previous policy packages of the industrial and competitive renaissance for which their advocates strove. Unless that dent can be made, and made quickly, it will presumably not be long before New Labour will begin to pay the electoral price of promising so much and of delivering so little.

Time will undoubtedly show that New Labour *has* been loyal to its electoral promises, in this policy field as in others; and that is immensely to its credit. Time will probably also show that the policy promises to which it has been so loyal were actually inadequate to the task for which they were proffered. This opens a space again for the argument that New Labour would have served us better by refocusing that loyalty on different and more radical promises.

References

Beckett, M. (1997), *Speech at the Launch of the CBI's Report of its National Manufacturing Council* (23 September), London.
Beckett, M. (1998), *Speech to the EU's Industry Council* (6 May), London.
Blair, T. (1996), *Speech to the Singapore Business Community* (January), Singapore.
Blair, T. (1997a), 'Britain will be Better with New Labour', *New Labour: Because Britain Deserves Better*, London, Labour Party.

Blair, T. (1997b), *Speech to the TUC* (September).

Blair, T. (1998), 'Foreword', *Fairness at Work*, London, The Stationery Office.

Byers, S. (1999), 'Wealth Creation is the Priority', *Guardian* (3 February), p. 9.

Darling, A. (1997), 'A Political Perspective' in Gavin Kelly, Dominic Kelly, and Andrew Gamble (eds), *Stakeholder Capitalism*, London, Macmillan.

Driver, T. and Martell, L. (1998), *New Labour: Politics after Thatcherism*, Cambridge, Polity Press.

DTI (1998), *Our Competitive Future: Building the Knowledge Driven Economy*, London, Cm 4176, London, The Stationery Office.

Giddens, A. (1998), *The Third Way*, Cambridge, Polity Press.

King, D. and Wickham-Jones, M. (1998), 'Training Without the State: New Labour and Labour Markets', *Policy and Politics*, 26(4):439–55.

Labour Party (1996), *New Labour: New Life for Britain*, London, Labour Party.

Labour Party (1997), *New Labour: Because Britain Deserves Better*, London, Labour Party.

Leadbeater, C. and Mulgan, G., 'Labour's Forgotten Idea', *Financial Times* (2 October), p. 16.

Marquand, D. (1995), 'Escape to the Future', *Guardian* (1 May), p. 15.

10

New Labour and the global economy

Rorden Wilkinson

Intrinsic to the modernisation of the Labour Party has been a marked shift in the general orientation of the Party's economic policy. Part of that shift has been a commitment to work within what the Party leadership has come to understand as the narrow confines of the contemporary global economy. This shift has, in turn, located New Labour's foreign economic policy squarely within a prevailing neo-liberal global orthodoxy: one which accepts that economic prosperity is best realised through domestic deregulation, industrial competitiveness, and trade and investment liberalisation.

This chapter explores the emerging detail of this neo-liberal foreign economic policy. In doing so, it argues that the key to understanding New Labour's neo-liberalism lies in its interpretation of globalisation. New Labour perceives globalisation as a series of processes which narrow the parameters within which government action can take place and, consequently, has sought to construct a foreign economic policy which captures and reworks key features of neo-liberalism in such a way so as to 'benefit' Britain. To illustrate this, the chapter first examines New Labour's understanding of globalisation. Second, it locates New Labour's manifesto commitments within this understanding. Third, it examines New Labour's interaction with key global forums and issues. Fourth, it looks at New Labour's position on the international regulation of labour and capital. And finally, by way of a conclusion, it asks how successful New Labour has been in achieving the objectives set out in its manifesto.

New Labour and globalisation

The concept of globalisation is itself problematic and the literature on it is voluminous. To date, there is little agreement among either specialists or commentators as to what globalisation actually is, or whether it is a new phenomenon or merely the acceleration of a series of processes already long-established in the global political economy. That said, in its broadest sense the term 'globalisation' refers to the increasing inter-dependence and inter-connectedness of all

---

Box 10.1   *New Labour's manifesto pledges on foreign economic policy*

- Accept the 'global economy as a reality and reject the isolationism and 'go-it-alone' policies of the extremes of right or left'
- Reject state-ownership and market fundamentalism in favour of a partnership between industry and government directed at 'enhancing the dynamism of the market, not undermining it'
- Generate economic stability to promote investment
- Promote dynamic and competitive business and industry at home and abroad
- Put environmental considerations at the heart of 'policy-making' in areas such as international trade negotiations
- Be a reliable and powerful ally in international institutions
- Pursue a leadership role in international institutions and the global economy
- Attach a higher priority to combating global poverty and underdevelopment
- Promote internationalism, not isolationism and protectionism

---

aspects of international economic life, such that events in one region will necessarily have an impact, to greater or lesser degrees, far beyond their immediate geographical area. In the dominant neo-liberal understanding of the contemporary globalised economy, much is made of the collapse, in the early 1970s, of the Bretton Woods system of fixed exchange rates, and the rapid developments in telecommunications technologies thereafter. Against that background, global movements of capital are understood to have accelerated massively, as business interests seek to take advantage of cost differentials in less developed parts of the world. National currencies, no longer guaranteed relative fixity under the umbrella of currency convertibility, have become increasingly open to the whims and desires of currency speculators and financial markets have grown to become ever more diverse and sophisticated. As a consequence, so the argument goes, success in the prevailing global climate requires that national structures be tailored to the needs of a highly mobile set of capital-owning private institutions, and government policy restricted to initiatives that can attract such capital into the national economy.

New Labour's understanding of globalisation and, by extension, the global economy, owes much to this interpretation of recent technological and institutional trends. The increasing liberalisation of trade and the deregulation of capital and labour markets are understood as natural and irreversible responses to the increasingly global activities of business. Furthermore, the collapse of the former Soviet Union and the Eastern Bloc are seen as evidence of

the fallibility of the socialist project (Giddens, 1998:1–26). In sum, these developments are perceived to inhibit the government's ability to regulate the
national economy. New Labour's strategy has been to accept these trends as
long-term features of the global economy and develop strategies whereby
Britain can increase its competitiveness while at the same time carve out a
leading role in the new (and increasingly important) international economic
and financial regulatory bodies. As Mandelson and Liddle put it in 1996:

> We live in a world of capital mobility. Multinational companies have a vast array
> of choices as to where to locate new investment. . . . But whereas capital is mobile,
> labour is much less so. Decisions about where new investment is made are primar-
> ily determined by the skills and attributes of the local population. Governments
> can best promote economic success by ensuring that their people are equipped
> with the skills necessary for the modern world . . . In an economy of rapid change,
> skill requirements change too . . . [accordingly the] skill base should . . . be broadly
> defined. (Mandelson and Liddle, 1996:98–9)

That said, New Labour's re-orientation to meet the perceived needs of the prevailing global economic climate is more than just a pragmatic shift. It is also based
on the assumption that an increasingly liberalised global economy is broadly
beneficial. Indeed, Tony Blair has emphatically expressed support for free trade
and economic liberalisation on several occasions (Blair, 1998a;1997a;1997b).
The pursuit of a free-trade agenda in the post-war period, he has argued, has contributed 'massively to global prosperity' (Blair, 1998a). Moreover, New Labour
has repeatedly stated that it believes the primary means of ensuring an increase
in global prosperity is to actively pursue a further reduction in tariffs and other
barriers to trade, as well as to seek ways in which investment flows can be liber-
ated (DTI, 1999a). Intrinsic to this vision of the route to global prosperity is New
Labour's emphasis on promoting the right kind of British industry to take advantage of an increasingly liberalised global economy and, in particular, on the promotion of a new entrepreneurial spirit (Blair, 1998b).

It would be incorrect, however, to characterise New Labour's foreign (and
domestic) economic policy as a simple embrace of neo-liberalism. Though New
Labour has committed itself to follow what it perceives to be the logic of globalisation and operate within the parameters it is deemed to dictate, it has also
committed itself to pursuing this agenda in conjunction with the promotion of
certain environmental, social and developmental issues. It has committed itself,
that is, to a kind of *socialised* neo-liberalism. Many of the policy statements
and declarations of intent emanating from the Department for International
Development (DfID), the Foreign and Commonwealth Office (FCO), the
Department of Trade and Industry (DTI), and the Treasury have sought to place
social, developmental and environmental issues at the heart of Britain's foreign
economic policy. Yet, in pursuing these goals, the further liberalisation of trade
and investment flows are invariably presented as the key and prior concern,
with global social, developmental and environmental responsibility acting as

---

Box 10.2   *Key manifesto themes*

- To accept the neo-liberal orientation of the global economy.
- To place social, environmental and developmental considerations at the heart of foreign policy.
- To pursue a leading role in global economic institutions.

---

subordinate if useful (electoral and popular) additions to the overall package. For example, strategies to assist the development of Southern states revolve around creating greater space for their participation within the multilateral trading system, rather than a wholesale rethink of development policies (see also Chapter 18). The pursuit of sustainable development and environmentally conscious industry is seldom divorced from the need to increase the volume and value of global trade, or the pursuit of greater market share. The key to safe-guarding and promoting the position of labour is deemed to be an extension of global liberalisation, not the regulation of capital through the strengthening of international law.

Manifesto pledges

Contrary to the assertions of some commentators (Vickers, 1999), New Labour's foreign economic policy was well thought out prior to taking office. While Labour lacked the experience of government, its commitments clearly articulated the leadership's perception of the prevailing global climate as well as its intended responses to the perceived constraints. Three broad themes can be identified in New Labour's global economic manifesto commitments:

- *First*, an acceptance of the confines of the global economy
- *Second*, the placing of development and environmental considerations at the heart of its external policies; and
- *Third*, a willingness to engage with the gatekeepers of the global economy – the global economic institutions – in such a way as to support their work and to develop a leading role for the UK within them.

These three roles are, of course, highly inter-related. To enable Britain to take a leading role, government policies were to be constructed in such a way as to actively engage with, rather than stand apart from, the global economy. Furthermore, in recognition of recent social disquiet at the advance of the global economic agenda, attention had also to be directed at social and environ-mental considerations. In order to ensure that these policies were successful and embedded in the global landscape, supportive and active engagement with global economic institutions was essential. It is in the pursuit of these goals that New Labour has conducted itself since the May 1997 election.

New Labour and the global economic forums

New Labour's foreign economic policy has, in large part, emerged through a series of events and forums that have taken place since coming to power. Each has witnessed the further development of New Labour's stance and an increasing confidence in both its posture and desire to take a leading role in shaping the global economic landscape. But this development has always been consistent with the Party's understanding of the global economy and its manifesto commitments.

The 1997 Commonwealth Heads of Government Meeting (CHOGM) in Edinburgh provided the first opportunity for a clear illustration of New Labour's foreign economic policy in action. Tony Blair used the meeting, and the preceding Commonwealth Business Forum (Blair, 1997a), to voice his 'passionate' belief in free trade and the pursuit of further economic liberalisation. Furthermore, Margaret Beckett, in outlining the six key areas in which she perceived that Commonwealth co-operation could be improved, emphasised the need to help developing countries meet the entry requirements for the World Trade Organisation (WTO) (DTI, 1997). This emphasis was reflected in the agenda of the meeting, which focused primarily on trade, the economy, investment and sustainable development, though the position of Nigeria within the Commonwealth (following its suspension in 1995 for human rights abuses) and the conflict in Sierra Leone were also discussed. Aside from the support for the economic liberalisation agenda, Tony Blair also made clear the Government's determination to see its influence bolstered in the full sweep of relevant global forums. The Commonwealth, Blair told his fellow heads of state, 'should be a force for free trade' and an arena wherein its members can work together to facilitate the further liberalisation of trade in forthcoming WTO meetings (Blair, 1997a).

The Commonwealth Economic Declaration issued at the conclusion of the Conference was itself indicative of New Labour's central policy concerns. It opened with a note on the opportunities and challenges of globalisation, eulogising the 'engines of growth' provided by expansions in trade and investment flows, new technologies and the 'spread of market forces' and the need to spread the benefits of globalisation to those areas that have so far been excluded (Edinburgh Commonwealth Economic Declaration, 1997:paragraph 1). Furthermore, it embodied the very essence of Blair's vision of a third way. The Declaration committed the Commonwealth to market principles, trade and investment liberalisation, partnerships between governments and the private sector as the major requirement of wealth creation, as well as (finally) to the need to develop human and physical resources and pursue gender equality and good governance (Edinburgh Commonwealth Economic Declaration, 1997:paragraph 3). The Declaration's structure also reflected the priorities within New Labour's foreign economic project. Trade and investment occupied the first half of the Declaration, while the environment and development occupied the second.

New Labour's pattern of seeking a leading role in global economic policy-making continued through to the Presidency of the European Union. During the UK's six-month tenure of the Presidency in the first half of 1998, three important global economic forums took place, all of which enabled New Labour to consolidate the character and direction of its foreign economic policy. These were: the second Asia-Europe Meeting (ASEM2), the Birmingham meeting of the world's eight leading industrial powers (G8), and the Geneva Ministerial Meeting of the WTO.

The first of these, ASEM2, was the second in a series of meetings between Europe and Asia directed at building economic linkages between the two regions. In his opening remarks to the Meeting, Tony Blair again reiterated the substance of New Labour's project, emphasising the straitjacket of globalisation and the need to work within its constraints. He spoke enthusiastically of the need to continue the process of trade and investment liberalisation, and to do so even against the background of the deepening financial crisis in East Asia. Setting his face firmly against calls for greater trade and capital regulation in the wake of that crisis, he stated:

> We must also resist demands that we should look inwards in times of difficulty. Our joint aim must be to open up more markets. To reduce barriers to trade, increase investment and promote competition. Based on greater economic stability, transparency and confidence in financial markets. In that way we shall all benefit. Europe will benefit from an open Asia. Asia will benefit from an open Europe. (Blair, 1998c)

The nuclear tests of India and Pakistan ensured that the content of the May 1998 G8 Summit (the seven leading industrial states plus Russia) was not quite as had been envisaged (Foreign and Commonwealth Office, 1998). Nonetheless, in an interview on the eve of the Summit, Tony Blair reiterated the inevitability of embracing globalisation, of pressing for an open global economy, and equipping individuals to survive the rigours of the global market. He also emphasised the need to move away from government policies that subsidised domestic industries in order to shelter them from the global economy. Blair argued that the embracing of globalisation was both inevitable and desirable in terms of greater trade and international exchange. The role of government was 'not to pile up big budget deficits and hope for the best' but 'to run a prudent financial policy and combine that with government intervention to equip people and business to survive and compete in this new global market'. He continued thus:

> I would say the activities of government should not be designed to [prevent] firms competing in the global market. That is not an intelligent response in the end and it won't work, because the global market is upon us. If we try and shelter companies from the global market then all that will happen is that they may survive better for a few years but then they will go under eventually because of the pressures of global competition are such that [this] will happen. What you can do is to equip them and the individuals working for them better to survive the rigours of that global market. That is to me what the third way is. (Kettle, 1998)

Box 10.3 *'Promoting Shared Prosperity': selected extracts from the Edinburgh Commonwealth Economic Declaration, 25 October 1997*

'Today's globalised world poses both opportunities and challenges. Expanding trade and investment flows, driven by new technologies and the spread of market forces, have emerged as engines of growth. At the same time, not all countries have benefited equally from the globalisation of the world economy, and a significant number are threatened with marginalisation. Globalisation therefore needs to be carefully managed to meet the risks inherent in the process.

We believe that work, peace, security and social stability cannot be achieved in conditions of deep poverty and growing inequality. Special measures are needed to correct this, and in particular to help the integration of . . . small states and the Least Developed Countries, in the global economy and address the uneven development that threatens many countries . . .

We also believe that commitment to market principles, openness to international trade and investment, the development of human and physical resources, gender equality, and good governance and political stability remain major components of economic and social progress; and that wealth creation requires partnerships between governments and the private sector.

We welcome the progress made in recent years in dismantling trade barriers and establishing a rule-based international trading system. However, significant barriers to trade in goods and services remain, and the benefits of the expansion of world trade are still unevenly shared . . .

In discussing the causes, consequences and possible resolution of the Asian financial crisis, the G7 (in effect, the G8 with Russia excluded because of fears that it would be contaminated by the crisis) reached a consensus. This reflected both the reluctance of the troubled states to implement the full range of liberalisation policies as well as the possibility that the global financial architecture may have contributed to the crisis. New Labour generally, and Tony Blair in particular, quickly endorsed these explanations as well as the G7's proposals for averting future crises (see Box 10.4).

As Box 10.4 shows, the final area identified by the G7 was the enhancement of the role of international financial institutions and co-operation between them. It is within this context that Tony Blair sought to further New Labour's leading role. Speaking at the United Nations General Assembly, on 21 September 1998, Blair argued that the Asian crisis had highlighted shortcomings in the International Monetary Fund (IMF) and World Bank. He called for substantive reform of the organisations, with the possibility of a partial merger (*Financial Times*, 1998a; see also Giddens, 1998:145; Blair,

We believe that investment flows can bring substantial benefits, and that sound macro-economic policies and financial systems, strong regulatory and supervisory frameworks and political stability are essential in encouraging inward flows. At the same time, we recognise that volatility in such flows can greatly complicate economic management . . .

We welcome the improving growth prospects in many parts of the developing world. . . . At the same time, we remain concerned at the persistence of extreme poverty in many countries and the lack of capacity to reduce it . . .

We have a shared interest in protecting our environment, a global resource in which all countries have a stake. The costs of protecting it should be borne in accordance with shared and differentiated responsibilities. It is therefore incumbent on the global community to strengthen co-operation to achieve sustainable development, so that we can protect our planet for future generations . . .

In pursuance of these commitments, we agree to enhance the Commonwealth's role in building consensus on global economic issues and on an equitable structuring of international economic relations.

We also agree to sustain and where possible increase bilateral assistance among our members; and to ensure the flow of resources to the Secretariat and its various Funds . . .

We believe the Commonwealth can play a dynamic role in promoting trade and investment so as to enhance prosperity, accelerate economic growth and development and advance the eradication of poverty in the 21st Century. We plan to pursue this with vigour.'

Box 10.4   *G7 proposals for crisis aversion*

1 Increasing transparency
2 Helping countries prepare for integration into the global economy and for free capital flows
3 Strengthening national financial systems
4 Ensuring that the private sector takes responsibility for its lending decisions
5 Enhancing further the role of the International Financial Institutions and co-operation between them

---

1998d). This would ensure that a single institution would regulate the global financial system in a manner congruous with the pursuit of open markets and greater transparency in international financial dealings, while removing the problems associated with two organisations dealing with the same issue.

> **Box 10.5**   *Tony Blair on the challenges facing the global economy*
>
> * 'First, we must spread the benefits of globalisation
> * Second, we must keep markets open and fair
> * Third, we need to extend trade liberalisation
> * Fourth, we must . . . ensure that this is not done at any cost
> * Finally, we must maximise the benefits of the electronic age and the borderless economy'
>
> *Source:* Blair, 1998a.

Following on in quick succession from the G8 Summit was the Second Ministerial Meeting of the WTO. Tony Blair, speaking at the Ministerial Meeting, was candid about his vision of the global economy, and the main challenges facing the international community:

> The question now is not so much whether there should be free trade, but how best to manage what I believe is an irreversible and irresistible trend so that all countries and all peoples can benefit. . . . Everywhere, on all fronts of human existence, all people face the challenge of change. Technology transforms their workplaces. Globalisation alters the structures in which they work. Financial markets that with the push of a button move sums of money beyond contemplation across international frontiers with stunning rapidity, can move whole economies. These are powerful impulses of economic change that leave people feeling powerless and insecure about their future. . . . Our choice is clear. To resist change, let it happen or act together to manage its consequences so that our people are equipped for change and given the chances and security they need. Resistance is easy to demand, but won't work and will spoil the good that globalisation can bring. Laissez-faire will leave us divided and bitter. Working together to maximise the good and minimise the bad is the only realistic option. Nowhere is that clearer than in the way we trade with each other. (Blair, 1998a)

Blair went on to identify 'five key tasks', which are outlined in Box 10.5.

At the Ministerial Meeting the proximity of New Labour's foreign economic policy concerns to those of business became abundantly clear. One of the key debates which has dogged the WTO since its establishment in 1995 (and to some extent its predecessor, the General Agreement on Tariffs and Trade (GATT)), has been the issue of whether to require producers to adhere to a set of core labour standards when engaged in the production of goods and services for trade (Wilkinson, 1999; Hughes and Wilkinson, 1998; Haworth and Hughes, 1997; Lee, 1997). Such standards would relate to freedom of association, the right to collective bargaining, the prohibition of forced labour, restrictions on the usage of child labour, and non-discrimination in employment. The First Ministerial Meeting of the WTO in Singapore in 1996 witnessed much discussion on this issue. Speaking for the previous Conservative Government, Ian Lang argued that while the UK fully supported the rights of workers, a legal acknowledgement of such would sit uncomfortably within the WTO. Support for the free-trade agenda, he suggested, would naturally bring about an improvement of the material position of workers (Lang, 1996; see also Wilkinson, 1999:175–6). Instead, Lang argued that the appropriate place for the discussion of such issues was the International Labour Organisation (ILO) and not the WTO. Echoing Lang's sentiments, the WTO responded by issuing a Declaration that attempted, at one and the same time, to support the principal of core labour standards, but distance the Organisation from any responsibility in this issue.

The Singapore Ministerial Declaration did not, however, put a satisfactory end to the debate (Hughes and Wilkinson, 1998:378–9). Indeed, the Organisation's attempt to dodge the issue while at the same time appearing to support the notion of core labour standards, generated much ambiguity. Allied with the election of New Labour, this generated hope that the new Government would reverse Britain's position on the issue and join with the US in pushing for further discussion of the issue. However, speaking at the WTO's Second Ministerial Meeting in Geneva in May 1998, Blair acknowledged the need to press for the 'world-wide observance of core labour standards', but failed to support a re-examination of the issue within the Organisation. Indeed, implicit in his comments was the assertion that worker rights had little place within an organisation designed to promote freer trade. It seemed, then, that little separated the positions articulated by the Major Government and New Labour on this key issue.

The international regulation of labour and capital

New Labour's position on the labour standards issue is perhaps best articulated in the November 1997 White Paper on International Development (DfID, 1997). Here we can find clues to the tactics behind New Labour's refusal to modify the UK's position to any significant degree. Paragraph 3.36 of the White Paper commits the Government to pressing the EU to 'reaffirm at the WTO ministerial conference . . . its commitment to support the ILO's work in promoting labour standards'. Here the Government seeks to pursue the issue within the WTO through the EU (as the European Commission negotiates on behalf of the European 15), rather than taking a stand on this issue. This serves three purposes. First, it deflects heat away from the UK over such a controversial issue. Second, it enables New Labour to demonstrate its, albeit unsatisfactory, commitment to this issue without overtly taking a controversial stance. Third, in the event of a resumption of dialogue on this issue within the WTO, it enables New Labour to claim a share of the victory. Furthermore, the uncontroversial nature of this stand better enables New Labour to take a leading role within the WTO. Indeed, when pressed, Lord Clinton-Davies, the Minister for Trade and Industry prior to New Labour's first cabinet reshuffle, was candid about the damage that grandstanding on such an issue might cause to British industry (One World Action, 1998:26). What emerged most clearly from this issue was New Labour's emphasis on putting the rights of business first, while only paying lip service to the need for a degree of social responsibility.

The underlying pro-business orientation of New Labour's approach to the global economy can be further illustrated with reference to another controversial issue that has received much public attention – that of the Multilateral Agreement on Investment (MAI). Negotiations for an MAI began within the Organisation for Economic Co-operation and Development (OECD) in May 1995. The purpose of this Agreement was to increase the global flow of investment, and build upon existing (though insubstantial) agreements, such as the WTO's Agreement on Trade-Related Investment Measures (TRIMs). Initially, the agreement was to apply only to the 29 members of the OECD, though it was also to be open to signatories from outside. The MAI encountered enormous opposition, however, from a vast coalition of trade unions, non-governmental organisations, grass-roots movements, and governments from developing as well as developed states, because of the secrecy surrounding the negotiations and the social and environmental impact of such an agreement. The primary bone of contention was the MAI's emphasis on the complete removal of barriers to investment in signatory countries – a removal which was deemed to erode the ability of governments to regulate the inward flow of foreign investment and the establishment of production facilities by multinational corporations. This generated the fear that, in the absence of capital controls, investors would seek out the most cost-effective region to settle in and thus take advantage of low labour costs and lax environmental regulation. Some feared that states would increasingly seek to attract inward investment and dislodge it from other areas, by placing increasing pressure on labour and environmental costs – the so-called 'race to the bottom'. However, the withdrawal of the French Government from the negotiations in October 1998, and the enormous pressure exerted on the OECD and its member-states by the opposition coalition, effectively put an end to the OECD-sponsored MAI.

That said, support for a re-negotiated MAI within another forum, the WTO, has been steadily growing (DTI, 1999b). In the light of this and the initial OECD negotiations, the House of Commons Environmental Audit Committee and the Select Committee on Trade and Industry were requested to examine the issue. The conclusions of both Committees serve to highlight further the Government's position, as well as the underlying pro-business sympathies and concerns of its third way. The reports recognise the growing trend for businesses to seek to operate transnationally (Select Committee on Trade and Industry, 1999:paragraph 14), and the need to support these activities. Both reports state repeatedly that renewed negotiations for an MAI should proceed, with the provision that consideration 'on an equal footing' be given to environmental and social issues (Environmental Audit Committee, 1999:paragraph 70), and that the rationale for an MAI be clearly stated (Select Committee on Trade and

Industry, 1999:paragraph 28). Both reports also highlight the Government's commitment to a 'liberal rules-based system of investment' (Select Committee on Trade and Industry, 1999:paragraph 15; Environmental Audit Committee, 1999:paragraph 61). Here again, the supposed dictates of globalisation are used to support the pursuit of a policy directed at liberalising investment flows, while paying lip-service to the needs of labour and the environment. Furthermore, both reports recognise the need to create greater opportunities for developing countries to participate in any future negotiations for an MAI, rather than understanding that the removal of capital controls in these countries will open them up to business interests seeking low cost production. Clearly, the basic thrust of New Labour's stance on the MAI lies firmly with business.

Conclusion

So how, then, do we judge New Labour's foreign economic policy so early on in its tenure? First, New Labour's electoral strategy of trying to appeal to both business and the electorate at large has been carried through into its global economic policy. Second, these catchall policies have brought with them an embrace of neo-liberalism and hence a marked shift to the right in comparison to previous Labour Party economic policy. Third, this embrace is based on a partial and, arguably, inadequate understanding of globalisation. It is an understanding that has concentrated on the global economy as defined by business interests, rather than on the socio-economic consequences of changes in production triggered by unregulated capital flows. And fourth, New Labour's global policies have also been designed to locate Britain firmly among the leading policy-makers of the IMF, World Bank and WTO. As such, New Labour has largely fulfilled its manifesto commitments, with the caveat that in doing so it has demonstrated that its third way is not really an equal partnership between business, the environment and society. New Labour's third way still puts business interests first. Whether the centre of gravity of Labour's foreign economic policy will eventually move away from its heavy bias towards business already seems unlikely; but if it does not, much of the radical promise of New Labour's entry into power will be quickly lost.

References

Blair, T. (1997a), *Speech to the Commonwealth Business Forum* (22 October), London.

Blair, T. (1997b), *Speech to the Lord Mayor's Banquet* (10 November), Guildhall, London.

Blair, T. (1998a), *Speech to the Second Ministerial Meeting of the World Trade Organisation* (19 May), Geneva.

Blair, T. (1998b), 'The Third Way', French National Assembly (24 March), Paris.

Blair, T. (1998c), *Opening Remarks to the Second Asia–Europe Meeting* (3 April), Queen Elizabeth II Conference Centre, London.

Blair, T. (1998d), *Speech to the 53rd United Nations General Assembly* (21 September), New York.

Blair, T. (1998e), *Speech given at Lambeth Palace, London, for the Department for International Development* (28 July).

DfID (Department for International Development) (1997), *Eliminating World Poverty: A Challenge for the 21st Century*, London, Department for International Development, November.

DTI (1997), 'Commonwealth of Opportunities for Business', Press Release, 23 October.

DTI (1999a), 'Brian Wilson Welcomes Parliamentary Report on MAI', Press Release, 5 January.

DTI (1999b), 'Ministers Call for International Investment Rules to Promote Sustainable Development', Press Release, 8 February.

Edinburgh Commonwealth Economic Declaration (1997) *Promoting Shared Prosperity*, 25 October.

Environmental Audit Committee (1999), *First Report – the Multilateral Agreement on Investment*, London, The Stationery Office.

Financial Times (1998a), 'Blair to Urge Full IMF Overhaul', 21 September.

Financial Times (1998b), 'UK Aims to Take Leading Role at Heart of Europe', 2 October.

Foreign and Commonwealth Office (1998), *G8 Birmingham Summit, Background Brief*, March.

Giddens, A. (1998), *The Third Way*, Cambridge, Polity Press.

Haworth, N. and Hughes, S. (1997), 'Trade and International Labour Standards: Issues and Debates over a Social Clause', *Journal of Industrial Relations*, 39(2):179–85.

Hughes, S. and Wilkinson, R. (1998), 'International Labour Standards and World Trade: No role for the World Trade Organisation?', *New Political Economy*, 3(3):375–89.

Kettle M. (1998), interview with Tony Blair, 'Britain and the US: Why We Can Make a Difference', *Guardian*, 15 May.

Lang, I. (1996), Statement to the First Ministerial Meeting of the WTO, Singapore, 9 December.

Lee, E. (1997), 'Globalisation and Labour Standards: A Review of Issues', *International Labour Review*, 136(2):173–89.

Mandelson, P. and Liddle, R. (1996), *The Blair Revolution: Can New Labour Deliver?*, London, Faber and Faber.

One World Action (1998), *Can Trade be Democratic? The Challenges for Trade Unions*, London, One World Action.

Select Committee on Trade and Industry (1999), *Third Report – The Multilateral Agreement on Investment*, London, The Stationery Office.

Vickers, R. (1999), 'The Lure of the Third Way: Labour between Power and Principle', paper presented at the 1999 International Studies Association Annual Conference, Washington D.C., 19 February.

Wilkinson, R. (1999), 'Labour and Trade-Related Regulation: Beyond the Trade-Labour Standards Debate?', *British Journal of Politics and International Relations*, 1(2):165–91.

11

New Labour and the environment

Stephen Young

Labour's main commitment on the environment was included in Blair's intro-duction to the manifesto: 'We will put concern for the environment at the heart of policy-making, so that it is not an add-on extra, but informs the whole of government, from housing and energy policy through to global warming and international agreements' (Labour Party, 1997:4). This commitment was fleshed out as follows:

> The foundation of Labour's environmental approach is that protection of the envi-ronment cannot be the sole responsibility of any one department of state. All departments must promote policies to sustain the environment. (Labour Party, 1997:28)

The manifesto referred to 'sustainable' and 'sustainability', rather than focusing specifically on sustainable development. It picked out integrated transport as the policy required 'above all' by the idea of a sustainable environment. However, the manifesto did reflect the Party's understanding of the concept of sustainable development set out in a earlier detailed report (Labour Party, 1993), and an important speech by Blair in February 1996 after he became Leader.

The Labour leadership thus came to power understanding that sustainable development was a broader concept than conventional ideas about what envi-ronmental policy covered (see Box 11.1). In the 1990s, many politicians, policy-makers and commentators continued to see the environment in the way they had during the 1970s and 1980s – an issue marginalised as an optional add-on extra in a policy ghetto separated from mainstream economic and social policy.

Distinguishing the environment from sustainable development

The concept of sustainable development had been promoted by the 1987 Brundtland Report (World Commission on Environment and Development, 1987), and popularised at the 1992 Rio Earth Summit. Briefly, the concept's central idea is that humanity's actions and government policies need to focus

---

149

Box 11.1   *Core commitments on sustainable development in Labour's 1997 manifesto*

- Environment to be at the heart of policy-making informing the whole of government, and not just an add-on extra
- All departments to promote policies to sustain the environment
- Developing an integrated transport strategy at all levels to provide genuine choice to meet transport needs
- New Environmental Audit Committee in House of Commons to ensure high environment standards across government

---

on protecting the planet and the surrounding atmosphere from further damage, so that future generations can have access to equivalent resources and opportunities to those enjoyed by existing generations. This involves considering not just the environmental aspects of policies, but their social and economic dimensions as well. However, sustainable development remains a contestable concept, and how governments do, and should, respond has been much debated (Baker *et al.*, 1997; Jacobs, 1997). Box 11.2 summarises the Labour Government's interpretation of the concept in a document published early in 1998 (DETR, 1998a). It also sets out what ministers saw as the four key objectives of sustainable development. These highlight the social and economic dimensions, and divide the environment into two aspects – protection and resource management. These four objectives were subsequently used in a number of reports, including *A Better Quality of Life: A Strategy for Sustainable Development for the UK* (DETR, 1999a). During the 1997–99 period, greens were especially critical of the phrasing of the 'maintenance of high and stable levels of economic growth and employment'. Although ministers argued that this meant economic growth being stable and environmentally sustainable, they occasionally reverted to 'sustainable growth'.

The environment came at point eight in Labour's ten-point covenant: 'we will safeguard our environment, and develop an integrated transport policy to fight congestion and pollution' (Labour Party, 1997:5). However, this is potentially misleading. It is important to understand that there are two answers to the question as to where the environment came in the list of Labour's priorities in 1997. First, Labour went into office trying to use sustainable development as a guiding principle 'at the heart of policy-making' – a phrase subsequently often used by ministers.

Secondly, the environment was also dealt with in specific ways under different headings all through the manifesto. As it explains:

> Throughout this manifesto, there are policies designed to combine environmental sustainability with economic and social progress. They extend from commitments at local level to give communities enhanced control over their environments, to

---

initiatives at international level to ensure that all countries are contributing to the protection of the environment. (Labour Party, 1997:28–9)

Putting them in separate boxes (11.1 and 11.3) highlights the distinction between the core sustainable development commitments in the manifesto, and the more specific environmental pledges.

Box 11.2 *Labour's interpretation of sustainable development*

Sustainable development is concerned with achieving economic growth, in the form of higher living standards, while protecting and where possible enhancing the environment – not just for its own sake but because a damaged environment will sooner or later hold back economic growth and lower the quality of life – making sure that these economic and environmental benefits are available to everyone, not just to the privileged few.

Labour's interpretation stresses four key objectives rather than a definition:
- *'Social progress that recognises the needs of everyone'*. Promoting economic and environmental policies is inadequate if some groups or areas are excluded. Thus it is important to restrict the damage to health from poverty, bad housing and pollution.
- *'Effective protection of the environment'*. Acting to limit global threats such as climate change; promote health by improving air quality; and protect old buildings, wildlife and landscapes that people value and enjoy.
- *'Prudent use of natural resources'*. Non-renewable resources such as oil have to be used efficiently while alternatives are developed. Renewable resources like water have to be managed carefully so they are not endangered.
- *'Maintenance of high and stable levels of economic growth and employment, so that everyone in Britain can share in high living standards and greater job opportunities'*. If Britain is to prosper, it needs a skilled workforce, businesses to invest and adequate infrastructure.

Source: DETR, 1998a.

Box 11.3 *Specific environment commitments in Labour's 1997 manifesto*

Transport
- More effective regulation of railways; and a new rail authority to give coherent strategic management
- New public/private partnership to improve London underground

---

- Proper bus regulation at local level with more bus lanes and council/operator partnerships
- Strategic review of the roads programme
- Review of Vehicle Excise Duty
- Public/private partnerships to improve road maintenance

Energy
- Reducing VAT on heating to 5 per cent
- Promoting energy conservation – home energy efficiency schemes linked to Environment Task Force
- Promoting cleaner, more efficient energy use and production
- Strong drive to promote renewables
- 20 per cent CO_2 reduction by 2010

Local government
- Placing a new duty on councils to promote the economic, social and environmental well-being of their areas
- Encouraging all councils to adopt plans to protect and enhance their local environment
- Environmental protection to be one of the responsibilities of London's strategic authority and its mayor

Other issues
- Tough and efficient regulation of utilities
- Giving 250,000 under 25s opportunities for work, education and training – Environment Task Force to be one of four options
- Establishing an independent Food Standards Agency
- Moratorium on large-scale sales of Forestry Commission land
- Greater freedom to explore open countryside
- Greater protection for wildlife
- Promoting animal welfare
- Free vote in Parliament on banning hunting with hounds
- Review of distribution of lottery proceeds
- Proposed Millennium Commission to support environmental, education and public health projects

EU and international issues
- Reforming Common Agricultural Policy
- Overhauling Common Fisheries Policy
- Strengthening co-operation within the EU on environmental issues
- Providing leadership in the international community to promote common action to safeguard the global environment
- Leading the fight against global warming and working for new climate change protocol at Kyoto
- Giving a much higher priority to combating global poverty

Box 11.4   *The Greening Government Initiative*

- Cabinet Committee on the Environment established; chaired by Deputy Prime Minister; explicitly charged with co-ordination of sustainable development issues
- Network of Green Ministers established; chaired by Minister for the Environment; reporting to the above Cabinet Committee; individual Green Ministers responsible for promoting environmental appraisals of proposals within their departments, and greening their department's operations – as on waste and purchasing.
- Sustainable Development Unit (SDU) established within DETR to work on producing a new sustainable development strategy; co-ordinating the government's Greening Government Initiative and approach on Local Agenda 2I (LA2I); and injecting consideration of environmental issues into policy appraisals across Whitehall.

Sources: DETR Press Release, 31 July 1997; EAC, 1998, Vol. II:1–4; DETR, 1998b.

Institutional developments

One of Blair's first actions on taking office was to merge the Departments of Transport and of the Environment to create the DETR. This was an important part of Labour's approach to carrying out the manifesto, and of its attempt to control the Whitehall department that had aggressively promoted road building from the 1970s onwards. DETR's main responsibilities are the environment, local government, planning, regional development, urban regeneration, roads, railways, integrated transport, housing, construction, London, countryside, water and energy efficiency. The Deputy Prime Minister, John Prescott, was appointed Secretary of State, with Michael Meacher as Minister for the Environment. The institutional aspects of the core sustainable development commitments (as shown in Box 11.1) were carried through in July 1997, via the Greening Government Initiative. The main elements are summarised in Box 11.4. They were slightly amended after an early report from the Environmental Audit Committee (EAC) (DETR, 1998b). The EAC had been set up – as promised in the manifesto – to monitor how far each department embraced sustainable development, and to assess environmental performance across Whitehall. It was thus paralleling the work of the Public Accounts Committee in relation to spending programmes. Prescott anticipated it becoming a 'terrier to bite our ankles' (EAC, 1998, Vol. II:paragraph 2).

A number of agencies set up earlier by the Conservatives were left in place. The British Government Panel on Sustainable Development and the UK Round Table on Sustainable Development carried on operating in an advisory capacity, as did Going for Green on the environmental education front. The Environment Agency, with its wide-ranging remit, continued to be influential. It handled the talks with trade associations over the implementation of the Integrated Pollution and Prevention Control (IPPC) directive. New bodies were established. Some, like the Regional Development Agencies (RDAs) were created through legislation. Some restructuring took place in Wales and Scotland as part of the devolution initiative. Similarly, in England the Countryside Commission and the Rural Development Commission were merged to form the Countryside Agency. Groundwork continued its greening of rundown sites, but in November 1999 it was converted from a foundation to a federation. The future role of the Royal Commission on Environment and Pollution was under review throughout 1999.

Towards new sustainable development policy frameworks

This section examines the ways in which Labour tried to promote, albeit to a limited extent, holistic, cross-sectoral approaches from May 1997 to May 1999. This goes beyond the idea discussed above of taking economic, environmental and social dimensions into account. 'Holistic' is shorthand for developing a cross-sectoral approach on issues involving different departments and agencies. Tackling climate change, for example, involves action by government bodies on a number of fronts. These include managing finite energy sources effectively, developing renewables programmes, promoting green taxes, using more energy efficient construction materials and layouts, and restricting the growth in road traffic.

Transport

On the policy front the most important attempt to promote sustainable development came in the 1998 White Paper on integrated transport, *A New Deal for Transport* (DETR, 1998c). The details are summarised in Box 11.5. The centrepiece was the proposal that councils should prepare five-year Local Transport Plans (LTPs) after consulting widely with business, local groups and operators. The aim is that LTPs will cover all modes; include green transport strategies prepared by major employers; set out integration proposals; tackle air pollution; and promote traffic reduction, public transport use, and through-ticketing. The investment in infrastructure will be partly funded by an innovative proposal to give councils powers to generate new revenue streams from road congestion and workplace parking levies. This clearly established the principle of hypothecation in the transport field. The idea was that environmental taxes would be seen to be earmarked to pay for public transport projects that tackle the problem of traffic congestion. The White Paper marked an ambitious attempt to move away from the traditional 'predict and provide' approach, away from building roads to meet forecast demand, towards developing holistic, integrated approaches to manage demand.

Box 11.5 *Summary of Labour's 1998 integrated transport proposals*

Promoting integration at the national level
- Commission for Integrated Transport to monitor progress on implementing the White Paper, develop policies, set targets and advise on public spending priorities
- National public transport information to be available by phone and internet from January 2000

Promoting integration at the regional level
- Regional Transport Strategies to be prepared in the light of national policies by regional planning conferences working with Government Offices for the Regions, Regional Development Agencies, Highways Agency, Strategic Rail Authority, infrastructure providers and operators
- In London Mayor to produce integrated transport strategy covering all modes which will be implemented by new executive body Transport for London: latter to work with boroughs and be accountable to elected mayor

Promoting integration at the local level
- Councils to draw up five-year Local Transport Plans starting in 1999 covering financial years 2000/01–2004/05
- Councils to get new powers to levy workplace parking and road use charges, and to invest the revenue in public transport

Buses
- Better enforcement of bus lanes; 540-mile London bus priority network
- Quality Contracts giving operators chance to bid for exclusive rights for some routes while accepting council's targets
- Quality Partnerships with operator offering quality service, and council improved traffic management
- National minimum standard enabling the elderly to travel at half fare or less

Cycling
- 1996 National Cycle Strategy targets endorsed: to double 1996 journey total by 2002, and double it again by 2012
- Better provision for cyclists at interchanges and in road lay outs

Railways
- Strategic Rail Authority to promote rail use for freight and passengers; integrate rail with other modes; and prepare longer-term competition framework between operators as new franchises come up for negotiation

- Stronger role for independent Rail Regulator in reviewing amounts Railtrack charges operators for access; and enforcing Railtrack's network licence to maintain and improve infrastructure
- Franchising Director to get additional funds to promote integration, and address capacity constraints at 15 pinchpoints listed in Annex F of the White Paper

Roads
- Shift of emphasis from new schemes, to managing and maintaining existing network, with broader criteria applied to improvement projects
- Highways Agency to establish regional traffic control centres, becoming network operator rather than road builder, with new emphasis on up-to-date information for drivers
- Pilot road toll schemes

Source: DETR, 1998c.

Several other proposals were pushed through during the 1997–99 period that complemented the White Paper. Some of the bus initiatives went ahead, and measures were taken to tighten up the regulation of the railways (DETR, 1998c:40–3, 97–9). Several of the budget measures, summarised in Box 11.6, were aimed at getting people out of their cars. The reformed Private Finance Initiative was used to refurbish and extend the London underground via a public/private partnership approach. This fulfilled the commitment to retain a single service in the public sector. More than £1 billion pounds was committed to the existing system over the 1998–2000 period. A third of this is new money, levering in about £15 billion over 15 years (DETR, 1998c:106). Finally, the roads review resulted in 48 schemes proceeding; 40 being dropped and 51 being reconsidered against the new, wider criteria of accessibility, safety, economy, environment and integration (DETR, 1998d:40, Annexes B and C).

Budgets and economic instruments

Box 11.6 summarises the green tax aspects of the three budgets that Brown introduced in Labour's first two years. The initial emphasis was on rhetoric and reviews. A *Statement of Intent on Environmental Taxation* accompanied the July 1997 budget. It stated unequivocally: 'Tax reform will be used to achieve environmental objectives' (Treasury, 1997:1). Some claimed the 1999 budget was the greenest ever. The decision to implement the Marshall Report (Marshall, 1998) by introducing a Climate Change Levy – or energy tax – on industry from 2001, was the most significant decision. It is expected to be revenue-neutral, as it will be offset by cuts in National Insurance contributions. But in collecting a forecast £1.75 billion, it represents by far the most serious attempt to get industry to reduce its carbon emissions to date. It aims to cut emissions by 1.5 million

Box 11.6   *The green dimensions of Brown's first three budgets*

July 1997
- Reduce VAT on domestic fuel from 8 per cent to 5 per cent
- Environment Task Force included as part of Welfare to Work package
- Road fuel duties increased by 6 per cent
- Commitment to continue fuel price escalator and increase it from 5 per cent p.a. to 6 per cent
- Conservatives' proposal to reduce Vehicle Excise Duty (VED) for lorries with clean exhausts confirmed – and extended to buses

July 1998
- Landfill tax up from £7 a tonne to £10 from April 1999
- VAT on energy insulation materials cut from 17½ per cent to 5 per cent
- Lord Marshall to head Task Force on the potential use of economic instruments to reduce industry's use of energy and emissions of greenhouse gases

March 1999
- VED for private and light goods vehicles up £5 to £155 from June 1999
- VED for cars with engines up to 1100cc reduced to £100
- VED for new cars to be linked to CO2 emissions from autumn 2000
- VED frozen for 98 per cent of HGVs, and cut by £1000 for HGVs and buses with clean engines
- VED reduced by 55 per cent for vehicles involved in road/rail transport schemes
- Road fuel duties up by average of 6 per cent in line with escalator, creating 11.6 per cent increase in diesel duty
- Measures to encourage diesel users to switch to cleaner fuels
- Company car tax increased 1999–2002 by removing incentive to drive further to get more allowance; from 2002 this tax to be linked directly to cars' CO_2 emissions
- Removal of existing tax penalties on employers trying to promote green commuting – works buses, discount fares, bicycles; related capital and other allowances introduced
- Climate Change Levy (energy tax) to start in April 2001 with details in Finance Bill 2000; will apply to gas, coal, electricity used by business, agriculture and public sector for energy, but not to fuels used for generation, transport or domestic purposes
- £1 per tonne p.a. escalator introduced on Landfill Tax taking it from £11 in April 2000 to £15 in April 2004; inert waste used for landfill restoration to be exempt from October 1999

tonnes. It also fits the strategy, identified by Meacher, of cutting labour taxes when taxing pollution (*UK Environment News*, February 1998, p. 3).

Climate change and energy

After Kyoto, Labour committed itself to a legally binding target of a 12½ per cent reduction in greenhouse gas emissions at 1990 levels by 2012. This super-seded the manifesto commitment of reducing CO_2 emissions by 20 per cent by 2010, although ministers continued to refer to the 20 per cent figure as politi-cally binding. Some detected differences between the commitment of the DETR ministers to the twenty per cent figure, and the doubts voiced within the Department of Trade and Industry (DTI) and the Treasury. In October 1998, the DETR published *UK Climate Change: A Consultation Paper on Climate Change* (DETR, 1998e). It drew together the work of the Cleaner Vehicles Task Force, the budget and transport decisions and ministers' work on establishing greater diversity in energy supply, to counter the growth of gas-powered stations. In September 1998, 261 renewable energy projects were announced under the fifth Non Fossil Fuel Obligation scheme. A review of policy was developed to identify the changes needed to produce 10 per cent of UK electricity from renewables by 2010. Spending on energy efficiency programmes went up from £109m in 1998–99 to £223m in 2001–02 (*UK Environment News*, August 1998). The new London mayor will have to produce reports on London's con-tribution to climate change targets. The legislation implementing the EU direc-tive on Integrated Pollution Prevention and Control (IPPC) was due to be enacted in 1999. Finally, following the manifesto statement, 'We see no eco-nomic case for the building of any nuclear power stations', a review of nuclear power was set up (Labour Party, 1997:17). By the autumn of 1999 the extent to which all this activity would produce practical plans that would amount to a serious attack on climate change was not yet clear.

Labour's strategy on sustainable development as a whole

The Conservatives had fulfilled their Rio commitment on Agenda 21 by pub-lishing *Sustainable Development: The UK Strategy* (Department of the Environ-ment, 1994). Labour published consultation documents on updating this strategy (DETR, 1998a), and on sustainability indicators (DETR, 1999b), before producing their own follow-up to Rio – *A Better Quality of Life: A Strategy for Sustainable Development for the UK* (1999a). Its proposals are summarised in Box 11.7.

New Labour's strategy is not a comprehensive action plan, with costed pro-grammes, targets and a clear timetable. However, it is potentially significant because it establishes a more advanced monitoring process than the Conserva-tives had. A Sustainable Development Commission will be set up in 2000. Its functions will be to monitor overall progress towards sustainable development, build consensus-based solutions, review the overall impact of policies and to make recommendations to government (DETR, 1999a:paragraphs 5.25 and

Box 11.7   *Summary of* 'A Better Quality of Life' *(DETR, 1999a)*

Interpretation of sustainable development

Chapter 1 sets out the same four objectives summarised in Box 11.2. This is supplemented in Chapter 4 by a list of ten principles and approaches that will guide policy development:

1 'Putting people at the centre', so they can 'enjoy a better quality of life'.
2 'Taking a long term perspective . . . to safeguard the interests of future generations'.
3 'Taking account of . . . a wide range of costs and benefits, including those which cannot easily be valued in monetary terms'.
4 'Creating an open and supportive economic system' in which trade, growth and greater resource efficiency can flourish.
5 'Combating poverty and social exclusion', so all can fulfil their potential; and tackling widespread third world poverty.
6 'Respecting environmental limits' to avoid irreversible damage, thus protecting freshwater resources or limiting climate change.
7 Operating the precautionary principle so that decisions based on assessing the costs and benefits of action are transparent.
8 Anticipating early on 'where scientific advice or research is needed'; assessing it from a 'wide-ranging set of viewpoints'.
9 Ensuring that all have access to justice, to information, and to participation in transparent decision-making processes.
10 'Making the polluter pay' so there is an incentive for producers to reduce the damage they do to the environment.

Future sustainable development priorities (para. 10.3)
• Investing 'in people and equipment for a competitive economy'.
• Reducing 'the level of social exclusion'.
• 'Promoting a transport system which provides choice . . . minimises environmental harm and reduces congestion'.
• Making 'larger towns and cities better places to live and work'.
• 'Directing development, and promoting agricultural practices to protect and enhance the countryside and wildlife'.
• 'Improving energy efficiency and tackling waste'.
• Promoting sustainable development internationally with others.

Headline indicators (Chapter 3)
The strategy includes a 'quality of life' barometer with a toolkit of 13 headline indicators to monitor progress towards sustainable development. Ministers want each to move up, except 6–10 inclusive and 14 which need to go down:

1 'Total output of the economy (Gross Domestic Product)' – growth to be achieved 'alongside improvements in the other indicators'. 'We need more growth not less', but 'that growth must be of a higher quality . . . achieved while reducing pollution and use of resources'.

2 'Investment in public, business and private assets', to include social investment in things like buses and hospitals.

3 'Proportion of people of working age who are in work'.

4 Proportion of 19-year-olds with educational qualifications.

5 Life expectancy – years of healthy life to look forward to.

6 'Homes judged unfit to live in'.

7 'Level of crime'.

8 Emissions of greenhouse gases per head of population.

9 Total number of days when air pollution is moderate or high.

10 Volume of road traffic.

11 Proportion of rivers 'of good or fair quality'.

12 Populations of farmland and woodland birds – they are in long-term decline, and are 'good indicators of the health of the wider environment'.

13 Numbers of 'new homes built on previously developed land.'

14 Volume of waste – more recycling for instance, improves resource efficiency and reduces the need for landfill sites.

15 (An indicator measuring 'satisfaction with quality of life', is to be developed.)

About 110 more detailed second-tier indicators are listed through Chapters 5–9.

Key actions and commitments
Chapter 5 sets out ways of building sustainable development into policies and decisions made by public and private organisations. Chapter 6 focuses on promoting a growing economy while reducing environmental impacts. Chapter 7 considers the creation of better communities to live and work in. Chapter 8 focuses on protecting and managing the environment and natural resources and Chapter 9 looks at the international dimensions. About 90 key actions and commitments are listed. Some are new commitments – creating a Sustainable Development Commission. Most fall into two categories:

1 *Previously announced Labour initiatives* – New Deal for Communities; Transport White Paper details; energy labelling for new housing; waste strategy; council crime reduction strategies; promoting urban forests; improved access to the countryside.

2 *Issues where policy details are yet to be finalised* – Extending the renewables programmes; developing the work of the Cleaner Vehicles Task Force;

converting reports on issues like tourism and sustainable distribution
into action programmes; tightening air quality objectives.

The targets vary
- *Specific* – Annual report on anti-poverty and social exclusion; energy
  labelling for housing; review targets for recycled aggregates; mandatory
  and voluntary labelling.
- *Broad and aspirational* – Promoting continual improvements in resource
  efficiency; welfare reform; lifelong learning; taking better account of the
  needs of women; improving public awareness.
- *Quantitative* – Water companies to reduce leakage by 26 per cent by 2000
  from 1996/97; 5 per cent of electricity to be generated from renewables
  by 2003; 6 sectoral sustainability strategies by the end of 2000.
- *Non-quantitative* – Council planning and housing strategies to incorporate sustainable development objectives; strengthened local partnerships
  and capacity building.

10.13). In addition, annual reports will be published from 2000 on, setting out
progress on the headline indicators, and 'accounting for the action that
Government has taken, and proposes to take, in the priority areas' (DETR,
1999a:paragraph 10.11). The whole strategy will be reviewed in 2004.

Other Whitehall attempts at holistic thinking

Ministers have tried to adopt holistic, cross-departmental approaches on a
number of issues. Welfare to work and the New Deal for Communities have the
potential to link out-of-work people to sustainable development projects in their
neighbourhoods. In July 1998, £600 million was earmarked over four years for
150,000 young people working on the Environment Task Force (*UK Environment
News*, July 1998). Other examples include the work of the Social Exclusion Unit
on deprived housing estates, the Health and Education Action Zones and developing services for the under 8s and for those living in rural areas. These are all
issues involving different departments and agencies. Ministers have used
different phrases to describe such lateral, cross-sectoral thinking: 'holistic
government', 'corporate approach', 'strategic policy-making', and 'joined-up
thinking'. Local councils are often key players here, responsible for the implementation of changed national frameworks. In addition, Blair's determination to
reform the process of government, as shown by the *Modernising Government*
White Paper (Prime Minister, 1999), provides a potentially significant boost to
the development of holistic approaches.

In the short term, the Best Value approach that replaced Compulsory
Competitive Tendering at the local level and the addition of sustainable development criteria for assessing the Single Regeneration Budget (SRB), both had the
potential to promote holistic ideas. The bill to establish Best Value was included

in the 1998–99 session. In the longer term, two other pieces of legislation could become significant. The commitment to place a new duty of well-being on local councils was followed through in the local government White Paper, *Modern Local Government* (DETR, 1998f). Similarly, the manifesto proposals in relation to London went into the White Paper on the governance of London (DETR, 1998g). This proposed giving the mayor a statutory duty to promote sustainable develop-ment, together with responsibility for producing land-use, transport and air-quality strategies. The Greater London Authority Bill – due to be enacted in 1999 – also gives the mayor powers to introduce road congestion charges and work-place parking levies. The revised Planning Policy Guidance Notes (PPGs) on transport, house building on brownfield sites, regional planning and other issues began to appear, creating a new framework for land-use planning (for a full list see DETR, 1999c:Annex A). Over time, the sustainable development dimensions will become more significant and have a cumulative impact on councils.

There was no clear pledge on Local Agenda 21s (LA21s) in the manifesto, only a general commitment to 'encourage all local authorities to adopt plans to protect and enhance their local environment'. LA21s have the potential to pull the threads together at the local level, integrating these and other programmes into more holistic strategies and in July 1997, Blair committed the Government to getting all councils to prepare LA21s by December 2000. This was followed by a report advising councils how best to proceed (DETR, 1998h). An autumn 1998 survey of 469 UK councils showed that 130 had produced LA21s and 163 planned to do so by 2000 (Improvement and Development Agency, 1999). The number of councils with LA21s was included in the *Better Quality of Life* list of second tier indicators, as shown in Box 11.7. However, this strategy doc-ument emphasised the new duty of well-being and appeared to downplay LA21s (DETR, 1999c:paragraph 7.80).

Other incremental developments

Domestic issues

The Government easily carried out its manifesto commitments in two areas. First, the 1998 National Lottery Act set up the New Opportunities Fund of £1 billion to finance one-off initiatives in environment, education and health, as well as addressing other New Labour criticisms of how the Lottery had been operated under the previous government (Labour Party, 1997:30–1; Prime Minister, 1998:71). Second, the moratorium on large-scale sales of Forestry Commission land was maintained (Prime Minister, 1998:101). Other commit-ments were more difficult to progress far. The decision was taken to establish an independent Food Standards Agency (Department of Health, 1998), but the legislation was subsequently postponed. The Government also courted unpop-ularity when following scientific advice and banning beef on the bone. Meacher responded to popular concerns over genetically modified food in 1999 by wid-ening the membership of key advisory committees.

Some of the utility regulation also had environmental consequences. In May 1997, Prescott ordered OFWAT to impose mandatory targets to reduce leakage from water company pipes for five years, as part of a ten-point plan. Within two years, the amount of water lost from leakage before reaching the tap had been cut from 30 per cent to 22 per cent. Groundwater abstraction regulations were also tightened in 1999.

On four other issues progress was disputed. The pledge to protect wildlife led to consultation papers about the more effective protection of Sites of Special Scientific Interest (SSSIs). Meacher committed the Government to future legislation, but this measure appeared a long way down the queue. Government credibility on these issues was damaged by incidents like the U-turn on the Cardiff Bay barrage, even though steady progress was made on biodiversity action plans. The legislative situation was also unclear with regard to the 1999 announcement that there would be a right of access to four million acres of non-cultivated, open country. A Private Members Bill to ban hunting with hounds was introduced, but ran out of time. The Government claimed it had carried out its commitment, blaming the Bill's opponents for 'employing delaying tactics' (Prime Minister, 1998:68 and 106). But critics claimed ministers did not make Parliamentary time available because they had been frightened by the media profile of the pro-hunting Countryside Alliance. Similarly, animal rights supporters have been very critical of the small token measures taken to promote animal welfare (Prime Minister, 1998:68).

EU and international issues

Labour was in a good position to fulfil its manifesto commitment to strengthen co-operation within the EU on environmental issues, as Britain took up the Presidency of the EU for the first six months of 1998. Almost immediately on coming to office, Blair had been able to show the Government's approach while negotiating the EU Treaty at Amsterdam. The most important issue dealt with during Britain's Presidency was following up the Kyoto agreement, and working out how to divide up the EU's 8 per cent 'bubble' contribution to CO_2 reductions between the Member States. As President, Britain chaired meetings, organised conferences and ran seminars on everything from atmospheric pollution to zoo standards. This helped push debates along and spread best practice, especially in connection with the directives on air pollution, wastewater, Environmental Impact Assessment, IPPC, incineration and landfill.

From a narrower, self-interested perspective, Britain got the BSE ban lifted on beef from Northern Ireland, negotiated slightly tighter controls over fish stocks and started negotiations on the Common Agriculture Policy, albeit within what critics saw as too limited a framework. Ministers also agreed to stop dumping chemical and nuclear waste at sea, thus reversing the Conservatives' approach.

The commitment to help lead the fight against global warming was carried out at Kyoto especially by Prescott, and a year later at Buenos Aires. Soon after becoming Prime Minister, Blair made a strong speech at the UN conference

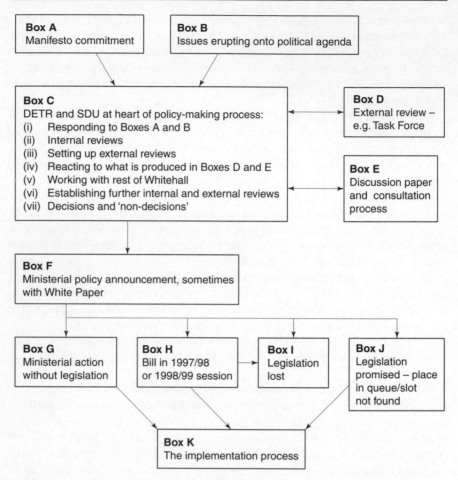

Figure 11.1 *Monitoring Labour's progress on environmental and sustainable development issues*

reviewing the five years since Rio. It reflected ideas elaborated in the international development White Paper (Department for International Development, 1997. On this see also Chapter 18).

Progress on the manifesto

Figure 11.1 is designed to help analyse the extent to which Labour carried out its manifesto commitments on the environment and succeeded in responding to the wider challenge of sustainable development during its first two years in office. Manifesto commitments start in Box A. Other issues – like food scares – arriving on the agenda and influencing the way the government proceeded are represented by Box B. Box C presents the DETR's pivotal role. This involves dealing, through the ministerial team and the Sustainable Development Unit (within DETR), with the Cabinet Office, the Cabinet Committee on the Environment, the Green Ministers Committee, quangos like the Environment Agency, and with other ministries. The most important have been the Treasury, the DTI (over energy), and the Ministry of Agriculture (over agri-environment and other rural issues). DETR responds to what comes from Boxes A and B. It carries out some reviews internally. It decides which topics to put out to arm's length review via a Task Force or similar committee, as represented by Box D, and sets out the terms of reference. It assesses the reports that come back. This can lead to additional inquiries into newly identified issues in Box D; consultation papers in Box E; and policy announcements in Box F. Occasionally when considering issues, non-decisions are made to shelve them. In Box G, ministers take action when new legislation is not needed. Box H provides a fast track into the legislative programme. Box I is there as hiccups occur. For example, the Private Member's Bill to abolish hunting with hounds was dropped in the sense that the Government did not make time for it to complete its stages. In Box J, there is a queue of issues that failed to get into the first two legislative programmes. Some – such as the transport White Paper – have priority. Other bills – SSSI protection, for example – will only be introduced when opportunity arises. Beyond that, there is the quagmire of Box K – the implementation process.

Transport provides a good illustration of the implementation problems that lie ahead. The LTPs, and the Quality Partnerships and Contracts, can only be done on a voluntary basis until legislation makes them statutory. Some of the proposed bodies also need new legislation. In the meantime, a shadow Strategic Rail Authority has been set up. By early 1999, ministers were looking for greater control over Railtrack's investment plans because of criticisms of its short-term approach. Sixteen of the 25 rail franchises do not come up for renegotiation until the period February 2003 to April 2004. Five of the rest are not due for renewal until 2111–12 (DETR, 1998c:96). The tactic of early renegotiation with companies that are consistently missing franchise targets seems limited. Furthermore, the White Paper was only a partial set of proposals: Annex A lists 18 documents that were to be published later, and the text refers to still more (paras 3.53, 4.86). The consultation paper on the fundamental issue of road charging was subsequently published with a deadline for comments of the end of March 1999. This will be followed by a white paper, which will join the long legislation queue. In the meantime, the Government is recruiting councils to run pilot projects on congestion charging and workplace parking levies. The manifesto was against the EU's proposal to raise the Heavy Goods Vehicle weight limit from 40 to 44 tonnes, and this issue has been handed on to the yet-to-be-created Commission for Integrated Transport to study (paras 3.164–8).

Virtually all the manifesto promises have been carried through to Boxes F, G and H, though public/private approaches to roads maintenance did not make much headway. A number of issues are stuck in Boxes D and E, examples being possible taxes on aggregates and pesticides. Considerable uncertainty remains over Boxes J and K as a second wave of issues has started to come on stream. A consultation document on waste (DETR, 1998i) will lead to a white paper late in 1999, with legislation probably to follow. The Greening Government Initiative has put the promised machinery changes in place. But the attempts at holistic approaches and operationalisation of the four objectives of sustainable development, summarised in Box 11.2, have been more limited and faltering. Simply including sustainable development in the terms of reference for Single Regeneration Budget bids, the RDAs and other new bodies (DETR, 1998b) is quite different from making holistic approaches work at the implementation stage.

Serious policy implementation was on a limited scale during New Labour's first two years. But in the second half of its first term, four initiatives will start to interact: the Greening Government Initiative, as it beds down; the attempts at holistic, joined-up thinking; the emerging sustainable development policy framework; and the monitoring process established by the *Better Quality of Life* strategy. Together, they have the potential to produce significant, cumulative change. This does not depend just on money and the balance of the steering mechanisms used. Initially, it depends more on the operationalisation of a different way of thinking.

Comparing New Labour with the Conservatives and old Labour

Blair's Government took the rhetoric further than the Conservatives on sustainable development, understood the social dimension, and widened the scope of the debates surrounding the concept considerably. The four initiatives identified in the preceding paragraph were all solid extensions of the Major Government's approach. New Labour's values and attitudes were fundamentally different on the environment from old Labour's. Both in office and opposition in the 1970s and 1980s old Labour had consistently put economic and social priorities ahead of what it saw as optional environmental concerns.

Assessment criteria

At the next election, Labour's progress on issues covered in this chapter can be measured against Prescott's own priorities (DETR, 1999d:2–4 and 16). These are: delivering practical plans on integrated transport and climate change; modernising local government; successfully establishing the RDAs; combating social exclusion; and improving the quality of life in urban and rural areas. In addition, the Comprehensive Spending Review increased DETR resources by 18 per cent over the financial years from 1999–2001 to 2001–02. The use of these funds can be analysed in relation to Prescott's priorities, as well as the 90 key actions and commitments in the *Better Quality of Life* strategy (see Box 11.7). Success with 'joined-up thinking' can be judged through the annual reports promised in the *Modernising Government* White Paper (Prime Minister, 1999:66).

From a radical green perspective, however, Labour's first two years delivered little. This chapter closes with some suggested criteria for judging the extent to which Labour will have been able to promote sustainable development in a serious way by the time of the next election.

- To what extent has the framework provided by the *Better Quality of Life* strategy promoted the four key objectives, as outlined in Box 11.2? How well have the seven priorities and ten principles listed in Box 11.7 stood up to the day-to-day pressures facing the Government? Are adequate targets and indicators in place, making it possible for the Sustainable Development Commission to monitor progress effectively so remedial action can be taken where necessary?
- A lot of what ministers have done relates to highlighting what others can do – individuals, councils, firms and trade associations, but how effective is the balance of steering mechanisms in changing the behaviour of industry and individuals'? Examples include economic instruments, legal controls, consensus-building approaches, and voluntary compliance in response to improved information.
- To what extent are coherent programmes being effectively implemented with regard to specific policy areas? For example, is the Government investing to reduce demand – investing in public transport to reduce car use, in energy efficiency measures and so on?
- How effectively has the Greening Government Initiative been sustained? To what extent have holistic, joined-up thinking approaches become established across government?
- How far have holistic, sustainable development approaches permeated down to regional levels – to the Welsh Assembly, to the Scottish Parliament, and, in England, to the regional planning conferences and RDAs?
- To what extent has the pledge given in the transport field – 'we are committed to devolving decisions to the most appropriate level' (DETR, 1998c:4.67) – been carried out? More broadly, have councils been able to use the duty of well-being both proactively and effectively?

Note

This research has been supported with funding from the UK Economic and Social Research Council (R000221956) and the Norwegian Research Council, through the Centre for Research and Documentation for a Sustainable Society (ProSus), Oslo.

References

Baker, S., Kousis, M., Richardson, D. and Young, S.C. (1997), *The Politics of Sustainable Development*, London, Routledge.

DETR (Department for the Environment, Transport and the Regions) (1998a), *Sustainable Development: Options For Change*, London, DETR.

DETR (1998b), *The Government Response to Environmental Audit Committee Report on the Greening Government Initiative*, Cm 4109, London, The Stationery Office.

DETR (1998c), *A New Deal for Transport: A Better Deal for Everyone*, Cm 3950, London, The Stationery Office.

DETR (1998d), *A New Deal for Trunk Roads in England*, London, DETR.

DETR (1998e), *UK Climate Change Programme: A Consultation Paper on Climate Change*, London, DETR.

DETR (1998f), *Modern Local Government: In Touch with the People*, Cm 4014, London, The Stationery Office.

DETR (1998g), *A Mayor and a New Assembly for London*, Cm 3897, London, The Stationery Office.

DETR (1998h), *Sustainable Local Communities for the 21st Century: Why and How to Prepare a Local Agenda 21 Strategy*, London, DETR.

DETR (1998i), *Less Waste, More Value*, London, DETR.

DETR (1999a), *A Better Quality of Life: A Strategy for Sustainable Development for the UK*, Cm 4345, London, The Stationery Office.

DETR (1999b), *Sustainability Counts*, London, DETR.

DETR (1999c), *Modernising Planning: A Progress Report*, London, DETR.

DETR (1999d), *DETR Framework for the Future: The Three Year Strategy*, London, DETR.

Department of Health (1998), *The Food Standards Agency: A Force for Change*, Cm 3830, London, The Stationery Office.

Department of International Development (1997), *Eliminating World Poverty*, London, The Stationery Office.

Department of the Environment (1994), *Sustainable Development: The UK Strategy*, Cm 2426, London, HMSO.

EAC (Environmental Audit Committee) (1998), *The Greening Government Initiative*, 2nd Report, HC 517, Session 1997/8, London, The Stationery Office.

Improvement and Development Agency (1999), *Local Agenda 21 Survey 1998*, London, Improvement and Development Agency.

Jacobs, M. (ed.) (1997), *Greening The Millennium: The New Politics of the Environment*, Oxford, Blackwells.

Labour Party (1993), *In Trust for Tomorrow*, London, Labour Party.

Labour Party (1997), *New Labour: Because Britain Deserves Better*, London, Labour Party.

Marshall, Lord (1998), *Economic Instruments and the Business Use of Energy*, London, Treasury.

Prime Minister (1998), *The Government's Annual Report 1997/8*, Cm 3969, London, The Stationery Office.

Prime Minister (1999), *Modernising Government*, Cm 4310, London, The Stationery Office.

Treasury (1997), *A Statement of Intent on Environmental Taxation*, London, Treasury.

World Commission on Environment and Development (1987), *Our Common Future*, Oxford, Oxford University Press.

12

New Labour's education policy

Gail Stedward

How education came to be New Labour's number one priority

In some contrast to the conscious lowering of expectations in other policy areas, in opposition New Labour's mantra of 'education, education, education' and Tony Blair's often-repeated assertion that education was the Party's 'number one priority', considerably raised expectations for change and improvement under a Labour government. How did the issue of education attain this primary status? A number of reasons can be identified.

In the first place, education has always enjoyed an important role in Labour Party policy and politics, and has featured prominently in Labour government policy. In the dramatically changed economic and ideological landscape of the late 1990s, education has become especially important as a legitimate site for government intervention, as is explained below. While some have argued that the Labour Party in 1997 was merely following the lead on education set by its Conservative predecessors, a closer analysis of developing Labour policy on education, both in government and in the period of opposition, shows this not to be the case. It is true that while in government the Conservatives gave education a privileged place on the agenda, most notably in the 1987 election campaign and in the subsequent watershed Education Reform Act 1988, which introduced, amongst its measures, a national curriculum. However, the idea of a core curriculum was previously raised in Callaghan's 'Great Debate' on education in 1976, such that when the Conservatives showed interest in the issue, Jack Straw, then Labour's education spokesman, was able to accuse them of stealing Labour policies (Demaine, 1992:241). Similarly, the importance of parents working in partnership with schools was raised in 1977 in the Taylor Report *A New Partnership for Our Schools* and endorsed in Labour's 1988 policy pamphlet *Parents in Partnership* (Demaine, 1992:244). Right at the beginning of Labour's long period in opposition, in October 1979, Neil Kinnock, then shadow spokesman on education, told the Socialist Education Conference:

Box 12.1   *'We will make education our number one priority'*

New Labour's Manifesto contained a ten-point 'contract with the people', the first point of which was:

1. *Education will be our number one priority, and we will increase the share of national income spent on education as we decrease it on the bills of economic and social failure.*

The more detailed commitments on education in manifesto were:

- Cut class sizes to 30 or under for 5, 6, 7 year-olds
- Nursery places for all 4 year olds
- Attack on low standards in schools
- Access to computer technology
- Lifelong learning through a new University for Industry
- More spending on education as the cost of unemployment falls

---

We have to use this period of opposition to make education a central issue of political debate and public demand. It has to be a finger in the fist of the next Labour Government. We must ensure that it gains the importance of economic, industrial and energy policy. That is an elementary necessity if we are to make our society more harmonious, more articulate, more reasoning, more tolerant, more democratic. That is a fundamental priority if we are to survive economically. (Cited in Centre for Contemporary Cultural Studies, 1981:256)

As dedicated accounts of the Labour Movement and education show (see for example Simon, 1965;1974), education has always had a special place in the Labour Party in terms of both individual and working class advancement and egalitarian ideals. However, another thread can be traced. As the post-war boom began to show signs of slump, the Labour Party began to focus more on the relationship between education and the economy. John Vaizey, an academic economist and one of Tony Crosland's informal 'independent advisers' (Crosland in Boyle, Crosland and Kogan, 1971), was active in promoting the ideas associated with 'human capital' development (Vaizey,1958;1962;1963). The influence of these ideas can be seen in the Robbins Report (1963) on the expansion of higher education and in the Plowden Committee's (1967) report on *Children and their Primary Schools*. They are also evident in Labour's slogan 'investment in people', adopted in 1961 and used in the 1964 manifesto. In the National Plan of the following year, the view of education as a route to general economic improvement as well as individual betterment was made explicit (Centre for Contemporary Cultural Studies, 1981:108). In the 1970s, the Alternative Economic Strategy stressed the importance of developing the potential of people as an important contributor to competitiveness. The emphasis on investment in human capital is clearly articulated in the Labour Party

170

literature of the 1980s and 1990s as Labour shifted towards 'supply side social-ism' (Thompson, 1997). So the idea of the economic potential of education is not then a novel product of New Labour but rather a nascent theme in Labour's education policy trajectory, which has tended to be overshadowed by the social aspect. What is new is that education was placed at the *centre* of the New Labour project for the renewal of Britain – as a key component of industrial and employment policy (on this, see also Chapter 9).

New Labour's 'third way' emerged in a political climate (and wider global competitive environment) which blocked any active state policies in relation to capital ownership and industrial investment. Consequently, the Labour Party in opposition was pushed inexorably towards a concentration of its economic and industrial policy on the resetting of labour markets, labour institutions and labour skills. In the process, education policy gathered a new importance as a replacement for discredited policies of industrial regulation and capital control. It is no coincidence that this recalls Clinton's strategy of education as the spur to economic growth (on this, see also Chapter 3). It was during the policy realignment from 'capital' focused policies to 'labour' focused ones, that leading members of the New Labour leadership first encountered the now widely-dis-cussed 'new growth theory'. The emergence of new growth theory constitutes a further force pulling New Labour towards a repositioning of education policy as a primary component of economic policy. The 'new' growth theory substi-tutes human capital for technological change, as 'an alternative, or at least a complementary, engine of growth' (Lucas, 1988:17). It emphasises the *endog-enous* nature of human capital and its development (Lucas, 1988; Romer, 1986; Skott and Auerbach, 1995). In new growth theory, economic processes such as globalisation and increased International competition demand invest-ment in the endogenous resource of human capital; and education impacts adversely on economic performance if it fails to produce workers with the req-uisite industrial skills. In the hands of the new growth theorists, education policy has a central role to play. It becomes *the* tool of government: charged to inculcate attitudes, develop skills and competencies which, in assisting workers to learn and to do their jobs more effectively, ultimately contribute to economic prosperity. In the process, as Robert Reich put it, the new growth theory ends the 'cleavage between economic and social policies' (Reich, 1983); and offers centre-left politicians a new programme for economic survival in the age of globally-mobile capital funds and technologies.

New Labour's vision for education is ambitious, but in keeping with its new economic orthodoxy, the aspirations and policy commitments have been made within the context of an acceptance of a stringent general resource framework. From the outset, the education policies proposed by New Labour have reflected an uneasy mix of Conservative consumerism and individualism, exemplified for instance by parents' choice, and appeals to traditional Labour concerns with collectivism and citizenship, such as the restated commitment to comprehen-sive education. The successful union of these divergent philosophies may be thought of as the quintessence of New Labour, a catch-all, election-winning strategy – whether this union can be achieved in governmental practice will be assessed at Labour's mid-term in power.

Promises and problems

Education policy retained the high profile of the election campaign with the Government's first actions.

Cut class sizes for 5–7 year olds

Three weeks after coming into office, New Labour took the first steps to deliver on this early pledge, made in 1996. The Education (Schools) Bill abolished the assisted places scheme established by the Conservatives in 1980, with the savings earmarked for reducing infant class sizes. Andrew Rawnsley presciently noted that the Government, having set up these articles of faith with the electorate, would bend over backwards to honour the promise on class sizes, regardless of the consequences (*Observer*, 31 May 1998). By mid-term in office, David Blunkett could boast that the pledge was half-way delivered: 'fewer than 200,000 children aged 5–7 in classes with more than 30 by the start of the school year in September, compared with 485,000 in January 1998'. He forecast that the manifesto promise would be delivered in full by September 2001, one year earlier than promised. However, one ironic consequence of the drive to cut infant class sizes is the increase in class sizes for 8–11 year olds as resources are redeployed to honour the pledge (*Guardian*, 5 March 1999).

Provide nursery places for all 4 year olds

Action on this manifesto promise was also swift. In a clear departure from the policies of their Conservative predecessors, New Labour abolished nursery vouchers and announced a new system of provision based on 'co-operation rather than competition' between providers (DfEE, 1997a). Local education authorities were instructed to convene Early Years Forums and prepare Early Years Development Plans. By September 1998 the pledge had been implemented. However, the trend established under the nursery voucher scheme – of primary schools lowering their reception class age to catch 4 year olds, with the result that voluntary sector pre-school playgroups closed – has continued (Pre-School Learning Alliance, 1999). Research, published in the US and ongoing in the UK (*Observer*, 4 October 1998), on the importance of play rather than formal education in early years as a foundation for successful formal learning later, suggests that the provision of places for 4 year olds in primary schools may have unintended consequences for the Government's long-term aims (but not 2002 targets) on numeracy and literacy. Voluntary playgroups (which rely on maternal involvement) also intersect with two other New Labour concerns: 'good' parenting and lifelong learning. Research by the Pre-School Learning Alliance shows that adult participants learn about child development and gain a wide range of transferable skills (*Guardian Education*, 19 May 1998). Government concern at the continued closure of voluntary playgroups is reflected in the establishment of an independent review of the issue (DfEE, 1999).

Access to computer technology

Echoing the optimism and zeal for new technology of Wilson in 1964, Blair announced plans to create a 'National Grid for Learning' in his speech to the 1996 Party Conference. Implementation of the policy appears to be repeating the disillusionment of that earlier era. The election manifesto promised an agreement with British Telecom to link schools to the internet free of charge and 'to make access charges as low as possible' (Labour Party, 1997:7). Since Labour took office, only 12 per cent of primary schools have gone on-line because the BT deal is offered only with its most expensive link service (*The Guardian*, 2 March 1999). The scheme to train teachers in IT has been criticised as ill conceived by teachers' unions, the Liberal Democrats and IT academics, principally on the grounds that the majority of teachers lack access to hardware and do not have even basic computer skills (*Guardian Education*, 2 February 1999).

More spending on education

Notwithstanding the early activity on education across all its sectors, New Labour's first year in office represented a period of 'Phoney War', waiting for the outcome of the comprehensive spending review in July 1998. Then, even with David Blunkett as one of the winners in the competition for funds, the 'extra' £19 billion of education spending over three years allocated by the spending review will not raise the proportion of GDP spent on education above that of the Conservatives in their final term (*Guardian*, 15 July 1998). Indeed, spending as a proportion of GDP actually fell under Labour, as David Blunkett admitted to the Commons Select Committee on Education; from 4.9 per cent under the Conservatives to 4.7 per cent (*Financial Times*, 8 July 1998). Furthermore, House of Commons library figures show that the extra funding in 2001–02 will be worth only £3 billion rather than the £19 billion over three years claimed by the Government (*Observer*, 17 January 1999). At mid-term, New Labour in power has not met its manifesto commitment to reverse the trend, set by the Conservatives, of cutting government spending on education as a share of national income (Labour Party, 1997:8). In fact, the trend has continued. Whether the Government can arrest this and meet its carefully worded promise that 'Over the course of a five-year Parliament, as we cut the costs of economic and social failure we will raise the proportion of national income spent on education' (Labour Party, 1997:9), is a moot point.

Lifelong learning

Lifelong learning – encompassing education and training of adults in workplaces and in educational institutions – was enunciated, but not elucidated, in the manifesto. The promise of improving and broadening access to education and training, through new initiatives such as 'Individual Learning Accounts' and the 'University for Industry', put a modern spin on Britain's perennially debated problem of a comparatively low skilled, poorly educated workforce and concomitant economic under-performance. The problem has always been one of the failure of mass education and training to equip the majority for work, in contrast to the success in the creation of a highly educated elite. The economic consequences of this have been the focus of particular concern in the last twenty years as employment in low skill, low wage industries has increasingly given way to high skill, high wage employment (OECD, 1995). The notion of lifelong learning is New Labour's solution to the problem – not just a statist measure to redress the shortfall of mass education and skills, but to underline the need for an *individual* capacity and willingness to respond to changes in patterns of employment.

Helena Kennedy's (1997) report, *Learning Works*, echoed the notion of 'thwarted potential' and emphasised the importance of the further education (FE) sector in addressing the problem. David Blunkett may have been instinctively sympathetic to the pivotal role of FE in the whole education project, noting that it could contribute not only directly to employment potential, and, in the re-education of parents, also to the ambitious schools targets set by New Labour, as parents would be better equipped to help their children (*Guardian*, 2 July 1997). Nonetheless, the sector's hope for a significant injection of resources was not forthcoming. Despite the rhetoric of the importance of the sector, Kennedy's original intention, that the priority given to FE should be backed up with a transfer of resources from the higher to the further education sector, was not taken up. Meanwhile, the paper on lifelong learning, *The Learning Age* (1998), originally billed as a white paper and subsequently demoted to a discussion document, failed to match the expectations raised by its initial promotion. John Edmonds, General Secretary of the GMB, voiced this disappointment, noting that, without significant financial and policy intervention by the Government, the initiative was bound to replay the failures of previous voluntary training policies (*Guardian*, 26 February 1998). The incentive contained in the 1999 budget – that employers' contributions to individual learning accounts will be tax-free – will do little to redress this.

The University for Industry, scheduled to launch in April 1999, comprises local consortia of universities, colleges, employers, local authorities and other relevant organisations who will co-ordinate recruitment and learning for students in their area or sector (*Guardian Higher*, 16 March 1999). It is an example of New Labour's espousal of public–private partnerships. The University for Industry may provide one way of meeting the Government's aim of increasing participation in FE and higher education (HE) without increasing resources or provision to the extent lobbied for by those sectors. This is because lifelong learning is predicated on distance learning and part-time study, rather than the conventional model of full-time participation by 18–21 year olds. The 1999 budget underscored this model with the allocation of £500m over three years to the education budget, from a total of £1.7b to establish community-based IT training in schools, colleges and libraries and to link this with adult education expansion through the University for Industry (*Guardian*, 10 March 1999).

The media, and consequently, the electorate's equation of education with schools, has undoubtedly contributed to the long-standing position of FE and training as a side-show to the main event. New Labour has not challenged this. Indeed, in its own rhetoric on education it has contributed to the concentration of attention and consequently resources on the high profile school sector. The specific targets and promises made by New Labour on schools contrast with the more general pledges for FE and training. Thus far, a pattern of incremental reform is apparent, characterised by pilot schemes and a limited introduction of innovations. For example, the IT learning centres will initially be concentrated in inner cities and maintenance allowances to encourage full-time participation in education for 16–18 year olds will be piloted. Full policy implementation for FE and training is still some way off and the patchwork of provision so far falls well short of a national, comprehensive training strategy. Meanwhile, according to DfEE figures, the proportion of 16–18 year olds in full-time education or training has fallen in England. At the end of 1997, 74 per cent of 16–18 year olds were engaged in some form of education or training, the lowest proportion since 1992 (*Guardian Higher*, 27 October 1998). The promise of lifelong learning, even in its reductionist form as a euphemism for continuing education, has yet to be fulfilled.

School standards

In some way all the New Labour education initiatives are linked (rhetorically, at least) with raising educational standards. Standards in schools has been the key area of the Government's education policy. Its priority was illustrated by the subject of the Government's first White Paper *Excellence in Schools* and by the splitting of the original Education Bill (whose HE fees proposal faced certain opposition in the Lords – discussed below) to create the School Standards and Framework Bill. This large piece of legislation, with 124 clauses and 30 schedules, is the foundation for New Labour's approach to raising standards. It is an approach characterised by three key features: new targets for literacy and numeracy, assessment of both pupils and teachers and increased central powers.

New targets for literacy and numeracy

The Secretary of State for Education and Employment has staked his job on the attainment of publicly stated targets: 'By 2002, 80 per cent of our 11 year olds will have reached the required standard in literacy and 75 per cent in numeracy' (David Blunkett, *Guardian Education*, 8 July 1997). In a bid to accomplish this, Blunkett waived the national curriculum so that pupils could concentrate on literacy and numeracy. Then, in September 1998 the National Literacy Project was introduced in English primary schools, with a central prescription of a daily 'literacy hour' and the teaching methods to deliver it. Following the work of the Numeracy Task Force, a similar numeracy hour was introduced in September 1999. At the time of writing, meeting the targets is some way off. The 1999 league tables, showing the results of the national tests for 1998, revealed that 64 per cent of pupils achieved the target for English and 57.9 per cent for maths (*Guardian*, 23 February 1999).

Assessment

The assessment of both pupils and teachers is to be achieved through testing, inspections and publication of league tables. New Labour's one concession to the contested status of this approach has been to introduce the concept of value added to the analysis of the data collected. The aim is to measure what a school has contributed to each pupil's progress and attainment. However, in order to do this, baseline testing at age 5 has been introduced, leading to worries of selection from the outset of a child's school career. This concern was amplified when the newly appointed junior minister for school standards, Charles Clarke, stated his approval for setting according to aptitude at this age (*Guardian*, 8 September 1998). While New Labour has criticised, and adapted accordingly, the content of the league tables, it has conspicuously failed to question the concept of tables as a useful measurement of standards. Likewise, the very notion of standards is narrowly interpreted; both the Conservatives and New Labour have correlated standards with 'scholarly, academic, subject-based achievement . . . measured by traditional forms of timed, written tests' (Torrance, 1997:321). While this notion was not unimportant to old Labour (witness the Great Debate), considerable emphasis was placed on 'the many other personal, practical and *social* outcomes of schooling' (Torrance, 1997:321 emphasis added). In the New Labour universe, a concern with the quantitative rather than the qualitative outcomes of education is apparently ascendant.

Increased central powers

As illustrated by the literacy and numeracy strategy, the Government's measures are predicated on setting the means as well as the ends of policy. The new Standards and Effectiveness Unit at the DfEE deals directly with schools as well as local education authorities (LEAs). Ministers have been empowered to intervene in LEAs and schools that are judged to be failing. In addition to sending in 'improvement teams' to LEAs, closing down schools and reopening them under 'Fresh Start', the Secretary of State can establish 'Education Action Zones' (EAZs) in response to bids from local partnership 'forums' of parents, education authorities, schools, voluntary organisations and businesses. The idea of EAZs has proved particularly controversial, as it sets up a direct challenge to LEAs as a model for local education management in the twenty-first century and represents a radical departure in Labour education policy. The zones are explicitly 'testbeds for innovation', a point reiterated by Tony Blair, David Blunkett and Stephen Byers, then Minister for School Standards, who placed EAZs in the context of the Government's search for a new third way in public services (*Guardian*, 3 March 1998).

In style of operation, New Labour has resembled the Conservatives in the previous decade. There has been a lot of tough talking (within days of taking office Blunkett had 'named and shamed' 18 failing schools), legislation to increase central powers and reduce discretion at the local government level, emphasis on standards and criticism of the teaching profession. While the philosophy underlying the role of education and its importance on the government agenda may differ between New Labour and the Conservatives, the continuity in their style was underlined by the appointment of the confrontational (and Conservative-appointed) Chris Woodhead as joint vice chair of the Standards Task Force and his reappointment as Chief Inspector of Schools, despite his deep unpopularity with the teaching profession. At the same time, the appointment (in the event, only briefly) of the emollient Tim Brighouse, Chief Education Officer of Birmingham, as Woodhead's co-vice chair, echoed old Labour's better relationship with educators. The approach of these two advisers could hardly be more different (for example, see the *Guardian*/Institute of Education debate, *Guardian Education*, 3 March 1998). Their differences of view on key issues – the best methods to raise standards and the role of LEAs – resonate with the struggles over education policy development in the New Labour Party.

Funding Higher Education

The Dearing Committee's Enquiry into Higher Education, set up in 1996 by the Conservative Government with cross-party support, effectively excluded HE from the election campaign. New Labour's manifesto made cursory reference to the sector, noting that the current system of student maintenance required review, but made no mention of tuition fees. Constituting the first review of HE since the Robbins Report in 1963, Dearing's remit was wide, but, in the context of the massive growth in student numbers, the dominant political issue was funding. New Labour in power swiftly rejected Dearing's proposal on fees and maintenance grants in its immediate response to the Report and announced its own preferred option of means-tested fees and loan repayments (DfEE, 1997b).

The introduction of tuition fees and the abolition of grants marked a distinct break with the ideology of old Labour, for whom 'free education' had been a shibboleth (notwithstanding the continued trend of significantly greater middle class participation in HE). The Government placed the decision to introduce fees in the context of its espousal of 'new realism' and 'hard choices' in a globally competitive environment, in which human capital is the key to international competitiveness (DfEE, 1997b). The Government also reiterated what was to become a familiar theme: 'rights and responsibilities go hand in hand.

The investment of the nation must be balanced by the commitment of the individual' (DfEE, 1997b).

Opponents of the Government's decision were quick to point out the anomalies in the fees policy. In particular, gap year students would have fees imposed on them retrospectively (having deferred their university entry for one year) and students enrolling in Scottish universities would pay more in tuition fees because of the longer four-year degree course. The gap year issue was quickly resolved when the Government relented on imposing fees on those affected; its 'first major U-turn' (*Observer*, 17 August 1997). The 'Scottish anomaly' took rather longer to resolve. Reports of confrontations at Conference and back-bench rebellion circulated, but skillful compositing and the tight discipline of New Labour ensured that the Government's real opposition lay in the House of Lords. The Bill finally proceeded after the Lords agreed not to inflict a fourth successive defeat on the Government when Blunkett conceded an independent review – to be completed by April 2000 – of fee arrangements for English, Welsh and Northern Irish students studying in Scotland. The Government agreed that the results of the review would be 'morally binding'. The 'Scottish anomaly' is likely to take on a new lease of life in the new Scottish parliament where, of the four major parties, only Labour supports tuition fees.

New Labour's stance on the introduction of tuition fees was radical not just in the context of a break with old Labour, but also in its willingness to tackle an issue which successive Conservative governments had feared. In 1984 even Keith Joseph had retreated and Kenneth Baker had subsequently referred to the 'ticking time bomb' he had left behind in 1988, having doubled student numbers but not investment (*Guardian Higher*, 2 September 1997). That the measure was broached and carried with relatively little opposition, is an indication of just how much the political and social climate has changed since Labour was last in power. The decision that the expanding HE sector could not be funded solely from general taxation, the invocation of an *individual* benefit from HE and, more particularly, the individual's responsibility to repay directly in monetary terms the benefit received, illustrates the shift towards viewing education as a commodity, with students as consumers. The notion of a wider social benefit from education was overshadowed by a new individual contract with the state, with the state as a credit broker rather than an agent of redistribution. The New Labour state recognises the importance of education to compete in the international marketplace and, with education as the linchpin of its economic policy, the relationship between citizen and state looks more like an economic than a social contract.

Conclusion

At mid-term in power, New Labour's record on education is a mixed one. This is not surprising, given the breadth of education policy and the range and detail of New Labour's initiatives. The record is mixed both in terms of meeting the promises made to the electorate and also in terms of the ideological flavour of the Government's policies. On keeping promises, inevitably at this stage in the Government's life, it has not fulfilled all of the pledges made to the electorate, some of which have been explicitly tied to a full five-year term of government. While there have been some high-profile achievements, such as the provision of nursery places for all 4 year olds one year earlier than promised, there have also been some unforeseen consequences of policies. Given its reputation for spin and presentation, it is no surprise that New Labour's wording of pledges and promises sometimes verges on the casuistic. Increasing education spending, for instance, is ultimately tied to a 'decrease . . . on the bills of economic and social failure' (Labour Party, 1997:4). It is not too cynical to suggest that this is less a hostage to fortune than an escape clause. The same could be said of meeting the targets for numeracy and literacy by 2002, on which the Secretary of State for Education and Employment has staked his job. It is very likely that the next general election will be held before the data to assess his credibility is published, whether he means the 2002 test results (not available until 2003) or the 2001 test results published in 2002.

In ideological terms the New Labour record is equally mixed. One of New Labour's first actions in power was to abolish the assisted places scheme, which Labour has opposed since its introduction by the first Thatcher Government. While old Labour would have gone further and coupled this with removal of charitable status from private schools, the 'modernisation' trajectory saw the latter policy dropped from manifestos after the Left's high water mark in 1983. Thus, by 1997, the New Labour Minister for School Standards was able to talk about partnership with and learning lessons from the independent sector (*Guardian Education*, 7 October 1997). However, the independent sector began to forecast an increase in the social *exclusiveness* of its intake in the wake of the withdrawal of the assisted places scheme. If they are right, the outcome will be, to say the least, somewhat paradoxical for a government committed to the enhancement of social inclusion.

The New Labour programme for education reform has certainly built on many of the foundations laid down by the preceding Conservative governments. As noted above, this is not to say that the Labour Party simply adopted Conservative policies; rather, a new consensus has emerged between the parties on issues such as raising school standards. But New Labour has also gone much further in some areas: the introduction of university tuition fees for instance, the development of Education Action Zones or the intent to introduce performance-related pay for teachers. Such initiatives are also a clear break with old Labour. In these terms then, of a willingness to innovate, New Labour has shown a real degree of radicalism. At the beginning of this chapter, it was noted that the education policies proposed by New Labour were an interesting amalgam calculated to maximise the Party's appeal across the electorate. At mid-term, the New Labour Government appears to have succeeded in holding this together – perhaps this is what is meant by the third way.

References

Boyle, E., Crosland, A. and Kogan, M. (1971), *The Politics of Education*, Harmondsworth, Penguin.

Centre for Contemporary Cultural Studies (1981), *Unpopular Education*, London, Hutchinson.

Demaine, J. (1992), 'The Labour Party and Education Policy', *British Journal of Educational Studies*, 40(3):239–47.

DfEE (Department for Education and Employment) (1997a), 'Way Forward for Early Years Education Announced', Press Release, 22 May.

DfEE (1997b), 'Government Responds to Dearing Committee Report on Higher Education', Press Release, 23 July.

DfEE (1999), 'Hodge Announces Details of Pre-school Review', Press Release, 15 April.

Kennedy, H. (1997), *Learning Works: Widening Participation in Further Education*, London, FEFC.

Labour Party (1997) *New Labour: Because Britain Deserves Better*, London, The Labour Party.

Lucas, R. E. (1988), 'On the Mechanics of Economic Development', *Journal of Monetary Economics*, 22:3–24.

OECD (1995), *Literacy, Economy and Society*, Paris, OECD.

Pre-School Learning Alliance (1999), 'Pre-School Learning Alliance Welcomes Government Intervention', Press Release, 17 March.

Reich, R. (1983), *The Next American Frontier*, Harmondsworth, Penguin.

Romer, P. M. (1986), 'Increasing Returns and Long-Run Growth', *Journal of Political Economy*, 94:1102–37.

Simon, B. (1965), *Education and the Labour Movement 1870–1920*, London, Lawrence and Wishart.

Simon, B. (1974), *The Politics of Educational Reform 1920–1940*, London, Lawrence and Wishart.

Skott, P. and Auerbach, P. (1995), 'Cumulative Causation and the "New" Theories of Economic Growth', *Journal of Post Keynesian Economics*, 17(3):381–402.

Thompson, N. (1997), *Political Economy and the Labour Party*, London, UCL Press.

Torrance, H. (1997), 'Assessment, Accountability, and Standards: Using Assessment to Control the Reform of Schooling' in A. H. Halsey, *et al.* (eds), *Education: Culture, Economy and Society*, Oxford, Oxford University Press.

Vaizey, J. (1958), *The Costs of Education*, London, Allen and Unwin.

Vaizey, J. (1962), *Education for Tomorrow*, London, Allen and Unwin.

Vaizey, J. (1963), *The Control of Education*, London, Allen and Unwin.

13

New Labour and welfare reform

David Purdy

Welfare reform lies at the heart of New Labour's project. Since taking office, the Government has set about transforming the management of benefits and claimants in a bid to get 'welfare to work', has launched numerous local pilot schemes, has developed a national strategy for childcare, has conducted a review of pension provision and, to date, has published eight key papers on various aspects of welfare reform. The aim of this chapter is to take stock of these initiatives, placing them in a wider historical and political context and assessing their strengths and weaknesses. After dissecting the case for welfare reform, it traces the evolution of New Labour's distinctive approach to social policy, examines the New Deal for people of working age and concludes with an account of the Government's policies for parents, children and retirement pensioners.

The case for welfare reform

Until the 1980s, when people spoke of the 'welfare state' they usually had in mind the whole range of state-sponsored programmes concerned with social security, education, health care, housing and the personal social services. The primary target of 'welfare reform', however, is the social security system and, in particular, the provision of benefits for people of working age who, for various reasons, are not in paid work. In-work benefits are not usually considered problematic, while tax expenditures are commonly ignored altogether. The shifting conventions that fix the boundaries between childhood, youth, working life and retirement pass similarly unremarked and, although feminists have had some success in getting unpaid caregiving and domestic labour recognised as work, the idea that people can produce goods and services of value to others, besides themselves, *outside* the framework of paid employment, has still not been fully acknowledged.

Although it is widely accepted that 'welfare isn't working', opinions differ about what exactly is wrong. The existing social security system is variously criticised for being unaffordable, ineffectual, degenerate, outmoded and divisive. The first of these charges is hard to sustain, in Britain's case at any rate. Demographic fears that there will soon be too few workers supporting too many pensioners are unfounded. Even if the future workforce forms a smaller proportion of the population than today's, it is also likely to be richer and hence better able to bear the cost of state pensions. Moreover, even without reform, a growing number of old people expect to receive private pensions and hence will be paying a larger share of total tax revenue than today's elderly. In any case, thanks to Conservative retrenchment in the 1980s, the projected rise in Britain's pensions bill is far gentler than that of other comparable countries, including the US.

Current trends in welfare spending also do not give any cause for alarm. To be sure, from 1973–74 to 1995–96, real spending on UK social security programmes rose at an average annual rate of 3.4 per cent, while GDP grew at a rate of only 2 per cent. As a result, the proportion of GDP devoted to social security (excluding housing-related benefits) rose from 8 per cent to 11 per cent (Evans, 1998:306–7, Table 7A.1). By European standards, however, this ratio is low: among the member-states of the European Union, only Greece, Ireland, Portugal and Spain spend less on social security as a proportion of GDP. Moreover, from now on, provided the economy's underlying rate of growth is maintained, the share of resources devoted to social security is set to decline.

Thus, the case for welfare reform is not that the existing system is unaffordable, but that it is badly designed. What this charge means depends on who is making it and what they think social security is for. It is generally accepted nowadays that the state should try to prevent or relieve poverty. Something must, therefore, be amiss if spending on social security rises, but the incidence of poverty grows. Views differ, however, about what *else* the state should be doing. Some people, mainly on the right, believe that public policy should foster the work ethic, and blame the present system for encouraging 'welfare dependency'. Others, mainly on the left, seek to promote social solidarity through a system of taxes and transfers from which all citizens are entitled to benefit, regardless of their means, and to which all are obliged to contribute, according to their capacity. Whatever the *normative* goals of social security, moreover, it seems reasonable to insist that the *institutions* through which it is delivered should at least be compatible with other aspects of economic and social organisation. On this count, the Beveridge social insurance model stands condemned. Designed for a world of full employment, job security, stable marriages, traditional gender roles and two-parent, one-earner families, the model has been overtaken by mass unemployment, flexible labour markets, rising divorce rates, gender convergence and the growing diversity of family and household forms.

Not that the Beveridge model was preserved in aspic. Under Mrs Thatcher, in particular, the role of social insurance was steadily eroded, while spending on means-tested benefits grew dramatically, accounting, by 1995–96, for 23 per cent of total social security spending (over 30 per cent if housing benefits are included). National Insurance benefits still accounted for just under half the total, compared with almost two-thirds in 1979–80, but three-quarters of these payments went on retirement pensions (Evans, 1998:Tables 7.3 and 7A.1). The Beveridge ideal of a basic, but comprehensive and inclusive social insurance system had never, in truth, been realised and, indeed, was not, at bottom, coherent. What began to emerge under the Conservatives was a residual welfare state which provided a low-level safety net for the poor, while encouraging the majority of citizens to take care of themselves.

The genesis of New Labour: politics and policy, 1992–97

In the absence of any viable programme for restoring full employment, re-regulating the labour market and revamping social insurance, there were three broad options for social security policy: to press on with the market revolution and complete the transition to a residual welfare state; to protect the poor by conventional measures of redistribution; and to recast the welfare state in a 'productivist' mould, encouraging, helping and, if necessary, forcing those deemed capable of work to adapt to market forces, providing employers with a suitably skilled and motivated labour force and preserving social cohesion. Ideologically opposed to the first of these options and instinctively inclined towards the second, after its unexpected and traumatic defeat in the 1992 general election, Labour eventually embraced the third.

The manifesto on which Labour fought the 1992 election included pledges to restore the value of child benefit, raise the basic pension and re-introduce the link between pensions and earnings that the Conservatives had abandoned in 1981. At £3.3 billion a year, the estimated cost of these measures was more than the Party was promising to commit to education and health, arguably more urgent priorities and more popular among voters too, judging by popular reactions to the Liberal Democrats' proposal to 'earmark' an extra penny on income tax for spending on education. Worse still, Labour proposed to raise the ceiling on employees' National Insurance contributions. Though justified on grounds of fairness, this commitment had little appeal for middle income voters and prompted tabloid headlines warning of 'Labour's tax bombshell'. And with the economy still in recession and unemployment mounting, Labour's plans for a National Minimum Wage provoked anxiety rather than enthusiasm among low paid workers.

By historical standards, this platform was a very mild version of 'tax and redistribute'. But after Labour's fourth consecutive election defeat, the credibility of its traditional approach to the welfare state was thrown into question and John Smith, the Party Leader, convened an independent Commission on Social Justice to conduct a wide-ranging review of taxation and social policy. Chaired by Sir (now Lord) Gordon Borrie and serviced by the Institute for Public Policy Research, the Commission published its final report in October 1994, just three months after Tony Blair's victory in the Party Leadership election that followed John Smith's death. Since the Commission was a non-party body, the Labour leadership was subsequently able to draw on its broad analysis without being bound by its recommendations.

The Commission's central argument was that welfare policy had to adapt to seismic shifts in economy and society (Commission on Social Justice, 1994). In a world of free trade, mobile capital and perpetual innovation, where ways of living and working were in flux, neither deregulation nor redistribution could secure economic success with social cohesion. What was required was a new kind of welfare state dedicated to promoting investment in human and social capital and providing collective support for individual self-help. Specific proposals included:

- interest-free, income-contingent loans for full-time students to replace maintenance grants and cover one-fifth of tuition fees;
- measures to reduce long-term unemployment and increase economic activity rates, including a well-resourced and claimant-friendly employment service, investment in childcare facilities, sheltered employment projects in areas of economic blight and wage subsidies to induce employers to hire and train jobless workers;
- a National Minimum Wage plus reforms of the tax and benefit system to sharpen work incentives;
- steps to make National Insurance more inclusive and less disadvantageous to women by lowering the participation threshold and extending the system of credited contributions;
- a new pensions settlement involving a larger role for private, funded pensions and an enhanced guaranteed minimum income for everyone over retirement age;
- an increase in child benefit paid for by taxing child benefit payments to higher rate taxpayers.

While New Labour subsequently distanced itself from this blueprint, the report was influential and anticipated later attempts to chart a 'third way' beyond left and right. One of its central themes was that economy and society form an integrated complex. Hence, just as the trend of economic growth constrains social spending, so welfare arrangements affect economic performance. This general idea suggested that micro-economic social engineering might be to New Labour what Keynesian macro-economic management had been to old Labour. Similarly, the Commission argued for active partnership between state and civil society, with government acting as enabler, facilitator and broker rather than as direct service provider or remote financial controller.

American models also influenced new Labour's approach to welfare reform. Key policy advisers such as David Miliband and Ed Balls had studied at Harvard and maintained close links with their American counterparts. Deputations of Labour MPs crossed the Atlantic to learn about 'workfare' programmes in Wisconsin and California and the term 'welfare dependency' found its way into Party rhetoric. Faced with the undoubted fact that some people remain on benefits for long periods of time, some Labour spokesmen came near to suggesting that social security actually generates anti-social attitudes and behaviour such as fecklessness and fraud. In fact, the evidence suggests that, given the prevailing demand for labour, particular individuals are at risk of becoming long-term benefit recipients because of their prior characteristics, not that people become dependent as a consequence of receiving benefit (Shaw *et al.*, 1996).

In the run-up to the 1997 election, issues of cost and affordability remained at the forefront of public debate. Determined to avoid a re-run of 1992, Labour set about discarding its 'tax and spend' image and made a pitch for 'Middle England'. Stressing the costs of economic failure and the limits of taxpayer tolerance, the Party promised a fundamental change in the direction of welfare policy, away from passive support for jobless claimants towards active efforts to improve their chances of securing employment within a more prudently managed and stable economy. The programme which, above all, epitomised this approach was the New Deal – an ambitious, if not entirely novel, plan aimed at four main target groups: the young unemployed, the older long-term unemployed, lone parents and partially disabled people of working age. The name recalled Roosevelt's efforts to rescue the American economy from the Great Depression of the 1930s, though New Labour firmly repudiated deficit-financed job creation schemes in favour of fiscal rectitude, monetary discipline and labour supply activation.

The New Deal rapidly became New Labour's flagship policy and, as it was to be funded from the proceeds of a windfall tax levied on privatised utilities, formed the only exception to the Party's pre-election commitment to stick to Conservative spending limits during its first two years in office. On most other issues, the Party avoided specific commitments. Gordon Brown's one attempt at a 'tough choice' before the election – a proposal to means test child benefit paid to parents of 16 and 17 year old children in full-time education – proved too contentious and was shelved. In the event, Labour's 1997 election manifesto contained only two firm pledges: to retain the basic retirement pension and to uphold the 'universality' of child benefit. There was, of course, a general commitment to welfare reform, but what this entailed was left vague. Party spokesmen repeatedly claimed that, in time, the New Deal would yield savings on benefit outlays that could be diverted to the education budget. Nothing was said, however, about how large this dividend was likely to be or about how long it would take to materialise, while the evidence that US 'workfare' programmes had succeeded in cutting welfare rolls, but had also led to increased spending per welfare recipient, was simply ignored. Thus, New Labour arrived in office with welfare reform as one of its top priorities, alongside education, yet without any clear or agreed idea as to what this commitment entailed for specific social security programmes.

Table 13.1   *Expenditure on New Deal programmes*

Programme	Planned expenditure (£ millions)	Per cent of total
Young unemployed (18–24)	2620	73
Older long-term unemployed (25+)	450	13
Lone parents	190	5
Disabled	200	6
Partners of the unemployed	60	2
Childcare	40	1
Total	*3560*	*100*

Source: HMSO (1998a).

The New Deal in action

As soon as it took office, the new Government set about instituting the New Deal. Advisory national task forces were established in England, Scotland, Wales and Northern Ireland, with representation from major employers, trade unions, local government and the voluntary sector. Operational responsibility was assigned to the Employment Service because, according to ministers, it was organised on a national basis and was used to implementing new programmes quickly. However, the Government recognised that if it was to win the confidence of claimants, the Service would have to shed its 'benefit police' image and become a 'gatekeeper of opportunity', combining the functions of benefit administration, job placement and personal counselling. Similarly, to secure the co-operation of employers and harness the experience of other organisations concerned with human resources and urban regeneration, local partnerships had to be built. And to furnish a benchmark for monitoring the work of the Employment Service, some New Deal areas were run by private employment agencies.

Out of £5.2 billion raised by the windfall tax, £3.6 billion was allocated to New Deal programmes. (A further £1.3 billion was invested in schools, with smaller sums going to initiatives such as the University for Industry.) The break-down of New Deal expenditure is shown in Table 13.1. The largest single pro-gramme is the New Deal for the young unemployed. Since April 1998, all unemployed young people aged 18–24 have been guaranteed places on this programme. After a 'gateway' period of up to four months, during which clients receive intensive appraisal and counselling by a personal adviser who stays in touch throughout, those who have not been placed in an unsubsidised job are offered one of four options:

1   a subsidised job, normally with a private sector employer, who receives £60 a week for up to six months and must offer suitable training either on the job or through day release (in some cases, self-employment may be an accept-able substitute);

2   a six-month placement with a voluntary organisation, receiving a wage or
    benefit plus £15 a week, together with proper provision for training, as in the
    first case;
3   a six-month placement with an environmental task force on similar terms;
    and
4   full-time education for up to 12 months on an approved course. (This option
    is only available to young people with no vocational qualifications.)

The Government insists that there is 'no fifth option'. Young people who reject
New Deal offers without 'good cause' lose the whole of their benefit for two
weeks. A second or subsequent refusal attracts a four-week penalty. These sanctions are harsh, but so far have rarely been invoked. Their purpose, according
to ministers, is to emphasise that claimants have responsibilities as well as
rights. They may also be intended to reassure taxpayers that public funds are
being put to good use.

The New Deal for the older unemployed is aimed at those over the age of 25
who have been out of work for over two years. Participation is mandatory and
clients undergo an 'advisory interview process' with a personal adviser. Those
who fail to find a job within six months are offered one of two options: subsidised employment for up to six months, with employers receiving £75 a week for
each eligible worker they hire; or a full-time vocational training course lasting
up to 12 months, during which entitlement to benefits is retained. There is
'follow through' provision for those who subsequently return to unemployment. In the 1999 budget, the Chancellor announced a New Deal for the over-
50s unemployed, offering personalised advice and financial support for those
who move from unemployment or inactivity into full-time or part-time work.

The New Deals for lone parents and disabled people were initially voluntary.
Under the Welfare Reform and Pensions Bill still before Parliament at the time
of writing, however, *all* benefit claimants of working age will be obliged to
attend interviews at their local job-centre, both when they make their first
claim and at regular intervals thereafter, though lone parents and disabled claimants will not be penalised for refusing job offers. The introduction of this
'single, work-focused gateway' emphasises how far New Labour has shifted its
sights. In place of the old goal of full employment, conceived as a condition of
the labour market in which the number of unemployed jobseekers equals the
number of unfilled job vacancies or, alternatively, as the lowest rate of unemployment compatible with a stable rate of inflation, the aim of public policy is
now to maximise labour force participation and enhance the employability of
socially disadvantaged groups.

Despite the emphasis on building local partnerships, some critics have
argued that the New Deal is still too top-down and insensitive to local conditions
(Peck, 1998). The introduction of 'Employment Zones' may correct this bias.
These are area-based initiatives aimed mainly at people over 25 who have been
unemployed for over a year, though lone parents and disabled people may also

take part. The idea is to enable local partnerships to combine different funding streams so as to provide their clients with 'personal job accounts' that can be used flexibly to support a variety of employment-related activities. This model is less prescriptive than the New Deal and offers greater local discretion over the use of funds and the framing of work plans. It also complements the efforts of the Social Exclusion Unit to co-ordinate across government departments, and links up with the Government's New Deal for Communities, a programme which has been allocated £800 million to test out innovative, long-term and locally designed projects for regenerating small neighbourhoods with high concentrations of multiple deprivation.

Strenuous efforts are being made to overcome barriers to employment such as lack of work experience and lack of affordable childcare. According to Bennett and Walker (1999), the Government's plans engage, to varying degrees, with 31 of 38 such barriers identified in the literature (Gardiner, 1997). Particular attention has been given to 'making work pay' through the introduction of a National Minimum Wage and through reforms of the tax and benefit system, which are described in the next section. One barrier that has not yet been tackled, however, is the treatment of housing costs. This is said to be an important source of financial disincentives, though it needs to be borne in mind that purely hypothetical comparisons of in-work earnings with out-of-work benefits tell us nothing about how people actually behave.

It is too early to judge the effectiveness of the New Deal. As we have seen, its aim is to improve the employment prospects of people who are, or risk becoming, disconnected from the labour market. Despite a barrage of information on the numbers of programme participants and their eventual destinations, a complete economic cycle will have to elapse before it becomes possible to separate out short-term, cyclical influences on labour market activity from longer-term, structural forces. In recent years, most entry-level jobs have been part-time or temporary and, in either case, low paid. We simply do not yet know how many New Deal participants will climb up the 'ladder of opportunity', how many will remain stuck on the lowest rung and how many will move from welfare to work and back again (the so-called 'revolving door' syndrome).

Preliminary indications are broadly favourable. The Employment Service has warmed to its new role and, in general, the New Deal has been welcomed by young people and by agencies working with disadvantaged groups, though attitudes may change if voluntary programmes are made compulsory and the sanctions regime is tightened. Atkinson (1999) reports that voluntary participants in the programme for 18–24 year olds formed 8 per cent of the total, double the number initially expected. Comparing those who entered the 12 pilot schemes that began in January 1998 with their counterparts in other areas, he finds that 18 per cent more had moved into jobs by the end of the year. On the other hand, more young people went into full-time education than originally expected, perhaps in order to avoid less palatable options. And a worrying large minority of New Deal clients have disappeared from Employment

Service records to 'unknown destinations', mostly – it is presumed – in the underground economy.

Of course, empirical indicators do not prove causal efficacy. Policy interventions may be wrongly credited with outcomes that would have occurred anyway. In this connection, it is worth noting that the rate of long-term unemployment in Britain peaked in 1993 at 4.4 per cent of the labour force and, by early 1998 before the New Deal was in place, had fallen to 2 per cent. Perhaps, contrary to the theory underpinning the New Deal, as enunciated by Layard (1996), the long-term unemployed are not so unemployable that a strong economic recovery will not pick them up. Conversely, while supply-side policies may help to sustain a boom by relieving skill shortages and restraining wage increases, they offer no defence against a deep and prolonged recession. For the same reason, without complementary action to stimulate the demand for labour, the New Deal lacks credibility in depressed areas where unemployment remains high even when the national economy is buoyant (Peck, 1998).

This said, it may be possible to develop the New Deal in ways that offer protection against cyclical downturn and regional decline by extending job subsidies, for varying periods and with suitable safeguards, to the so-called 'third sector' or social economy. This domain of campaigning and advocacy groups, non-profit and voluntary bodies, charities, trusts, housing associations, self-help projects and local exchange and trading schemes (LETS) offers fertile ground for efforts to combat social exclusion and kindle the spirit of community. Third sector organisations operate on a voluntary basis and are motivated not by the pursuit of profit, but by values of solidarity, reciprocity, caring and inclusion. They cater to needs that are either not met at all, or not met so well, by conventional forms of market or state provision. They are well placed to channel public support towards disadvantaged groups who are excluded from mainstream employment. And being free from the relentless pressure to compete and expand that drives capitalist enterprise, they are attached to the communities they serve and cherish the environment they inhabit.

Of course, the scope for creating jobs in the social economy depends on whether finance can be raised to sustain them, whether through borrowing to cover capital costs or taxation to cover recurrent costs, and this is subject to fiscal and ideological constraints. Cyclical swings in budget balances and the prevailing anathema against even short-term deficit finance inhibit the use of the social economy as an anti-cyclical shock absorber. More generally, without a serious effort to adopt more popular forms of taxation and persuade taxpayers that social economy projects offer good value for money, tax resistance may carry the day. There are, in any case, dangers in using public funds to promote third sector employment. It may undermine existing public services and compromise civic independence and vitality. Nevertheless, as ever more areas of social life, from sport and the arts to childcare and education, fall under the sway of market forces, the idea of redressing the balance in favour of non-market forms of production and consumption is ethically and politically appealing.

Parents, children and pensioners: remixing the economy of welfare

One of Tony Blair's first appointments on becoming Prime Minister was to make Frank Field Minister for Welfare Reform. His brief was to 'think the unthinkable'. At the time, this was hailed as an inspired move. An iconoclastic Christian Socialist, former Director of the Child Poverty Action Group and Chairman of the House of Commons Select Committee on Social Security, Field was the Tories' favourite Labour MP. He believed that means-tested benefits discourage work, penalise thrift and encourage fraud, and sought to revive the ideals of self-help and mutual assurance. In retrospect, his appointment appears misguided. It gave a middle-ranking minister, with a fancy job title, responsibility for policy development over the head of the Secretary of State for Social Security, Harriet Harman. It also aggravated turf wars with other departments. The Treasury, in particular, was bound to scrutinise welfare reform proposals for their spending implications, and having handed over control of interest rates to the Bank of England, Gordon Brown was keen to develop a new role in shaping social policy. Reports of rifts between the three ministers began to appear only months after the election (*Guardian*, 26 September 1997).

However, the new Government's first serious crisis arose not from its own agenda, but in response to a leftover Conservative policy. In the 1996 budget, Peter Lilley, the outgoing Secretary of State for Social Security, had announced the Government's intention to remove special treatment for lone parents. Two benefits were at risk: the 'Lone Parent Premium', a means-tested benefit payable to out-of-work lone parents who were eligible for Income Support; and 'One Parent Benefit', a flat-rate transfer paid to lone parents in work. In opposition, Harriet Harman had denounced this measure, but in government her position was undermined by New Labour's self-imposed spending straitjacket. Savings from the cuts, estimated at £300 million in the first year and £600 million eventually, had been built into Conservative spending plans. While these sums were trivial by comparison with a total social security budget of £100 billion, the Government decided to proceed with abolition, against the advice of its own Social Security Advisory Committee which had recommended delay pending further research on lone parents' living costs.

In its defence, the Government cited the New Deal for lone parents, though this was still at the pilot stage. Harman's supporters also claimed that in return for agreeing to defend the policy against hostile media and Parliamentary criticism, she had squeezed an extra £300 million out of the Treasury to finance after-school clubs, part of an evolving national childcare strategy to which she was strongly committed. With opinion polls showing a three-to-one majority against the cuts, the Government's stance provoked its first major backbench rebellion. Forty-seven Labour MPs voted against the Government, by no means all of them on the Left, and many of those who voted with the Government did so with heavy hearts.

The Government had demonstrated that its pledge to stay within Tory spending plans was genuine, but had aroused deep misgivings among its supporters about the purpose of welfare reform. To make matters worse, a few days before the Commons vote on lone-parent benefit cuts, a paper was leaked from the Department of Social Security floating the possibility of means-testing the Disability Living Allowance (DLA), a non-contributory benefit claimed by just under 2 million disabled people of working age and designed to cover the costs of care and mobility. The disability lobby was already unhappy with the 'Benefit Integrity Project'; a programme initiated by the Conservatives to investigate the awards made to some 450,000 DLA recipients. The possibility that benefits might be withdrawn from those who, though not poor, were undeniably worse off than non-disabled people on the same income, but with lower living costs, provoked understandable outrage.

In a bid to demonstrate that welfare reform was driven by principles, not cuts, the Government launched a 'Welfare Roadshow', a series of meetings for Labour Party members in each of nine regional centres. Its most cogent argument, however, was Gordon Brown's March 1998 Budget. The lone-parent benefit cuts were not restored, but the Government announced the introduction of two new in-work benefits delivered through the tax system: the Working Families Tax Credit (WFTC), available to all working parents on low incomes, and the Childcare Tax Credit, a subsidy for childcare costs available to families earning up to £20,000 a year. For good measure, child benefit scales were raised and, in the following year's Budget, the Married Couple's Tax Allowance, worth £200 a year, was replaced by a new Children's Tax Credit, worth £416 a year, with effect from April 2001. As a result of these measures, parents who in 1997 were receiving £11 a week for their first child, will in 2001 be receiving £23 a week.

Modelled on the US Earned Income Tax Credit, the WFTC offers a more generous replacement for Family Credit. Starting in October 1999, families with full-time wage earners are guaranteed a minimum income of £200 a week. The total cost is estimated at £5 billion, twice the amount spent on Family Credit, and 1.4 million families are expected to benefit, twice the number claiming Family Credit. The Childcare Tax Credit enables working lone parents and couples where both partners are employed to reclaim up to 70 per cent of their childcare costs, subject to a ceiling of £100 a week for one child and £150 a week for two or more children.

As a tax expenditure rather than a cash transfer, the WFTC will boost the take-home pay of the working poor without increasing the benefits bill. It is thus easier to justify to Middle England. It may also enable people moving from welfare to work to feel more self-reliant than if they simply switch from one benefit to another. On the downside, the WFTC may transfer income 'from purse to wallet'. Family Credit is paid directly to mothers and although families can still choose to have the WFTC paid as a cash benefit to a non-earning spouse, it seems probable that many will opt for payment through the wage packet. Another drawback is that under the UK's PAYE system, tax credits will be administered by employers, alerting them to payments of which they have hitherto been unaware and giving them an incentive to keep pay low. The claim that the WFTC will improve work incentives is also open to doubt (Mendelson, 1998).

However, taken together with the measures unveiled in the National Childcare Strategy announced in May 1998, the new tax credits provide hard evidence that the Government is serious not just about tackling family poverty, but about making childcare a central concern of public policy. One of its most frequently cited statistics is that between 1979 and 1995 the proportion of working age households with no one in employment rose from one in ten to one in five. A prime cause is the lack of public provision for childcare. To tackle this problem, the Government proposes to introduce 8000 new homework clubs (or 'study Support Centres'), with places provided free to users, and 40,000 additional places in out-of-school clubs, for which users will be charged; to encourage non-employed single parents to train as careworkers; to establish tighter regulation of childcare providers, including nanny agencies; and to guarantee nursery places for all 4 year olds from September 1998.

The Government is unfazed by criticism that paying some women to look after other women's children is the modern equivalent of paying neighbours to take in each other's washing. Nor does it worry that the jobs created will be low paid and unskilled: its overriding priority is to promote social inclusion through paid employment. Its policies are, however, drawing market forces into an area of social life from which they have hitherto been largely excluded. This risks converting unpaid, informal care into a paid service. It also discriminates against those parents – single, married or cohabiting – who, for whatever reason, prefer to stay at home with their children, at any rate during the pre-school years.

With the continuing disarray of the Conservatives and Labour's commanding lead in the opinion polls, the Government began to play down expectations of major savings from welfare reform. Nevertheless, welfare finance continued to exercise ministers and lay at the heart of the conflict between Frank Field and the Treasury. Despite his reputation as the darling of the Right, Field is a social democrat, not a neo-liberal. While retaining the Basic Retirement Pension as an inflation-proofed safety net, he wanted to replace the State Earnings-Related Pension Scheme (SERPS) with a system in which all employed and self-employed persons would be obliged to contribute to a second pension, but provision would be organised by the private sector on a funded basis. Without compulsion, free riding by people who had failed to save enough would cause resentment. But compulsion was also problematic. Personal pensions are notoriously costly to market and manage and, without expensive state subsidies, offer a poor investment for people with low earnings or interrupted employment histories. Moreover, the transition to a new pension regime would impose a double burden on current workers, forcing them to pay both for today's state pensioners and for their own future private pensions. Field was willing to grasp these nettles; the Treasury was not.

Thus, having dutifully thought the unthinkable, Field had his ideas dismissed as unworkable. As he himself subsequently remarked of his time as Minister for Welfare Reform: 'it was like grafting someone else's organ on to a body. The chances of rejection are pretty great' (*Guardian*, 3 August 1998). In the end, when Harriet Harman was sacked in the ministerial reshuffle of July 1998, Field asked for her job and resigned after being refused it. His post disappeared with his departure, and the new Secretary of State, Alastair Darling, formerly Chief Secretary to the Treasury, was given the job of producing feasible plans for the reform of pensions and housing benefit.

The Green Paper on pensions which finally appeared in November 1998 rejects extra compulsion and recommends a new, additional form of private pension, thereby further complicating an already complex system (HMSO, 1998b). Its proposals fall into three parts. First, the poorest pensioners are to benefit from a Minimum Income Guarantee which will be regularly uprated in line with earnings, and action is promised to increase the take-up of means-tested Income Support for the one million pensioners who currently fail to claim it. Second, the Government proposes to replace SERPS by a new State Second Pension to be phased in over five years. For anyone earning up to £9000 a year, this will provide twice as much as SERPS, and arrangements for crediting contributions will be extended to caregivers with earnings below the National Insurance threshold and to disabled people with incomplete contributions records. Third, people earning between £9000 and £18,500 a year will be offered the inducement of higher National Insurance rebates to join funded second pension schemes. Those whose employers do not provide occupational pensions or for whom existing personal pensions are unsuitable, will be able to contribute to a Stakeholder Pension. This is a new type of collectively structured, but privately organised scheme which, it is envisaged, could be established by groups of employers, financial services companies, trade unions or other membership organisations.

At present, total state and privately financed payments to pensioners amount to some £60 billion a year (at 1997 prices), equivalent to about 9 per cent of GDP. Of these payments, 60 per cent come from the National Insurance Fund and 40 per cent from private sources. The Government's aim is to reverse these proportions. This is a hazardous undertaking. Altering the balance between public and private pensions diverts funds from a circuit that flows from workers to pensioners via the state, to one that flows from workers to the stock market via private pension schemes. But with a larger volume of funds seeking placement in a financial system that elevates short-term speculation over long-term commitment, the probable consequence is increased financial instability, which could, in turn, damage the 'real' economy.

Furthermore, if people are encouraged to think primarily of their own personal futures and to ignore the wider forces which they are powerless to control as individuals, but which may be susceptible to collective management, they will acquire no sense of belonging to a community of fate, confronting risk together. During the formative years of the welfare state, such communities took root in the soil of class and nation, fed by the experience of industrial conflict and world war. The generations that lived through this epoch are now passing away, and there seems little chance of recreating the solidarities that shaped their world in a post-industrial, cosmopolitan society marked by multiple, intersecting social divisions. Equally, unless the effort is made to build institutions which give people a sense that they are *citizens* with a common body of rights and responsibilities, not just private persons leading separate lives, or even members of groups based on sectional interests and values, there seems little chance of creating a society which is not only adaptable and prosperous, but also cohesive and secure.

References

Atkinson, J. (1999), *The New Deal for Young Unemployed People*, Institute for Employment Studies, University of Sussex.

Bennett, F. and Walker, R. (1999), 'Will Work Work?', *CRSP Briefings*, Centre for Research in Social Policy, University of Loughborough, p. 4.

Commission on Social Justice (1994), *Social Justice: Strategies for National Renewal*, London, Vintage.

Evans, M. (1998), 'Social Security: Dismantling the Pyramids?' in H. Glennester and J. Hills (eds), *The State of Welfare* (2nd ed.), Oxford, Blackwell, pp. 257–307.

Gardiner, K. (1997), *Bridges from Benefit to Employment*, York, York Publishing Services.

HMSO (1998a), *New Ambitions for Our Country: A New Contract for Welfare*, Cm 3804, London.

HMSO (1998b) *A New Contract for Welfare: Partnership in Pensions*, Cm 4179, London.

Layard, R. (1996), 'Preventing Long-term Unemployment: An Economic Analysis' in D. Snower and G. De La Dehesa (eds), *Unemployment Policy: Government Options for the Labour Market*, Cambridge, Cambridge University Press.

Mendelson, M. (1998) *The WIS that Was: Replacing the Canadian Working Income Supplement*, York, Joseph Rowntree Foundation.

Peck, J. (1998), *New Labourers: Making a New Deal for the Workless Class*, paper presented at the annual conference of the Royal Geographical Society/Institute of British Geographers, 5–8 January 1998, Guildford.

Shaw, A., Walker, R., Ashworth, K., Jenkins, K. and Middleton, S. (1996), *Moving Off Income Support: Barriers and Bridges*, DSS Research Report 53, London, HMSO.

14

New Labour and health

Bruce Wood

Background to power

In contrast to several other key policy areas, uncertainty of new Labour's policy direction was particularly marked in the case of health for three reasons. First, by 1997 the Thatcher/Major legacy of a National Health Service (NHS) based on quasi-markets following their 1989–91 reforms had become well entrenched. A majority of the more than 30,000 general practitioners (GPs) had become 'fundholders' and all provider units had become NHS trusts: in all these cases some autonomy accompanied the new status. The system of annual contracts between purchasers (health authorities and GP fundholders) and providers (NHS trusts) was several years old and had become embedded as, in effect, a routine managerial process. Though in opposition Labour had consistently and strongly opposed the 1989–91 reforms, the resulting quasi-market based on the purchaser–provider split and the consequent contractual relationships, it would not be a simple task to dismantle the machinery now in place. Second, Labour's criticisms had not included clear statements of its preferred alternative structures for the NHS. The last few years in opposition had been characterised by discontinuity of health policy leadership with a rapid turnover of shadow health secretaries (Robin Cook moved on after the 1992 election campaign fiasco of 'Jennifer's ear', to be followed by both Margaret Beckett and Chris Smith in fairly quick succession). In short, the incoming government had no blueprint for further health reforms and would need to formulate one before it was possible to take radical action. Thirdly, this discontinuity was extended by Blair's surprise appointment of Frank Dobson as the new Secretary of State for Health. Though he had been a junior health spokesman back in the 1980s his views in 1997 on health policy priorities were quite unknown and there was no immediate action plan in the Labour election manifesto for him to implement.

What Dobson did have as his opening agenda were the manifesto commitments and 'contract with the people' pledges outlined in Chapter 1 (see Box 1.2 in Chapter 1 and Appendix 1 at the end of the book). These amounted to a commitment to put health towards the top of the Blair Government's agenda, alongside education and employment. In so far as these promises included detailed targets, they were quickly to prove something of a poisoned chalice. The 'five early pledges' included 'cut NHS waiting lists by treating an extra 100,000 patients as a first step by releasing £100m saved from NHS red tape'. Beneath the usual rhetoric of politics lay three words – 'cut waiting lists', which were to haunt Dobson right through the first two years. Health policy analysts pointed out that such a commitment flew in the face of almost fifty years of evidence of steadily increased NHS waiting lists, despite a host of earlier political promises to tackle them. Indeed, there had been regular injections of extra funds to appease public opinion when periodically waiting lists attracted media criticism (in fact the 1989–91 reforms resulted from Thatcher's personal handling of this very issue). Such cash injections were usually in the winter when weather-related emergency hospital admissions rose at the very time that managers were having to contemplate temporary bed closures because of the requirement to balance the books before the end of the financial year in March.

Health reform was listed in fifth place in the expanded manifesto list of commitments, styled the 'contract with the people'. Here Dobson inherited a much freer hand as this promise was much less specific, with no numbers attached, and so was easier to meet later: 'We will rebuild the NHS, reducing spending on administration and increasing spending on patient care.' Whether this necessarily involved major structural reforms was unclear and early speculation by leading health policy analysts of Dobson's likely approach ranged from radical organisational upheaval through to focusing on public health and prevention of illness policies, leaving acute care largely unscathed. There was, however, general agreement amongst observers that the 1989–91 reforms could not simply be repealed or reversed and replaced by the 'old' NHS system (often described as 'command and control'). The new structures were too well established, and they had not been a total failure in terms of their impact on efficiency in particular. Additionally, though appearing to introduce market forces into the NHS, they had actually strengthened central controls over local health boards and that was likely to be attractive to the new minister seeking to cut waiting lists and administrative costs.

The immediate agenda

The first two years of the new Labour Government saw some progress on meeting all the seven manifesto commitments (see Box 14.1), though at varying pace and in some cases progress was particularly slow. The routine politics of health tend to be characterised by a continuous succession of what may be labelled as 'micro-issues', especially when the media can create human-interest stories. Like all his predecessors, Dobson soon found himself handling an array of immediate crises as part of the routine political process. Arguably, this succession of issues is used by governments to deflect attention away from the two core health issues of rationing and of total expenditure levels (see

---

Box 14.1   *Health: the 1997 manifesto pledges*

- 100,000 people off waiting lists
- End the internal market
- End waiting for cancer surgery
- Tough quality targets for hospitals
- Independent food standards agency
- New public health drive
- Raise spending in real terms each year; spend money on patients not bureaucracy

Source: Box 1.4 of this book.

Wood, 1999). Dobson quickly discovered that the structure of the NHS allowed him to announce and take the credit for good news, but ensure that any blame was devolved to purchasers and providers in the field (Klein's apt description of NHS politics, Klein, 1995:127). Dobson's long political experience, including a spell as shadow spokesman in the 1980s, gave him some valuable background. His innate political instincts were that doctors could be collectively criticised and attacked, but not nurses; that there was too much 'red tape' but the fault lay with the Thatcher quasi-market reforms and not with NHS managers; and that he could initially get away with apologising for the apparent failure to meet the pledge of reduced waiting lists. This he did by repetitively and frequently promising that the 'early pledge' would be met within the time of the first parliament (this political tactic in effect successfully redefined the word 'early' as now meaning 'within four to five years').

There was a steady flow of immediate news stories and early good news announcements, such as persuading the Chancellor to release some modest amounts of cash for waiting list and winter pressure initiatives (an annual tradition inherited from the Tories), announcing the retention of the historic central London St Bartholomew's ('Barts') Hospital and stopping closures of some small rural cottage hospitals. But, beneath these lay an underlying agenda of four key issues on which Dobson had to decide whether and, if so, how to act. These were:

1 whether or not to embark on major structural reform of the NHS to meet the commitment to end the internal market;
2 how to tackle the doctors over the well-known Labour antipathy to GP fundholding;
3 what to do about the global NHS budget given the Blair/Brown public commitment to keeping overall public expenditure under constraint, potentially in conflict with the manifesto promise to 'increase spending in real terms each year'; and

4 how to handle concerns about rationing in and by the NHS (this had become something of an ongoing public debate following the 'Child B' court case in Cambridgeshire).

Important as they were, other issues to receive early attention – such as the review of public health policy and the replacement of Tory appointees on health authority and NHS trust boards – were in reality of secondary importance once Dobson had announced that an NHS White Paper was being drafted for autumn 1997 publication. And the final health manifesto pledge to establish an independent food standards agency took a back seat in the early months of new Labour in power, though it was moved forward later, in early 1999.

In fact, the December 1997 White Paper (Secretary of State for Health, 1997) and the follow-up July 1998 Green Paper (NHS Executive, 1998) skilfully tackled no less than three of the four key issues listed in the paragraph above (again in a tradition inherited from the Tories). Nonetheless, there was to be no explicit discussion of 'rationing', the word banned by Virginia Bottomley when she was Secretary of State and feared by all health ministers claiming to support the NHS founding principle of free treatment whenever it is clinically needed. Financial policy was also kept separate from these policy documents and was to be part of the 'comprehensive spending review' promised by the Government in mid-1998. Thus, within 18 months of taking office, a series of proposals for wide-ranging NHS reform and for expenditure increases had been formulated and announced and was awaiting legislative implementation. Particularly important in this initial process was the decision to focus further NHS reforms around two criticisms of the service that New Labour inherited. Dobson chose consciously to focus his reform plans on three key issues:

1 improving *quality* of care;
2 increasing *efficiency*; and
3 improving the *information* on which policy decisions were to be taken in the NHS.

This choice of agenda in effect became the Dobson contribution to the health service.

Dobson's reform plan

The 1997 White Paper, *The New NHS: Modern, Dependable*, focused on quality and efficiency. Its 86 pages were scattered with a mixture of populist initiatives (such as a proposal for annual large-scale surveys of patient opinion and the establishment of a nationwide freephone Helpline staffed by health professionals) and proposals for new organisational arrangements designed to meet the pledge to end the internal market and to extend the use of evidence-based medicine through new national-level institutions. The rhetoric was one of 'bright ideas', modified by suggestions that there would be no radical upheaval. Thus, no less than seven times, it was claimed that the Dobson plan was 'going with the grain' (Harrison and Wood, 1999 outline the approach in more detail).

Though GP fundholding was to end, this was the only local institutional casualty. Health authorities as planners, quality monitors and commissioners of services (but not as purchasers it seemed) would continue; so would provider NHS trusts. The emphasis, however, would move from competition and annual contracts to New Labour phraseology of 'partnership' and 'long-term service agreements', thus enabling the claim to be made that, despite the continuing separation of payers from providers, the internal market would indeed be ending. It was not easy to argue this convincingly, however, because the GP community was to be satisfied through the universal introduction of a new tier of commissioning bodies, to be styled Primary Care Groups (PCGs). Though PCGs would be statutorily accountable to district health authorities, they would operate at four levels of maturity. The highest level four would give them considerable autonomy by making them a new species of NHS trusts. In addition, they seemed likely to be dominated by doctors with only token nursing, lay and district health authority membership on their boards.

The key new national institutions proposed in the White Paper were a National Institute for Clinical Excellence (NICE) and a Commission for Health Improvement (CHI). The former would enhance quality by developing clinical guidelines which were evidence-based, while the latter was to undertake both regular and urgent reviews (i.e. inspections) of local services, reporting direct to the Secretary of State. The emphasis was on quality and on using robust statistical data of treatments, and trusts, district health authorities and PCGs would have a statutory responsibility for ensuring the quality of care through monitoring local clinical activity in a process to be styled as 'clinical governance'.

The plethora of proposals in the White Paper added up to a package politically astute enough to offer a degree of satisfaction to every interested party. Opponents of the internal market naturally welcomed the ending of contracts and GP fundholding, whereas proponents saw most of the market machinery surviving and noted semantic changes (the use of 'commissioning', 'partnership' and the like) which overlay the retention of a planning–providing split that was not unlike the market approach. GP interests were largely met in that they would play a major role in 'commissioning' hospital services and retain their professional self-employed status through the new PCG machinery. More public participation and better public access to urgent services like cancer care was also promised in the documents, the latter a manifesto commitment. Only the hospital doctors could be seen as potential losers as their professional clinical autonomy, a form of self-regulation traditionally operated at the level of the individual consultant, would come under pressure from both local clinical governance arrangements and NICE policy promulgations, such as clinical guidelines based on evidence-based clinical research studies.

This clever juggling act was made the more possible because the White Paper contained very few details about its 'bright ideas'. The arrangements for PCGs and their precise relationship to and with district health authorities was left particularly vague and unclear. The remit and memberships of NICE and CHI were unspecified, as were the precise arrangements for local clinical governance. Thus, initial debate was incoherent, reflecting the pursuit of different agendas. A follow-up Green Paper in July 1998, *A First Class Service: Quality in the New NHS*, answered some questions. However, much was still left to be determined later: for example, the legislation and regulations needed to establish new statutory bodies such as NICE and CHI, and the size and exact geographical configurations of PCGs and their precise memberships and powers. The Green Paper also addressed the issue of efficiency by centring on the interests of patients in being treated fairly. Thus it repeatedly condemned what were styled 'unacceptable variations in services across the country' and proposed to introduce a programme of National Service Frameworks (NSFs) which both set explicit standards and established performance measures which all providers would be expected to meet in a particular clinical area, such as cancer care, mental illness or heart attacks.

The Green Paper went on to seek comments on more than 20 different questions. Many of these were as much matters of broad philosophy or principle as they were of detail. Thus, 'how might we best work with the health professions to modernise and strengthen professional self-regulation?' and 'how best can partnerships between all the agencies involved in National Service Frameworks be fostered?' were among them.

By summer 1998, it was clear that the two documents had established an implementation agenda that required primary legislation. Nonetheless, a host of decisions to be taken during the actual implementation process would be crucial to the final design of the reformed NHS. This would clearly take some years to conclude and would probably involve significant modifications to these Dobson plans or statements of intent. In many ways, this was reminiscent of the post-1989 approach, when successive Tory secretaries of state opportunistically altered crucial details, such as the criteria for both NHS trust and GP fundholder status, so as to create a reform momentum seemingly based on volunteers (see Harrison and Wood, 1999 for details of this scheme of 'incentivised implementation'). They developed entirely new initiatives such as the Patient's Charter and 'league tables' of performance indicators as integral parts of the new market system. Dobson also began showing signs of an interest in using incentives to develop new relationships, as evidenced by his call for local bids to be designated as 'health action zones' (HAZs). With promises of additional funding to those whose bids succeeded, almost every health authority felt it necessary to apply for HAZ status.

Another aspect of his approach reminiscent of his predecessors was the wish to make speedy progress on those aspects of change that did not require legislation. He established a timetable for the establishment of PCGs (by April 1999). This placed district health authorities negotiating with large numbers of GPs (on average more than 300 each) and civil servants drafting detailed guidance on such matters as financial and organisational accountability procedures (model financial instructions and standing orders, and the like) under great pressure to meet the Dobson deadline. Decisions in principle about the numbers and boundaries of PCGs had to be taken locally, in advance of full knowledge of the practical consequences. Many district health authority officers were working in an atmosphere of uncertainty about their personal future. This was due to uncertainty about whether there was any future role for health authorities to play in areas of the country where all PCGs seemed likely to qualify for level four status and early transition into free-standing new primary care trusts which would appear to make health authorities redundant bodies.

Increasing the NHS budget

As indicated earlier, meeting the manifesto commitment to increasing spending on the NHS was not covered in the Dobson plans for structural reform, but was left to be determined in conjunction with the Chancellor during his promised 'comprehensive spending review'. The outcome of that review was announced in July 1998. Though undoubtedly good news for the NHS, the headline-grabbing approach adopted by Chancellor Brown so misled people initially that the detailed outcome (a very substantial budget increase over a three-year period) probably did less for morale in the NHS workforce than it might have done. Brown's alleged '£21 billion' increase in the total NHS budget quickly was revealed to include double and treble counting of money as the extra sums allocated in years one and two were recounted later as part of the new baseline for the subsequent years. Thus, a £2 billion increase in year one became counted as a £6 billion increase over the three years of the announcement.

When the crudity of that mathematical sleight of hand is put aside it became clear that NHS expenditure for 1999–2002 was planned to rise faster than it had done during the Tory governments after 1979, and considerably faster than in the 1992–97 period of the second Major Government. Interestingly, however, the proposed increase was very close to the levels of increase in the 1990–93 years, when the Tory governments spent heavily to ensure that their reforms were implemented 'successfully'. Though his White and Green Paper reform plans frequently foresaw savings to fund the new 'bright ideas' contained in them, Dobson must have known that past NHS reforms (1974, 1989 and, even more so, 1948) had always been costly, and much of this 21 billion would be needed as a sort of 'reforms war chest' into which he could dip to oil the wheels of implementation.

Given the uncertainties surrounding his plans, discussed above, Dobson seemed unlikely to have available enough resources to meet the aspirations of large numbers of nurses, therapists, technicians and support staff whose pay levels remained relatively modest and who had hoped for more generous treatment from an incoming Labour government. The 'Catch-22' situation that they found themselves in was this: salary increases of any substance are likely to depend more on efficiency savings elsewhere in the NHS budget than on one-off public spending increases. Though savings may be possible on some items like drugs (antibiotics, for example), the NHS budget has always been dominated by staff costs; hence, only job cuts can free up funds for salary awards. Unsurprisingly, though untypically for a politician who liked to be seen as blunt and outspoken about rights and wrongs, Dobson was very cautious in making any statements about NHS salaries, and made no clear promises beyond general expressions of sympathy towards the nurses and other direct carers of patients.

An interim assessment

Box 14.1 listed the seven key commitments contained in the 1997 manifesto and they provide obvious benchmarks for an interim assessment of progress. The first proved, not surprisingly, to be a poisoned chalice: the 'early pledge' to cut waiting lists by 100,000 quickly became a likely area of failure. Within nine months of taking office, the Blair Government presided over an *increase* of around 100,000 in the standard NHS waiting list figures, from 1.15 to 1.25 million patients (the standard numbers refer to patients who have been placed by specialists onto lists for future treatment as hospital in-patients). As indicated earlier, this was entirely predictable and a continuation of historical trends. Indeed, the increase would almost certainly have been even higher but for the good fortune of two successive mild winters in 1997–98 and in 1998–99. Though lists dropped marginally, by 45,000, in the summer months of 1998, the chances of meeting the target of a reduction to around 1 million remained slim, despite Dobson's skilful redefinition, noted earlier, of 'early' as meaning 'within five years'. This failure to cut lists is certainly not for want of effort nationally and locally: during the summer of 1998, all district health authority and NHS trust boards were required to produce detailed plans for coping with winter 1998–99, and the network of NHS regional offices had to approve those plans individually. Hence, intense pressure on local managers remains, even if the goal is unattainable without a major redefinition of the concept of a 'waiting list'. This intense pressure on managers appeared to be getting results when, in spring 1999, the lists finally dipped below the level the Blair Government inherited in May 1997, and Dobson continued to try to redefine the concept by claiming that waiting times before admission had fallen. However, the opposition parties simultaneously attempted to include waits for out-patient appointments in the data, as these were alleged to be continuing to rise.

The debate was further muddied by the inevitability of different results area by area, allowing MPs to voice varying concerns about the NHS performance depending on the location of their constituency. An authoritative expert task force on the definition of 'waiting lists', which might have taken some of the heat out of this ongoing debate (figures are published monthly), did not appear to be seen as an option by the Government.

The second item, ending the internal market, had been tackled in Dobson's White and Green Papers of 1997 and 1998, though full implementation of their proposals would take some years to complete. In spring 1999, the major legislation required was placed before Parliament with the target of approval and royal assent by the end of the year. Here, the Dobson strategy of focusing on 'quality' as the basis of the proposed organisational reforms was politically sound: it is an incontestable concept in the political rhetoric of health debates. It reflected his style of adopting a seemingly 'common sense' approach to complex problems, and allowed him to play on his strengths of plain speaking communication (a style he arguably shared with Deputy Prime Minister John Prescott). To be able to categorise, criticise and label all opponents of almost any of the proposed changes as 'anti-quality' was no mean political feat.

However, health care and the NHS is a good deal more complex than this simplistic labelling might suggest and the Dobson proposals for ending the internal market have some fundamental weaknesses to them which will have to be resolved during the implementation process. These include the potentially flawed assumption that by utilising 'evidence-based medicine' through the work of the new National Institute for Clinical Excellence, cost-efficiency savings will accrue. The assumption here is that the NHS undertakes more episodes of what are sometimes labelled as 'unnecessary treatment' than it has gaps in provision. There is a good deal of information, not hard to find, to suggest that there is quite strong evidence of unnecessary care being provided. In summer 1998, for example, a study indicated that GP prescriptions included up to £15 million a year for antibiotics when they were of no use because the condition was a virus and not bacteriological – several million pounds could be saved here without reducing quality. Earlier concerns have been about such matters as the rate of caesarean-section births, of treatment for 'glue ears', and so on, as well as questions about the extent to which the NHS should provide cosmetic surgery, tattoo removal and the like.

These possible instances of efficiency savings are real enough, but all international comparisons suggest that evidence-based treatment protocols are often just as likely to add to expenditure than to result in savings. Treatment levels, especially the incidence of surgery, are relatively low in the UK, making the scope for savings correspondingly relatively modest. Far more worrying to the Dobson approach must be that the NHS has been widely recognised as having gaps and variable provision geographically in a number of specialist areas, including the well-documented cases of cancer and fertility treatment. The former is indeed the subject of Labour's third pledge in Box 14.1. In the case of cancer and the promise of improved and quicker access to specialist doctors, the Calman-Hine Cancer Service Framework is quoted with approval in the 1998 Green Paper as a pioneer role model for the proposed new series of National Service Frameworks. Ironically, in view of aspirations for savings, it requires considerable extra expenditure on new centres of excellence to ensure more equitable access to specialist centres and doctors. Controversially, in this case the Government announced that at least £100m would come from the National Lottery.

This experience of greater cost pressures is certain to be replicated when National Service Frameworks for other clinical areas of specialism are drafted. For example, the long-term care of the elderly was removed from the NHS by the Thatcher and Major Governments. The (Sutherland) Royal Commission reported on this early in 1999 and recommended returning responsibility to the NHS for the medical and nursing costs of this care. Immediate government response was cautious, Dobson being understandably reluctant to pick up the large costs involved. A further set of cost pressures associated with improved quality of care involves the historical reluctance of the NHS to invest in new technology or to prescribe new and often expensive drugs. Thus, access to the latest state-of-the-art screening and diagnostic equipment (magnetic resonance imaging and so on) is geographically variable. People with long-term and incurable conditions, such as multiple sclerosis and Alzheimer's disease, have been far less able to access new drug regimes such as beta-interferon and aricept than have their American equivalents. Again, a National Service Framework is highly likely to lead to increased treatment rates and hence spending levels. Some 200 patients' associations representing other specific medical conditions include many seeking more specialised facilities at a much higher cost. A typical example is the Stroke Association, which claims that better local access nationwide to specialist stroke units would save a large number of lives (see Wood, 2000).

The government's public expenditure proposals for the lifetime of the 1997 parliament (the 'extra 21 billion pounds') represented an important shot in the arm for the NHS and provided valuable ammunition about Dobson's commitment to 'reinventing' the health service in the wake of 18 Tory years. The crass initial announcement about the extra money apart, this was handled well in that discretion lay with the Secretary of State as to the distribution of these extra monies. Furthermore, they arrived in the wake of White and Green Paper proposals which included several 'bright ideas' and populist policy initiatives, such as the 24-hour NHS Helpline, in need of sources of funding.

Finally, Dobson clearly identified the medical profession as a potential major obstacle to radical reform and he responded carefully, mixing trenchant criticism with attempts to get their support for his proposed reforms. The concept of PCGs was one instance. By focusing on protracted discussions about their exact composition, powers and hierarchy (whether a GP should chair their board, for example) the minister appeared to gain grudging acceptance by the profession for the PCG concept in 1998. This was in spite of the fact that PCGs represented a threat to the traditional autonomy of GPs and to the separation of the primary medical care budget (effectively open-ended since 1948) from the hospital close-ended budgetary allocations. Through spring and summer of 1998, the British Medical Association appeared indecisive about whether or not to oppose PCGs outright, thus losing the initiative to the Government.

In contrast to this caution was Dobson's opportunism following the disastrous finding of high death rates after paediatric surgery in Bristol. Though the General Medical Council (the licensing body for doctors) took strong action in 1998 by striking-off and suspending the key doctors, the failure of the profession locally to take earlier action provided Dobson with the opportunity to publicise the importance of his proposals for better clinical governance, to attack the apparent excessive loyalty and deference within the profession, and to announce a review of the Council's powers and legal autonomy of doctors, after first holding a public inquiry into events in Bristol. From this one series of grim events in one hospital came the possibility of radical reforms to the structure of medicine, and the profession was in no position to publicly oppose Dobson's moves.

In summary, a secretary of state whose appointment surprised virtually everyone and who was widely tipped to be a victim of the first cabinet reshuffle had, within 18 months, produced proposals for wide-ranging reforms to the organisation and the culture of the NHS through ending the competitivism and short-termism of the internal market. He had also put the medical profession onto the defensive, pursued a range of populist policies, fielded the daily 'crisis' issues pretty capably, and presided over the announcement of a substantial funding increase. Failure to reduce waiting lists continued to dog him, and there remained serious doubts amongst experts as to the coherence of his reform plans and the viability of funding service developments through savings. These latter doubts could comfortably be contained until after the next general election, though the waiting list issue remained a more heavily and immediately poisoned chalice, incapable of satisfactory resolution in line with the unwise manifesto promise.

Though progress had clearly been made on most of the manifesto pledges, there were two of them where little happened in the first two years: food standards and public health. In January 1999 the proposed Food Standards Agency was finally announced but arrangements for funding it ran into a storm of criticism. One-third of its expected £120 million annual budget was to be met by a £90 annual flat-rate levy on each food retail and catering business, with a small corner shop paying as much as a large supermarket. There were signs that the Government might rethink this, following lobbying by the small business interests, but it seems that the Agency will only be established after the Government has been in office for three years or more, as legislation is required.

The record of public health activity has also been slower than expected, and key issues like tobacco advertising saw the Government backing away from taking positive action in the case of the sponsorship of international sporting events, such as the Formula One and the world snooker championships. A promised major public health white paper was heralded as a follow-up to a 1998 green paper *Our Healthier Nation*, but remained unpublished in June 1999.

A third pledge, to cut spending on bureaucracy, is harder to evaluate. By June 1999, ministers were beginning to claim savings of up to one billion pounds (actually of £200 million a year multiplied up over a five-year period, in a further example of the double-counting referred to above), but they were careful not to be explicit. Auditing the calculation of these savings might be controversial and the Dobson reforms were certain to add new costs in areas like the administration of PCGs, or the running of the new National Institute of Clinical Excellence and the Commission for Health Improvement.

References

Harrison, S. and B. Wood (1999), 'Designing Health Organisation in the UK, 1968–1998. From Blueprint to Bright Idea and "Manipulated Emergence", *Public Administration*, 77(4): 751–68.

Klein, R. (1995), *The New Politics of the NHS* (3rd ed.), London, Longmans.

NHS Executive (1998), *A First Class Service: Quality in the New NHS*, London, Department of Health.

Secretary of State for Health (1997), *The New NHS: Modern, Dependable*, Cm 3807, London, Stationery Office.

Wood, B. (1999), 'The Politics of Health' in Jones, B. (ed.), *Political Issues in Britain Today* (5th ed.), Manchester, Manchester University Press.

Wood, B. (2000) *Patient Power? The Politics of Patients' Associations in Britain and America*, Buckingham, Open University Press.

15

New Labour and 'law and order'

Inderjeet Parmar

Introduction

'Law and order' has, in recent decades, been the quintessential Conservative issue. Labour has been accused either of being silent or 'soft' on crime and successive public opinion polls have invariably indicated a significant Conservative lead. The Tory Party was 'the party of law and order.' Successive general election defeats, however, along with the triumph of Thatcherism, internal reform within the Labour Party (Hay, 1994; Smith, 1994), the doubling of recorded crime since 1979 and strong criticism of Tory policies by senior judges and police chiefs, profoundly altered the political balance of power on law and order. Today, New Labour is 'the party of law and order'.

'Tough on crime, tough on the causes of crime' was the winning formula developed by Tony Blair, as shadow home secretary (1992–94), that finally wrested control of the crime and punishment agenda from the Conservatives. This was a significant achievement in itself and was rendered even more remarkable by the fact that the level of recorded crime was actually decreasing for the first time since 1953 (Straw, 1997). Tony Blair's formula summed up the mix of 'Old' and 'New' Labour that has come to dominate the current government's thinking on law and order politics. 'Tough on crime' bore witness to 18 years of Tory rule characterised by 'get tough' rhetoric, increased police powers, stiffer sentences and a growing prison population. But 'tough on the causes of crime' signalled the continuing significance of the 'gentler' tone of old Labour, that crime was not purely driven by maladjusted individuals bent on destruction and lawlessness, that it had social causes beyond the offender (Straw, 1997; Labour Party, 1997). New Labour promised, therefore, to punish the offender as well as tackle the root causes of criminal behaviour. New Labour, with its seemingly 'balanced' and 'moderate' approach to crime, successfully harnessed the public's growing disenchantment with the Conservatives (King *et al.*, 1998).

This chapter has three broad aims. The first is to describe Labour's election pledges and the policies designed to implement them. The second is to describe

---

Box 15.1   *New Labour's manifesto commitments on law and order*

- Tackle youth crime – fast-track persistent offenders
- Zero-tolerance policing encouraged
- Break the drug/crime connection
- Constructive prison regimes
- Relieve social deprivation to attack the causes of crime
- Make racial harassment/violence an offence
- Reform the Crown Prosecution Service
- Ban handguns

Source: The Labour Party, 1997.

---

how Labour has dealt with significant law and order 'events' as they have emerged (for example, the Stephen Lawrence case and police corruption), in order to explore New Labour's values in this policy area. The third aim is to evaluate the impact of its policies on crime. This chapter is, of necessity, more descriptive than evaluative because policies in an area such as law and order take several years to bear fruit. Nevertheless, it will identify trends that permit as full an evaluation as practicable at this stage.

Labour's election pledges and policies

The 1997 manifesto stressed a commitment to policing and improved conviction rates, i.e. punitive measures, which squared with the 'tough on crime' aspect of Labour's approach to the issue. Some of the promises also addressed 'the *causes of crime,*' albeit in a 'narrow' sense of the term. 'Zero-tolerance policing' and the policy on drug misuse, for example, both suggest this interpretation because, as research shows, tolerance of petty offences and the consumption of illegal drugs lead to serious crime. In addition, the manifesto emphasised the need to fight crime through a broader set of policies designed to 'relieve social deprivation' (Labour Party, 1997). In practice, this has emerged as the 'New Deal' to decrease youth unemployment and as the Social Exclusion Unit's (SEUs) remit to examine the causes of economic and social marginality. Inevitably, these policies fall outside the jurisdiction of the Home Office but some of them must be considered briefly in their relation to law and order. This permits the evaluation of the fears of liberal critics who suggest that New Labour has jettisoned the 'causes' aspect of the formula and, in conjunction with its focus on zero-tolerance policing, has taken up the authoritarian approach of its Conservative predecessors (Dennis, 1998; Campbell, 1998). Ultimately of course, Labour's aims, like those of their Conservative predecessors, are a reduction in crime *and* a reduction in the public's anxieties about crime.

Box 15.2   *Major provisions of the Crime and Disorder Act*

- Fast-tracking of persistent young offenders
- Final police warning to replace discredited repeat caution system
- Parenting orders and counselling sessions
- Reparation orders to make good harm caused by offenders
- Local child curfew schemes
- Reduction of age of criminal responsibility to 10 years
- Local authorities to set up multi-agency strategy for youth crime and justice
- Police powers against truancy
- Anti-social behaviour orders
- Drug offender treatment and testing
- Sex offender orders
- Higher penalties for racially-aggravated offences
- Abolition of death penalty

1998 Crime and Disorder Act

At the heart of New Labour's approach to law and order lies the Crime and Disorder Act (CDA) of 1998. This law is wide-ranging – covering youth crime, treatment for drug offenders, 'race' crime, anti-social behaviour, and the role of local agencies in crime fighting.

A principal concern of the CDA is juvenile crime, which accounts for a disproportionate number of recorded offences (teenagers account for around 28 per cent of all violent crime, 40 per cent of burglaries and a third of criminal damage offences). Re-offending is another, and several initiatives have been undertaken to try to deal with the problem. Finally, 'fast-track' sentencing is to be encouraged in order to ensure that persistent offenders are processed quickly, thereby protecting the community more effectively (Graham, 1998). More controversially, the CDA empowers the courts and other agencies to issue parenting orders and local child curfew schemes, which could require parents to attend counselling sessions. The age of criminal responsibility has also been reduced to include children aged 10–13 years, and the police have been empowered to take truants to school. The Home Office, which has piloted these schemes in several localities since October 1998, plans to apply them nationally by 2000–1.

Under the terms of the CDA, local authorities are required to establish Youth Offending Teams to ensure local provision of youth justice, to oversee the implementation of 'youth justice plans,' curfews, personal offender 'action plans', all in a bid to promote a 'multi-agency' approach to juvenile delinquency. In a further initiative that tries to 'nip crime in the bud' (of central importance to

---

zero-tolerance policing), the CDA empowers local agencies to issue 'reparation orders' to 'make young offenders face up to their crimes and the consequences of their actions' (Mandelson and Liddle, 1996). A national Youth Justice Board has been created to oversee the whole system.

The approach of the CDA is in line with zero-tolerance policing. The stress on targeting crime 'hotspots' and 'persistent offenders' is part of the systematic approach of zero-tolerance policing, which was endorsed at Labour's 1998 Party conference. The multi-agency approach of involving local councils, health authorities, the police, social services and probation services is also part of the same strategy. Its aim is to ensure that responsibility for 'policing' is broadened out to other agencies, is responsive to community concerns and retains public support.

The CDA also tries to sever the link between drug-dependence and crime by providing powers to the courts to offer testing and treatment to young offenders. The seriousness of the Government's attitude to the problem of drug misuse and crime was further evidenced by the appointment of Britain's first 'drug czar', Keith Hellawell, to co-ordinate a multi-agency approach that cuts across jurisdictions to tackle the problem. To tackle 'anti-social behaviour' the CDA empowers local agencies to issue an order to prevent the particular behaviour taking place for a minimum of two years. The principal purpose of this is to empower citizens in their attempts to stay the hands of local 'trouble-makers', such as racist and un-neighbourly individuals. The CDA also introduced new assault, harassment and public order offences with higher penalties where a crime can be demonstrated to have been 'racially aggravated'.

Reform of the Crown Prosecution Service

The Crown Prosecution Service (CPS), which was formed in 1986, had faced severe criticism for administrative incompetence, failure to prosecute corrupt police officers, and excessive bureaucratisation, forcing the resignation of the Director of Public Prosecutions (DPP) Dame Barbara Mills in 1998. Labour promised to reorganise the CPS to improve co-operation with police services, improve efficiency and enhance public confidence in the Service. In July 1998, following the Glidewell Report and the Comprehensive Spending Review, the Government announced that the CPS was to be decentralised into 42 areas coterminous with police districts and its budget increased by £30 million. Since the CPS had been found to be mismanaged, a new post of chief executive (under the authority of the Director of Public Prosecutions) has been created alongside the appointment of 42 'area business managers', with the aim of permitting the legal professionals to concentrate exclusively on casework. A further decentralising measure was the appointment of 42 local Chief Crown Prosecutors – in effect local Directors of Public Prosecutions – to enhance local accountability and the prospects for local partnerships with the police, courts and judiciary. The Glidewell Report recommended that the CPS take charge of prosecutions immediately after police had charged a defendant. Thereafter, the CPS would, through units consisting of lawyers, caseworkers and police, prepare and present cases to the courts.

Through such reforms, the Government aims to halve the time it takes to prosecute persistent offenders, permitting the CPS to focus on more serious crime and increase public confidence in the criminal justice system (Graham, 1998). The Government also hopes that its reforms will improve the career structure, stature and morale of CPS personnel.

Prisons

The crisis of a rapidly rising prison population – there were 65000 inmates in 1998, a 25 per cent increase from 1996 – demanded a radical overhaul of Labour's attitude to privatisation. New Labour's policy shifted from robust opposition to private prisons in 1994, to one of inviting bids for two new ones by 1998, and the renewal of the contract to privately run a third. Of course, the Government could not repudiate the previous government's contractual obligations, but there has been an important shift in New Labour's thinking. Private prisons are now a part of the permanent landscape of the criminal justice system. Labour's election manifesto, however, merely offered to audit resources, encourage constructive prison regimes and reduce the drug problem by continuing random testing (introduced by the Conservatives) and providing voluntary testing units in every prison.

The Prison Service has implemented random drug tests in all prisons, attempts to ensure an average of 22.5 hours' (per prisoner per week) purposeful activity, and also to ensure 2200 completions of programmes designed to prevent re-offending. In addition, young prisoners are eligible for the Government's New Deal programmes, in a scheme being piloted in 11 establishments until April 2000. The aim, of course, is to reduce re-offending rates by giving pre-release prisoners access to education, training and advice, and immediate access to the 'gateway' of the New Deal.

The Government's current spending plans, however, do not allow for any further investment to maintain *existing* levels of regime activity per prisoner. In addition, there will be little or no money to extend drug treatment programmes (currently being piloted in 59 prisons) to the whole prison system or to finance voluntary drug testing units in every prison. The latter represents a clear case of breaking an election promise on the part of New Labour. In its defence, the Government could argue that it inherited long-term problems from the previous Conservative Government, including the inevitable increases in the prison population brought about by the Crime Sentences Act of 1997, which made harsher sentences mandatory for certain serious offences. It is clear to the Prison Service, however, that unless there is further investment, prisoners will spend more time in overcrowded cells, less in constructive activities or in 'facing up to their offending behaviour', and that, ultimately, greater levels of discontent and disorder may result.

Box 15.3 *The New Deal for Communities*

- New national strategy for long-term commitment to tackle poverty
- 18 minister-headed special action teams to implement strategy
- Community partnerships in specifically-targeted areas
- Further £700m for 500 additional schemes
- Co-ordination by Cabinet-level SEU

Relieving social deprivation to attack the causes of crime

The Social Exclusion Unit (SEU) was formed to identify and tackle the causes of social inequality which, according to Blair, involves low educational achievement, joblessness and crime, a series of 'joined up problems [that] demand joined up solutions' (Cabinet Office, 1997). A Basic Skills Agency survey in 1998 showed appalling levels of educational failure among young offenders: 70 per cent could not complete a job application form; 64 per cent had been habitual school truants; and 55 per cent admitted to having committed crimes during periods of truancy. Consequently, the SEU made the reduction of truancy and school exclusion rates, and improved numeracy and literacy, major priorities in the effort to reduce juvenile delinquency. So far, the centrepiece of the SEU's efforts is the £800 million, three-year 'New Deal for Communities' that initially focuses on 17 'pathfinder' districts in cities across Britain, to improve housing, education, health, job and training prospects, and reduce crime rates.

The initiatives of the SEU, listed in Box 15.3, form an important part of the shift in British politics that New Labour represents. Political recognition of the problems of poverty and of the poor is the first step in a programme of urban regeneration that may result in the amelioration of the worst excesses of the *laissez-faire* attitudes of Conservative governments. It is also, however, a far cry from the politics of old Labour given the relatively meagre resources devoted to the SEU compared with the huge programmes of nationalisation, house building and urban renewal of the post-war years. The SEU's real claim to novelty, however, lies in the targeting of funds to specific areas, with specific plans of action drawn up by local agencies with clearly defined and realisable aims and objectives. The SEU may spend much less than old Labour and involve the private sector, as the Conservatives favoured, but it also takes a 'hands on', technocratic approach to the problem.

New Labour and 'law and order' events

An evaluation of the Government's performance requires consideration of its handling of events not entirely of its own making. Two such instances are briefly considered below: the racially motivated killing of Stephen Lawrence (along with the ensuing controversy over 'institutional racism' in the police service) and the issue of police corruption. Analysis of these enables a better understanding of the core values, policy style, substantive actions and effectiveness of New Labour's approach to law and order.

The death of Stephen Lawrence

Stephen Lawrence was stabbed to death in London in April 1993 by a group of white youths. The ensuing police investigation, which faced severe criticism for incompetence, racism and corruption, was the subject of an independent judicial inquiry. Headed by Sir William Macpherson, this was the most wide-ranging inquiry into police–ethnic minority relations since the Scarman Report of 1981. It identified 'the lessons to be learned for the investigation and prosecution of racially motivated crime', making 70 recommendations for reform. A report by the Police Complaints Authority (PCA) had also pointed up numerous shortcomings in the original investigation, including such things as the failure to place identified suspects under immediate surveillance, to take eye witness accounts seriously, to conduct adequate house-to-house enquiries and to act upon surveillance data to prevent suspects disposing of possible incriminating evidence. This case opened up a wider political debate about the policing of racial crime and the under-representation of ethnic minorities in the police service. In the course of the public inquiry into the Lawrence case, several chief constables admitted the existence of racist attitudes among their officers, with the chief of Greater Manchester Police describing the problem in his area as 'institutional racism'.

Sir Paul Condon, Commissioner of the Metropolitan Police, expressed his regrets about the case and expressed the desire to discipline several of the officers implicated (most of whom had retired by 1998). However, his force came under further suspicion when it was alleged that officers giving evidence to the Macpherson inquiry had been 'coached' beforehand from a written document. His denial that 'institutional racism' existed in his force further alienated him from the Lawrence campaign and was authoritatively dismissed by the Macpherson Report. Both the Macpherson and PCA reports, however, ruled out *self-conscious* racism and corrupt police connections (with one of the suspects) as causes of the errors made during the original investigation. *Racist stereotyping* (of blacks as criminals or suspects rather than victims), the Macpherson Report argued, caused the police to fail to administer first-aid to Stephen Lawrence, and to treat his friend, Duwayne Brooks, as a suspect. In general, the Report expressed support for the view that black people in Britain were 'over-policed and under-protected'.

According to Jack Straw, the Macpherson Report constituted a challenge to 'the police service and the rest of society' in the Government's attempts to build 'an anti-racist society'. It was 'the core task of policing' to provide a fair and just service to all sections of a 'multi-ethnic and multi-cultural society.' More concretely, Straw published an Action Plan (Home Office, 1999), to implement

Box 15.4   *The Home Secretary's Action Plan to combat racism in the police*

- Police using racist language or behaviour to face dismissal under new code of practice
- Race Relations Act to be extended to cover police service (and all other public services)
- Racism awareness training for all police
- New targets for recruitment of ethnic minority officers
- Freedom of Information Act to cover police administration and operations
- Racial incidents in schools to be recorded and reported to parents, governors and local education authorities
- Anti-racist (citizen) education to be part of schools' national curriculum
- Home Office to study feasibility of an independent authority to investigate complaints against the police

Source: Home Office, 1999.

many, though not all, of the Macpherson Report's recommendations. Its key objectives are listed in Box 15.4. The process is to be overseen by a steering group under Straw's leadership, consisting of bodies such as the Black Police Association, the Commission for Racial Equality, the CPS, the Association of Chief Police Officers (ACPO) and the Metropolitan Police.

New Labour's handling of racially motivated crime has been severely tested by the Lawrence case. Overall, Home Secretary Straw's reputation has been enhanced because it was he who ordered the Macpherson inquiry, made racially-aggravated offences statutorily punishable with stiffer sentences, promoted greater recruitment of ethnic minorities by the police and set targets for local forces. Indirectly, Straw was responsible for making the issue of 'institutional racism' in the police service a subject of national significance, and for establishing new race relations training provision for the police service in 1999 (before the release of the Macpherson Report). Straw has received support from many quarters for his role in trying to make good, in a concrete way, the promise of the Scarman Report on police–minority relations in the 1980s. Instead of racial awareness being a mere 'optional extra' for police forces, Straw has elevated it to 'the core of modern policing'.

Corruption in the police

The issue of police corruption also resurfaced independently, especially in London's Metropolitan Police. According to the PCA, serious corruption within the police service was 'on an upward cycle' (PCA, 1997–98). In response, Scotland Yard established a 125-strong anti-corruption branch, the Complaints

Investigation Bureau (CIB), only twenty years after the last major purge of corrupt officers under the leadership of Sir Robert Mark (Chief of the Metropolitan Police, 1997–98). In the latest drive against corruption, between 20 and 40 officers may be charged for accepting bribes or 'recycling' drugs, i.e. selling to the public drugs that were seized in police raids. In January 1998, the homes of 19 serving and former Flying Squad officers were raided for evidence, although Condon has stated that there may be up to 250 corrupt officers in his force, some of whom had accepted bribes of up to £80,000. Two main categories of corruption concern the police and public: first, deals between officers and, mainly, drug dealers, over seized money, intelligence files and 'tip-offs' that allow criminals to go free; and, secondly, officers stealing drugs or money from known criminals directly.

It is not only the Metropolitan Police, however, that is concerned about corruption in its ranks. Even the architect of zero-tolerance policing in Britain, Detective Superintendent Ray Mallon, was suspended during an investigation into 'alleged corruption and other irregularities' in the Cleveland Police Force. Corruption and malpractice concerns have also been expressed by other police forces, including West Midlands, and by the Association of Chief Police Officers, although they have been rejected by the rank-and-file organisation, the Police Federation. The PCA also raised concerns about allegations of racial and sexual harassment, another indicator of malpractice within the police service (PCA, 1996–97). In several cases of domestic violence, for instance, officers had formed sexual relationships with victims while others had harassed the women they had been assigned to protect. Female officers, particularly those assigned to male-dominated special squads (such as CID), were most likely to face sexual harassment. Financial compensation paid by the police to settle cases has been substantial. The Metropolitan Police paid out almost £5 million between 1996 and 1998. Greater Manchester Police paid over £10 million in damages and legal costs in one case alone, namely the case against Kevin Taylor, a personal friend of the former Deputy Chief Constable of Greater Manchester Police, John Stalker.

Finally, evidence of a widespread culture of exaggerating 'clear up' (detection) rates and under-recording of actual crime rates within the police service was publicly exposed in early 1999. According to an investigation of Nottinghamshire Police by officers from Bedfordshire, such practices were rife throughout the former's jurisdiction, indicating a force-wide policy of under-recording. Even more damning was the claim by the former Chief Constable of South Yorkshire, Richard Wells: 'I don't think you could be on the same planet and not be aware that it is an issue for *all police forces*.'

The combined result of the Lawrence Report, police corruption inquiries and the publicity surrounding the cases of racial and sexual harassment within the police service, was a crisis in the police service as a whole. The process of reform, therefore, was unlikely to be without friction and pain. Jack Straw had to tackle the difficult problem of criticising the police for past failures at the

---

Box 15.5   *New police disciplinary procedures*

- Civil standard of proof at disciplinary hearings (balance of probabilities rather than beyond reasonable doubt)
- Officers acquitted in criminal court may be disciplined for same offence
- Cases of officers committing serious criminal offences to be heard internally within 6 weeks, in advance of criminal proceedings
- Hearings may be held despite absence, through illness, of accused officers
- Forfeiture of police pensions for misconduct under review
- Availability of post-retirement disciplinary sanctions under review
- Ending of 'right to silence' in disciplinary hearings under review

---

same time as maintaining police morale and support, which explains his continued public statements to the effect that the problems of the police arise from a small minority of 'bad apples'. Straw's main response to the crisis was the introduction of new police disciplinary procedures in April 1999 (see Box 15.5), following the Government's submissions to the Home Affairs Select Committee report on police complaints and discipline.

There does now appear to be an opening for New Labour to exploit, in its desire to reform the culture and practices of the police service. The Lawrence case and internal corruption scandals, in addition to the new managerial culture within the police, provide an opportunity for Jack Straw to proceed with far-reaching changes at this time. As with so many other areas of policy, only time will tell whether New Labour succeeds.

Evaluation of New Labour's policies

It is difficult to evaluate a set of policies that have only recently been translated into legislation, such as the diverse sections of the Crime and Disorder Act or the reform of the CPS and, especially, the impact of the New Deal for Communities and for Young People. A further difficulty arises in separating the impact of the policies of the previous government from that of the policies of the present administration.

One thing is clear, however: the Labour Party is now considered the party of law and order. New Labour has appropriated the 'get tough' rhetoric and approach of the Conservatives, added social causation and technocratic zeal to the formula, and won the public's confidence (King *et al.*, 1998). Whether or not this will remain the case depends on the longer-term impact of New Labour's policies on crime rates and on public anxieties about crime.

According to figures from both the police and the British Crime Survey (BCS, 1998), the crime rate has fallen. The exposure of attempts by police forces to 'cover up' the true crime figures, of course, may undermine the claim of falling

---

crime levels. The BCS, however, based on victim surveys and not police figures, *also* reveals falling crime levels. Between October 1996 and October 1997, recorded crime fell by 6 per cent to 4.8 million offences, the first such fall since the BCS began in 1981. Between 1993 and 1997, there was a 15 per cent decrease, with burglaries falling by 25 per cent. Violent crime fell 17 per cent between 1995 and 1997 and car theft by a quarter. The fear of crime also decreased: in 1998, only 18 per cent of the public believed that there was a 'lot more' crime, compared with 34 per cent in 1992. These figures show that Labour inherited a national climate of improving crime figures and have continued that trend (Pilkington, 1998) rather than initiated it. But it is also New Labour, rather than the Conservatives, that is likely to reap the political dividends if the decrease in crime continues.

Another early success for New Labour was the banning of handguns and the surrender of almost 180,000 firearms by members of the public, under the provisions of the Firearms (Amendment) (No.2) Act 1998. Labour's aim of being tough on crime and on its causes found expression in its encouragement of zero-tolerance policing, the provisions of the CDA, and through the New Deal and the work of the SEU.

The CDA promised to 'fast-track' persistent juvenile offenders, aiming to cut the number of days from arrest to sentence by half (from 142 to 71) by 2002. 'Fast-tracking', the rationale of which was recommended originally by the Audit Commission during the John Major era, appears to be working. Between May and December 1997, the average time between arrest and sentencing was reduced from 142 to 135 days. The target for the end of 1998 was 100. The CDA was also aimed at reparation and community-based sentences, i.e. at making offenders face up to the harm caused to victims. In this respect, the CDA's effects merit being closely monitored, informed, as they were, by a highly successful multi-agency programme in Northampton that significantly cut re-offending rates.

With regard to racial harassment, the CPS's monitoring of the police and courts will permit the evaluation of the long-term impact of the CDA's provisions in this area. There are currently several areas of policing that are of concern to ethnic minorities. One such area is zero-tolerance policing and its racially unequal application, particularly in inner city areas; another is the unacceptably high number of racial attacks in Britain (Bradley, 1998). Such concerns may be at least partially addressed by Labour's current policies, *if* the CDA's provisions actually work and *if* more black and Asian police officers are recruited and retained. The current position suggests, however, that progress is likely to be very slow. According to Her Majesty's Inspectorate of Constabulary, only three (Metropolitan Police, South Wales, and West Yorkshire) of England and Wales' 43 police forces were making 'sufficient efforts' to recruit, promote or retain black officers.

The effects of Jack Straw's efforts to root out police corruption cannot be evaluated at present since they will take several years to 'bed down'. In response to a number of recommendations from the Select Committee on Home Affairs, Straw agreed to new procedures to point up poor police performance, to apply a 'balance of probabilities' standard of proof in disciplinary cases and to reduce the level of legal representation for officers in order to cut delays. Public spending limits, however, prevented Straw from increasing the budget and independence of the PCA, which remains reliant on serving police officers to conduct investigations of serving officers. On the issue of police malpractices associated with the under-recording of crime figures, Jack Straw introduced new 'counting rules' in April 1998 that made mis-recording more difficult.

Finally, the Government's 'New Deal' directed billions of pounds into addressing, in part at least, the problems of social deprivation and exclusion. According to preliminary figures, over 30000 people found jobs as a result of the New Deal for Young People, while more than 127000 participated in the scheme up to October 1998. There were concerns, however, that the New Deal would run into problems if, as expected, an economic downturn occurred and because of the low levels of educational attainment that it is aimed at. Even more importantly, from the perspective of its crime reduction objective, was the concern that compulsory government schemes drive many people off welfare rolls and into the 'drugs economy.' Such people may then contribute to higher levels of crime, subverting the intentions of the government (Peck, 1998).

Conclusion

How new, then, are New Labour's law and order policies? Do they in fact differ from those of the Tories and of old Labour? While there is much in New Labour's thinking that is inherited from the Tories, there is also significant discontinuity. What is 'new' is the acceptance within government, and not merely in its public rhetoric, that crime and disorder have causes in addition to purely individually centred ones; that there are also social factors at work. This is important in a number of ways: first, it opens up public debate to a broader set of arguments, challenging and moderating the view that harsher penalties alone are sufficient to deal with delinquency. It brings *society* back in to public argument about the appropriate response to criminality, after several years in the political and ideological wilderness. Secondly, it opens up the possibility of social programmes either run, co-ordinated or inspired by, government, an idea which had also fallen into disrepute. Finally, accepting social causes is also politically astute: it feeds into a widespread attitude that always questioned the New Right's view that crime was a purely individual phenomenon, adding to the general discontent with the Tories as being 'out of touch', uncaring, arrogant and ideologically-driven. Labour won support for its policies, therefore, because it embraced a commonsensical middle ground between a regime of 'short, sharp shocks' and 'traditional' social democratic views on crime and punishment.

In some respects, New Labour's recent stress on robust policing and punishment differs little from what some *old* Labour governments were, on occasion, forced to do, e.g. preside over and justify coercive policing of strikes and demonstrations as necessary to restore the 'rule of law'. Both society and the Party, however, have changed radically since the 1970s, as the roles of the trades unions and of the Left in New Labour politics reflect. New Labour is committed to attacking the social causes of crime, as was old Labour, but with the difference that it seeks vigorously to address not only economic deprivation, but also social factors that allow individuals greater opportunity to commit crime, such as truancy and school exclusions. The latter have consequences for literacy, numeracy and social skills and lead directly into higher likelihood of joblessness. Other social factors that concern New Labour include the environment of policing in high-crime areas, the previous tolerance of 'low-level', so-called petty offences and the role of parents and communities in nipping juvenile delinquency 'in the bud'. Such an interpretation of social causes permits experimentation with a variety of strategies that involve reparation and drug treatment orders for young offenders. While the Conservatives rightly claim that New Labour has, effectively, stolen their policies in a number of law and order-related initiatives, the fact is that their approach was not as 'hands on' as that of the Blair Government.

Whether or not this constitutes evidence of a 'Third Way' (Giddens, 1998) – a fully coherent social, economic and political philosophy lying between orthodox social democracy and neo-liberalism – remains to be seen. What is apparent, however, is that New Labour has the energy and vigour of a radical force attacking the problems of law and order with pragmatism and technocratic optimism. In this respect, 'what works', not ideological loyalties, are the watchwords of New Labour.

References

Bradley, R. (1998), 'Public Expectations and Perceptions of Policing', Policing and Reducing Crime Unit, Police Research Series Paper 96, London, Home Office.

British Crime Survey (1998), *The 1998 British Crime Survey*, London, Home Office.

Cabinet Office (1997), *Social Exclusion Unit: Background and Structure*, London, Cabinet Office.

Campbell, B. (1998), 'The Mad, the Bad and the Angry: Men, Crime and Public Order', paper delivered to Social Policy Department Seminars on the Third Way, 11 November 1998, University of Manchester.

Dennis, N. (ed.) (1998), *Zero Tolerance: Policing a Free Society*, London, Institute of Economic Affairs.

Giddens, A. (1998), *The Third Way. The Renewal of Social Democracy*, Cambridge, Polity Press.

Graham, J. (1998), *Fast Tracking of Persistent Young Offenders*, Research and Statistics Directorate, Research Findings No. 74, London, Home Office.

Hay, C. (1994), 'Labour's Thatcherite Revisionism: Playing the 'Politics of Catch-up', *Political Studies*, 42:700–7.

Home Office (1999), *Stephen Lawrence Inquiry. Home Secretary's Action Plan*, London, Home Office Communication Directorate.

King, A., Denver, D., McLean, I., Norris, P., Norton, P., Sanders, D. and Seyd, P. (1998), *New Labour Triumphs. Britain at the Polls*, Chatham, N.J., Chatham House Publishers, Inc.

Labour Party (1997), *New Labour: Because Britain Deserves Better*, London, Labour Party.

Mandelson, P. and Liddle, R. (1996), *The Blair Revolution. Can New Labour Deliver?*, London, Faber and Faber.

Metropolitan Police (1997–98), *Annual Report*.

PCA (Police Complaints Authority) (1996–97), *Annual Report*.

PCA (Police Complaints Authority) (1997–98), *Annual Report*.

Peck, Jamie (1998), 'Reintegrating the Workless Classes: New Labour, New Deal', paper delivered to Social Policy Department Seminars on the Third Way, 25 November 1998, University of Manchester.

Pilkington, C. (1998), *Issues in British Politics*, London, Macmillan.

Smith, M.J. (1994), 'Understanding the "Politics of Catch-up": the Modernisation of the Labour Party', *Political Studies*, 42:708–15.

Straw, J. (1997), 'Towards the Responsible Society', *The Superintendent*, 8 (Summer):3.

16

New Labour policies for the media and the arts

Peter Humphreys

Creative Britain

The Department for Culture, Media and Sport (DCMS) is the former Department of National Heritage, re-named by New Labour. The DCMS is responsible for sport and tourism, and also the millennium, as well as the media and arts. This chapter is only concerned with the latter. Any one seeking guidance about what drives New Labour policy for the media and arts is advised to look for it in a book called *Creative Britain* written by Chris Smith, the DCMS Secretary of State. The book is essentially a collection of reworked speeches from the Minister's first year in office. One theme comes across particularly strongly: the Government recognises the crucial economic importance to the regeneration of Britain of the 'creative industries' (Smith, 1998).

One of the New Labour Government's first acts in the media and arts field was to establish, in June 1997, the Creative Industries Task Force (CITF), one of the numerous such policy advisory task forces set up by New Labour since coming to office. The CITF brings together Departments of State – notably the DCMS, Department of Trade and Industry (DTI) and the Treasury, as well as 'key people drawn from the industries themselves . . . cutting across traditional divides in Whitehall, uniting government and industry in a partnership approach, and setting out the agenda of specific issues to be addressed' (Smith, 1998:11). The key aim of the Task Force was to create a government/industry network that would 'assess the value of the creative industries, analyse their needs and iden-tify ways of maximising their economic impact'. Indeed, the first task of the CITF was to produce a 'map' of the creative industries. Published in November 1998, this identified current activity in each creative industry, their potential for future growth and key obstacles and threats to that potential growth (DCMS, 1999a:50). More recently, in April 1999, Chris Smith published an independent research report that the DCMS had commissioned into Britain's TV export performance (DCMS, 1999b) and established a CITF inquiry team specifically to pursue the report's recommendations and to investigate how to improve exports of British-made television programmes (DCMS, 1999c).

Box 16.1 *New Labour's manifesto commitments on the media*

'Labour aims for a thriving, diverse media industry, combining commercial success and public service. We will ensure that the BBC continues to be a flagship for British creativity and public service broadcasting, but we believe that the combination of public and private sectors in competition is a key spur to innovation and high standards. The regulatory framework for media and broadcasting should reflect the realities of a far more open and competitive economy, and enormous technological advance, for example with digital television. Labour will balance sensible rules, fair regulation and national and international competition, so maintaining quality and diversity for the benefit of the viewers.'

Source: Labour Party, 1997.

All this reveals much about New Labour's priorities for the media and the arts, and might be taken as a sign of continuity with the market-oriented policies of the Conservatives. Furthermore, in the field of broadcasting policy New Labour dropped any ideas it once toyed with for an early radical regulatory overhaul, and devoted itself instead to the pragmatic advancement of policies already introduced by the Conservatives, notably for promoting digital broadcasting. Arguably, New Labour's evolutionary approach to the digital era is highly appropriate. Labour's press policies hardly differ from those of the Conservatives. The same is true of media ownership. New Labour's emphasis on promoting increased efficiency has a distinctly 'Thatcherite' echo. At the same time, however, New Labour has made much of its commitment to the issues of improving quality, promoting social inclusiveness, widening access to culture, and the devolution of decision-making. In these latter fields, New Labour has made a modest, but nonetheless significant, impression. Through its policies for both the BBC and Channel 4, New Labour has confirmed its commitment to public service broadcasting, arts funding has been modestly increased and arts decision-making has been devolved.

New Labour broadcasting policy

Manifesto commitments and achievements

New Labour's pre-election strategy for media policy concentrated on broadcasting, saying nothing about the press. As Box 16.1 shows, New Labour's 1997 manifesto promised support for the BBC's central public-service role, whilst underlining the need for media policy and regulation to be appropriate to the demands of a modern, competitive economy. Elsewhere, New Labour made it very clear that Channel 4 (C4), which Thatcherites had wanted to privatise, would remain a public service broadcaster. New Labour also stressed that it would promote the digital revolution.

While in opposition, there had been serious discussion within New Labour leadership circles about a radical overhaul of broadcasting regulation, notably through the establishment of a new 'OFCOM', which would supposedly be more appropriate to regulation of the 'converging' communications sectors. This radical policy had been advocated by media policy experts in the Institute of Public Policy Research (Collins and Murroni, 1996). It was also advocated by (then) OFTEL Director-General Donald Cruickshank. However, the Queen's Speech following New Labour's election victory contained no mention of a new OFCOM. Indeed, the speech contained very little at all of direct relevance to the media. It soon became very clear indeed that the New Labour Government intended to proceed carefully and cautiously with media policy.

In July 1998, the Government produced its first annual report. New Labour media policy could boast of achievements on two 'fronts':

- 'Promoting new public service programmes and services – through the changes to the Channel 4 funding formula and our approval of new public service channels from the BBC';
- 'Working with the industry to harness digital technology – consulting on a date for analogue switch-off and co-operating with the regulators to give the industry greater certainty about decisions' (The Government, 1998:70).

The first of these two policy 'fronts' represented fulfilment of New Labour's promised support for public service broadcasting. The Conservatives' Broadcasting Act 1990 had enabled C4 to finance itself through selling its own advertising, but the Act had also established an insurance system against the possibility that C4's advertising sales might not cover its costs. Accordingly, ITV (strictly called Channel 3) companies would provide a safety net against the payment of an annual 'insurance premium' by C4. However, C4's self-financing had meanwhile proved to be an unexpected commercial success. The insurance formula had resulted in the independent sector public service broad-caster paying private ITV companies as much as £87 million in 1996. The Conservatives' Broadcasting Act 1996 had already envisaged phasing out this funding formula; therefore New Labour was in fact merely accelerating the process.

As for the new BBC channels, in 1997 BBC Worldwide, the Corporation's commercial division, signed up for a joint venture with the private company Flextech (parent company: the US cable TV giant, Tele-Communications International Inc.) to produce several advertising and subscription funded satellite and cable TV channels. In March 1998, the BBC signed a £340 million deal with the US media company, Discovery Channel (Peak and Fisher, 1999:172–3). The Government's approval for such deals signified clearly New Labour's intention to continue with the Conservatives' policy of encouraging the BBC to develop its international commercial activities, albeit in the worthy cause of generating new income for public service broadcasting. The BBC has also launched a number of new public service channels for the new technologies, starting in 1997 with a 24-hour news service, News 24. For allowing the latter development, the Government incurred the displeasure of Rupert Murdoch since in his view News 24 represented unfair competition for Sky News because the licence-funded BBC could provide News 24 free to cable TV operators. In 1998, the BBC introduced two new digital public service channels, BBC Choice and BBC Parliament. BBC Knowledge, a digital channel dedicated to learning, followed in 1999. Also, in 1997 the BBC launched BBC Online, which by 1998, according to the BBC's annual report, quickly became the most visited internet site in Europe. Following a survey indicating strong public support for the concept, Chris Smith granted his approval for the continuation of the publicly-funded online service (BBC, 1999:20, 29).

Funding the BBC

All governments have to grapple with the difficult issue of funding the BBC: governments never relish the prospect of increasing the user licence fee that is levied on all TV households in the country. In December 1998, DCMS Secretary Chris Smith confirmed that the Government would continue to adhere to the five-year formula introduced by the Conservatives in April 1997. Although this involved initial inflation-plus increases in order to help fund the BBC's new digital services, licence fee increases for the five-year period as a whole would be set just below inflation as measured by the retail price index (DCMS, 1998a). For its part, the BBC has lobbied for a series of inflation-plus increases (Peak and Fisher, 1999:173). The BBC's finances are stretched, notwithstanding the annual £2.1 billion (in 1997–98) that it gains from the licence fee. This figure, which at first sight might appear very large, is actually insufficient given the Corporation's commitment to quality and comprehensive service provision, including digital broadcasting services, and also the inflation in recent years of broadcasting costs. Not least, this is because of the dramatic rise in the cost of strategic programme rights, like those for popular sports fixtures (during the 1990s, the BBC has lost the rights to live premier league football to BSkyB, Formula One motor racing to ITV and, most recently, live Test Match cricket to C4 and BSkyB).

Consequently, Smith established a special committee to investigate supplementary ways of funding the BBC in addition to its licence fee, which would remain the Corporation's principal source of revenue at least until the year 2006 (when its Royal Charter is due for renewal). The committee was also to review the balance between the Corporation's public service and commercial activities. The committee was chaired by top British economist Gavyn Davies, a former member of the Treasury's independent forecasting panel and a City figure close to New Labour. In 1997, Mr Davies had co-authored a book commissioned by the BBC (Graham and Davis, 1997) in which he argued that new technology actually '*increases*, not *decreases*' the need for well-funded public service broadcasting. The committee duly submitted its report in August 1999. Controversy centred on the proposition that the best way to improve funding for the BBC should be to levy over the period of the development of the new technology a higher licence fee for digital television viewers. The commercial sector was united in its opposition to this recommendation, arguing that it would slow down consumer up-take of the new technology (digital satellite and digital terrestrial platforms were launched in 1998, digital cable was due to follow in 1999/2000). The report also invited controversy by suggesting that the BBC should sell up to 49 per cent of BBC Worldwide and the bulk of BBC Resources Ltd. Moreover, it should submit its accounts to the scrutiny of the National Audit Office. On receiving the report, DCMS Secretary Chris Smith immediately launched a public consultation on the future funding of the BBC, and the committee's proposals, lasting until 1 November.

Digital broadcasting

The second policy 'front' mentioned in the Government's first annual report was digital TV. Smith has identified the move to digital as one of New Labour's most important media policy goals. In fact, the New Labour Government has largely inherited its predecessor's policy for digital broadcasting. The Conservatives had been keen to promote digital broadcasting and their Broadcasting Act 1996 had introduced a regulatory regime for digital terrestrial broadcasting. However, New Labour finds itself faced with an arguably trickier problem than establishing a regulatory framework for digital broadcasting, namely: How to kick-start the digital market? How to persuade consumers of the attraction of yet more channels, when multi-channel TV is already provided by analogue satellite (BSkyB) and cable TV systems? In May 1998, the Culture, Media and Sport Committee, chaired by Gerald Kaufmann, who has been notably impressed by the communications 'revolution', challenged the Government to announce a planned switch-off of analogue television by 2010 by which deadline all broadcasting should be digital. The analogue frequencies could then be sold for other purposes such as mobile telephony. However, critics pointed out that there is no need to determine a date for a future switch-off of the analogue system, which could in theory continue to co-exist with digital as long as consumers wanted it to. A planned switch-off is clearly in the interest of an influential digital lobby of manufacturers, investors and retailers who see such a policy as a means to drive the digital market (Elstein, 1998:9).

Inheriting this thorny issue, and under pressure from powerful players in the media industry, Smith commissioned a report, by the National Economic Research Associates consultants, to explore the issue. Their report (DCMS, 1998b), published in February 1998, concluded that the shut-down of analogue TV transmissions appeared to be feasible within a 10–15 year time frame, that is between 2008 and 2013. The Government now faces a pressing dilemma. If it announces too early a date for an analogue switch-off, it risks being discredited and the announcement being ignored by consumers, since it has made clear that it will not switch off analogue until as many homes as now receive analogue signals (over 99 per cent) are equipped to receive digital. However, if the Government fudges the issue or announces too open a date then it would be unlikely to have any effect on consumer behaviour, and this would certainly harm the industrial and commercial prospects for digital broadcasting. Characteristically, Smith's response to the Commons Culture, Media and Sport committee was to refuse 'to rush prematurely into an announcement of a date which cannot be met' (Elstein, 1998:9).

Despite such difficulties and dilemmas, the Government's commitment to the fastest practical introduction of the new technologies – and moving Britain into the 'Information Age' – was illustrated by the joint publication by the Department of Trade and Industry (DTI) and the DCMS of *Broadband Britain: A Fresh Look at the Broadcast Entertainment Restrictions* (DTI/DCMS, 1998a). This announced that, in fulfilment of its manifesto commitments, the Government would progressively lift the restrictions that the Conservatives had placed on British Telecom (BT) and other Public Telecommunications Operators (PTOs) from conveying and providing entertainment services to residential customers. The purpose of these restrictions – which the Conservatives themselves had intended to review in 2002 – had been to promote investment in the then infant UK cable sector and give it a chance to compete against the power of established national players like BT. The cable sector having successfully taken off, these restrictions were now felt to be becoming an increasingly unnecessary constraint on BT's and other telecommunications companies' investment in developing the country's broadband capability, the much vaunted 'information superhighway'. According to *Broadband Britain*, PTOs and other operators should immediately have the possibility of providing entertainment to the 17 per cent of British homes outside cable franchise areas, and they should be allowed to compete throughout the whole country from 1 January 2001. According to Smith, the timetable would give cable operators adequate time to convert to digital and continue their network build before they face open competition, whilst encouraging PTOs to provide entertainment services to those parts of the UK currently under-served by the cable industry (DTI, 1998). A Statutory Instrument to make the changes necessary under the Broadcasting Act was duly approved by Parliament on 11 January 1999, this being the only change to broadcasting legislation required to implement *Broadband Britain* (DTI/DCMS, 1999:3.59).

The future of broadcasting: a New Labour Broadcasting Act?

The New Labour Government has been in no great hurry to produce a Broadcasting Act of its own. It has produced a Green Paper: *Regulating Communications: Approaching Convergence in the Information Age* (DTI/DCMS, 1998b). This document, significantly published jointly by the DTI and the DCMS, 'sets out the Government's preliminary views and reasoning on the likely implications of digital convergence for the legal and regulatory frameworks covering broadcasting and telecommunications'. The DTI/DCMS Green Paper came some eight months after the publication of the European Commission's (EC's) Green Paper on convergence. The Commission's paper had caused considerable controversy because it appeared to suggest that broadcasting might soon be subsumed into telecommunications, and could therefore be regulated with a lighter touch, mainly along economic lines (EC, 1997). The New Labour Government's response – co-authored by the DTI and DCMS – to the EC's Green Paper had welcomed the stimulus to debate it provided, but underlined the member-states' competence for media regulation, and recommended an 'evolutionary, rather than revolutionary' approach for the UK (DTI/DCMS, 1998c).

According to the DTI/DCMS (1998b), the public policy objectives that underpin regulation combined serving the consumer interest and supporting universal access with securing effective competition and industry competitiveness. The Government seeks to promote quality, plurality, diversity and choice, while at the same time encouraging investment in services and infrastructure and providing efficient management of scarce resources such as the radio spectrum. The Green Paper might best be summarised as recommending incremental adjustment. It does, though, invite comment on a number of possible eventual regulatory models:

- 'separate regulators for infrastructure and for content-providing industry;
- separate regulators for economic and competition issues on the one hand and for cultural and content issues on the other;
- either of these or other possible models, subject to a co-ordinating body spanning both areas of regulation (including perhaps a wider range of content/cultural regulatory bodies) to ensure coherence and consistency;
- a single, fully integrated regulator whose internal organisation might be split along the lines suggested in the first two points' (DTI/DCMS, 1998b:6).

The Government itself believes the current regulatory framework – with special regulators for broadcasting – to have 'sufficient flexibility to meet our aims for some time to come', although it keeps an open mind about the need for reform at some future stage. At the same time, the DTI/DCMS Green Paper announced that the existing principal regulators – the Office of Fair trading (OFT), Office of Telecommunications (OFTEL) and the Independent Television Commission (ITC) – would in future co-operate more closely and produce greater regulatory consistency on overlapping areas.

As for the place of public broadcasting in the age of digital convergence, the Green Paper stated very clearly:

> Public service broadcasting will remain important as a benchmark of quality and as a guarantee of plurality, diversity and impartiality across the whole range of programming. There can be no certainty that the market will provide the necessary incentives to meet consumer expectations in these respects, and there will be a continuing need to ensure that they are secured through other means. (DTI/DCMS, 1998b:4)

In June 1999, reporting the results of its consultation on the convergence Green Paper (DTI/DCMS, 1999), the Government confirmed that it would 'continue with the evolutionary approach to adapting communications regulation set out in the Green Paper'. It noted that this had attracted general support whereas 'there was no clear consensus for a particular regulatory structure in the longer term'.

During its presidency of the European Union, the Government staged a major European conference on broadcasting policy. The European Audiovisual Conference, held in Birmingham over three days in early April 1998, was attended by around four hundred of the most senior figures in the European media policy community. Entitled 'Challenges and Opportunities of the Digital Age', the conference focused mainly on the digital convergence of the media and telecommunications sectors and the attendant regulatory issues, including the future of public service broadcasting. Significantly, in his concluding speech, Chris Smith underlined his belief that in the digital era there remained 'a continuing major role for public service provision' and that the 'market, left to itself, simply will not deliver social policy, competition, or cultural policy aims' (EC, 1998:77).

Media ownership rules and competition policy

The liberalisation of media ownership rules

Notably absent from New Labour's 1997 manifesto had been any mention of media ownership. This was indicative of just how far New Labour had moved from old Labour. For years in opposition, there had been rumblings within the Labour Party about the need for stricter press ownership rules, notably to combat the power of the media mogul Rupert Murdoch. Even the final report of Labour's Policy Review for the 1990s had noted how 'a few proprietors now control the newspaper industry' and signalled the intention 'to refer newspaper ownership . . . to [a] strengthened Monopolies and Mergers Commission' (Labour Party, 1989:60). But that was in the days before New Labour, and before New Labour's positive new relationship with Murdoch. In 1995, Labour MP Chris Mullin introduced a Media (Diversity) Bill that aimed to prevent a single media proprietor – like Rupert Murdoch – from owning more than one national newspaper. It would also have prevented newspaper owners from owning more than 20 per cent in any TV company. However, Mullin's Bill was not supported by the New Labour leadership, and it did not succeed (Leys, 1998:16).

Meanwhile, through a series of steps culminating in the Broadcasting Act 1996, the Conservatives incrementally relaxed the UK's media ownership rules, including cross-media restrictions, in order to permit British media companies to expand, to become internationally competitive, and to invest in the new technologies, notably digital broadcasting (Gibbons, 1998). In fact, though, in opposition New Labour's stance on media ownership had actually

---

Box 16.2   *New Labour's manifesto commitment on competition policy*

'As an early priority we will reform Britain's competition law. We will adopt a tough "prohibitive" approach to deter anti-competitive practices and abuses of market power.'

Source: Labour Party, 1997.

---

been more liberal than that of the Conservatives. Despite generally loosening cross-media rules, the Conservatives were still seeking to preclude newspaper companies enjoying a national market share of 20 per cent or more from expanding into terrestrial (though not cable, satellite, or digital) broadcasting. This limitation would affect both Rupert Murdoch's News International and Mirror Group Newspapers. In an amendment to the Bill, however, the New Labour shadow front bench actually proposed scrapping the 20 per cent limit, arguing that any percentage limit was arbitrary and that decisions on takeovers could be safely left to the competition authorities (Gopsill, 1996:1–3).

At the time, the obvious explanation was that New Labour was keen to support the Labour-leaning Mirror Group as well as pursue a policy of appeasing Murdoch. However, it could also be explained by New Labour's conversion to the cause of business. Lewis Moonie MP, then a front bench National Heritage spokesman, explained his preference for 'complete deregulation and allowing the Office of Fair Trading and the Monopolies and Mergers Commission to sort things out'. For Moonie, cross-media ownership was a good thing: 'The whole point [was] to ensure the creation of bigger companies that could compete abroad' (Foot, 1996). New Labour's stance provoked a back-bench revolt, led by Chris Mullin, who tabled a rebel amendment advocating a 10 per cent threshold for cross-media restrictions. Predictably, both – the New Labour front bench's and Chris Mullin's – amendments to the Conservatives' Broadcasting Act 1996 were defeated, the former by 302 to 232, the latter by 73 to 303 with most Labour MPs abstaining (Gopsill, 1996:1–3).

Newspaper price wars and competition in the newspaper sector

Upon coming to power, New Labour has honoured its commitment to tightening up competition policy (see Box 16.2), but it has failed to satisfy everyone that it will bite in the media field. A controversy soon blew up over the New Labour Government's Competition Bill. There had been fairly widespread concern for some time that the News International-owned *Times'* alleged 'price war' against competitors was causing serious damage to the *Independent.* The non-Murdoch press – notably the *Independent, Telegraph* and *Guardian* newspapers – was pressuring for action to prevent 'predatory pricing', that is selling newspapers below cost price.

While the Government's Competition Bill did align UK competition rules with Articles 85 and 86 of the European Union Treaty by prohibiting the abuse of dominant position in a market, numerous critics felt that the Government had failed to cater adequately to the character of the media sector where pluralism and diversity had a special value and where normal definitions of market dominance should be supplemented by special restrictions. Therefore, in February 1998 a cross-party group of peers – among them Gordon Borrie, a former Director-General of Fair Trading and an adviser to Labour on media policy – introduced an amendment to the Competition Bill with a view to strengthening its predatory pricing provisions with respect to the newspaper industry. The OFT had examined the issues in 1993, 1994 and 1996 under existing competition laws and had not found grounds to act against News International's pricing policies. Hence, in the view of supporters of the Lords amendment and MPs like Chris Mullin (see below), there was a need for stricter rules against predatory behaviour in the newspaper industry.

However, the New Labour Government opposed the amendment, arguing that it was both unworkable and unnecessary. New Labour peers were instructed to vote against it. During the debate, the Government was more or less directly accused of kow-towing to Murdoch, while Competition Minister Lord Simon argued that there was no case for using the Bill to target an individual company or sector of the market. The *Guardian* editorialised ironically thus: 'Labour is imposing a three-line whip against the amendments even though they simply reflect what Labour was saying [about predatory pricing] before the election. The suspicion is that Mr. Blair is diluting his former intentions in order to keep Mr. Murdoch's papers including the Sun on Labour's side. There could be few more monstrous claims' (*Guardian*, 9 February 1998, p. 14).

To the Government's annoyance, the vote on 9 February went in favour of the amendment: 121 (of whom 26 were crossbenchers) to 93. Twenty-three Labour peers rebelled against the Government line by voting for the amendment, including Lord Hattersley, the recently appointed Labour peer Lord David Puttnam (the eminent film producer and founder member of the CITF) and, of course, the aforementioned Lord Borrie. Others abstained. Only 81 Labour peers voted for the Government. Thirty Conservative peers defied their party line, which had been to abstain, by voting for the amendment. The Liberal Democrat peers, 42 in all, their largest recorded vote in the Lords, all voted in favour of the amendment. The Competition Bill duly returned to the Commons, where the Government with its huge majority could be confident of overturning the amendment.

At committee stage, the controversial Lords amendment was duly removed from the Bill. Nonetheless, some influential Labour MPs were still prepared to defy the Government line when the Bill was debated at its Commons report stage. Giles Radice, chair of the Treasury Committee (and staunchly New Labour), tabled an amendment seeking a more rigorous definition in the legislation of the market dominance that would trigger concern about anti-competitive behaviour, but not going so far as to single out the newspaper sector for special treatment. Chris Mullin, chair of the home affairs select committee, also tabled an amendment that effectively reinserted the substance of the original Lords amendment. Mullin's amendment explicitly singled out anti-competitive behaviour in the newspaper sector and sought to lower the test of dominance to ownership of a 'significant' share of the domestic newspaper market. The debate focused on the alleged 'predatory pricing' of the *Times* (and occasionally the *Sun*), and also on whether or not the amendments were specifically 'anti-Murdoch' (*Hansard*, Vol. 315, No. 202, 8 July 1998:pp. 1136–69). After a vigorous debate, Giles Radice withdrew his amendment. A vote was taken on Chris Mullin's amendment and unsurprisingly it was defeated: 68 MPs voting for it; 301 voting against it. Bar 23 independent spirits, New Labour voted en masse against it (Giles Radice among them). Finally, as the Bill completed its passage through Parliament in October 1998 the Government defeated by 116 to 87 a last attempt in the Lords, led by Liberal Democrat Lord McNally, the peer who had tabled the original Lords amendment, to give the authorities tougher powers to act against anti-competitive behaviour in the newspaper sector (*Lords Hansard*, 20 October 1998: col 1345–69).

Competition issues in the media field

Notwithstanding the Competition Bill controversy over the predatory pricing amendments, New Labour policy against media concentration has clearly been predicated on a tougher application of competition policy. Along with the need for internationally competitive media companies, this had been the principal justification for New Labour's support for relaxing media-specific concentration controls. There are indeed indications of increasingly active competition policy in the media field:

- In September, BSkyB, controlled by Rupert Murdoch's News International, made a controversial takeover bid for Manchester United. Critics argued that the bid raised the question of fair competition between football broadcasters. In October, on the recommendation of the OFT, the then DTI Secretary Peter Mandelson referred the £623 takeover bid to the Monopolies and Mergers Commission (MMC). Following the latter's recommendations, in April 1999 the new DTI Secretary Stephen Byers blocked the takeover bid on competition grounds. The takeover, it was argued, would give BSkyB an unfair advantage over other broadcasters in negotiations over premiership football programme rights. The MMC also took the view that the takeover would reinforce the growing inequalities between Britain's football clubs. The DCMS had made clear its reservations about the takeover bid in its submission to the MMC. Following his Manchester United ruling, Stephen Byers declared that he would refer a bid proposed in December 1998 by NTL, one of the UK's largest cable television operators, to take control of Newcastle United to the independent Competition

Commission, the MMC's successor, whereupon NTL promptly dropped its £160 million takeover plan.

- In January 1999, the OFT took an action to the Restrictive Practices Court against the Premier League of Britain's top football clubs. At issue was whether the League should be able to negotiate on behalf of all of its 20 member clubs collective agreements, such as the current £743 million deal awarding exclusive live broadcasting rights to BSkyB and highlights to the BBC until the year 2001. The OFT considered the deal to be anti-competitive and would have liked to see the football rights market opened up. However, in July 1999 the Court ruled that the Premier League's exclusive deal with BSkyB was nonetheless in the wider public interest. The current system assured the Premier League clubs a level of income that allowed them to improve the quality of their stadia and their playing squads. The system allowed the Premier League to achieve an equitable division of television revenue between its member clubs. The Court also argued that competition between broadcasters was partly dependent upon them being granted exclusive rights.

- In 1998, the OFT embarked upon a fourth inquiry into alleged predatory pricing by News International following complaints from the *Independent*, the *Daily Telegraph* and the *Guardian* against *The Times*. So far three such inquiries had all found in favour of News International (see above). In May 1999, however, John Bridgeman, Director-General of Fair Trading, declared that *The Times* had deliberately made loss-making price cuts which had affected competition in the daily newspaper market between June 1996 and January 1998 when the Monday edition was sold for 10p, but that News International had agreed to provide a detailed business justification for any future price cuts (OFT, 1999).

Privacy and the press

The circumstances leading up to and surrounding Princess Diana's death in August 1997 triggered a renewal of a controversy that had dogged the Conservatives. Tabloid excesses during the 1980s had led the Conservatives to instigate the Calcutt inquiry that produced its first report in 1990, recommending the establishment of the Press Complaints Commission (PCC), a self-regulatory body of the press industry. At the time, this measure was presented as a last chance for the tabloid press to mend its ways. However, when a second Calcutt report in 1993 criticised the PCC for being 'over-favourable to the industry' and recommended the introduction of a statutory regime for press privacy, the Conservatives balked at taking any such action (Humphreys, 1996:58–61). Princess Diana's death led to renewed calls for privacy legislation, but most newspapers expressed strong objections to such a measure on the grounds that it would interfere with press freedom. Instead, newspaper editors voluntarily tightened up the PCC's code of conduct, taking effect on 1

January 1998 (Peak and Fisher, 1999:286–7).

The New Labour Government welcomed the new code. Like the Conservatives, New Labour favoured self-regulation to enactment of a privacy law. At the same time, the Government was committed to, and in the process of, enacting two European-based laws, both of which had implications for privacy: namely, the incorporation of the European Convention of Human Rights (ECHR) into UK law through its Human Rights Bill, and its Data Protection Bill. In the face of demands for privacy legislation, the Government argued that, following incorporation of the ECHR into UK law, privacy could be adequately protected through the courts. When the Human Rights Bill commenced its Parliamentary process in November 1997, much of the media launched a campaign against this 'back door privacy law'. The problem was that Article 8 of the ECHR, protecting privacy, was in tension with Article 10, which safeguarded free speech (Peak and Fisher, 1999:286).

In February, the controversy heightened over statements made by New Labour's Lord Chancellor, Lord Irvine, interviewed in the *New Statesman*, apparently in support of privacy provisions that would compel newspapers to prove a public interest before publishing stories such as that concerning the private life of Foreign Minister Robin Cook. Downing Street quickly distanced itself from Lord Irvine's position, insisting that no New Labour privacy law, by the front or back door, was in prospect and that the matter would continue to be dealt with through the PCC. As a result, Lord Irvine immediately toned down his line, merely emphasising the need for the PCC to take a tougher line on privacy. Subsequently, the Human Rights Bill was amended in such a way as to compel judges to pay particular regard to freedom of expression when ruling on privacy cases. Similarly, under pressure from the media industry, the Government included a special exemption for the media in its 1998 Data Protection Bill, which the media industry had equally feared would amount to a 'back door' privacy law. The exemptions protected the media on the grounds of 'the special importance of freedom of expression' and publication 'in the public interest'. Compliance with the PCC code would be a key test. Investigative journalism would be safeguarded (Peak and Fisher, 1999:288).

New Labour policies for the arts and culture

The first year of New Labour in power was a period of considerable disappointment in the arts sector as the Government adhered to its predecessor's spending plans. Representatives of museums, orchestras and theatres across the country – most notably Sir Peter Hall – continued to complain of under-funding and to warn of imminent collapse. One newspaper article even asked: 'What on earth is going on? Is Labour, the historic ally of the arts, turning into their deadliest enemy?'. It pointed out that even during the economic crisis ridden years of the Callaghan Labour Government (1976–79), Arts Council funding had increased by 20 per cent. Now the Government's support for the Arts Council

---

Box 16.3   *New Labour's manifesto statement on the arts and culture*

'The arts, culture and sport are central to the task of recreating the sense of community, identity and civic pride that should define our country. Yet we consistently undervalue the role of the arts and culture in helping to create a civic society – from amateur theatre to our art galleries. Art, sport and leisure are vital to our quality of life and the renewal of our economy. They are significant earners for Britain. They employ hundreds of thousands of people.'

Source: Labour Party, 1997.

---

for the year 1998–99 was £184 million, one million less than during the year 1992–93. In real terms, a significant cut in spending had occurred over the intervening years and New Labour had not even made a start to remedy it. DCMS Minister Chris Smith's line appeared to be 'Just be patient. Have faith' (Billington, 1998). Criticising the fact that the Arts Council's 1998–99 allocation actually marked a cut of just under 1 per cent on the previous year, its departing Conservative chairman Lord Gowrie reportedly accused New Labour's arts funding of being 'niggardly and atavistic' (Glaister, 1998). Sir Peter Hall observed that the New Labour Government 'managed to find £750m for the [millennium] Dome, yet the Greenwich Theatre closed for want of £150,000' (O'Sullivan, 1998).

Boosting funding, gaining value for money, widening access

The mood in the arts world generally improved suddenly when in July 1998, following Chancellor Gordon Brown's Comprehensive Spending Review (CSR), Smith was able to announce £125 million in extra arts funding for the three years 1999–2002 (DCMS, 1998c). Nonetheless, before very long Peter Hall had announced the formation of an informal body of critics of New Labour arts, the 'Shadow Arts Council'. When the Arts Council revealed its new grant allocations, it was now criticised for failing to match New Labour's radical rhetoric about increasing access to the arts with practice. It was accused of over-concentrating resources on big companies, while keeping around half of small and medium-sized companies on standstill funding (Glaister, 1999). On the other hand, Melvin Bragg, a long-time member of the National Campaign for the Arts, challenged New Labour's critics for failing to recognise its achievements 'under an enthusiastic and dogged Chris Smith . . . [T]he first shoots of success should be . . . acknowledged' (Bragg, 1999).

Altogether, the CSR increased funding for the DCMS by a total of £290 million for the three years 1999–2002 (DCMS, 1998c), but it came with strings attached. Like other departments, the DCMS will be required to produce Public

---

Box 16.4   *The QUEST brief*

'QUEST will identify, evaluate and promote good practice in delivering results, and will provide independent advice to the Secretary of State on the performance of sponsored bodies in meeting our objectives.'

Source: DCMS, 1999a:18.

Service Agreements (PSAs) showing how its spending will meet Government objectives such as promoting quality and widening access to culture with increased efficiency and effectiveness. Similarly, the DCMS will produce Funding Agreements with sponsored bodies. In December 1998, Smith duly announced the establishment by the DCMS of a new standards and efficiency body called the Quality, Efficiency and Standards Team (QUEST). This will be a small 'core team' of civil servants supported by experts from the DCMS sponsored bodies, the wider field of culture, local Government and the private sector (DCMS, 1999a:18). QUEST will provide performance indicators for all the bodies funded by the DCMS and is explicitly 'designed to help DCMS and its partners to get the best return in outcomes on the ground for the public money invested' (DCMS, 1999a:8).

In addition, in its 1999 annual report, the DCMS announced its intention to rationalise a number of its structures. This would include the creation of a single body – British Film – to replace the various overlapping bodies hitherto involved in film finance. British Film would 'help channel Lottery funds more effectively into all parts of the film-making process and . . . co-ordinate Government support for film'. Overall, British Film is expected 'to deliver a coherent strategy for the development of film culture and the film industry' (DCMS, 1999a:11, 19). In May 1999, Smith announced that over the next three years the new body, now called the Film Council, would be legally designated a Lottery distributor in October 1999 and become fully operational from April 2000. Over the next three years, it was expected to channel at least £145 million of public and lottery money into film (DCMS, 1999d). To help boost film finance further, New Labour has established a Film Finance Forum, as a 'conduit between the film industry and City financial institutions' (DCMS, 1999a:55). Furthermore, Gordon Brown announced in his first budget a 100 per cent tax write-off for three years for British films up to £15 million. He subsequently extended the scheme by two years (*Guardian*, 24 July 1998, p. 6).

The Arts Council has already seen a big reorganisation under New Labour. Its membership and decision-making structures have been rationalised by its Labour-appointed chairman Gerry Robinson, the chief executive of Granada. Its regional devolution, with Regional Arts Boards gaining extended responsibilities, is also seen as being conducive to New Labour's goal of widening access to the arts. Similarly, a New Audiences Fund for the Arts of up to £5 million, administered by the Arts Council, aims to 'help arts organisations to broaden their audiences; to bring new people to the arts; [and] to encourage young people to widen their experience of the arts'. Moreover, funding has been directed at 'areas of proven cultural and social deprivation'. Over 100 such projects have been supported (DCMS, 1999a:44).

The National Lottery has also been reorganised. In July 1998, the National Lottery Act was enacted. Among other things, including the rather cosmetic replacement of OFLOT with the National Lottery Commission as the new regulator, the Act provided for the establishment of a National Endowment for Science, Technology and the Arts (NESTA), as a new support organisation for British creative enterprise. Smith has since issued new directions to Lottery distributors that will 'change the bias for capital projects towards a greater focus on people and access'. It appears that Lottery arts funding is to be redirected to promote New Labour's goal of making the arts more widely accessible (DCMS, 1999a:70–3). As a result of the CSR, the DCMS was able to specify a 'guaranteed share of Lottery income from 2001 for the arts, sport, heritage and charities worth some £ 200–250 million a year each' (DCMS, 1998c). However, the overall share of the Lottery funds available to the arts will fall because the National Lottery Act 1998 allows Lottery funding to be used to support health, education and the environment (DCMS 1999a: 70–3; for a critical perspective, see Select Committee on Culture, Media and Sport, 1998).

Conclusion

A year into office, Chris Smith was criticised by the House of Commons Select Committee on Culture, Media and Sport for not being strong enough, especially in his dealings with the Treasury (see Box 16.5). Yet, as seen, the DCMS did not fare badly from the CSR. Moreover, it is not easy to be 'tough' with the Treasury, especially if the Department's past spending on the arts has long been associated with cultural elitism. To his credit, Smith has tried to identify the arts with less elitist, more popular, socially inclusive and pluralist purposes. Furthermore, if the department has been under-funded, the fault lies with New Labour's budgetary conservatism rather than Smith.

Another criticism made by the Select Committee on Culture, Media and Sport has been that the DCMS is not suited to responsibility for the media in the multi-media, digital age, and that a new Department of Communication is required, unifying the media interests of the DTI and the DCMS and creating a stronger voice for communications policy within Government (see Box 16.5). In the age of 'convergence' of the communication sectors, there may be something to recommend this kind of radical change. But convergence is a hotly contentious term. It is by no means evident either that it is occurring as fast as some argue, or that it will abolish the special characteristics of different communications sectors. The media will always have a special social and cultural importance. They will always be uniquely significant for democratic pluralism.

Box 16.5   *Criticism of the DCMS by the House of Commons Select Committee on Culture, Media and Sport*

On being tough with the Treasury:
'We note the Department's commitment to enhance its influence within Whitehall and to highlight the economic and cultural importance of the sectors which it sponsors. However, a commitment is not an achievement and unfortunately the Department has not enhanced its influence in the way it says it would like to do. The Secretary of State should now make it his highest priority to advance the Department both within Cabinet and by taking a much tougher attitude in his negotiations with the Treasury . . .'

On the need for a new, separate Department of Communication:
'. . . we are concerned that "creative Britain" provides an inadequate label for what should be the [DCMS'] focus. In our most recent Report we judged that the intertwining of technological and cultural factors in the media and information technology sectors justified the establishment of a separate Department of Communications.'

Source: SCCMS, 1998.

Moreover, what would happen to the arts if media were hived off to another ministry? Would their voice in Government thereby be weakened? Would the interests of public service broadcasting, and the other non-commercial, cultural considerations of media policy, be adequately represented inside a 'high-tech', telecommunications-orientated, industry-centred, Department of Communication? Most Western European countries have a ministry of culture as well as a ministry for telecommunications. Smith has been criticised for his cautious approach to the digital age, but there is a very strong case for adopting an evolutionary, pragmatic approach. Certain interests in the communications industry may want a radical regulatory overhaul – effectively, a further wave of deregulation of broadcasting in the direction of a 'telecommunications model' – but this would be to risk many of the past public service achievements of British media policy. Finally, Smith would seem to be as good a defender of public service broadcasting as could be hoped for. The shortfalls of New Labour media policy – for instance, in the field of inadequate media ownership and competition rules, or the lack of privacy legislation – are squarely to be laid on New Labour rather than on an individual minister's shoulders.

References

Billington, M. (1998), 'Smith's Line Has Always Been One of Jam Tomorrow', *Guardian*, 7 February, p. 5.

Bragg, M. (1999), 'I Love You All – But I Wish You'd Stop Playing the Same Old Whingeing Game', *Guardian*, Arts, 16 February 1999, pp. 8–9.

BBC (1999), *Annual Report and Accounts 98/99*, London, BBC.

Collins, R. and Murroni, C. (1996), *New Media, New Policies*, Cambridge, Polity Press.

DCMS (1998a), 'Television Licence Fee Will Rise According to Five Year Formula', DCMS Press Release 310/98, 15 December.

DCMS (1998b), *Television: The Digital Future. A Consultation Document*, DCMS, May.

DCMS (1998c), 'Chris Smith Details Biggest Ever Increase in Cultural Funding', DCMS Press Release 167/98, 24 July.

DCMS (1999a), *Annual Report 1999*, London, DCMS.

DCMS (1999b), *Building a Global Audience: British Television in Global Markets*, report written by David Graham Associates, London, DCMS.

DCMS (1999c) 'Chris Smith Announces Inquiry Team to Investigate Ways to Boost the Sale of British TV Programmes Overseas', DCMS Press Release 105/99, 26 April.

DCMS (1999d), 'New Film Council on Target to Begin Work in April 2000', DCMS Press Release 139/99, 19 May.

DTI (1998), 'Broadcast Entertainment Restrictions to be Lifted', DTI Press Release 23 April.

DTI/DCMS (1998a), *Broadband Britain: A Fresh Look at the Broadcast Entertainment Restrictions*, DTI/DCMS.

DTI/DCMS (1998b), *Regulating Communications: Approaching Convergence in the Information Age*, DTI/DCMS.

DTI/DCMS (1998c), *UK Government Response to the Commission Green Paper on Convergence*, http://www.ispo.cec.be/convergencegp/ukgov.html.

DTI/DCMS (1999), *Regulating Communications: The Way Ahead. Results of the Consultation on the Convergence Green Paper*, DTI/DCMS.

EC 1997, *Green Paper on the Convergence of the Telecommunications, Media and Information Technology Sectors, and the Implications for Regulation*, Brussels, European Commission, COM(97)623.

EC 1998, *Proceedings of the European Audiovisual Conference*, Brussels.

Elstein, D. (1998), 'Facing the Big Switch-Off', *Media Guardian*, 15 June.

Foot, P. (1996), 'Sour Note, Moonie Tune', *Guardian*, 15 April, pp. 16–17.

Gibbons, T. (1998), 'Aspiring to Pluralism: The Constraints of Public Broadcasting Values on the De-Regulation of British Media Ownership', *Cardozo Arts and Entertainment Law Journal*, 16(2–3):475–500.

Glaister, D. (1998), 'Dome Rises As Axe Falls Again on Arts Cash', *Guardian*, 17 January 1998, p. 3.

Glaister, D. (1999), 'Arts Subsidies: ACE Rhetoric, Pity About the Grants', *Guardian*, 16 February 1999, p. 15.

Gopsill, T. (1996), 'Meanwhile Back on the Benches . . .', *Free Press*, 93, August, pp. 1–3, London, Campaign for Press and Broadcasting Freedom.

Government, The (1998), *The Government's Annual Report 97/98*, Cm 3969, London.

Graham, A. and Davies, G. (1997), *Broadcasting, Society and Policy in the Multimedia Age*, Luton, John Libbey Media/University of Luton Press.

Humphreys, P. (1996), *Mass Media and Media Policy in Western Europe*, Manchester and New York, Manchester University Press.

Labour Party (1989), *Meet the Challenge, Make the Change: A New Agenda for Britain*, London, Labour Party.

Labour Party (1997), *New Labour: Because Britain Deserves Better*, London, Labour Party.

Leys, C. (1998), 'Controlling the Waves', *Red Pepper*, No. 47.

OFT (1999), 'Newspaper Pricing: News International Gives Assurances', OFT Press Release PN 17/99, 21 May.

O'Sullivan, J. (1998), 'Betrayed: the Luvvies Labour's Lost', *Independent*, 23 May 1998, p. 4.

Peak, S. and Fisher, P. (1999), *The Media Guide, A Guardian Book*, London, Fourth Estate.

Select Committee on Culture, Media and Sport (1998), *Culture, Media and Sport – Fifth Report*, London, HC 468–I, 1998–99 Session.

Smith, C. (1998), *Creative Britain*, London, Faber and Faber.

17

European policy: fresh start or false dawn?

Simon Bulmer

Introduction

The election of the Blair Government in May 1997 presented two challenges to Labour. The first was to show how far the party had travelled since its internal divisions over European policy when last in power in the 1970s and the bloodletting that ensued in the early 1980s when in opposition. Was its pro-Europeanism merely tactical: designed to highlight the Conservative Government's internal divisions? The second challenge was to demonstrate an ability to carry out a competent and constructive policy within the European Union (EU) in line with its manifesto commitment (see Box 17.1). Was Tony Blair simply 'John Major with a smile', as some perceived him on the continent? Or did the new Government herald a fresh start in Britain's European diplomacy?

This chapter is organised into five parts:

- An examination of how Labour's policy had been transformed by the mid-1990s
- An assessment of the challenge for the new Government in reconstructing relations with EU partners
- An exploration of the manifesto commitments
- A detailed review of Labour's policy in power, including during the UK presidency of the EU in 1998, and
- An evaluation of achievements and prospects for the future.

The transformation of Labour's European policy

The Labour Party's policy on integration has been far from consistent (Newman, 1983; George and Haythorne, 1996). Under Harold Wilson, Labour had applied for membership of the European Communities (EC) in 1966. But by the time of the 1983 general election, ten years after Britain's accession to the EC, the party's policy had shifted to a commitment to withdrawal. This

---

Box 17.1   *New Labour's manifesto commitments on Europe*

- to hold a referendum on participation in the single currency; and
- to lead reform of the EU.

Source: Labour Party, 1997.

---

policy had already been a major contributory factor to the creation of the Social Democratic Party (SDP) (see Appendix 1 for a review of manifesto commitments since 1979).

The party's return to a policy of support for European integration took place gradually under the leadership of Neil Kinnock. Among the reasons were:

- the electoral challenge of the SDP/Liberal Alliance;
- the trade unions' conversion to support for integration;
- the failure of the French Socialists under Mitterrand to achieve socialist reflation in one country and the consequent growth of support for a positive international strategy for achieving the economic objectives of the Labour Party;
- and a shift to pro-Europeanism on the part of some key figures, such as Kinnock, and the move of some pro-Europeans, such as John Smith and then Tony Blair, into more prominent party posts.

But was this conversion genuine?

One way of addressing this question is through analysing the views of Labour parliamentarians. Baker and Seawright (1998a) undertook a survey in 1996 of Labour MPs and MEPs, providing important findings on the extent of conversion. Their findings show a party that is supportive of integration and the pursuit of a range of policies by means of a European strategy. The findings contrast strongly with those from a similar survey of Conservative MPs and MEPs, which revealed a greater preponderance of Euro-scepticism amongst the former alongside strong divisions between Europhiles and sceptics on key policy issues (Ludlam, 1998). The Labour survey showed that MPs elected from the 1987 general election onwards were more pro-European than those in earlier cohorts were. Nevertheless, divisions remained at Westminster, especially over the question of sovereignty and monetary union, but there was a strong consensus on supporting the social dimension of the EU. Of course, the survey took place before the May 1997 election, so the picture will doubtless have changed with the turnover of personnel and an influx of newly elected MPs. Labour MEPs, the largest contingent within the Socialist Party Group in the European Parliament (EP) 1994–99, had cultivated strong contacts with their counterparts in other member-states.

A second way of examining whether the conversion was genuine is to examine the positions on integration taken by the party leadership and those close to it. Tony Blair himself had promoted a pro-European policy as leader of the opposition. In a speech at Chatham House in April 1995, he argued that Britain's global influence was dependent in turn on influence in the EU (Blair, 1995). A positive tone was set, but there was little policy detail beyond a commitment to strengthening a 'people's Europe'. The details began to emerge over the subsequent period, for example in proposals for EU institutional reform. A further distinctive feature of New Labour's European policy that had already emerged in 1996, was a strong business orientation. Labour's Business Agenda for Europe was released in May 1996 and placed completion of the single European market as the first goal, with participation in the Social Chapter the fifth (of six) goals. A final indication of Blair's European policy is set out in Peter Mandelson and Roger Liddle's influential book, *The Blair Revolution* (1996:157–82). It contains a full chapter on European policy and puts forward a positive agenda based on three principles: eastern enlargement to strengthen European security, democracy and socio-economic progress; deeper co-operation and the pooling of sovereignty where advantages do not threaten national identity; and strengthening the EU's legitimacy.

By the time of his election in May 1997, Tony Blair had become accustomed to meeting fellow leaders of EU socialist parties (in the Party of European Socialists) ahead of European summit meetings (the European Council). Indeed, also taking into account contacts through the European Parliament, the party was better connected with fellow democratic socialists and much more Europeanised in its approach than ever before.

Reconstructing Britain's credibility in the EU

The second challenge for the incoming Government concerned the rebuilding of relations with EU partners. The Major Governments had secured some successes in pursuing Conservative policy in the EU (Teasdale, 1998). However, such successes as the opt-outs from the Social Chapter and monetary union, or securing assurances on subsidiarity, were largely achieved through obstructing integration. In supporting the 1995 EU enlargement (to include Austria, Finland and Sweden), the strengthening of the single market and a relatively liberal world trade agreement, the Conservative Government secured more constructive European policy achievements. But by the last months of his premiership the Major Government's European policy had alienated many of its partners. The principal causes were the obstructionist approach adopted in negotiations for a successor to the Maastricht Treaty and the breakdown of relations over the handling of the BSE crisis. However, there had already been criticism of the handling of the British presidency of the EU in 1992. The problem of finding continued membership of the Exchange Rate Mechanism (ERM) unsustainable in the markets, had culminated in 'Black Wednesday' in September 1992. The latter, of course, proved to be a decisive moment in the British electorate's loss of trust in the Conservatives.

These developments had caused a serious deterioration of relations with EU partners. The German Chancellor, Helmut Kohl, warned of European integration being obstructed by 'the slowest ship in the convoy'. The notion of differentiated integration – whereby some member-governments could opt for more rapid European integration – became a Franco-German priority in part as a response to British obstructionism. In the latter weeks of the Major Government, the EU's Intergovernmental Conference (IGC) on treaty reform virtually ceased work in the hope that a more constructive government would be elected. Against this background it was little wonder that Labour's victory was greeted with acclaim on the continent.

Manifesto commitments

What was the electoral platform of 'New Labour'? The two specific manifesto commitments were, as noted in Box 17.1, to hold a referendum on participation in the single currency; and to lead reform of the EU.

The broad context for Labour's European policy stance was twofold. First, it supported a vision of 'Europe [as] an alliance of independent nations choosing to co-operate to achieve the goals they cannot achieve alone'. A 'European federal superstate' was opposed. In this respect, the language of Labour's European policy was little different from that of the Conservative Government, whose 1996 White Paper on the IGC stated, 'the success of the European Union . . . can be achieved if the EU develops as a Union of nations' (Foreign and Commonwealth Office, 1996:4). Secondly, the manifesto saw three options for Britain in the EU: withdrawal; staying in but on the sidelines; and staying in but playing a leading role. The argument was that the first position would be disastrous for jobs, inward investment and international influence, while the second position represented Britain's existing role in the EU: marginalised by the BSE crisis and obstructionism in the IGC negotiations. Hence the manifesto commitment to play a leading role in EU reform. Substantively, this did not represent much of a change of policy from Conservative *aspirations*.

To flesh out the commitment to play a leading role, including during the UK presidency in the first half of 1998, the manifesto specified a number of areas for attention (see Box 17.2). Of these specific objectives, the last represented a clear contrast with Conservative policy; objectives 1 and 3 represented no change; whilst 2, 4 and 5 represented changes in the detail. Specifically, the detailed changes were: the commitment to, and nature of, institutional reform as part of eastern enlargement under 2; possible differences in understanding 'openness and democracy' as well as the commitment to proportional representation (PR) under 4; and a more positive commitment towards extending qualified majority voting (QMV) under 5.

Policy on the single currency was tactically designed for the election. The commitment to a referendum aimed to exploit the serious divisions within the Conservatives. John Major's Government was seeking to keep options open on

---

Box 17.2 *New Labour's policy on Europe: areas for action*

1 Rapid completion of the single market and enforcement of its rules as a means of strengthening European competitiveness and the opportunities for British firms
2 A high priority for enlargement of the EU to central and eastern European countries and Cyprus, with accompanying institutional reforms to facilitate a functioning, enlarged Union
3 Reform of the Common Agricultural Policy (CAP) and of the Common Fisheries Policy
4 Greater openness and democracy in EU institutions and support for a PR system in elections to the EP;
5 Retention of the veto on matters of national interest, e.g. taxation, defence, immigration, budgetary and treaty changes but extension of QMV in 'limited areas where that is in Britain's interests';
6 Signing up to the Social Chapter which should become a means of promoting employability and flexibility rather than high social costs.

Source: Labour Party, 1997.

---

membership of the single currency as a way of holding his party together. For Labour, there was a recognition that to rule out membership of a successful monetary union would be to put Britain on the sidelines of the EU's major policy initiative. However, for Labour to join the single currency, there would have to be 'genuine convergence among the economies that take part' and agreement in the Cabinet, in Parliament and, finally, in a referendum.

Labour in power

New Labour came to power with a Cabinet that featured committed pro-Europeans in key positions of government: the Prime Minister himself, Chancellor Gordon Brown and the Minister Without Portfolio, Peter Mandelson. The Deputy Prime Minister, John Prescott, and the Foreign Secretary, Robin Cook, were converted Europhiles. However, Jack Straw, the Home Secretary, and David Blunkett, the Secretary of State for Education and Employment, were the most Euro-sceptic of the key players in the Cabinet (see profiles in Anderson and Mann, 1997). The most unconventional appointment relevant to EU policy was that of Sir David Simon, the former chairman of British Petroleum, to the post of Minister for Competitiveness in Europe, located in the Department of Trade and Industry (DTI) but with a base also in the Treasury.

Behind the personalities there was little change to the formal machinery of government for the handling of European policy (Bulmer and Burch, 1998).

However, the Cabinet Office European Secretariat was able to play a more pro-active role in the benign policy climate of the new Government. Furthermore, the role of the Prime Minister's Policy Unit has been strengthened, where European policy is the responsibility of Roger Liddle.

The Amsterdam Treaty

The IGC on treaty reform had occupied the Labour Party in two ways prior to entering government. First, it needed to have a policy on the IGC in order to par-ticipate in Parliamentary debate. Secondly, as an anticipated election victory approached, the Party needed to assess the prospects for negotiating the policy with other member-governments, since reforms require unanimous agree-ment.

In respect of the first goal, Tony Blair set up a small working party to develop a party position (Labour Party, 1995). Thinking on the IGC emerged during 1996, with the broad thrust of the details being towards the eventual manifesto contents. Already at the end of 1996 Robin Cook had appointed Sir Michael Butler, a former British Permanent Representative to the EU, to tour member-state capitals and establish how Labour's plans fitted with those of other governments. In addition, in the run-up to the election senior Whitehall officials had been briefing the Labour Shadow Cabinet in keeping with accepted practice, so there was no initial policy vacuum. In the Cabinet Office's European Secretariat, close attention was paid to Labour's position paper on the IGC and to its manifesto commitments, in order to see how they could be translated into negotiating positions in the six weeks before the Amsterdam summit.

From Labour's perspective the outcome of Amsterdam seemed to vindicate its claims that it could achieve more, including defending the national interest, through positive diplomacy. The new approach was evident in the arrange-ments ending the British 'opt-out' through incorporation of the Social Chapter, in supporting an employment chapter in the treaty, in advocating a strength-ening of the European Parliament's powers, in pressing for increased majority voting in the Council on certain policy areas and in support for the strengthen-ing of EU human rights provisions. On all these matters, the previous Conservative Government had been obstructionist. On other matters, Labour more stubbornly defended national interests: on the right to retain border con-trols within the proposed area of freedom justice and security; in resisting the widening of the Court of Justice's powers; in blocking majority voting in the Council on Justice and Home Affairs co-operation and limiting it in the Common Foreign and Security Policy; and in blocking the development of a European defence identity through incorporation of the Western European Union into the EU. In most of these areas where the new British Government demonstrated continuity, it was not isolated. Overall the outcome for Labour's objectives was broadly satisfactory.

Last but not least, with its massive majority the Blair Government was able to secure swift ratification of the Amsterdam Treaty. This contrasted with the trials and tribulations of Major in securing ratification of the Maastricht Treaty.

European Monetary Union (EMU)

A first development relating to EMU had occurred within days of Labour taking office. This was the decision on 6 May 1997 by the Chancellor, Gordon Brown, to give the Bank of England operational responsibility for setting interest rates. Although in essence a domestic decision, it did place the UK on track towards one of the requirements of EMU. The major UK policy decisions on EMU were to follow in the autumn of 1997. On 27 October, Brown announced the Government's policy in the Commons. Although it made no specific commitment to join EMU, it differed from the Conservative Government's policy of keeping options open. Brown made it clear that there was no constitutional objection to membership and that, in principle, 'a successful single currency within a single European market would be of benefit to Europe and to Britain' (Brown, 1997). The key issue of principle for the Government was the national interest, which would be defined by the Treasury's assessment of five economic tests:

- whether there can be sustainable convergence between Britain and the economies of a single currency;
- whether there is sufficient flexibility to cope with economic change;
- the effect on investment;
- the impact on the financial services industry;
- whether it is good for employment.

If all these tests were met satisfactorily, the Government would recommend membership. Gordon Brown made clear that Britain could not meet these criteria by 1999, when the states participating in EMU locked their currencies to form the single currency, the Euro. Moreover, Brown stated that 'barring some fundamental and unforeseen change in economic circumstances, making a decision, during this Parliament, to join is not realistic'. However, the Chancellor made clear that preparations for the single currency were to begin. On the policy level, the Government would seek to meet the five tests, for example through its 'Getting Europe to Work' initiative and pursuing an anti-inflation policy. At the same time, Lord Simon took responsibility for preparing business for the Euro.

The policy was certainly in line with the Labour manifesto. The most crucial of the five tests is that on economic convergence between the UK and the continent, since the cycles have not been synchronised in the past. The other four tests are more difficult to substantiate and thus give the Government more discretion. Two other observations should be made. First, non-participation at the start of the single currency has undoubtedly restricted the Government's ability to play a key role in the EU, thus weakening its efforts in respect of that manifesto goal. Secondly, the Government was slow to take the debate on EMU to the British public. While business needs to be informed about the Euro whether Britain joins or not, the Blair Government has taken a defensive position over a wider campaign ahead of a referendum out of deference to the known opposition of the Murdoch and Black press such as the *Sun* and *Sunday Telegraph*. In February 1999, Tony Blair launched the 'national changeover plan': a programme of how the transition to joining the single currency would come about. And while Blair's language became more positive about the Euro, it was still a rather defensive position.

The presidency

The presidency of the EU covered the first six months of 1998 (also see Henderson, 1998; Ludlow, 1998). As with any country's presidency much of the business is pre-programmed – perhaps 70 per cent of it. The remainder is split between unexpected crises and initiatives on the part of the presidency state. The objectives of the presidency – discussed in advance with the Liberal Democrats in the Cabinet Joint Consultative Committee – were stated on several different occasions by different ministers, albeit with some inconsistencies. They can be summarised as aiming to:

- preside over the key decisions to launch the single currency;
- inaugurate the enlargement process and the associated budgetary and policy reforms (known as Agenda 2000);
- pursue an agenda of economic reform emphasising employability, a more effective single market and making Europe more competitive ('the third way');
- strengthen EU activity in combating crime and environmental protection;
- make EU foreign policy more effective;
- continue the process of establishing the UK as an influential and constructive partner in the EU; and
- involve the British people in the presidency.

In evaluating the outcome, it is worth pointing out that Labour had the good fortune of no major crises. This was a striking contrast with the 1992 presidency when John Major had to contend with the European and domestic ramifications of the Danish rejection of the Maastricht Treaty and the ERM crisis. Both were unanticipated events and blew that presidency off course (Ludlow, 1998). Labour's record was, in general, good.

The single currency proved not to be as tricky an issue as anticipated. By the time of the special summit in May 1998, there was little ambiguity about the 11 member-states who both met the criteria for membership and wished to participate. In that respect, the launch was smooth. It was much less so in respect of appointing the President of the European Central Bank. A row blew up on the eve of the summit as to whether the favoured candidate of the Germans, the Dutch central banker Wim Duisenberg, or the French candidate, M. Trichet, should secure the appointment. Tony Blair had to preside over a political 'fix' –

still contested – under which Duisenberg may stand down half way through his term. It was an unedifying episode, which raised questions about an otherwise smooth presidential operation. The other area where the Government was not so successful was in seeking to have a place within the decision-making arena of the Euro-zone. The French Government was opposed, arguing that only the governments of states participating in the single currency should be permitted to attend. Accordingly, the first meeting of the 'Euro-11' took place towards the end of the presidency but with the Austrians chairing the meeting because of Britain's exclusion. This meeting indicated the limit to the Government's credibility in claiming leadership in the EU.

The launching of the enlargement process was also successful. On the associated reforms, the Government sought to establish a deadline of March 1999 for the key decisions. Beyond this, progress was hampered during the presidency, in part because of the German Federal Government's inability to secure a coherent policy ahead of its September 1998 election.

On economic reform the Chancellor had already put forward British proposals at the November 1997 Luxembourg employment summit. The Government was able to accelerate progress on employment action plans, securing some move in EU policy towards its domestic ideas on lifelong learning, benefit changes to encourage people to enter the labour market and so on. Steps were also made towards reform of capital markets, encouragement of entrepreneurship through removing burdens on business and improving transposition rates in the single market. This agenda, largely the responsibility of Lord Simon, also secured successes in bringing British and EU policy closer together. It is also worth mentioning that Tony Blair made two key speeches on 'the third way': to the Dutch Parliament in The Hague and to the *assemblée nationale* in Paris, the latter in French. Although opaque and rhetorical in nature, these speeches did try to engage with mainstream continental approaches to economic management and thus departed from the more strident 'lecturing' of European partners undertaken by Conservative predecessors.

Conservative governments had been very wary of EU powers over Justice and Home Affairs co-operation. Under Labour, a more pragmatic line has been adopted. During the presidency, the Government successfully promoted a more open decision-making approach as well as maintaining the pace of decision-making in a policy area where the UK – both historically and under Tony Blair – has been less than fully committed. Labour's utilitarian approach has entailed co-operating where there are clear benefits, such as on combating crime or fraud, but wishing to retain frontier controls on immigration. On the environment, achievements were also pragmatic and less evident but included agreement on how to implement the Kyoto agreement on greenhouse gases.

Overall, the new Government's performance in the presidency was a creditable one. The broad picture was one of managing the EU well, and of rebuilding a constructive relationship with partner states. Ludlow attributes the positive achievements to 'the overall efficiency of ministers and officials, a modest, but far from useless, record of successes, and, above all, a change in tone' (Ludlow, 1998:574). On the negative side, however, were the rather poorly focused efforts to develop a debate about a 'people's Europe', the inclination for spin-doctors in London to overdo the achievements of the presidency, and the (for fellow governments) tiresome language of Britain 'leading' in Europe. The last of these sat ill at ease with the clear fact that the new Government could not play the central role in the EU that Tony Blair coveted because of non-participation in the central project, namely the Euro.

Beyond the presidency

Before the end of the presidency, Tony Blair had already recognised that the Government had to do more if it were to play a fuller part in the core debates of the EU. A seminar on the 'Future of Europe' was convened at the end of May to try to think creatively about strategic issues, which have been neglected for many years by successive governments owing to domestic political divisions over integration. Subsequently, Robin Cook and the Foreign and Commonwealth Office (FCO) began to reflect on strategic issues, such as reform of the EU's institutions. Two particular areas of emphasis seemed to emerge from Tony Blair's emphasis. One was a realisation, noted also in a think-tank report on British leadership in Europe (Grant,1998), that one area where the UK could justifiably claim a leading role in Europe is in matters of defence. In order to do so, however, a change of policy would be needed. At the October 1998 informal EU summit in Portschach, however, Tony Blair surprised his colleagues precisely with a proposal for stronger European defence identity. Moreover, shortly thereafter, at an Anglo-French summit in St. Malo, the British and French Governments agreed on closer bilateral defence relations. How much Blair's proposals achieve remains to be seen, especially since developments in Kosovo changed the context of the debate.

This Anglo-French development reflected the second area of emphasis arising from Blair's initiatives, namely an evaluation of Britain's key bilateral alliances within the EU and an effort to strengthen them. Much emphasis seemed to be placed on the prospects of an election victory by the German Social Democrat Chancellor-candidate, Gerhard Schröder. In the event Schröder was elected in September 1998 to head a red-Green coalition. Tony Blair's efforts at developing relations with the new government had mixed results, principally because the new German Government comprised conflicting views on European policy. Efforts to develop a close relationship between Schröder's ministerial 'fixer', Bodo Hombach and Trade and Industry Secretary, Peter Mandelson, were affected by the latter's enforced resignation in December 1998. Furthermore, the new SPD Finance Minister, Oskar Lafontaine, prioritised a Keynesian economic policy as a kind of corrective for the counter-inflationary course that the previous predominantly centre-right governments had set for EMU at Maastricht in 1991. This policy placed Lafontaine closer to his French counterparts rather than to Tony Blair's emphasis on the need for more flexible labour markets as the way to create more jobs in the EU. Apart from on matters military, relations between the Jospin Government in France and the Labour Government were characterised by different directions on strategies for the Left and French suspicions about Blair's admiration for the policies of the Democrats in the US.

In March 1998, two developments suggested that this emphasis on alliances might pay dividends. First, the resignation of Lafontaine over policy differences in the German coalition resolved intra-coalition tensions in favour of Schröder, whose policy of the 'new centre' resembles Tony Blair's preference for the 'third way'. It also strengthened an Anglo-Saxon orientation for Schröder's Government. Within days the European Commission had resigned en bloc as a response to a report on mismanagement and fraud. In the ensuing negotiations, Tony Blair was able to mobilise his European contacts and play a key role in advocating the former Italian Prime Minister, Romano Prodi, as Commission president. Prodi also has sympathies with the 'third way'. What was clear from this episode was that Tony Blair cultivated key bilateral contacts with his counterparts: something he has encouraged his ministers also to do.

Finally, Tony Blair had to secure a satisfactory settlement for the UK in the Agenda 2000 reform package designed to get the EU ready for eastward enlargement. At the Berlin summit in March 1999, the EU agreed to a more modest set of reforms than originally expected. From the UK's perspective reform of the CAP did not go far enough but the core of the British budget rebate was defended.

European policy in context

In many areas of economic policy there has been an attempt to ensure that European policy reflects domestic priorities. In foreign policy, too, Robin Cook had to try to get EU support for his ethical foreign policy, for example (see Chapter 20). This survey of European policy cannot address all the interconnections with other policies. However, there is one key area of the wider Blair 'project' that warrants brief attention because of its strong European dimension: constitutional reform. The introduction of PR for the June 1999 European elections honoured a specific manifesto commitment on the EU. Less immediately connected to European policy is the recasting of the state: through devolution in Scotland and Wales, the Northern Irish peace process, and limited regionalism in England. None the less, these developments will have an impact on how the UK is represented in the EU. Indeed, European integration has contributed to some extent to each of these processes. Thus, now the new quasi-federal UK is in operation, European policy may once again become contested, albeit because of territorially-based bargaining, such as between Edinburgh and London. A final area of constitutional reform bears upon European policy, namely the modernisation of the House of Commons. In November 1998, reforms were put forward in a White Paper with a view to improving the mechanisms for scrutiny in the Commons (House of Commons, 1998). These new mechanisms were put into effect almost immediately. In the context of reform of the House of Lords, particular attention is being paid to the House's important contribution to control over the EU. When these constitutional reforms are all fully operational, the Blair Government will also have brought about a significant reform of how the British polity interacts with the EU.

Conclusion

How, then, has Labour fared in its first two years or so of European policy? First, it has avoided any major conflagrations with its EU partners and has made good progress towards repairing the damage brought about by the BSE crisis under John Major's Government. Included in this, is the progress that the Government has secured towards lifting the ban on exports of beef from the UK. Secondly, it has been able to achieve positive results on most of its manifesto commitments. In terms of its reform agenda, it has been reasonably successful. It has sustained progress on the single market and EU enlargement and contributed to institutional reform through the Amsterdam Treaty. It also signed up to the Social Chapter, although this policy area has become much less dynamic in recent years. The main failure has been on the Common Fisheries Policy, where reform has been negligible (but would have been very difficult to achieve). Reform of the CAP has not gone far enough and may not meet World Trade Organisation rules, but that shortcoming is attributable to the interventions at the March 1999 Berlin summit of the French president, Jacques Chirac, rather than to the efforts of the UK Government.

Thirdly, on EMU the manifesto commitment was modest: simply the promise of a referendum on membership. It is clear that this task is most likely one for Labour's second term, since the real objective is not just holding a referendum but securing a successful endorsement for joining the Euro. Tony Blair has realised that non-participation in the single currency represents a major barrier to increased influence in the EU. Much preparatory work remains ahead of that referendum. In mid-October 1999 Tony Blair launched a cross-party campaign for 'Britain in Europe', regarded as the first stage of cultivating public opinion for a referendum on the single currency in a second Labour term. However, a committee of junior ministers, chaired by Joyce Quin, actively examined how the European issue can be better presented in public debate. Fourthly, the Labour Government has certainly changed the tone of British European policy; it has regarded the EU as an opportunity rather than a threat. However, its efforts to 'lead' the EU were a misguided attempt to engage with the (failed) discourse of the Major Government. They reflect a long-standing inability of British governments to adjust to medium-power status. Moreover, the use of this discourse merely underlined the fact that the UK cannot be absent from the single currency, the EU's principal project, if it wishes to be an influential player.

Weighed against these judgements, however, the Labour Party's performance in the June 1999 European elections was poor and raised new questions about its policy. First, the Government could not escape some blame for the low turnout – a mere 24 per cent – with Blair himself pre-occupied with the situation in Kosovo. Labour had expected to suffer electoral losses due to the shift from the first-past-the-post system – from which the party had benefited in 1994 during the Major Government's unpopularity – to PR. However, by securing only 28 per cent of the vote (in contrast to 44 per cent in 1994, its strength in the European Parliament declined dramatically from 62 to 29 MEPs. This result prompted a postmortem, especially given Labour's weak performance in some of its heartlands, and fresh consideration to the Government's tactics over the timing of a referendum on the single currency.

Although the European election result marred its record, the new Government's European policy may indeed be adjudged a 'fresh start'. But the ultimate test – winning a referendum on the single currency – is yet to come.

References

Anderson, P. and Mann, N. (1997), *Safety First: The Making of New Labour*, London, Granta Books.

Baker, D. and Seawright, D. (1998a), 'A "Rosy" Map of Europe? Labour Parliamentarians and European Integration' in D. Baker and D. Seawright (eds), *Britain For and Against Europe: British Politics and the Question of European Integration*, Oxford, Clarendon Press.

Blair, T. (1995), 'Britain in Europe', Address to the Royal Institute of International Affairs, Chatham House, London, 5 April, London, Labour Party.

Brown, G. (1997), 'Statement on EMU by the Chancellor of the Exchequer', 27 October, http://www.hm-treasury.gov.uk/pub/html/press97/p126_97.html.

Bulmer, S. and Burch, M. (1998), 'Organising for Europe: Whitehall, the British State and European Union', *Public Administration*, 76(4):601–28.

Foreign and Commonwealth Office (1996), 'A Partnership of Nations: The British Approach to the European Union Intergovernmental Conference 1996', Cm 3181, London, HMSO.

George, S. and Haythorne, D. (1996), 'The British Labour Party' in J. Gaffney (ed.), *Political Parties and the European Union*, London, Routledge.

Grant, C. (1998), *Can Britain lead in Europe?*, London, Centre for European Reform.

Henderson, D. (1998), 'The UK Presidency: An Insider's View', *Journal of Common Market Studies*, 36(4):563–72.

House of Commons (1998), 'The Scrutiny of European Union Business', Cm 4095, London, The Stationery Office.

Labour Party (1995), 'Future of the European Union: Labour's Position in Preparation for the Intergovernmental Conference 1996', Interim Report, Labour Party, 14 September.

Labour Party (1997), *New Labour: Because Britain Deserves Better*, London, Labour Party.

Ludlam, S. (1998), 'The Cauldron: Conservative Parliamentarians and European Integration' in D. Baker and D. Seawright (eds), *Britain For and Against Europe: British Politics and the Question of European Integration*, Oxford, Clarendon Press.

Ludlow, P. (1998), 'The 1998 UK Presidency: A View from Brussels', *Journal of Common Market Studies*, 36(4):573–83.

Mandelson, P. and Liddle, R. (1996), *The Blair Revolution: Can New Labour Deliver*, London, Faber and Faber.

Newman, M. (1983), *Socialism and European Unity*, London, Junction Books.

Teasdale, A. (1998), 'Britain's Successes in the European Union 1973–98' in M. Fraser (ed.), *Britain in Europe: The Next Phase* (2nd ed.), London, Strategems Publishing.

18

New Labour and international development

Ralph A. Young

Though development aid remains a secondary sector within the broad domain of British policy-making, New Labour has brought to this area a commitment to reform that makes the Blair administration the most potentially innovative since the first Wilson Government in 1964. On assuming power, it restored independent ministry status to Britain's aid agency for the first time in nearly 22 years, and returned the ministry to Cabinet rank for the first time in 30. In appointing Clare Short as the new Minister for International Development, Tony Blair chose an experienced Labour politician but one with a well-honed reputation as an outspoken reformer on the left of the Party who would clearly play an activist role in exercising her responsibilities.

While the initial policy commitments taken on by the Blair Government were generally modest in scale, the new Department for International Development (DfID) had within six months of the May elections produced the first White Paper on Britain's overseas aid strategy since 1975. Boldly entitled *Eliminating World Poverty: A Challenge for the 21st Century*, this document committed the Government to reversing the decline in Britain's aid spending and taking on a highly ambitious set of development objectives (DfID, 1997). Yet despite so positive a beginning, it remained uncertain that the development of British aid policy would follow a course that would prove distinctive from that marking the evolution of Britain's aid programme under previous governments. The new institutional framework within which aid policy would be developed might well not prove sustainable, and in the view of some analysts could actually weaken Britain's performance in this area. Nor was it clear, despite the range of important initiatives incorporated in the new ministry's agenda, that the Labour Government's strategy for international development properly addressed the existing shortcomings in Britain's aid programme.

A brief history of British aid

Britain's commitment to Third World development has an impressive historical pedigree through its imperial roots in the 1929 Colonial Development Act and the Colonial Welfare and Development Acts of 1940 and 1945. Yet prior to the middle 1960s, British aid was anchored to a framework of assumptions limiting the state's role primarily to investment in physical and social infrastructure, placing stress on loan rather than grant capital, and looking to the private sector to take the lead over productive investments. Though British colonies normally received official grants on attaining independence, aid ties were not expected to continue (White, 1998:152–3). Through the 1950s and early 1960s, British aid funding was channelled largely through multilateral programmes, and former colonies were otherwise encouraged to meet their capital requirements on a mainly non-concessional basis. As Lee notes, 'it took considerable time to shift the design of capital aid programmes away from the Treasury doctrines of colonial self-sufficiency' (Lee, 1967:254).

The rapid dismantling of Britain's African empire after the end of the 1950s, however, created an imperative towards a rethinking of Britain's approach to development aid. In its innovation of introducing a Ministry for Overseas Development in October 1964 – and passing the Overseas Aid Act in 1966 – the Wilson Labour Government was able to build upon planning already underway under the previous Conservative administration.

Over a following period of more than three decades, the development of Britain's aid programme has been maintained in a broadly consistent form by successive governments of very different policy persuasions. Indeed, one analyst could argue that in terms of aid commitments and policy stance, rhetoric more than substance separated New Labour's predecessors (White, 1998:151–2). Though this argument requires qualification in the case of aid levels, it appears a largely appropriate assessment of British aid in practice – and not least from the standpoint of the stresses and pressures that the aid programme has faced.

When the Ministry of Overseas Development was first established, it enjoyed no little advantage from its timeliness in starting to create a secure political niche. Its first minister, Barbara Castle, was an experienced reform politician with the warm backing of Harold Wilson (himself a co-founder of War on Want). Initially, her most pressing problems appeared to be the recruitment of suitably qualified staff and the domestication of a permanent secretary who, despite a liberal record as a former senior Colonial Office official and colonial governor, was reluctant to serve under a woman minister (Castle, 1994:342–4, 346–8). Relatively quickly, however, the problems that were to mark the development of the British aid programme became evident:

- the difficulties of protecting a limited aid budget from cuts, as government priorities altered;
- the problems of pressing the interests of a weak, modestly resourced ministry against those of more powerful rivals where policy overlapped;
- the difficulties of insulating development aid from the priorities of British business (which, reflecting imperial heritage, often had well-established links with the very areas on which the aid programme was focused);

- and, lastly, the problem of preserving the autonomy of an aid ministry from the colonising ambitions of its immediate neighbour, the Foreign and Commonwealth Office (FCO).

As developments unfolded, the original Ministry of Overseas Development preserved its cabinet status only until a cabinet reshuffle in August 1967. With the Conservatives returning to power in June 1970, the ministry lost its independence altogether, being soon placed under the FCO as the Overseas Development Administration. When Labour regained power in March 1974, Overseas Development recovered its separate ministry status (though not its Cabinet standing) under Judith Hart. By June 1975, however, the Secretary of State for Foreign Affairs had acquired the role of Minister for Overseas Development (and acted as its Cabinet voice), with the actual Minister simply assigned responsibility for the ministry's day-to-day management. Under Mrs Thatcher, the ministry became once more the Overseas Development Administration (ODA) within the FCO.

In part, of course, the calibre and experience of successive ministers and ministers of state helped provide some counterweight to the problems the aid programme experienced in establishing its independent existence. Barbara Castle was a committed and energetic minister well able to tackle the challenge of getting the new ministry off the ground. Judith Hart sought to re-establish the ministry's separate identity in the middle 1970s with a new White Paper – *The Changing Emphasis in British Aid Policies* – that underlined the changed understandings and priorities of the international development effort (Ministry of Overseas Development, 1975). Judith Hart and Reg Prentice also helped to provide continuity through their several periods at the head of Overseas Development (she on three occasions and he on two). Yet, it should be noted that on average individual Labour ministers spent only a limited time in this post – a little more than 14 months; their Conservative counterparts, by contrast, averaged over 52 months, and one served as Minister of State for Overseas Development for no less than 94. Nor can this latter fact be assumed simply to reflect the marginality of the aid portfolio under the Thatcher and Major Governments. After 1986, Chris Patton and Lynda Chalker took a keen interest in development issues, and were generally well respected within the academic development community in Britain. Lady Chalker, in part through the role she played as British Government trouble-shooter in Africa during its turbulent political transition following the close of the Cold War, was able to establish a measure of influence that helped moderate pressures to reduce aid funding and reinvigorated the ODA's poverty focus after 1994. The principle was also accepted that ODA should be more directly involved in trade, investment and other economic policies of relevance to developing countries (Foreign Affairs Committee, 1996:5). Thus, at some levels at least, the agenda associated with DfID was already in place before New Labour came to power.

Though by 1996 the ODA's funding represented only 0.26 per cent of GNP, roughly half the level at which it had stood when Labour lost power in 1979, the ODA had thus managed to remain intact and, within its modest means, effective. Recognition of a separate status and specialised role remained; ODA retained an individual entry in official listings of Whitehall agencies while being linked to the FCO through three joint departments (Aid Policy, Economic Advisers and Economic Relations). As one writer was able to note, the agency carried forward from a difficult period a reputation for 'a high level of staff commitment, an excellent balance of relevant professional skills, and . . . a "thinking" organisational culture'. It was also 'one of the most decentralized of aid agencies in terms of location and responsibility for decision-making' (Cox and Healey, 1998:233).

New Labour's policy pledges

The creation of DfID in May 1997 marked the re-establishment of the aid programme's autonomy. The only new department of state created by the incoming Blair Government, its establishment had been given prominence among Labour's commitments to international development in the Party's 1997 election manifesto. It accompanied promises to reverse the decline in Britain's aid spending and give international development issues much higher priority on the Government's policy agenda. As with the Conservative and Liberal manifestos, there was also a reaffirmation of Britain's engagement to eventually achieve the United Nations aid target for developed countries of 0.7 per cent of GNP.

The new department was placed under a minister who gave early indication of an intention not just to assert its independence but also, in line with Labour's election manifesto, to extend its role. Clare Short had the advantage of a ministerial unit which, if small, had been separated intact from the FCO. It had inherited from ODA responsibility for Britain's bilateral and multilateral aid programmes, including those directed to the so-called transitional economies of Central and Eastern Europe. With some 17 years' experience in overseas development, its permanent secretary had been promoted to his current position in 1994. Most other senior staff were carried over in their same posts. Clare Short also had the support of both Tony Blair and Gordon Brown, the new Chancellor of the Exchequer, and had seemingly smooth political relations with the key members of the new ministerial team at the FCO. She was thought as well to be popular among Labour Party activists, though on more than one occasion she had been slapped down by the Party leadership for seeming to court controversy by her statements to the media. Indeed, her initial appointment as shadow spokesperson on overseas development, some nine months before the May elections, had been viewed in the press as a demotion. She herself was a former civil servant, who in the early 1970s had served as private secretary to a Conservative Home Office minister and was well versed in the procedures and culture of Whitehall.

Box 18.1   *International development in New Labour's 1997 election manifesto*

New Labour promised to:
- create a new department of international development under a minister of Cabinet rank;
- 'bring development issues back into the mainstream of government decision making';
- 'start to reverse the decline in UK aid spending';
- maintain 'the UK's commitment to the 0.7 per cent UN aid target';
- 'shift aid resources towards programmes that help the poorest people in the poorest countries';
- 'work for greater consistency between the aid, trade, agriculture and economic reform policies of the EU';
- 'enhance the position of the poorest countries during the renegotiation of the Lomé Convention';
- 'support further measures to reduce the debt burden borne by the world's poorest countries';
- 'ensure that developing countries are given a fair deal in international trade'
- 'rejoin Unesco'.

Source: The Times, 1997, 330–1.

Though Clare Short's extensive experience as an opposition frontbench spokesperson had been primarily devoted to domestic policy areas, initial interviews made it clear that she was assuming office with a relatively well-defined (and populist) perspective on a range of development issues – not least Third World debt. She argued in public that the new aid agenda would be wholly poverty-focused, and that any dependence on British foreign policy objectives not relevant to this agenda would be cut. This was in marked contrast to her predecessor Lynda Chalker, who had shown considerable dexterity in co-ordinating the two sets of priorities. Short insisted that the wide range of the new Department's brief would involve injecting its concerns into the policy process, forcing other ministries to address the priorities which her department existed to promote. From the outset, she made clear that she would be both an initiator and a fighter. Yet, in one early interview she threatened to quit her post, while in another wondered if she would be able to long survive in a New Labour Cabinet (*Observer*, 31 August 1997, p. 23; BBC, 'Clare's New World').

The cluster of radical ideas at the core of the November 1997 New Labour statement on international development had been well marked out in advance by Clare Short, in interviews and speeches. The White Paper itself was the product of extensive consultations within Whitehall, and also with a range of voluntary agencies working in humanitarian relief and overseas development – 'after 20 years of political marginalisation' (Whaites, 1998:203). *Eliminating World Poverty* was actually the fifth White Paper on international development and Labour governments near the start of their tenures have produced all of the three regarded as substantial documents. In the 22 years since Judith Hart's White Paper, the terrain on which development programmes operated had been transformed by the ending of the Cold War, the appearance of the newly industrialising economies in east and southeast Asia, the debt crisis, the emergence of new development agendas associated with neo-liberal orthodoxies, and the recognition of major new issue areas like the environment. The 1975 White Paper had addressed the question of Third World poverty by focusing attention on rural development. *Eliminating World Poverty* was required to attempt a more nuanced approach by incorporating within its development perspective a recognition of the importance of environmental, 'good governance', and human rights concerns as well as acknowledgment of the powerful forces sustaining the process of economic globalisation.

In specifying the goals to which Britain's aid effort should be directed, the White Paper was indeed ambitious. Drawing on the principles agreed in the 1992 Rio Declaration on sustainable development and the recommendations published the previous year by the Development Assistance Committee (DAC) of the Organization for Economic Cooperation and Development (OECD), these were listed as the following:

- A reduction by one-half of the proportion of people worldwide living in extreme poverty by 2015
- The achievement of universal primary education in all countries by the same year
- The elimination of gender disparity in primary and secondary education by 2005
- A reduction by 2015 in maternal mortality rates by three-quarters, and in mortality rates for infants and children under 5 by two-thirds
- Access for all individuals of appropriate age to reproductive health care by 2015
- The implementation of national strategies for sustainable development in all countries by 2005 (with a reversal of the current decline in environmental resources by 2015) (DfID, 1997:21).

In seeking to contribute towards the achievement of such targets, the White Paper formulated a strategy resting upon the building of poverty-focused partnerships – with the governments of less developed countries, with multilateral agencies concerned with development, and, within Britain, with the voluntary sector and the academic community as well as with British business. It also rested upon active pressure to ensure policy consistency across the range of government policies affecting both developing economies and the transitional economies of Central and Eastern Europe (DfID, 1997:37–47, 50–67). It promised that

Britain would give strong support to human rights and accountable government and 'use our resources proactively to promote political stability and social cohesion' (DfID, 1997:7). It also committed Britain to pressing for a reduction of Third World debt to sustainable levels (DfID, 1997:71–4) and indicated that its poverty priorities would entail a shift of British aid resources towards meeting the needs of countries in South Asia and sub-Saharan Africa (DfID, 1997:38).

Eliminating World Poverty received warm praise for its broad strategic vision, but disappointment was also expressed over its overly cautious analysis of the constraints on Third World development, its failure to go farther than it did on some key issues, and the relative absence of specific recommendations about how British aid might contribute towards solving the development problems the White Paper identified. While commending the fluency and sophistication of its presentation of a range of complex development issues, two senior development specialists nonetheless criticised its 'unrealism and its retreat from specifics' (Hewitt and Killick, 1998:194). Yet, by building upon foundations laid by her Conservative predecessor, Clare Short managed to win the admission of the opposition spokesperson on international development that there was not much in the White Paper that the Conservative Party could disagree with. However, he also pointed to evidence that despite the efforts to harmonise the White Paper's priorities with the recent mission statement of the FCO, a great deal in the relationship between the two agencies remained unresolved (Goodlad, 1998:195, 198). Another observer detected the inhibiting hand of the Treasury in the gap between the ambitious objectives and the careful avoidance of specific recommendations entailing costly commitments for the British taxpayer (Waites, 1998:209–11). Again, it is clear that Clare Short's determination to end the practice of 'tied aid' (with British aid programmes being made conditional on the purchase of materials, equipment or services from British firms) was blocked at the drafting stage by the Department of Trade and Industry (BBC, 'Clare's New World'). Though the White Paper did promise the removal of the controversial Aid and Trade Provision introduced by the Callaghan Government in 1977, a new mechanism for tying aid surfaced within its recommendations. The final elimination of tied aid was only offered within the context of a commitment to work for multilateral action on this front (Morrissey, 1998; DfID, 1997: 41ff).

Despite such shortcomings, as well as the apparent occurrence of several 'U-turns' from positions which the Labour Party had adopted in opposition and the marked tendency to shape a development agenda in the rather limited terms of a 'welfare state' model, the White Paper did make a significant contribution to recasting the terms of debate over international development – not least in its efforts to re-establish the developmentalist state as a positive agent of change. There was certainly enough contained in its 148 paragraphs to indicate the direction of aid policy over the coming years, while the ambitious aims underpinning its recommendations offered a practical focus for a poverty-focused aid programme of necessarily modest scope given the scale of the problems being addressed. Most importantly, the White Paper existed. It provided a marker of New Labour's commitment to international development and a reasonably specific set of standards against which its future performance could be judged.

From promise to performance

The first 24 months during which DfID sought to give momentum to its strategies have been far from smooth. Notably, the Department received a substantial boost as a result of the Comprehensive Spending Review (CSR) in July 1998, but the CSR's fine print suggested a less munificent level of support from the Treasury than first appeared. The increased funding included money from the privatisation of the Commonwealth Development Corporation, then still at the planning stages, while the full package was tied to a set of 11 performance indicators which were, for the most part, closely linked to the OECD's poverty-reduction targets, and thus seemingly far beyond the Department's resources (DfID, 1999:10–11). The commitment to increase the Department's resources over the next three years from its current level of £2.326 billion to £3.218 billion was impressive, nonetheless. If conditions in the national economy permitted such a commitment to be sustained, it would represent an average annual increase in the Department's budget of 8.8 per cent in real terms, raising its capacity for aid provision from 0.26 per cent of GNP to 0.30 per cent.

An aid ministry inevitably has a complex character because of the diversity of its activities. The text of the Department's first annual report identified some 110 separate areas of activity; including those needing emergency aid, over 150 countries or British dependencies were receiving assistance (DfID, 1998a). The broad range of policy sectors that DfID's programmes spanned included several which, on the domestic front, would each have its own ministry. Moreover, programme areas in the development field are often marked by considerable variety due to the varying requirements of recipient countries. Nor was an army of officials available to manage such diversity. In the early 1990s, the former ODA had had a permanent staff of over 1600, which, by the time New Labour took power, had been reduced to around 1000. With extra funding under the CSR, it was expected to expand to just under 1300 by 2002, still a modest figure given the ambitious scope of the Department's programmes (DfID, 1999:142).

Internally, the Department has been undertaking a sector-by-sector review of its activities. With the White Paper making clear its acceptance of a connection between a pro-poor aid strategy, sound public policies and efficient delivery of public services, the Department was able to incorporate many of the previous government's concerns with macro-economic reform and public sector restructuring relatively smoothly into its own agenda (DfID, 1998a:13–19). Nonetheless, the Department marked out its new priorities at an early stage – including the suspension of new commitments under the Aid and Trade programme and a decision that Britain would rejoin the United Nations Education Scientific and Cultural Organisation (UNESCO) and reverse the Major Government's decision to quit the United Nations Industrial Development Organisation (UNIDO) (*Guardian*, 23 May 1997, p. 23; DfID, 1998a:52).

By the Department's second annual report (DfID, 1999), there was evidence of a considerable effort to refocus key activities and programmes:

• The health and population agendas were being reshaped
• The 'good governance' agenda was also being reshaped, with much greater emphasis being placed on human rights concerns
• A shifting of funds to strengthen African aid commitments had made Britain the largest bilateral aid giver to the region
• A broader strategy for transferring a greater share of bilateral aid funding to programmes targeted on low-income countries had been put in place, and by 2002 these were expected to receive more than three-quarters of British bilateral aid, as against the two-thirds share they had when Labour took office.

Though references to the 'partnership' model in the Department's first annual report had been limited largely to co-operation with multilateral development agencies, partnership had become a guiding theme in the second. Through relationships based on close dialogue with governments of low-income countries prepared to commit themselves to sustainable pro-poor development programmes, the Department was prepared 'in principle to embark on a deeper, long-term partnership, involving all forms of assistance' (DfID, 1999:18). For the first time, the country strategy papers based on such dialogue activity were to be published (and by early 1999 20 had been, 11 of these dealing with low-income countries). The approach stressed the avoidance of 'crude conditionality and reflects DfID's willingness to work within the framework of a recipient country's own strategies and objectives as well as its commitment to openness and transparency. Nonetheless, the Department has warned that partnership might 'involve intense dialogue and hard choices . . . future levels of support may vary greatly depending on the degree of commitment that the recipient government has to improve significantly the condition of the poor. Partnership is not a soft option' (DfID, 1999:19).

In December 1997, Clare Short, long an active campaigner on this issue, had signed the Ottawa Convention on Landmines on behalf of the British Government. In April 1998, DfID and the FCO produced a joint report on progress in the human rights field (DfID/FCO, 1998). The same month an important speech sought to lay out the principles which were to guide British humanitarian aid (DfID, 1998b). In August, DfID issued a critical examination of the effectiveness of the multilateral institutions to whose programmes her Departmental contributed; over 45 per cent of the total aid budget is currently committed in this way (DfID, 1998c). In November, the Department issued a policy statement on women and poverty elimination (DfID, 1998d). It also issued a second statement on partnerships with business in the pursuit of its development objectives (DfID, 1998e). The following month saw an important policy statement on the environment (DfID, 1998f). In February 1999, Clare

Short produced a plan for a radical overhaul of the European Union's aid machinery, having first enlisted support from the French and German aid ministers (*Guardian*, 23 February 1999, p. 15). With both of DfID's annual reports to date underlining the role of conflict in generating poverty, the Emergency Aid Department inherited from ODA has been transformed into the Department of Conflict and Humanitarian Affairs. In March 1999, Short produced a new initiative that would direct British aid into an unaccustomed field – the reform of Third World military institutions, particularly with an eye to improving mechanisms of civilian control (*Guardian*, 10 March 1999, p. 10; *Economist*, 13 March 1999, p. 47).

A preliminary assessment of progress

DfID remains an agency of modest status in the Cabinet pecking order. The Government rejected a recommendation of the House of Commons International Development Committee that the minister be made a member of the Cabinet Committee on Defence and Overseas Policy (International Development Committee, 1997a:vii; International Development Committee, 1998a:iv) – though she does on occasion attend meetings. Given the breadth of the Department's remit, it must seek active engagement with a variety of ministerial partners whose interests overlap but whose priorities are likely to be distinct from its own. There are numerous issue areas where this is the case, such as: women's issues, a new multilateral agreement on external private investment, a programme to enhance the participation of less developed countries in the international trading system, an improved multilateral framework for intellectual property legislation, the promotion of core international labour standards, the European Union's trade policies, and Third World debt (DfID, 1998a:39–46; DfID, 1999: 22, 56, 85). The Inter-Governmental Working Group on Development, established in November 1997 under DfID's chairmanship, had a formidable membership: the FCO, the Treasury, the Department of Trade and Industry (DTI), the Export Credits Guarantee Department, the Department of the Environment, Transport and the Regions, the Ministry of Defence, the Ministry of Agriculture, Fisheries and Food, the Department of Health, the Department of Education and Employment and the Cabinet Office.

Relations between Clare Short's Department and other ministries have not always been free from friction. At the outset, those with the FCO, for example, were marked by considerable strain. The loss of the former ODA brought a sharp reduction in the FCO's budget as well as removing from its control an often efficient tool for exercising diplomatic influence. Foreign Office officials were quick to make clear to the media their dissatisfaction with the new arrangements (*Economist*, 16 August 1997, p. 25). Yet a substantial area of overlapping responsibilities and interests remained, as the joint report on human rights underlined on the positive side and the Montserrat imbroglio did on the negative (International Development Committee, 1997b; 1998b). On the other hand, relations with the Department of Trade and Industry have been less seemingly marked by friction than anticipated and since August 1997 DfID has joined the FCO in giving advice on applications for export licences for arms (DfID, 1999:96). Clare Short's most important success came in the negotiations with the Treasury that allowed her Department to assume control of Britain's relations with the World Bank. In this area, she has collaborated closely with the Chancellor of the Exchequer, and has used her direct access to a key international forum for pressing the British case for more flexible arrangements for debt reduction for low-income Third World countries.

As a minister, Clare Short has shown a propensity for igniting public rows with comments whose consequences might have been better foreseen. Certainly the initial controversy in which she was embroiled – her scathing observation that the leaders of Montserrat, a Caribbean island then threatened by potentially devastating volcanic activity, might soon be demanding 'golden elephants' – was very damaging to her own position, as she herself later acknowledged (BBC, 'Clare's New World'). Subsequent controversies over statements she made on the question of the need for famine relief appeals for the Sudan, debt relief for countries affected by Hurricane Mitch, or over the need to admit more refugees from Kosovo to the UK have undoubtedly generated friction with those groups which should be counted among the Department's core constituencies. Such groups include non-governmental organisations involved in development or humanitarian relief, Labour backbenchers and, not least, the International Development Committee, which has defined for itself an activist role in producing eight separate reports in its first 18 months but which has occasionally felt provoked into short-tempered comment on her Department's performance, or her own. Short also angered the business community with whom the Department had been trying to build links by publicly refusing to lobby for British firms while on trips abroad (*Guardian*, 8 December 1998, pp. 10 and 20). Although she had a valid point to make, it was evident that established understandings of ministerial roles had been upset.

At the same time, Short has certainly been an energetic and enthusiastic minister, who has been deeply committed to her Department and who has been, perhaps, more of an innovator than any of her predecessors over the previous generation. She has sought to move the aid debate away from any conception of development assistance as mere charity and to define for it a more strategic conception anchored to a specific programme of poverty elimination. She has deployed the new dual focus on poverty and partnerships to assert her Department's independence from lingering expectations that aid might be deployed to further Britain's diplomatic or commercial interests as well as to move the development debate on, at least at official level, from what she regarded as the outdated certainties of neo-liberal orthodoxy. At the same time, her own positions were sometimes marked by considerable ambiguity – as in her statements at different times over the significance of globalisation (*Guardian*, 23 May 1997, p. 23; International Development Committee, 1998a:vi). Clare Short was certainly under no illusions as to the enormity of the tasks facing her Department. The achievement of the goal of halving the world's burden of extreme poverty by 2015 was possible, she told a journalist, but not likely; a much greater mobilisation of political will at the international level was necessary than had yet occurred (BBC, 'Clare's New World').

In the case of the ministry itself, it is probably a little early to attempt an assessment of its likely impact. Clearly the autonomy and independence it has acquired has been used to chart a distinctive course for Britain's aid agenda. DfID has been successful in pushing outward the previously relatively narrow boundaries of influence of Britain's aid programme, both within domestic politics and in external arenas. Winning a substantial funding increase under the CSR gave DfID an enhanced profile at a time when aid programmes elsewhere have generally been in decline; between 1991 and 1997 the aid ratio for the 21 member-states of the OECD's DAC dropped by a third, from 0.33 per cent of GNP to 0.22 per cent (Randall and German, 1998:7). Whether the new agenda will have much practical impact in terms of the goals set for the aid programme is a more difficult question. The direct measurement of the impact of aid programmes on poverty reduction is far from straightforward; in any case such an enterprise would certainly be premature at this stage.

Yet, we can already say that New Labour has succeeded in meeting most of its manifesto commitments in the sphere of international development. The two where progress has been least evident – a fairer deal for developing countries over international trade and greater consistency between the European Union's aid and its agricultural, trade and economic reform policies – are enmeshed in processes of international negotiation that will not produce concrete results for some time. But at the same time, concerns remain that the partnership strategy to which the aid programme has been anchored – a partnership based on dialogue between Britain and individual recipient countries on a supposedly equal basis – will turn out to be an illusory goal. Partnerships in the aid field inevitably become tilted towards the agenda of the aid provider (Maxwell and Riddell, 1998). On the other hand, Britain supplies only some 6 per cent of total aid flows, and 'these flows are frequently . . . modest in relation to the budgets of recipient countries' (DfID, 1999:26). Moreover, in at least two cases – Sierra Leone and the Sudan – humanitarian aid has not escaped the influence of Foreign Office priorities (Crawhall and Collinson, 1998:163; *Guardian*, 20 December 1998). The Department has certainly laboured to define a clear sense of institutional purpose and to demonstrate its capacity to exercise an independent role. But DfID is still some distance from translating all the goals it has set for itself into effective action.

References

Castle, B. (1994), *Fighting All the Way*, London, Pan.
'Clare's New World,' BBC 2, 15 February 1998.

Crawhall, N. and S. Collinson (1998), 'United Kingdom', in J. Randel and T. German (eds), with D. Ewing, *The Reality of Aid 1998/99: An Independent Review of Poverty Reduction and Development Assistance*, London, Earthscan, pp. 160–6.

Cox, A. and J. Healey (1998), 'The 1997 White Paper: Powerful Poverty Commitment, Imprecise Operational Strategy,' *Journal of International Development*, 10(2):227–34.

Department for International Development (DfID) (1997), *Eliminating World Poverty: A Challenge for the 21st Century*, Cm 3789, London, Stationery Office.

DfID (1998a), *Departmental Report 1998–1999*, Cm 3907, London, Stationery Office.

DfID (1998b), 'Principles for a New Humanitarianism,' keynote address by Clare Short to the ECHO/ODI Conference on 'Principled Aid in an Unprincipled World', London, DfID.

DfID (1998c), *Impact Assessment in Multilateral Development Institutions*, London, DfID.

DfID (1998d), *Breaking the Barriers: Women and the Elimination of World Poverty*, London, DfID.

DfID (1998e), *Partnerships with Business*, London, DfID.

DfID (1998f), *Biodiversity Matters*, London, DfID Environment Policy Department.

DfID (1999), *Departmental Report 1999: The Government's Expenditure Plans 1999–2000 to 2001–2002*, Cm 4210, London, Stationery Office.

DfID /FCO (1998), *Human Rights: Annual Report on Human Rights*, London, DfID/FCO.

Foreign Affairs Committee (House of Commons) (1996), *Second Report from the Foreign Affairs Committee, Session 1995–96: Observations by the Secretary of State for Foreign and Commonwealth Affairs*, Cm 3385, London, Stationery Office.

Goodlad, A. (1998), 'The View from the Opposition Benches', *Journal of International Development*, 10(2):195–201.

Hewitt, A. and T. Killick (1998), 'The 1975 and 1997 White Papers Compared: Enriched Vision, Depleted Policies?' *Journal of International Development*, 10(2):185–94.

International Development Committee (House of Commons) (1997a), *The Development White Paper*, Second Report, Session 1997–98, HC 330, London, Stationery Office.

International Development Committee (House of Commons) (1997b), *Montserrat*, First Report, Session 1997–98, HC 267, London, Stationery Office.

International Development Committee (House of Commons) (1998a), *Government Response to the Second Report from the Committee, Session 1997–98: The Development White Paper*, Second Special Report, Session 1997–98, HC 643, London, Stationery Office.

International Development Committee (House of Commons) (1998b), *Montserrat – Further Developments*, Sixth Report, Session 1997–98, HC 726, London, Stationery Office.

Lee, J. M. (1967), *Colonial Government and Good Government*, Oxford, Clarendon.

Maxwell, S. and R. Riddell (1998), 'Conditionality or Contract? Perspectives on Partnership for Development', *Journal of International Development*, 10(2):257–68.

Ministry of Overseas Development (1975), *The Changing Emphasis in British Aid Policies: More Help for the Poorest*, Cmnd 6370, London, HMSO.

Morrissey, O. (1998), 'ATP Is Dead. Long Live Mixed Credits', *Journal of International Development*, 10(2):247–55.

Randel, J. and T. German (eds), with D. Ewing (1998), *The Reality of Aid 1998/1999: An Independent Review of Poverty Reduction*, London, Earthscan.

The Times (1997), *The Times Guide to the House of Commons May 1997*, London, *The Times*.

Whaites, A. (1998), 'The New UK White Paper on International Development: an NGO Perspective,' *Journal of International Development*, 10(2):203–13.

White, H. (1998), 'British Aid and the White Paper on International Development: Dressing a Wolf in Sheep's Clothing in the Emperor's New Clothes?', *Journal of International Development*, 10(2):151–66.

19

New Labour and defence

Philip Gummett

The British are, by instinct, an internationalist people. We believe that as well as defending our rights, we should discharge our responsibilities in the world. We do not want to stand idly by and watch humanitarian disasters or the aggression of dictators go unchecked. We want to give a lead, we want to be a force for good. (George Robertson, MP, Secretary of State for Defence (1998a: para. 19))

Labour governments, unlike Labour oppositions, have always been strong on defence. When Churchill returned to power in 1951, he confessed himself dismayed as a parliamentarian, but delighted as Prime Minister, to discover how much Attlee had secretly spent on developing the atomic bomb. The unilateralist tendency of the late 1950s and early 1960s was resisted by Gaitskell, followed by Wilson, as part of a strategy for winning the electoral middle ground. Even though Wilson's Defence Secretary, Denis Healey, introduced substantial reforms (cancellation of several major projects, withdrawal from east of Suez), he still left a legacy that endured into the 1990s of armed forces that were performing a greater range of missions than any others in the world except those of the Superpowers and, possibly, France. Britain was maintaining independent strategic and theatre nuclear forces that were committed to NATO. It was providing for the direct defence of the UK while also maintaining a major army and air force contribution on the European mainland. It was deploying a major surface and submarine force in the Eastern Atlantic and the Channel. It continued to have a limited capability for operations outside the NATO area, including the defence of such territories as Hong Kong and the Falkland Islands.

In opposition, however, in the late 1970s and early 1980s, with the massive Reagan arms build-up in the US, his demonisation of the Soviet Union as the 'evil empire', and the parallel developments in Europe (cruise missiles) and especially the UK (cruise; Trident; and Mrs Thatcher's matching – even stiffening – of the Reagan rhetoric), there was a major revival of anti-nuclear sentiment, not least in the Labour Party. But the hundreds of thousands who took to the streets did not outweigh the electoral damage. Casting off the perceived millstone of unilateralism and, by association, general softness on defence, became a key goal of a new generation of Labour leaders.

To this endeavour was added an unexpected twist. The end of the Cold War called for radical rethinking of defence policy, including the size and shape of the armed forces and associated equipment policy. It also saw sharp downward pressure on defence budgets, and a complex and evolving alliance scene. Most fundamentally, it posed the question of who now was the enemy. As a news-paper editorial, discussing the future of the planned European Fighter Aircraft, succinctly put it: 'Who Will the Fighter Fight?'

For the Conservative Government, the need for fundamental rethinking was a problem. Anything that implied a major Defence Review (with capital letters) conjured up the unhappy memory of John Nott in 1981 presenting a contro-versial plan for restructuring, which included halving the Navy, only to be U-turned by the Falklands War. But, for Labour, the opposite was true: calling for a Review allowed them to duck specific questions about what they would do in office, while also criticising the Tories for being merely incrementalist in their response to the end of the Cold War, and for having a budget-led, rather than foreign-policy-led, approach to reshaping defence policy.

Hence, the manifesto for the 1997 election, and prior documents such as the 1995 *Strategy for a Secure Future: Labour's Approach to the Defence Industry*, con-tented themselves with a fairly short list of commitments (see Appendix 1). Chief among these was the maintenance of strong defence through NATO, the initia-tion of a strategic defence review, retention of the Trident nuclear missile force, a push for multilateral reductions in weapons of mass destruction, and the retention of a strong UK defence industry, with its expertise extended to civilian use through a defence diversification agency. In the eyes of the party managers and in its prominence within the manifesto, defence was kept low in the agenda. Before two years had passed, however, it was to rise to unexpected prominence.

Setting up the Review

On taking office, the new Government changed its defence team from that which had led this issue during the campaign. George Robertson replaced David Clark as Secretary of State. Robertson was an unknown quantity in this field. He was supported by Dr John Gilbert, a former chair of the House of Commons Defence Committee, with a reputation as a solid right-winger on defence. Robin Cook became Secretary of State for Foreign and Commonwealth Affairs, and would therefore interact with the defence team on wider security matters.

Early pronouncements insisted on the commitment to Trident, and confirmed the go-ahead for the largest current defence equipment project, the Eurofighter aircraft, being developed and built in co-operation with Germany, Italy and Spain. New Labour continued, as under the Conservatives, to block moves towards a greater EU role in defence at the inter-governmental conference that lead to Amsterdam revision of the Treaty on European Union. It also rejected

---

Box 19.1   *Strategic Defence Review – supporting essays*

STRATEGIC DEFENCE REVIEW
The titles of the supporting essays were:
• The Strategic Defence Review Process
• The Policy Framework
• The Impact of Technology
• Defence Diplomacy
• Deterrence, Arms Control and Proliferation
• Future Military Capabilities
• Reserve Forces
• Joint Operations
• A Policy for People
• Procurement and Industry
• Support and Infrastructure

Source: MoD, 1998b.

---

suggestions that European defence and security arrangements could be simplified and strengthened by incorporating into the EU the Western European Union (a collective security organisation that had been set up just before, and then overshadowed by, NATO, but which had been resurrected in the 1990s as part of the search to establish a distinctively European defence identity).

Within its first month in office, the Government set up the promised Strategic Defence Review (SDR), the results of which were published in July 1998. The process of the Review is itself worthy of comment, involving, as it did, a distinctively New Labourish style of consultation.

The starting point was the joint development by the Ministry of Defence (MoD) and the Foreign and Commonwealth Office (FCO) of a policy framework, subsequently published, along with other working papers, in a volume of essays that accompanied the review document itself (see Box 19.1). These were the product of working groups and consultations with former defence ministers and officials, industrialists, trade unionists, academics, former and current MPs, peers, scientists, non-governmental organisations (NGOs) and environmentalists. The Framework was tried out in seminars in London and Coventry in July 1997, attended by MPs, academics, representatives of NGOs, the media, as well as ministers and officials.

Additional input came in the form of over 500 submissions from 'outsiders', received in response to an open invitation, plus a further 100 from Service and civilian personnel within the MoD. In a related initiative, the Secretary of State set up a panel of 18 outsiders whose role was to test the conclusions emerging from the work. They included six former officials or Service personnel, the editor of Richard Crossman's diaries, three academics, three defence industrialists,

---

Box 19.2   *Defence diversification: Labour's thinking while in opposition*

Defence diversification
'Diversification is no longer a useful option, but a commercial imperative. It provides the opportunity to utilise industry's experience and skills in the development of alternative products for the advancement of civil society. Technological spin-offs from defence R&D remain at a low level of realisation and there needs to be a greater cross-fertilisation between the defence and civil sectors.'

'There is growing enthusiasm throughout the defence industry for Labour's proposal for a Defence Diversification Agency (DDA). Such an agency would provide information on long-term procurement plans and on best practice in diversification, assist in identifying new markets and areas for R&D, advise on the targeting of KONVER grants [an EU scheme for support of struggling defence-dependent regions], and co-ordinate renewal in highly defence dependent areas affected by base closure or industrial retrenchment.'

Source: Labour Party, 1995, pp. 21–2.

---

two journalists, a governor of the BBC, and the director of an NGO concerned with verification of arms control agreements.

Throughout the process, speeches, press releases and articles were used to 'keep the wider public in touch with progress' (MoD, 1998b, para. 26), together with parallel dissemination activities within MoD and the Services. As options began to be sharpened, a rolling process of meetings between the Defence Secretary and his ministerial colleagues, the Chiefs of Staff and senior officials, together with inter-departmental consultations (notably an inter-departmental group chaired by the Cabinet Office) was used to move towards conclusions. These were submitted to the Prime Minister on 27 March, with final conclusions announced on 8 July 1998.

In the meantime, steps had been taken on at least one other manifesto promise, namely, the commitment to establish a Defence Diversification Agency (DDA). This commitment was aimed principally at the trades unions, and arose from concern about sharp reductions in the scale of employment dependent on the defence industry (from 625000 in 1985–86 to 415000 in 1995–96) which, given the geographical distribution of the industry, disproportionately affected Labour constituencies.

Two quotations from the 1995 document *Strategy for a Secure Future* give the flavour of thinking while in opposition (Box 19.2).

What emerged, in March 1998, was a Green Paper that struck a somewhat different note. First, it noted that with the job losses already referred to above, and

---

a reduction in UK defence spending between 1985–86 and 1995–96 from £29.9 billion to £20.0 billion, 'the UK defence industry may already have absorbed most of the impact of the 'peace dividend' following the end of the Cold War' (MoD, 1998c: para. 9). Nevertheless, further rationalisation on a European scale was needed in order to maintain competitiveness with the US. Moreover, rapid technological change, and increased inter-dependency between military and civil technology, added to the importance of ready transfer of technology between the military and civil spheres. Indeed, 'as far as diversification from military to civil application is concerned experience shows that it is at the stage at which technologies are evolved that this is best achieved.' (MoD, 1998c: para.12)

This argument is soundly enough based in terms of academic understandings of technology transfer processes, and of the (limited) scope for conversion of factories from one purpose to another. It nevertheless represented a sharp change from the pre-election language, as illustrated above. Its consequences were that the proposed Agency would be set up as part of the Defence Evaluation and Research Agency (DERA), and would adopt a threefold approach:

> First, in order to encourage the widest possible exploitation of military technology by companies which service only civil markets, the DDA would provide knowledge of what is available, encourage access to DERA laboratories, stimulate transfer of MoD's Intellectual Property Rights and seek partnership with companies for programmes of co-development and adaptation. Second, in order to encourage diversification among companies active in servicing defence needs, it would draw upon the wealth of knowledge within MoD about future equipment needs, about technological trends . . . about relative market assessments, and make this database available . . . to industry. Thirdly, in order to encourage the transfer of suitable civil technology into military programmes, the DDA database would be provided to enable civil companies to discover the potential for their products in UK defence programmes. (MoD, 1998c: para. 17)

Thus did the focus shift, from a pre-election concern over support to a declining industry, to a post-election concern with developing a two-way process of technology transfer between the military and civil sectors.

Outcomes of the Review

Labour had stated before the election that the Review would be foreign policy led and, indeed, the resulting White Paper began by identifying national interests and goals, rather than consideration of military matters. It started from the position that Britain was a major European state and a leading member of the EU. In asserting the indivisibility of British security from that of its European partners, however, it *immediately* added 'and Allies', continuing:

> We therefore have a fundamental interest in the security and stability of the continent as a whole and in the effectiveness of NATO as a collective political and military instrument to underpin these interests. This in turn depends on the transatlantic relationship and the continued engagement in Europe of the United States. (MoD, 1998a: para. 18).

It is important not to underestimate the power of the historical legacy of transatlantic relations, which extended seamlessly into New Labour from the previous Conservative governments. There is a strong, and far from groundless, belief in the MoD and in the armed services that the UK is the most important defence 'player' in Europe. In the Gulf War, it supplied roughly as many forces as the rest of the non-US NATO countries combined, and of much higher quality even than the French. The same conflict also showed, however, how small is Europe's total capacity compared to the US, which supplied 90 per cent of the NATO forces, and most of the 'smart' equipment (O'Hanlon, 1997). A similar pattern was later seen in the 1999 war over Kosovo. Hence the crucial dilemma: how to keep the US on board but not be (too) subservient to it (on which subject, see Deighton, 1997, especially the chapter by Bayles).

The 50-year-old principle of defending interests in Europe by locking in the US thus remained, to no-one's surprise, the bedrock of British security policy, despite the siren voices across the Channel calling for a more distinctive European defence and security identity.

But Britain's vital interests, said the White Paper, were not confined to Europe. The economy is founded on international trade, with exports forming a higher proportion of GDP than for the US, Japan, Germany or France, and with a higher proportion of income being invested abroad than for any other major economy. Hence, Britain's economic interests and history gave it other international responsibilities, not least because 10 million British citizens lived and worked abroad. 'Our national security and prosperity thus depend on promoting international stability, freedom and economic development.' As a Permanent Member of the UN Security Council, 'and as a country both willing and able to play a leading role internationally', Britain had a 'responsibility to act as a force for good in the world' (MoD, 1998a: para. 21).

Against that background, the White Paper turned more specifically to the way in which the end of the Cold War had transformed the security environment, and how that environment might change up to the year 2015. It acknowledged that: 'The world does not live in the shadow of World War. There is no longer a direct threat to Western Europe or the United Kingdom as we used to know it, and we face no significant military threat to any of our Overseas Territories' (MoD, 1998a: para. 23).

Nevertheless, the security environment was not seen as benign. Indeed, over the past eight years, more British troops had been on active operations than at any one time during the Cold War – engaged in actions that ran from the Gulf War to the rescue of British citizens from crises overseas. (MoD, 1998a: para. 28). In addition, whereas for the past 200 years the dominant force in international affairs had been the nation state, for the next 20 years the risks to international stability were seen as more likely to come from such other factors as ethnic and religious conflict, population and environmental pressures, competition for scarce resources, drugs, terrorism and crime. On top of this, technology was seen as having a major effect on social change world wide, with

---

Box 19.3   *Pre- and Post-SDR UK defence missions*

Pre-SDR missions	**SDR missions**
Military Aid to the Civil Power in the UK	Peacetime Security
A challenge to the internal or external security of a Dependent Territory	Security of Overseas Territories
General War – a large-scale attack against NATO	Defence Diplomacy
A limited regional conflict involving a NATO ally	Support to Wider British Interests
A British contribution to NATO's and the WEU's new missions	Peace Support and Humanitarian Operations
A serious conflict which, if unchecked, could adversely affect European security, or pose a threat to British interests elsewhere, or to international security	Regional Conflict outside the NATO area
Other military assistance and limited operations, to support international order and humanitarian principles	Regional Conflict inside the NATO area
	Strategic Attack on NATO

Sources: MoD, 1995, p. 27; MoD, 1998a: para. 44.

---

security implications. Some of these might be felt through changes in military capabilities, others through new vulnerabilities to which advanced societies were exposed, such as information warfare, or biological weapons (MoD, 1998a: paras 29–34).

Within this framework, a revised set of defence missions was defined. These are shown, and compared with the pre-SDR missions, in Box 19.3. The main differences between the pre-SDR missions (themselves dating from reformulations under the Conservatives dating from 1992 and 1993) and the SDR missions, apart from the symbolic downgrading of the final two items, is the introduction of the category of Defence Diplomacy. This new Mission was intended to give formal recognition, and higher priority – indeed, to make it a core activity – to work in which MoD was already very experienced. This included an enhanced arms control programme, an expansion of its Outreach programme to Eastern Europe (providing attachments and training, and introducing concepts of accountability and civilian involvement in defence management), and wider education and training initiatives for overseas countries. It also implied a review of the requirements for defence attachés at embassies. (MoD, 1998a: paras 48–9). Of particular interest under the arms control heading, and offered as evidence of a desire to be more open about defence affairs, the White Paper also revealed for the first time the size of the UK's stocks of fissile material – the first nuclear weapons power in fact to do this. (MoD, 1998a: para. 72). The nuclear deterrent was to be further downgraded in importance, by halving the number of warheads to be carried by the Trident fleet (though one analyst suggests that this policy simply represented planned fitting out of Trident between 1998 and 2000, and that what was being abandoned was further planned growth in the next century: see Grove, 1998:8).

As for the consequences for the size and shape of the Armed Services, and their equipment, the watchwords were 'Jointness' and mobility. In the expectation that the forms of intervention likely to characterise the post-Cold War world would involve tri-service forces, a key aim was to build military capability around 'a pool of powerful and versatile units from all three Services which would be available for operations at short notice' (MoD, 1998a: para. 92). Consistent with the belief that 'In the post Cold War world, we must be prepared to go to the crisis, rather than have the crisis come to us' (MoD, 1998a: para. 6), these Joint Rapid Reaction Forces would depend, *inter alia*, on better long range air and sea transport. Two new large aircraft carriers were to be bought, in order 'to project power more flexibly around the world'. There would also be a joint helicopter command, while the Navy and Air Force were to develop a new joint force based on Harrier jets, equally able to operate from aircraft carriers or land bases. Logistics was also to be managed across all three Services, and a new army/air nuclear, chemical and biological reconnaissance regiment was to be set up. The whole would be able, in addition to maintaining commitments to Northern Ireland, to mount a Gulf War-type operation, or a Bosnian-scale operation plus a simultaneous but smaller deployment to some other crisis. (MoD, 1998a: para. 89).

Table 19.1 summarises the key equipment and personnel changes brought about by the Review. In addition, the Government was to go ahead with the order for 232 Eurofighter aircraft, and would bring into service a fleet of new attack helicopters, 'smart' weapons, and improved intelligence and reconnaissance equipment.

Defence procurement was also to be reformed, and a new system of 'smart procurement' introduced. Developed on the basis of an analysis by the consultancy firm McKinsey, the new system would adopt separate procurement processes for major and minor projects, adopt a through-life approach to projects covering both acquisition and in-service support, draw industry representatives into project teams, and streamline approvals procedures (MoD, 1998a: paras 154–8). It was subsequently announced that the MoD's Procurement

Table 19.1 Key equipment and personnel changes under SDR

	Pre-SDR	*SDR*
Trident missiles	65	58
Max warheads per Trident submarine	96	48
Attack submarines	12	10
Aircraft carriers	3 smaller	2 very large (from 2012)
Destroyers/frigates	35	32
Roll-on roll-off container ships	2	6
Mine sweepers	25	22
Offensive air support	177	154
C-17 heavy airlift planes	none planned	4
Tank regiments	8	6 larger
Regular Army	108000	112300
Territorial Army	56000	40000

Executive was to become a Next Steps Agency. More contentiously, DERA was to become the subject of a Public-Private Partnership – a proposal that was presented more sharply soon afterwards in the Chancellor's speech on the outcome of the Comprehensive Spending Review (CSR) (*Financial Times*, 15 July 1998; and see further developments of this proposal in *Financial Times*, 6 May 1999). This was in spite of a hostile reaction to the possibility of privatisation of DERA from the Commons Defence Committee earlier in the month (House of Commons, 1998a).

A provisional balance sheet

One measure of the success of the political management of the review process is that no significant dissent emerged from the armed forces or, indeed, from any other governmental quarter, bar some criticisms by the Commons Defence Committee of the cuts in the Territorial Army (House of Commons, 1998b). This is in sharp contrast to the lively dissent that accompanied earlier Reviews. For example, John Nott saw his Navy Minister resign; earlier still, James Callaghan, as Prime Minister, had been visited by the Chiefs of Staff in formal protest. To do this while also announcing a cut in the defence budget of £915 million in real terms over the next three years, and a reduction in percentage of GDP devoted to defence from 2.7 per cent in 1998–99 to 2.4 per cent in 2001–02, is a remarkable political achievement. On the other hand, it needs also to be recognised that the lack of dissent owed something to the fact that the cuts were not worse. Nevertheless, these reductions still represented an 'efficiency gain' of 3 per cent a year, and against a background in which, since 1990, the defence budget had already fallen 23 per cent in real terms, and the armed forces been cut by one-third. The consultation process had clearly 'worked', in this respect. As one well-informed analyst observed:

Most observers have given the SDR high marks for its intellectual breadth and consistency and welcomed the fact that it has provided us with a template that can evolve in response to new events and new ideas. The MoD is rather pleased with itself. (Clarke, 1998:3)

The Review was widely seen as representing a sensible rationalisation of the UK's force structure. It addressed problems of overstretch, altered the focus towards expeditionary operations rather than defence of the Central Front, provided the means for delivery of those forces, began some much-needed reorganisation onto a tri-Service basis, and addressed some long standing issues of the management of defence procurement. Quietly, and to general approval, the Review sealed the turn away from the aggressively competitive procurement climate that had been introduced in the 1980s, in what many observers believed to have been a mistaken interpretation of how 'real' businesses managed their supplier relations. Other sensible moves were improvements in medical and logistic support, areas that had suffered under the Conservatives who had been concerned to 'trim the tail without blunting the teeth', while overlooking the fact, as the SDR put it, that 'logistic support is the lifeblood of the forces' (MoD 1998a: para. 7).

On the nuclear front, it downgraded the deterrent, disclosed new information about the management of nuclear materials, and put down a marker for continued energetic British diplomacy in attempts to control the spread of nuclear weapons and, indeed, other weapons of mass destruction.

As Clarke, again, put it, the Review treated the MoD

more than ever before as a major company and seeks to gain greater efficiencies through de-stocking, outsourcing and more commercial asset management. It is certainly a 'review' in the management sense that it has looked hard at all areas of MoD operation, including equipment procurement, and tried to find ways of streamlining the operation. And it claims to be 'strategic' in the sense that it begins from a foreign policy baseline which establishes what the UK wants to achieve with its security policy and relates its force goals explicitly to that. (Clarke, 1998:3)

His criticism, however, concerned what the Review did not discuss or, at least, question: the centrality of the Atlantic Alliance, the nuclear deterrent, Eurofighter, and 'the view that the UK *should* aim to play such a prominent role in the world, or that UK interests will be best served by having the power to intervene' (Clarke, 1998:3). Hence, he concluded:

[The Review] was braver and went further than many had expected, with the promise of better management and co-ordination. The Labour Government should be congratulated for emphasising defence diplomacy, humanitarian response abilities and greater transparency. But the reluctance truly to examine the foreign policy assumptions and nuclear reliance represent a missed opportunity. (Clarke, 1998:7)

Interestingly, similar criticisms came from rather different political quarters. Writing in the *Financial Times*, and basing his argument on information that had begun to circulate in the months prior to publication of the SDR, Philip Stephens attributed the non-negotiability of Trident and Eurofighter to a pre-election lunch between Tony Blair and the editor of the *Daily Telegraph*, at which Blair was trapped into writing an article which set firm limits on what would be permitted of the review process. In the Cabinet debates over how deep the defence cuts should be in the CSR, moreover, Robertson had support, according to Stephens, from Margaret Beckett at DTI, and Clare Short: 'The old left demand for unilateral disarmament has given way to the belief that Britain needs military muscle to run an ethical foreign policy' (Stephens, 1998). As the sub-title to this article put it, 'Tony Blair's defence review has taken the politics out of the issue but has missed the opportunity to think 10 years ahead.'

More forcefully, the Bagehot column in *The Economist*, while admitting to no expertise in the subject, recalled the debates within the Labour Party under Wilson, Callaghan, Kinnock and Blair (pre-election), and recognised the shift towards nuclear deterrence and the Atlantic Alliance as combining 'good sense with good politics'. But, it continued, was it still such good sense by the time Labour had won the 1997 election? Given, as it colourfully put it, that the Territorial Army no longer faced the prospect of 'bayoneting Russian infantry on the cliffs of Dover', was not the traditional Tory insistence on strong defence looking a trifle more paranoid, and the traditional Labour dislike of defence spending a trifle less reckless? And did not proposals such as the purchase of two large aircraft carriers ('hugely expensive, hugely vulnerable, and far too precious to put in harm's way unless an overwhelming national interest is at stake') smack of a 'woolly and vainglorious' mentality? 'A truly radical review', Bagehot went on to note, 'would have asked why Britain needed much defence at all, once the threat to it had disappeared. This one seemed to have started by ruling big cuts out – provided that the word 'modernisation' could be slapped on to the final outcome' (Bagehot, 1998).

In short, the initial assessment seemed to be that the Review had done a good job within the framework set for it, but that the framework itself had not been sufficiently questioned, so that doubts remained about its fitness for purpose. Not a bad verdict, perhaps, but certainly one that left room for further evolution.

An alternative analysis might suggest that, given the history of electoral damage done by previous Labour policies on defence, it should not be surprising that the party, in government, chose to move cautiously. As Harold Macmillan once remarked, the art of politics can be compared to rowing a boat: the trick is to look firmly in one direction, while moving steadily in the other. In this regard, some of the appearances of the July 1998 SDR had already begun to look deceptive by the end of the year.

For example, despite Labour's general desire to play a leadership role in Europe, the SDR did little to advance the debate about European rationalisation, either of military forces and planning, or of procurement, or of overarching common foreign and security policy. Yet Robertson's commitment to consolidation of the European arms industry has been clear. Britain has long played an

---

Box 19.4   *Summary of the Declaration on European Defence,*
UK–French Summit, St Malo, 3–4 December 1998

- Provisions in the Amsterdam Treaty on a Common Foreign and Security Policy should be implemented fully for the EU to play its role on the international stage. The European Council must be able to take decisions on an intergovernmental basis, framing a common defence policy.
- The EU must have the capacity for autonomous action, backed by credible military force. Europeans will operate within the institutional framework of the EU and in conformity with their various obligations to NATO.
- There must be structures and sources of intelligence and analysis to enable the EU to take decisions and approve military action where the Alliance as a whole is not engaged. The EU needs access to suitable military means (taking into account existing WEU assets).
- Europe needs strengthened armed forces supported by a competitive defence industry and technology.
- Both states are determined to unite efforts to bring about these objectives.

Source: IISS, 1999, p. 37.

---

active part at both governmental and industrial levels, continued under Labour, in the manoeuvres to create a transnational European Aerospace and Defence Company (EADC), able to take on the American giants in this field. This remains a strong commitment, despite the setback caused in January 1999 when the decision of GEC to put its Marconi defence subsidiary on the market led British Aerospace to buy it rather than risk a US purchase but, in so doing, threw into disarray the talks about the EADC.

Moreover, with Britain not among the founder members of the Euro at its launch in January 1999, it made sense to play up its leadership credentials, along with those of France, as one of the key European states in matters of defence and security. Indeed, at the St Malo UK–French summit in December 1998, and in other speeches around the same time, Mr Blair moved significantly beyond both his party's pre-election position, and even that expressed in the SDR, and signalled his interest in developing a genuine European operational capability in defence, while remaining committed to the Atlantic Alliance.

Contrary to the Labour line in 1997, the view began to circulate that Britain might now support the fusion of the Western European Union (WEU) into the EU, thus linking decision making over European defence and security more closely into the inter-governmental politics of the EU. This prospect, by now actively promoted by Britain, took an important step forward in May 1999 when the ten member countries of the WEU agreed in principle to merge with the EU. It was expected that the EU summit in June 1999 would ratify this proposal (*Guardian*, 12 May 1999).

The crisis over Kosovo, and the onset in March 1999 of aerial attacks on Yugoslavia by NATO forces, confirmed both the correctness of judgement in the SDR over the type of war that was most likely to be fought in the immediate future, and the inability of Europe to respond to such crises without US leadership, weapons and intelligence gathering. It has been a remarkable feature of how far the Labour Party has moved its position in these matters and a clear demonstration of the solidity of Mr Blair's electoral position, that throughout the campaign Britain was the NATO member state most firmly committed to the action.

At the time of drafting of the SDR, in the early summer of 1998, neither Mr Blair nor Mr Robertson could have anticipated that the quotation cited at the start of this chapter might prove so prescient. Whether these sentiments have survived the Yugoslavian campaign, and whether Britain can develop with its European partners the new order to which Labour is now committed, and do so without weakening the Atlantic Alliance, are the key questions for the immediate future in the field of defence and security.

References

Bagehot (1998), 'George Robertson Punches Above His Weight', *The Economist*, 11 July, p. 35.

Clarke, M. (1998), 'How strategic was the review?', *Disarmament Diplomacy*, 28:3–4.

Deighton, A. (ed.) (1997), *Western European Union 1954–1997: Defence, Security, Integration*, Oxford, European Integration Research Unit.

Grove, E. (1998) 'Nuclear Implications Explained', *Disarmament Diplomacy*, 28:8–9.

House of Commons (1998a), Defence Committee, Sixth Report, Session 1997–98, *The Defence Evaluation and Research Agency*, London, The Stationery Office.

House of Commons (1998b), Defence Committee, Eighth Report, Session 1997–98, *The Strategic Defence Review*, London, The Stationery Office.

International Institute for Strategic Studies (IISS) (1999), *Strategic Survey 1998/99*, Oxford, Oxford University Press.

Labour Party (1995) *Strategy for a Secure Future: Labour's Approach to the Defence Industry* London, The Labour Party.

Ministry of Defence (1995) *Statement on the Defence Estimates 1995*, Cm 2800, London, HMSO.

MoD (1998a), *The Strategic Defence Review*, Cm 3999, London, The Stationery Office.

MoD (1998b), *The Strategic Defence Review: Supporting Essays*, Cm 3999, London, HMSO.

MoD (1998c) *Defence Diversification: Getting the Most Out of Defence Technology*, Cm 3861, London, The Stationery Office.

O'Hanlon, M. (1997), 'Transforming NATO: The Role of European Forces', *Survival*, 39(3):5–15.

Stephens, P. (1998), 'Short Range Target', *Financial Times*, 25 May.

20

New Labour's foreign policy

Peter Lawler

Pragmatism, prudence and a bipartisan disdain for dramatic shifts in policy fundamentals have been the principal hallmarks of British foreign policy throughout the century. It is against the backdrop of this tradition, that New Labour's commitment to bring fresh vision – and with it a more overt ethical content to British foreign policy – acquires its significance. Prior to the Second World War, the Labour Party offered an alternative foreign policy doctrine constructed around philosophical internationalism, international working-class solidarity, a critique of capitalism and an antipathy to power politics. The Labour government of 1945–51 decisively repudiated this. Since then, believers in an alternative foreign policy, while continuing to exist on the margins of party debate, have generally failed to disrupt the continuity between the foreign policies of post-war governments, of either persuasion, in anything other than detail. During the Thatcher era, the Labour Party in opposition recovered some fire in its belly regarding both foreign and defence policy (evidenced particularly by strong grass-roots support throughout the 1980s for non-nuclear defence), but this decisively hindered rather than helped its re-election prospects.

New Labour's foreign policy pronouncements prior to the 1997 election and since then have exhibited only traces of the radicalism of the old socialist alternative. That has been consigned, along with the old Clause 4, to history's dustbin. Nonetheless, Foreign policy was one of the 'four cornerstones' of Tony Blair's vision of a 'New Britain' (Blair, 1996:viii), enunciated prior to the 1997 general election, and his Government has explicitly committed itself to a comprehensive review of foreign policy and a revivification of Britain's internationalist credentials.

Principles and promises

The imperative to reform foreign policy was driven, arguably, by a number of factors. First, scholars and practitioners have long acknowledged that broad changes in the character of international relations – notably, increasing inter-dependence and globalisation – coupled with changes in Britain's relative power and standing demanded foreign policy innovation. Britain's post-1945 decline has been particularly pertinent in exposing the growing implausibility of a myth of exceptionalism. At the heart of that myth lay the presumption that even a post-imperial Britain remained a great power operating within three circles of influence: Commonwealth (replacing Empire), the Atlantic and Europe. This was famously questioned in 1962 by the then US Secretary of State, Dean Acheson, in his remark that Britain had lost an Empire but not found a role. Yet, the three circles imagery was still being articulated with vigour thirty years later by a Conservative Under Secretary of State for Foreign and Commonwealth Affairs (Lennox-Boyd, 1993). Even if the Thatcher Governments recognised key features of a changing external environment, they also exhibited a consistent reticence to let go of the past. True, Thatcher had little personal sympathy for the Foreign and Commonwealth Office (FCO) and its 'insatiable appetite for nuances and conditions which can blur the clearest vision' (Thatcher, 1993). Yet, her vision was predominantly built around a relentless and sometimes belligerent evocation of a recovered British exceptionalism, the practical impact of which was usually softened through the influence of her more moderately-minded foreign secretaries.

Under Major, pragmatism returned to the foreground. Indeed, the last Conservative Foreign Secretary, Malcolm Rifkind (1995), cut to the chase in declaring that 'I am not pre-occupied with agonising soul-searching about Britain's historical vocation . . . The best starting point is Lord Palmerston's dictum: "the furtherance of British interests should be the only object of a British Foreign Secretary".'

In contrast, New Labour's manifesto commitments and statements since taking power made it clear that British foreign policy is sorely in need of 'the vision thing'. In essence, this has entailed the reconstruction of Britain's image overseas. Instead of recalling a glorious (and imperial) past, New Labour set about presenting Britain as a confident 'young' country, with 'a lot to offer, especially in partnership with other countries' (Blair, 1996:xiii). Britain was still depicted as capable of operating a genuinely global foreign policy and possessing strong leadership capabilities, but these claims were mitigated by a greater emphasis on co-operative behaviour within multilateral institutions, most notably the European Union (EU), UN and the Commonwealth. As a recent commentary succinctly put it, 'Cool Britannia is in, rule Britannia is out' (Dunne and Wheeler, 1998:850).

A second factor impelling foreign policy reform arose from EU membership and the need to resolve tensions between Britain's presumption of natural *leadership* in Europe and the dictates of *membership* of a collective enterprise (on this, see also Chapter 17). Britain's famously 'awkward partnership' with Europe, arose in part from the strong – in some European eyes, excessive – commitment to the transatlantic relationship with the US. It also reflected the antipathy of many Conservatives towards the social market orientation of other member states and the post-nationalist implications of ever-greater union. Although clearly more in tune with the general tenor of European politics, The Labour Party has also been divided over the question of European integration. Not surprisingly, development of New Labour's European policy has been a more cautious, ambiguous and, arguably, audience-driven process in comparison to other dimensions of foreign policy.

An internationalist foreign policy

The third, more controversial, factor underpinning New Labour's foreign policy reform project emerges more directly from the Party and in particular the internationalist values historically associated with it. 'Labour has traditionally been the party of internationalism', declared the Party's election manifesto (Labour Party, 1997). Prior to this, the foreign policy section of the Labour Party's Policy Guide, released in October 1996, had brought the two themes of internationalism and leadership together. It condemned the Conservatives for:

* squandering Britain's 'unique assets' and its potential for leadership;
* misusing development aid money to seed lucrative arms deals;
* systematically reducing the overall aid budget;
* failing to press for reform of the world bank;
* failing 'to exercise British influence within international institutions on behalf of the world's poor and disadvantaged'. (Labour Party, 1996)

The Policy Guide committed New Labour to ensuring that 'Britain is at the centre of international decision making, not left at the sidelines'. It went on to claim that 'Britain is ideally placed to promote international security and prosperity and to work for human rights, democracy, economic development and the protection of the global environment.' To this end, Labour argued for a foreign policy built around working for 'the strengthening of international organisations', the making of 'the protection and promotion of human rights a key part of our foreign policy', and supporting 'democracy and good government throughout the world'. As much as it wanted to restore British influence in international politics, New Labour emphasised that the kind of influence that its Britain would carry was to be of a qualitatively different order. British 'leadership in the international community' was to be achieved through 'internationalism and engagement' (Labour Party, 1996).

Of course, New Labour was not the first to identify a concern with human rights as a dimension of British foreign policy. Inspired by the Carter administration in the US, the Callaghan Labour Government of 1976–79 sought to bring human rights more fully into British diplomacy and in 1992 the former Conservative Foreign Secretary Douglas Hurd established the first self-standing human rights policy unit in the FCO (Dunne and Wheeler, 1998:852) and introduced human rights training for diplomats. Furthermore, previous

Labour governments have exhibited elements of solidarity with other internationalist-minded states, in the area of development assistance for example (see Chapter 18).

The weight of tradition and habit seems, nonetheless, to have ultimately prevailed. The historical shrouding of the FCO from public and Parliamentary scrutiny helped to stifle substantive reformist moves. However, the vulnerability of conservative foreign policy to criticism in both practical and moral terms facilitated the eventual sundering of at least some of the ties of tradition. The publication in 1996 of the *Scott Report* on the 'arms-to-Iraq' affair, lent considerable last-minute weight to Labour's case for reform in the run up to the election. The report revealed the extent to which foreign policy, trade policy and even aid policy had become intertwined with a domestic political culture of secrecy and unaccountability, particularly in the pursuit of commercial outlets for Britain's arms-related industries.

The source of New Labour's most direct confrontation with foreign policy tradition lies in the declaration that it seeks to 'restore Britain's pride and influence as *a leading force for good in the world*' (Labour Party, 1997, emphasis added). Less dramatic, but perhaps no less significant, was New Labour's commitment to open up the institutions and process of British foreign policy to greater public scrutiny and Parliamentary accountability.

Policies and practice

In endeavouring to bring about change, restore ethical content *and* retain considerable continuity with the past, New Labour set itself a challenging foreign policy brief and the new Foreign Secretary got off to a quick start. Substantive policy commitments made by Robin Cook in the early months of the new Labour government included:

- putting human rights at the heart of foreign policy;
- the regulation of the Arms trade;
- a different approach to Europe;
- stronger commitment to multilateral activism;
- major reform of aid policy;
- a greater role for the FCO in trade promotion.

Cook's first act was to establish the broad framework that would guide New Labour's foreign policy over the next five years. Only ten days into his appointment, he launched a 'Mission Statement' for the FCO. The new mission of the FCO was to 'promote the national interests of the United Kingdom and to contribute to a strong world community' (FCO, 1998a:vi). This mission is intended to secure four benefits for Britain through a foreign policy guided by five 'strategic aims' (see Box 20.1).

As significant as the contents of the Mission Statement, was the manner of its release. In an overt attempt to bring the FCO at least partly out from under

Box 20.1   *The new FCO Mission Statement*

The mission of the Foreign & Commonwealth Office is to promote the national interests of the United Kingdom and to contribute to a strong world community. We shall pursue that Mission to secure for Britain four benefits through our foreign policy:

- *Security.* We shall ensure the security of the United Kingdom and the Dependent Territories and peace for our people by promoting international stability, fostering our defence alliances and promoting arms control actively.
- *Prosperity.* We shall make maximum use of our overseas posts to promote trade abroad and boost jobs at home.
- *Quality of Life.* We shall work with others to protect the World's environment and to counter the menace of drugs, terrorism and crime.
- *Mutual Respect.* We shall work through our international forums and bilateral relationships to spread the values of human rights, civil liberties and democracy which we demand for ourselves.

To secure these benefits for the United Kingdom we shall conduct a global foreign policy with the following strategic aims:

- to make the United Kingdom a leading player in a Europe of independent nation states;
- to strengthen the Commonwealth and to improve the prosperity of its members and co-operation between its members;
- to use the status of the United Kingdom at the United Nations to secure more effective international action to keep the peace of the world and to combat poverty in the world;
- to foster a people's diplomacy through services to British citizens abroad and by increasing respect and goodwill for Britain among the peoples of the world drawing on the assets of the British Council and the BBC World Service;
- To strengthen our relationships in all regions of the world.

The Government will seek to secure these strategic aims over the five years of this parliament.

The Government will use the professionalism, the expertise and the dedication of the staff of the FCO in Whitehall and abroad to achieve our Mission. I invite them to join us in working together to deliver these benefits for the British people.

Source: FCO, 1998a, pp. vi–vii.

the shroud of tradition, the Statement was presented with considerable media fanfare from within the FCO building itself. It was followed by a video made for the FCO by the British film director David Puttnam (which would subsequently be sent out to all British foreign posts) and a mass meeting with FCO staff. Cook's opening efforts to alter the FCO's public image were subsequently followed by an announcement of revisions to recruitment policy to encourage a greater intake from the state education sector, minority groups and women. In addition, the public was invited for the first time to come and inspect the lavishly renovated FCO headquarters in King Charles Street. Of course, such efforts could be dismissed as little more than populist stunts by a government that has attracted considerable criticism for its preoccupation with image. A more generous, and by no means implausible, reading would see Cook's efforts to make the workings of the FCO more visible as consistent with New Labour's commitment to more open and transparent government.

In launching the Mission Statement, Cook declared that 'this was an age of internationalism'. Clearly taking aim at the tradition of pragmatism, he went on to claim that the new mission moved the FCO beyond 'managing crisis intervention' and on to 'the delivery of a long-term strategy'. Furthermore, it also supplied 'an ethical content to foreign policy and recognises that the national interest cannot be defined only by narrow *realpolitik*'. Referring to the fourth benefit that the Mission intended to secure for Britain, Cook identified a 'national interest' in 'the promotion of our values and confidence in our identity'. This provided the impetus for the goal of securing 'the respect of other nations for Britain's contribution to keeping the peace of the world and promoting democracy around the world'. More pointedly, Cook claimed that 'the Labour Government does not accept that political values can be left behind when we check in our passports to travel on diplomatic business'. Accordingly, the Government 'would put human rights at the heart of our foreign policy'. In addition, the four benefits that the Mission was intended to realise provided 'the Labour Government's contract with the British people on foreign policy'. This theme was reiterated in internationalist form in the Mission's commitment to a 'peoples diplomacy', by which was meant the fostering of 'respect, understanding and goodwill for Britain among nations as well as governments' (Cook, 1997a).

To start out with a public exposition of guiding principles, underpinned by allusions to a public moral contract, did constitute a decisive break with the past and the theme of ethics and foreign policy was returned to frequently in the months that followed election victory. Cook returned to it only three weeks after the launch of the Mission Statement, in an address to the London diplomatic corps. Here he expounded upon the themes of international interdependence and the interconnectedness of 'the domestic sphere and international events'. 'Diplomacy', he argued, 'now encompasses the fundamentals of the lives of our peoples, their jobs, their beliefs of right and wrong, even the quality of the air they breathe' (Cook, 1997b).

Box 20.2   *'Putting Human Rights at the heart of British foreign policy': key commitments*

- Support for 'measures within the international community to express our condemnation of those regimes who grotesquely violate human rights and fail to respond to demands for an improvement in standards' (such as The Harare Declaration binding Commonwealth members to principles of human rights and good governance).
- Support for the use of sanctions by the international community against regimes violating human rights.
- Refusal to supply weapons and equipment to regimes which 'deny the demands of their peoples for human rights'.
- A commitment to ensuring that Britain's pursuit of increased trade did not undermine human rights, particularly regarding the use of child labour.
- Support for the establishment of a permanent International Criminal Court and the provision of more resources to existing International Criminal Tribunals (such as the tribunals on Rwanda and Yugoslavia).
- A commitment to publish an annual report on British activities promoting human rights.
- The incorporation of the European Convention of Human Rights into British law.

Source: Cook, 1997c.

Human rights

In July 1997, in a lengthy speech on 'Human Rights into a New Century', Cook reiterated the ethical dimensions of foreign policy once more. On this occasion, he outlined twelve policies that would put into effect Britain's commitment to human rights (Cook, 1997c). The key commitments are outlined in Box 20.2.

In announcing these policies, Cook eschewed engagement with debates about the universality of human rights, preferring to adopt what he called a 'down to earth' perspective wherein Britain had an obligation to pursue on behalf of others those rights 'which we claim for ourselves'. He also pointed to his government's establishment of a separate Department for International Development, headed by a minister with Cabinet status (on this, see Chapter 18). The new human rights policies were, Cook argued, 'an integral part of Britain's work in international development'.

The weeks that followed the announcement of new human rights policies proved to be difficult for the new foreign secretary. On the one hand, Britain's decision to snub the ceremony honouring Burma's admission into the Association of South East Asian Nations (ASEAN), because of the ruling junta's human rights violations, attracted praise from human rights monitoring organisations. On the other, Britain's relationship with another ASEAN member, Indonesia, attracted far less favourable commentary. The issue here was arms sales.

The arms industry

New Labour's policies on the British arms industry were bound to attract considerable attention. By the end of 1996, Britain had become the world's second largest arms exporter with annual exports totalling £5.1 billion pounds (25 per cent of the global market) and a domestic arms manufacturing sector employing 415,000 people. The industry had been in the public eye throughout the dying days of the previous Conservative administration, not only because of the publicity surrounding the 'arms to Iraq' affair, but also because the Scott Report had revealed the absence of any regulation other than statutory powers granted under wartime legislation. These powers, the report concluded, 'lacked the provisions for parliamentary supervision and control that would be expected and are requisite in a modern parliamentary democracy' (Scott, 1996:1759, K2.1). This was a deficiency for which both Conservative and Labour post-war administrations were culpable.

In June 1997, the then Junior Foreign Minister, Tony Lloyd, foreshadowed Labour's policies on the regulation of the arms trade, in a speech to an NGO seminar. It was announced that arms sales would come under comprehensive legislative control, governed by human rights concerns, as well as principles of transparency and accountability. In addition, the Government would issue an annual report on UK strategic exports (Lloyd, 1997). In response to a Written Parliamentary Question at the end of the following month, the Foreign Secretary announced the 'new criteria to ensure a responsible arms trade'. The first criterion constitutes a broad summary of the restrictive dimensions of the total package:

> An export licence will not be issued if the arguments for doing so are outweighed by the need to comply with the UK's international obligations and commitments, or by concern that the goods might be used for internal repression or international aggression, or by the risks to regional stability, or other considerations as described in these criteria. (FCO, 1997)

Subsequent criteria outline in some detail what the UK's 'international obligations and commitments' exactly are, including a wide range of international treaties and the government's own commitment not to export any form of anti-personnel landmine (APL). Furthermore, the Government declared that it would honour its pledge to improve transparency and accountability by publishing an annual report on strategic exports, would work towards common EU criteria for the control of arms exports and prohibit the manufacturing, selling, or procuring by British companies 'of equipment designed primarily for torture'.

In spite of their comprehensiveness (especially in contrast to what had existed previously), the announcement of the new criteria generated immediate and considerable critical commentary. This was for two principle reasons: the qualifying references to 'The United Kingdom's National Interests'; and, the Foreign Secretary's observation that the criteria would not be applied to export licences agreed to by the previous government. The implication of the latter point was clear enough: the government intended to honour arms sales agreements with Indonesia worth more than three hundred million pounds and involving trainer aircraft, armoured cars and water cannon. The *Guardian* (29 July 1997) declared that 'as was sadly expected' Cook had failed 'the ethical test', a judgement echoed by a number of NGOs and the defence spokesman of the Liberal Democrats. According to the *Independent* (29 July 1997), the new guidelines fell 'indisputably short of a watertight guarantee that British arms will not slip through the human rights net'. Particular targets for criticism included the requirement that 'full weight' should be given to the UK's national interests including the 'potential effect on the UK's economic, financial and commercial interests' and the 'potential effect on the UK's relations with the recipient country' (FCO, 1997).

The political dilemma confronting the government is apparent. Approximately 90,000 of jobs in Britain's defence manufacturing sector are dependent solely on exports. Furthermore, in 1996 £438 million of the UK's arms exports were accounted for by sales to Indonesia alone (*Guardian*, 29 July 1997; *Independent*, 29 July 1997). Not surprisingly, then, the 'ethical dimension' of New Labour's foreign policy came back into sharp focus during the Foreign Secretary's tour of South East Asia in August 1997. Again, he received mixed reviews from the domestic press and various interested NGOs, particularly with regard to the substantive content of Britain's commitment to bridge building and 'positive partnership' with trading partners who have poor human rights records and are in the market for British arms. In the case of Indonesia, Cook's 'six point plan' for improving human rights was dismissed by the *Financial Times* (2 September 1997) as 'window dressing', not the least because of such things as the paltry donation of £2000 worth of political science text books (in English) to the Jakarta Human Rights Commission. Against this, the fact that Cook received rebukes from both the Burmese and Malaysian Governments for raising human rights issues did at least suggest that he was endeavouring to move Britain somewhat beyond the pale of pragmatism. Similarly, Cook's decision to block two arms contracts with Indonesia in October 1997 lent some credence to his reform efforts, although their low value (about £1 million) rendered the decision largely symbolic in the eyes of his critics. That those decisions were followed almost immediately by the approval of 11 new contracts for Indonesia covering surveillance equipment, communications equipment, bombs and ammunition did not enhance the government's credibility in this area. Nonetheless, by the end of their first year in office, the government claimed that it had established 'a positive human rights partnership programme in Indonesia' (FCO, 1998a:xiii).

International activism

The policies on human rights and the arms industry attracted the bulk of press interest in foreign policy during the first year of the Blair Government. This was hardly surprising since it is within these domains that national interest and the Government's professed commitment to cosmopolitan duties beyond national boundaries intersect so acutely. A further component of new Labour's 'new internationalism', however, was a stronger general commitment to multilateral activism, particularly at the UN, in pursuit of two of the four benefits for Britain outlined in the FCO's Mission Statement: the security of the UK; and the enhancement of 'the quality of life'. These briefs cover a wide range of policy domains, including international environmental protection, arms control and disarmament and multilateral co-operation in the areas of drugs, terrorism and crime.

Because of its permanent seat on the UN Security Council, Britain has long been a major UN player. Few of these policy developments involve, therefore, a repudiation of Conservative practice, but more an increase in relative prominence, a shift in the priorities guiding the detail of policy, and a strengthening of the pre-existing ethical dimensions. In his first address to the UN General Assembly, in September 1997, the Foreign Secretary affirmed Britain's commitment to the UN and reiterated Britain's support for the reform of the UN's bureaucracy, financial structure and Security Council. The distinctiveness of New Labour's approach emerged in Cook's commitment to reverse the decline in Britain's aid budget, to work for a balance between developed and developing countries in a reformed Security Council, and his government's decision to rejoin UNESCO and not leave UNIDO (Cook, 1997d; see also Chapter 18).

A particular feature of the FCO since Cook's arrival has been a much more constructive relationship with non-governmental organisations (NGOs). Innovations include secondment of FCO staff to Save The Children and the Minority Rights Group, and recruitment of advisers (especially in the area of human rights) from NGOs to the FCO (Cook, 1998b; FCO, 1999:35, 78).

In its analysis of achievements against objectives, the 1998 FCO Departmental Report claimed that Britain had 'taken the initiative' or played a 'leading' or 'prominent' role on a host of international issues. These included: the ratification of the Comprehensive Test Ban Treaty (Britain and France were the first two nuclear powers to do so); the strengthening of the Biological Weapons Convention; development of the EU Code of Conduct on conventional arms transfers; the opening of political dialogue between the EU and Algeria; the maintenance of momentum in the Middle East peace process; and the securing of a programme to implement decisions of the 1992 Rio Conference (FCO, 1998a:xi-xiii). Britain also took a proactive role in the design and establishment of a permanent International Criminal Court (Cook, 1998a) and was one of the first signatories of the Ottawa Convention to ban APLs, although it only just made the ratification deadline.

In many respects, then, developments since the 1977 election support the Blair government's claims that it is refashioning Britain as a more multilaterally-minded, ethically-motivated international player which, in particular, takes a more constructive view of relations with the developing world. Equally, The *Guardian's* observation (12 May, 1997) that as 'the most radical member of Blair's Cabinet', Cook had 'blown the winds of change through Whitehall's stuffiest ministry' has proven to have real substance to it.

The FCO's award-winning World Wide Web pages (which have produced a quantum leap in the volume of available information), its commitments to annual reporting in key policy areas such as human rights or arms sales and annual open days have lent support to the claims of greater openness. The FCO is also working to modify the received image of the diplomatic service as being overwhelmingly made up of white males from public schools (by appointing Whitehall's first Minority Ethnic Liaison Officer, for example), although the conservatives had already begun to make some efforts in this area (FCO, 1999:81). The July 1999 cabinet reshuffle contributed further to the changing of the FCO's public image. In came Peter Hain, the veteran anti-apartheid campaigner and anti-nuclear activist, who was joined by John Battle, a former industry minister from the left of the Party and noted both for his opposition to the Gulf War and nuclear defence. The FCO also received Britain's first black minister, Baroness Scotland of Asthal.

Words and deeds

The fact that New Labour's foreign policy did, in many respects, break with a long past ensured that from the outset virtually every action of the Foreign Secretary would be construed by the media as a test of the new 'ethical foreign policy' (even if it was usually forgotten that the Foreign Secretary never used such an all-encompassing phrase).

One might well question whether Britain 'has really managed to square the circle in hard, high-profile cases like Indonesia and China where economics invariably conflict with hopes for improved human rights' (Black, 1998:13). But British efforts in places such as Algeria, Bosnia, Jordan, China and Pakistan – as reported in the FCO's first annual audit of British efforts in the human rights field (FCO/DfID, 1998) – were praised, albeit guardedly, by human rights NGOs. The praise was guarded largely because of Britain's continuing pursuit of markets for its arms industry and the inconsistency of this with the FCO's otherwise admirably holistic view of the human rights dimension of foreign policy (Black, 1998).

Equally, Cook's much cited defence of a 'third way' between 'the row and the kow tow', the successor to the much-debated idea of 'constructive engagement', suffers from being 'an ill-marked path, which tends to become invisible at awkward moments' (Neal Ascherson, *Observer*, 2 August, 1998, p. 26). Nonetheless, the second year of New Labour's foreign policy saw increasing recognition of a real difference between New Labour and previous conservative governments. As already noted, it would be erroneous to presume that a concern for human rights arrived only with New Labour; the difference lies more in the greater prominence and visibility of rights-talk in British foreign policy and a concomitant greater willingness to be publicly judged. Neal Ascherson (*Observer*, 2 August, 1998, p. 26) has claimed that the 'ethical dimension' had 'given a new background colour to British foreign policy. That amounts to success. But it is also why the failures stand out so clearly'.

The problem of consistency

As we have seen the British arms industry dogged New Labour's Foreign Secretary from the outset and it continues to do so. According to the Select Committee on International Development (SCID), 'the determined and principled control of arms exports is a litmus test of this Government's concern to prevent conflict and inject an ethical dimension into foreign policy' (SCID, 1999:1). The promised first annual report on arms ('strategic') exports was due by June 1998, but did not materialise until March 1999. Covering the period May to December 1997, the report showed that small arms had been exported to Bahrain, Sri Lanka, Turkey and Zimbabwe. According to Saferworld, such exports 'raise serious questions' in light of the Government guideline that arms should not be exported 'if there is a clearly identifiable risk that the proposed export might be used for internal repression'. The report also provides little detail of the licences issued for strategic components, spare parts and dual-use goods. The large number of such licences covering exports to India and Pakistan appears to risk breaching a further guideline: that export licences should not be granted if the intended recipient 'would use the proposed export aggressively against another country, or to assert force by a territorial claim' (Saferworld, 1999:1). In addition, some exports were authorised to destinations, such as Jordan and Singapore, notorious as transit routes for arms to Iraq and Iran. Toxicological agents, sub-machine guns and ammunition were exported to Hong Kong, in spite of its transfer to China in June 1997. What possible use, Saferworld also asks, could the Channel Islands have had 'for CS gas cartridges, stun grenades and "non-military" small arms'?

The *Independent on Sunday* (27 June 1999) has also reported that Royal Ordnance, a subsidiary of British Aerospace, the UK's largest weapons manufacturer, was the sole provider of RDX (the key component of APLs) to the US Army. The US has refused to sign the Ottowa Treaty banning APLs and although there are a range of possible uses for RDX, there was nothing in the contract to rule out the use of the British-supplied RDX in the manufacture of US APLs. The DTI refused to give details on the Royal Ordinance contract to the paper on the grounds of 'commercial confidentiality'. It may be the case that the DTI or the FCO do, in fact, thoroughly vet such contracts to ensure they do not breach Britain's international treaty commitments. It should be noted, however, that in July 1999 the SCID criticised the DTI for approving the export of arms to Indonesia and Eritrea and 'failing to apply the human rights and conflict concerns which are at the heart of (British) development policy . . . despite the protests of DfID' (SCID, 1999:2).

As was noted above, the Scott Report made much of the paltry legislative framework surrounding arms exports and New Labour made much use of the Scott Report. Yet, three years later, strategic export controls are still being operated under what the Select Committee on Trade and Industry (SCTI) (1999:1) called 'a barely refurbished piece of emergency legislation from 60 years ago' (the Import, Export and Custom Powers [Defence] Act 1939). At the time of writing, the government had yet to commit itself to a formal mechanism for parliamentary scrutiny of strategic exports. Against this, the Government has welcomed an unprecedented joint ad hoc enquiry by the parliamentary Defence, Foreign Affairs, International Development and Trade and Industry select committees into the annual arms exports report, as proposed by Saferworld (SCTI, 1999; Saferworld, 1999). That enquiry will report after the publication of the next annual strategic exports audit.

The 'Arms to Iraq' affair also resurfaced in July 1999, but this time not in a manner likely to enhance Cook's reputation. In opposition, Cook attacked the Conservatives for using 'gagging orders' (Public Interest Immunity Certificates, or PIIs) to secure the imprisonment of the businessmen involved in the scandal by withholding evidence that would have shown collusion by the security services. Using John Major's 'open government' code, the Guardian newspaper discovered that since coming to power not only has the New Labour government used PIIs almost twice as frequently as the Tories during the last two years of the Major Government, but that Cook had issued a gagging order against Paul Grecian, one of the businessmen involved in the original scandal, in order to prevent him gaining access to four documents he wanted to use in his legal case against Customs and Excise for malicious prosecution. In response to this, the Shadow foreign secretary, John Maples, described Cook's action as 'rich in hypocrisy and irony' (*Guardian*, 20 July 1999).

The 1998 'Arms to Africa' episode similarly cast the FCO and, ultimately the Foreign Secretary in a rather poor light. In February 1998, Sandline International, a private British military company, sent an unlicensed shipment of arms into Sierra Leone, intended for the use of the democratically elected President Tejan Kabbah who, in May 1997, had been ousted in an internationally-condemned coup. The British High Commissioner had given the shipment 'a degree of approval' even though it was in clear breach of a UN Security Council Resolution of October 1997. That resolution was implemented for the UK by an Order in Council, making it a criminal offence for any British citizen to supply arms to Sierra Leone. FCO officials had been informed of the impending shipment but 'did not immediately appreciate the full significance of the information' (Legg and Ibbs, 1998:1.5) The matter was only referred to Customs and Excise by the FCO after newspaper allegations that Britain was breaching the UN arms embargo. In April 1998, Sandline's solicitors wrote to the Foreign Secretary protesting the investigation on the grounds that the shipment had received approval from government officials.

By now a full-scale scandal was brewing and Cook immediately set up an investigation headed by Sir Thomas Legg, which published its report in July 1998. Although it exonerated all FCO ministers of any wrongdoing, while revealing them to be disturbingly out of touch with what was going on, it strongly criticised the FCO. The report's conclusions identified 'repeated, and partly systemic, failures of communication' arising from a series of 'management and cultural factors'. However, it also concluded that 'the officials were working hard and conscientiously, and should not be judged too harshly' (Legg and Ibbs, 1998:1.16–1.18).

Cook, along with his Junior Minister Tony Lloyd, was personally tainted by the affair after a Labour MP, Ernie Ross, leaked a draft of a highly critical report about it from the House of Commons Select Committee on Foreign Affairs. In fact, Lloyd had knowledge of the leak when he told Parliament that he had not seen the report prior to its publication. Cook also subsequently admitted that his department had received leaks of two other reports from the same committee. Although Cook claimed no impropriety was committed because he did not act on the illicit information, the Select Committee on Standards and Privileges Committee (SCSP) nevertheless later suspended Ross and severely reprimanded Cook (SCSP, 1999). As was widely expected, Lloyd was sacked from his post in the July 1999 cabinet reshuffle. Cook weathered the storm. Nonetheless, the scandal added to mounting speculation that he was not in full command of his own, apparently not fully competent, department.

Various other episodes also tarnished the renovated image of British foreign policy under New Labour. During the crisis over Iraq's obstruction of the UN arms inspection team in early 1998, Britain stood alongside the US in taking a particularly robust stance and threatening Saddam Hussein with force if he did not back down. 'For once', claimed Tony Blair, 'there is no third way' (*Observer*, 15 February 1998) and he had the support of the majority of the British public (*Guardian*, 10 February 1998). Nonetheless, Britain's stance attracted a deal of domestic and international criticism. At home, critics on the left of the Labour Party voiced concerns about Britain's militancy and unequivocal support for the US. From the conservative side, Lord Gilmour (Deputy Foreign Secretary, 1979–81) described Britain as 'America's sadly obedient poodle' and lambasted Blair for having 'exceeded even previous Conservative governments in his subservience to the US administration' (*Observer*, 15 February 1998). The theme of 'double standards' was frequently aired, in reference to the markedly less militant reaction by Britain or the US to the development of weapons of mass destruction elsewhere in the world and the fact that the US, like Saddam Hussein, also took objection to certain foreign nationals inspecting its facilities under the Chemical Weapons Convention. There was also some concern as to whether some weapons inspectors were engaging in intelligence gathering outside of their UN brief. A *Guardian* editorial (12 February 1998) asked 'who will inspect the inspectors?', going on to point out that the Anglo-American standpoint would create a damaging impression of double standards 'where it does most damage – in the Middle East'.

In essence, critics were questioning the fit between Britain's approach to the crisis and its claims to be engaging in a more multilateral, less confrontational form of foreign policy. Britain's held the presidency of the EU at the time and was criticised by the Netherlands (traditionally Atlanticist and also supportive of a tough stance on the inspections issue) for failing to consult adequately with other European states, thereby hampering the forging of a common EU standpoint (*Guardian*, 19 February 1998). Again, the implication was that Britain was leaning excessively towards the US viewpoint at the expense of Europe, partly undermining New Labour's claims that it was bringing a fresh approach to its dealings with the EU. The criticism was not shared by all EU members, it must be said; the German Chancellor explicitly rebutted it (*Guardian*, 19 February 1998).

Similar criticisms about the substance of British foreign policy were to re-emerge during the Kosovo crisis a year later, although, paradoxically, Britain's initial response to mounting evidence of Serbian atrocities attracted the charge of inaction, something not historically unfamiliar to the FCO. In light of Milosovic's actions in Kosovo, The EU decided to ban flights by the Yugoslav national airline (JAT) from 8 September 1998 onwards. Britain declined to follow suit claiming that the action was in breach of international law since only an 'injured state' could take reprisals, in this case the breaking of a 1959 air services agreement with Yugoslavia. 'Foreign Office ethics fly out of the window', declared the *Independent* (16 September 1998), which rounded on Cook for failing to tear up the agreement especially given that, while holding the EU presidency, Britain had appeared to be leading the campaign for a tough-ening of the EU stance towards Serbia. With talk of the European Commission being on the verge of prosecuting the UK for non-compliance, Cook ordered a review of the policy and just eight days after the EU ban came into force, Britain reversed its decision and banned flights by Yugoslav carriers.

What kind of internationalism?

In spite of the various incidents that caused some observers to question whether Britain had genuinely embraced a more overt ethical dimension in foreign policy, the debate has shifted increasingly to what the commitment to an 'ethical dimension' in foreign policy substantively entails. Few have doubted Cook's personal commitment to a revivified British internationalism, but how such an internationalism is interpreted at Number 10 has increasingly become a matter of speculation, especially given the Prime Minister's increasing prom-inence in the foreign policy arena. The confrontations with Iraq and Serbia have been catalytic in this respect. Indeed, by the end of the bombing campaign against Yugoslavia, headlines referring to 'Blair's war', or describing the Prime Minister along the lines of 'Commander Blair' or 'NATO's hardliner' were rife in both the British and international press.

Early signs of variations in emphases between Cook and Blair were evident in the Prime Minister's Guildhall speech in November 1997. Addressing 'the principles of a modern British foreign policy', Blair reiterated the theme of a 'New Britain' and made frequent if brief references to the new ethical sensibilities regarding the arms industry and human rights. The bulk of his speech, however, turned around the theme of British leadership, even if 'in these post-empire days (we cannot) be a super-power in a military sense'. More provocatively, Blair claimed that:

> There is a lot of rubbish talked about the Empire. In my view, we should not either be apologising for it, or wringing our hands about it. . . . It was, in many ways, a most extraordinary achievement and it has left us with some very valuable connections – in the Commonwealth, in the English language. (Blair, 1997)

He went on to identify five 'guiding light principles of a modern British foreign policy':

* to be a 'leading partner in Europe'
* to be 'strong in Europe and strong with the US'
* to have strong defence, not just to defend but 'for British influence abroad'
* to 'use power and influence for a purpose'
* to champion free trade.

Fully reminiscent of Margaret Thatcher's much remarked-upon affection for Washington, Blair's comments on the US were laudatory. 'Leaving all sentiment aside', he said, 'they are a force for good in the world. They can always be relied on when the chips are down.'

Since then, there has been considerable press commentary on Blair's close relationship with Clinton and his administration. The *Guardian* noted a few months later, under the heading 'Love across the Pond', that its own opinion surveys show that almost two thirds of the British public shared Blair's enthusiasm for the alliance with the US (*Guardian*, 10 February 1998). What is less certain is whether this enthusiasm is fully shared within the FCO or by Robin Cook. During the Iraqi crisis, it was reported that co-ordination between the FCO and Downing Street was singularly lacking and that foreign diplomats saw Blair as more gung-ho than his foreign secretary (*Guardian*, 20 February 1998, 23 February 1998). When the US launched strikes against alleged terrorist bases in Sudan and Afghanistan in August 1998, in response to the bombing of US embassies in Nairobi and Dar es Salaam, the FCO and Cook remained conspicuously silent while Blair issued a short statement unequivocally supporting the American action (FCO, 1998b).

It was during the Kosovo crisis, in a speech entitled 'Doctrine of the International Community', that Blair has most fully identified what he personally understood by an internationalist foreign policy (Blair, 1999). 'Globalisation', argued Blair, 'is not just economic, it is also a political and security phenomenon'. He went on to say that in place of ad hoc responses to global crises, 'we need to focus in a serious and sustained way on the principles of the doctrine of international community and on the institutions that deliver them'. This would cover reform of the global financial and trading systems, reform of the UN and its Security Council, reform of NATO, greater co-operation between the developed and developing worlds over the environment and 'a serious examination of the issue of Third World debt' (Blair, 1999). For Blair, internationalism requires a readiness to resort to armed intervention after five considerations have been undertaken: 'are we sure of our case'; 'have we exhausted all the diplomatic options'; is there a sensible and prudent military option; 'are we prepared for the long term'; and, finally, do we have national interests involved?' What was also clear was that Blair saw Britain, alongside the US, at the heart of this global reform process, the ideological core of which was to be derived from the notion of the 'third way' (Blair, 1999:7).

To say that the campaign against Milosovic was 'Blair's war' might be an exaggeration (*Guardian*, 12 June 1999), but most commentators seem to agree that the Prime Minister was the more hawkish of the two key leaders, even if the US provided the bulk of the military muscle. To what extent this was a product of Blair's more secure political position (strong domestic public and media support and a large parliamentary majority), or Clinton's relative weakness remains a matter of debate. In any case, by the end of the air campaign against Serbia, and in spite of the risks involved in taking a hard-line stance, Blair's international standing was significantly elevated. In spite of this, the marginalisation of Parliament during the Kosovo crisis concerned even ardent supporters of the Downing Street viewpoint. President Clinton enjoys the formal title of Commander in Chief, but cannot ignore Capitol Hill during war. 'Commander Blair', as the *Observer* noted (18 April 1999), very much ran his campaign from the Prime Minister's study with little recourse even to his Cabinet, save for the Foreign Secretary, Minister of Defence and, occasionally, the Minister for International Development.

Conclusion

There can be little doubt that, in many respects, New Labour has decisively transformed British foreign policy, not the least in restoring an overt internationalist and ethical dimension to it and rendering its underlying principles more visible than ever before. Under Cook's leadership, the FCO is also undergoing a visible process of institutional transformation.

It would be wrong to overdraw the differences between Blair and Cook's understanding of internationalism. During 'Operation Allied Force', for example, both appeared to be fully in tune with each other regarding the moral condemnation of Serbian aggression and the rectitude of NATO's campaign. Nonetheless, Blair's foreign policy vision exhibits a degree of certitude about the principles and policies underpinning the new British internationalism that marks it out from the more open-ended perspective outlined by Cook in the early days of the New Labour Government.

It is tempting to suggest, then, that two subtly distinct varieties of British internationalism are emerging, personified in the figures of Cook and Blair respectively. The first is a strongly rights and justice-oriented, multilateralist internationalism that emphasises Britain's *membership* of the international community and entails a decisive break with tradition, but retains a deal of continuity with 'old' Labour Party values. It is an internationalism that is dialogical in character and sits more comfortably with the notion of a fresh, more co-operative approach to Europe. It is also an internationalism that frames such decisions as the appointment of a human rights expert from Amnesty International (a 'new sort of diplomat' as Cook put it) directly to the British Embassy in Manila, in reflection of the promotion of children's rights as 'an integral part of what the Foreign Office does' (Cook, 1999).

The second variety evinces a more modest shift from the recent path although with no less conviction. It draws selectively upon internationalist language and themes but is firmly centered around an emphasis upon British *leadership* capabilities, an unequivocal commitment to the bilateral partnership with the US and the evocation of 'enlightened patriotism' (Blair, 1997). It is authoritative in style and entails a shorter step away from British foreign policy tradition and a larger step away from old Labour. It also runs the risk of alienating Britain's European allies as much as bringing them along with it. In its association with the increasing centralisation of foreign policy making in the hands of the Prime Minister and his inner circle, the second type also raises questions about the appropriate fit between New Labour's foreign policy, as it unfolds further, and the wider Blairite project of open, democratic and accountable government.

References

Black, I. (1998), 'Robin Cook's Tour of the Global Badlands', *Guardian* (22 April 1998) p.13.

Blair, T. (1996), *New Britain: My Vision of a Young Country*, London, Fourth Estate.

Blair, T. (1997), 'The Principles of a Modern British Foreign Policy', speech at the Lord Mayor's Banquet (10 May), London: FCO.

Blair, T. (1999), 'Doctrine of the International Community', speech to the Economic Club of Chicago (22 April), London: FCO.

Cook, R. (1997a), 'Opening Statement by the Foreign Secretary, Mr Robin Cook, at a Press Conference on the FCO Mission Statement' (12 May), London, FCO.

Cook, R. (1997b), 'Speech by the Foreign Secretary, Mr Robin Cook, to the London Diplomatic Corps Annual Reception' (11 June), London, FCO.

Cook, R. (1997c), 'Human Rights into a New Century', speech by the Foreign Secretary (17 July), London, FCO.

Cook, R. (1997d), 'A United Nations for the Twenty-first Century', speech to the 52nd United Nations General Assembly (23 September), London, FCO.

Cook, R. (1998a), Statement on the International Criminal Court to the House of Commons (20 July), London, FCO.

Cook, R. (1998b), 'Human Rights: Making the Difference', speech to the Amnesty International Human Rights Festival (16 October), London, FCO.

Cook, R. (1999), 'My Pledge to Help the Victims of Child Abuse', article in the *Express* newspaper (5 August), London, FCO.

Dunne, T. and Wheeler, N. (1998), 'Good International Citizenship: A Third Way for British Foreign Policy', *International Affairs*, 74:4, 847–70.

FCO (1997), 'Foreign Secretary Announces New Criteria to Ensure Responsible Arms Trade', FCO Daily Bulletin, London, FCO, 28 July.

FCO (1998a), *98 Departmental Report*, Cm 3903, London, The Stationery Office.

FCO (1998b), 'British Reaction to US Strikes in Sudan and Afghanistan: Statement by the Prime Minister, Mr Tony Blair', London, FCO, 20 August.

FCO (1999), *99 Departmental Report*, Cm 4209, London, The Stationery Office.

FCO/Department of International Development (1998), *Annual Report on Human Rights*, London, The Stationery Office.

Labour Party (1996) 'Leadership in the World', http://www.poptel.org.uk/Labour-Party/policy/leadership-m.html & leadership-a.html.

Labour Party (1997), *New Labour: Because Britain Deserves Better*, London, Labour Party.

Legg, Sir R. and Ibbs, Sir R. (1998), *Report of the Sierra Leone Arms Investigation*, London, The Stationery Office.

Lennox-Boyd, M. (1993), 'British Foreign Policy', speech to the English Speaking Union Summer Conference (13 July), London, FCO.

Lloyd, T. (1997), 'Controlling the Arms Trade: A New Agenda for the Twenty First Century', speech to the Saferworld and British-American Security Information Council (BASIC) (9 June), London, FCO.

Rifkind, M. (1995), 'Principles and Practice of British Foreign Policy', speech at the Royal Institute of International Affairs, Chatham House (21 September), London, FCO.

Saferworld (1999), 'Long Awaited Arms Report Published', London, Saferworld, http://www.gn.apc.org/sworld/news&views/arep.html.

SCID (1999), 'Executive Summary', *Sixth Report: Conflict Prevention and Post-conflict Reconstruction*, HC 55–I, 1998–99 Session.

SCSP (1999), *Eighth Report: Premature Disclosure of Reports of the Foreign Affairs Committee*, HC 607, 1998–99 Session.

SCTI (1999), 'Appendix', *Fourth Special Report: Government Observations on the Second Report from the Committee (Session 1998–99) on Strategic Export Controls*, HC 65, 1998–99 Session.

Scott, Sir R. (1996), *Report of the Inquiry into the Export of Defence Equipment and Dual-use Goods to Iraq and Related Prosecutions*, London, HMSO.

Thatcher, M. (1993), *The Downing Street Years*, London, Harper Collins.

Appendix 1

Changes in Labour Party Policies 1979–97

	1979 manifesto	1983 maniefesto
Economy		
(1) priority action	• full employment • price stability	• reduce mass unemploy-ment (to 1 million) • 'emergency plan of action'
(2) industry/City	• public ownership • planning agreements • state aid for investment • price commission • import limits to protect local industry • Girobank to compete with Big 4 banks • new regional development agencies	• undertake national economic assessment and draw up 5 year national plan • create tripartite National Planning Council • re-nationalise privatised assets • extend public ownership • establish National Investment Bank and reform Pension Trusts. Be prepared to nationalise clearing banks • negotiate development plans with leading companies • give government new industrial powers • develop regional development agencies • introduce exchange controls and import controls • strengthen price controls • strengthen consumer rights

1987 manifesto

- combating unemployment and poverty
- 'priority programme'

- call national economic summit
- public investment in repairing/building hospitals, schools, transport and sewers
- extend 'social ownership' of utilities, plus public stake in high tech industries
- strengthen regulatory structures around City of London
- repatriate British savings and investments overseas
- set up British Industrial Investment Bank
- establish strong regional development agencies
- create new Ministry of Science and Technology

1992 manifesto

- recovery from recession
- 'national recovery programme'

- 'a government with whom business can do business'
- rebuild industrial strength by enhanced allowances for companies investing in new machinery
- create Ministry of Science, to work jointly with industries and universities
- house building programme to generate employment
- create National Investment Bank, operating on strictly commercial criteria, to bring public and private sector together in long-term infrastructure projects
- strengthen regional development agencies
- new deal for small businesses

1997 manifesto

- economic stability to promote investment
- raise the trend rate of growth by strengthening wealth creating base
- government spending to stay within existing limits for 2 years
- tougher competition laws
- reinvigorating the private finance initiative
- establish one-stop regional development agencies
- strengthen capability in science, technology and design: prioritise new green technologies and business

	1979 manifesto	**1983 manifesto**
(3) unions/workers	• tripartite standing pay commission • major extension of industrial democracy • employment subsidy & job creation programmes • jobs/retraining for long-term unemployed • move to 35 hour week	• partnership with unions 'at the heart of our programme' • discuss minimum wage • repeal Conservative employment laws • extend industrial democracy and worker rights (including those of part-time workers, homeworkers, and women on maternity leave) • new statutory framework of training, with well-resourced MSC • reduce working time
(4) environment	• support 'Plan for Coal' • safeguards on nuclear waste • increase public stake in North Sea oil • reduce lead in petrol • produce annual 'state of the environment' report • develop co-ordinated transport policy	• prepare a new 'Plan for Coal', giving coal priority as the nation's fuel • begin massive conservation programme • stop Sizewell and PWR programme • re-assess need for nuclear power. Take whole nuclear industry into public ownership • eliminate lead in petrol • strengthen environmental controls • develop rail network, and create national transport authority to facilitate integrated transport planning

Society

(1) tax policy	• wealth tax • raise tax thresholds	• seek 'fundamental and irreversible shift in the balance of wealth and power in favour of working people and their families'

1987 manifesto	1992 manifesto	1997 manifesto
• repeal Conservative labour laws • strengthen rights against unfair dismissal for all workers; and restore the right to belong to a trade union • introduce national minimum wage, and restore provisions for fair pay • increase benefits for long-term unemployed • guarantee job/retraining to long-term unemployed	• fair treatment at work. No return to 1970s legislation. Ballots before strikes and for union elections to stay. No mass or flying pickets. Adoption of Social Chapter. Restoration of right to join union • a national minimum wage of £3.40 an hour • a training revolution to modernise skills (in a coherent national training policy)	• retention of key elements of 1980s trade union reforms • encourage partnership at work • support Social Chapter • establish a sensible minimum wage • retain advantages of flexible labour markets • move 250,000 young people out of welfare into work
• create new Ministry of Environmental Protection • initiate major energy conservation programme • cancel PWR at Sizewell • invest substantially in research into alternative energy sources • create local transport plans • invest in British Rail	• will embrace the goal of sustainable development: tough emission targets and pollution controls; privileging energy saving over energy sales • establish legal right to a clean environment • subject all government policy to environmental appraisal • restore public control of the National Grid • secure long-term future of coal (stopping 'dash for gas') • no new nuclear power stations • invest in modern public transport (mobilising private finance on high-speed rail links: rejecting plans to privatise British Rail)	• all departments to promote policies to sustain the environment • vital to this is an integrated transport policy • better regulation of privatised rail network and bus companies • new public/private partnership to improve the London underground
• restore 2p cut in income tax • reverse Tory tax cuts on top 5 per cent • introduce wealth tax	• new top tax rate of 50 per cent • increase personal allowances and wife's earned income allowance to take low paid out of income tax system • abolish poll tax	• no change to basic or top rates of income tax throughout the next parliament • long-term aim of 10p starting rate of tax • cut VAT on fuel

	1979 manifesto	**1983 manifesto**
(2) social security	• raise child benefit • raise pensions • new disability allowance	• shift resources to families (via increase child benefits) • raise pensions, and tie pensions to prices/wages (whichever is rising faster) • increase disability allowances
(3) education	• expand nursery education • complete comprehensive system • end public subsidies to fee-paying schools • reduce class size • universal education and training scheme for all 16–19 year olds, with income-related mandatory awards	• comprehensive provision for under 5's • prohibit all forms of academic selection • remove assisted places scheme and charitable status from private schools • no class size over 30 • 2 year student traineeships for 16+, with adequate student financial support • phase in one-year educational entitlement for adults without previous further/higher education
(4) health	• aim to abolish all health charges • phase out pay beds • streamline bureaucracy	• phase out charges • block development of two-tier health service

1987 manifesto	**1992 manifesto**	**1997 manifesto**
• increase child benefit (as part of anti-poverty programme) • raise pensions, and tie pensions to prices/wages (whichever is rising faster) • new disability benefits	• increase child benefit • raise pensions, and restore the link with prices/earnings, (whichever is rising faster)	• retain universal child benefit from birth to age 16, and uprate it 'at least in line with prices' • raise pensions 'at least in line with prices' • create new stakeholder pension schemes
• nursery education for all 3 and 4 year olds • proper recognition and reward for teachers • flexible and clear core curriculum • end 11+, and assisted places scheme • establish 2 year education and training programme for 16+	• additional funds for education, as a rising percentage of GNP • nursery education for all 3–4 year olds by 2000 • modernised school curriculum • improved school standards and national tests • end selection at 11+ and phase out assisted places scheme • new rights for parents, and for local managers of schools	• number one priority; resources to grow as proportion of national income as spending on unemployment falls • zero tolerance of underperformance; • private/public partnerships to improve school buildings • introduction of IT • nursery places for all 4 year olds • new standards in primary schools. Class size down to 30 for 5–7 year olds • grant maintained schools to remain, with 'open and fair' admissions policies • assisted places scheme to be phased out • cost of student maintenance at university to be repaid on income-related basis • new University for Industry
• reduce hospital waiting lists • end privatisation in the NHS • pay nurses adequate wages	• additional resources to NHS • no new health charges • retention of pay review bodies • new performance standards for health authorities, with incentive payments for high achievers	• raise spending in real terms each year • reform the internal market • set high quality standards • ban tobacco advertising • establish independent food standards agency

	1979 manifesto	**1983 manifesto**
Constitution		
(1) rights/law	• resource policing while attacking social causes of crime • extend law centres • strengthen system of family law • restrict discrimination • reform citizenship and immigration laws	• a new deal for women, with positive action, and strengthening of Sex Discrimination and Equal Pay Acts • repeal Police and Criminal Evidence Act, and disband Special Patrol Groups • improve legal aid scheme • improve prison system • lead major campaign against racial discrimination • protect gay rights
(2) structure of state	• establish a Scottish Assembly • introduce a Freedom of Information Act • abolish delaying power & legislative veto powers of the House of Lords • increase powers of large district councils • Continue direct rule, while seeking popular consent for a more democratic governmental arrangement	• establish a Scottish Assembly with tax-raising powers • introduce a Freedom of Information Act • abolish the House of Lords • introduce state aid for political parties • strengthen local democracy • agreed devolved administration in Northern Ireland, repeal of PTA, plus all-Ireland talks on long-term unification by consent

1987 manifesto	1992 manifesto	1997 manifesto
• introduce crime prevention grants	• protect people against crime: new crime prevention measures	• be tough on crime, and tough on the causes of crime
• put more police on the beat, and introduce 'safer estates' and 'safer transport' policies	• reform PACE	• fast-track punishment for young offenders
• increase funding to Criminal Injuries Compensation Board, and strengthen victim support schemes	• improve access to legal aid	• reform CPS to increase conviction rate
	• introduce stronger anti-discrimination laws	• zero tolerance approach to petty crime and neighbourhood disorder
• set up Ministry for Women	• appoint a Minister of the Disabled, and a Children's Minister	• strengthen victims' rights
• strengthen laws against racial discrimination	• create a Ministry for Women	• fresh parliamentary vote on handguns ban
	• strengthen Data Protection Act	• review system of legal aid
		• reform systems of immigration control and asylum seeking
• establish a Scottish Assembly, and stronger Welsh agencies	• establish a Charter of Rights	• incorporate European Convention on Human Rights into UK law
• establish a new elected body for London	• introduce a Freedom of Information Act	• hold referendums on Scottish and Welsh devolution
• introduce Freedom of Information Act	• establish a Scottish Assembly, elected on Additional Member System	• implement the Nolan recommendations; and ask Nolan to consider how political parties should be financed
• introduce state aid for political parties	• establish an elected Welsh Assembly	
• strengthen local democracy (and establish 'Quality Commission' to disseminate best practice)	• create a new regional tier of government in England	• review how best to reform the House of Lords; end rights of hereditary peers to sit and vote there
• support principles underpinning Anglo-Irish Agreement	• set up a new elected authority for London	• create independent commission on electoral reform
	• make donations to political parties public	• introduce a Freedom of Information Act
	• replace House of Lords with new second chamber	• strengthen local democracy
	• introduce fixed parliamentary term	• hold referendum on a new elected body for London
	• support principles underpinning Anglo-Irish Agreement; repeal PTA	• later, hold referendums on new regional bodies for England
		• support principles of the Downing Street Declaration and the Framework Document

	1979 manifesto	**1983 manifesto**
Foreign policy		
(1) Europe	• reform of CAP • strengthen democratic institutions in Europe against multinational capital • oppose moves to a federal Europe, and stay out of any monetary union	• withdraw from the EEC
(2) defence	• seek multilateral arms reductions • support NATO • reduce defence expenditure to level of main European allies • do not replace Polaris	• seek full implementation of existing disarmament agreements • establish a non-nuclear defence policy in the UK (cancel Trident, negotiate removal of Polaris) • reduce defence expenditure to level of main European allies
(3) world issues	• support international organisations in pursuit of peace and détente • resist apartheid in South Africa and Rhodesia • seek restoration & strengthening of human rights • seek just world trading system	• prioritise policies to help liberate people from oppression, want and fear • revive North–South dialogue • create separate Ministry of Overseas Development • give highest priority to protection of human rights, and deny aid to governments persistently violating these

1987 manifesto	1992 manifesto	1997 manifesto
• 'work constructively with our EEC partners to promote prosperity and combat unemployment' • reform CAP • resist EEC interference in our policy for national recovery	• use UK Presidency of EU to lift UK standing in Europe • end opt-out from Social Chapter • reform CAP • support widening of the Community • support strengthening of political control of European monetary institutions	• lead in Euope: to achieve rapid completion of single market; enlargement; reform of CAP; greater openness and democracy; retention of national veto on key issues; sign up to the Social Chapter • hold referendum on a single currency
• play key role in NATO • concentrate on non-nuclear defence role (decommission Polaris and cancel Trident) • concentrate on buying British-made equipment • maintain 50 frigate and destroyer navy, the European Fighter aircraft, and the modernisation of army equipment	• play key role in NATO • provide the necessary level of forces with the appropriate equipment and weapons • set up Defence Diversification Agency to ensure already planned defence cuts are used for rebuilding industrial base	• strong defence through NATO • initiate a strategic defence and security review • retain Trident • push for multilateral reductions in nuclear, chemical and biological weapons • retention of a strong UK defence industry, with its expertise extended to civilian use through a defence diversification agency
• stand up for freedom wherever it is oppressed • support human rights movement • set up a Department of Overseas Development and Co-operation with cabinet rank	• work in the UN for a strengthened non-proliferation treaty (nuclear, biological, chemical) and environmental controls • set up Human Rights division in the FCO • increase overseas aid to UN target level within 5 years • tackling poverty to be top priority of aid programme – focusing particularly on the needs of women • new Marshall Plan for former Communist countries	• no arms sales to governments using them for internal repression • high priority to combating global poverty and under-development. Cabinet post for new Department of International Development • make protection of human rights a central part of foreign policy • seek international agreements on environmental protection

Appendix 2

Main west European Labour, social-democrat and socialist parties affiliated to the Socialist International

Country	Party name	Acronym
Austria	*Sozialdemokratische Partei Österreichs*	SPÖ
Belgium	*Parti Socialiste (Walloon)*	PSB
	Socialistische Partij (Flemish)	BSP
Denmark	*Socialdemokratiet*	SD
Finland	*Suomen Sosialidemokraattinen Puolue*	SSDP
France	*Parti Socialiste*	PS(F)
Germany	*Sozialdemokratische Partei Deutschlands*	SPD
Greece	*Panelleniko Sosialistiko Kinima*	PASOK
Iceland	*Althyduflokkurinn*	AdF
Ireland	*Irish Labour Party*	ILP
Italy	*Partito Democratico della Sinistra*	PDS
Luxembourg	*Parti Ouvrier Socialiste Luxembourgeois*	POSL
Netherlands	*Partij van de Arbeid*	PdvA
Norway	*Det Norske Arbeiderparti*	DNA
Portugal	*Partido Socialista*	PS(P)
Spain	*Partido Socialista Obrero Español*	PSOE
Sweden	*Socialdemokratiska Arbetarepartei*	SAP
Switzerland	*Parti Socialiste Suisse*	PSS
UK	*(New) Labour Party*	(N)LP

Index

311